The Classic Italian
Cook Book

THE CLASSIC ITALIAN COOK BOOK

THE ART OF ITALIAN COOKING
AND THE ITALIAN ART OF EATING

Marcella Hazan

DRAWINGS BY GEORGE KOIZUMI

ALFRED A. KNOPF *New York* 1983

Knopf Edition Published February 27, 1976
Reprinted Twelve Times
Fourteenth Printing, December 1983
Copyright © 1973 by Marcella Hazan

The excerpt on *Bollito misto*, page 322, is from *The Passionate Epicure*, by Marcel Rouff, copyright © 1962 by E. P. Dutton & Co., Inc., publishers, and is used with their permission.

Library of Congress Cataloging in Publication Data
Hazan, Marcella.
The classic Italian cook book.
Includes index.
1. Cookery, Italian. I. Title.
[TX723.H34   1976]   641.5′945   75-39785
ISBN 0-394-40510-2

To Victor, my husband, *con tutto il mio amore e profonda tenerezza*. Without his confidence I would not have started this work, without his support I would soon have abandoned it, without his hand next to mine I could not have given it its final form and expression. His name really belongs on the title page.

Contents

Acknowledgments xiii

Preface xv

INTRODUCTION 1

SAUCES *Le Salse* 25

ANTIPASTI 31

FIRST COURSES *I Primi* 51

SECOND COURSES *I Secondi* 209

VEGETABLES *Le Verdure* 335

SALADS *Le Insalate* 403

THE CHEESE COURSE *Il Formaggio* 425

DESSERTS AND FRUIT *I Dolci e la Frutta* 427

AFTERTHOUGHTS 459

Index 461

Illustrations

PASTA-CUTTING TOOLS 22

COLANDER AND GRATER 22

PASSATELLI 70

MAKING AND ROLLING OUT PASTA DOUGH 114 TO 118

TAGLIATELLE, FETTUCCINE, AND MALTAGLIATI 118

PAPPARDELLE 122

MALTAGLIATI 122

ACTUAL SIZES OF PASTA TYPES 124

SCRIGNO DI VENERE 147

SLICED PASTA ROLL WITH SPINACH FILLING 153

CAPPELLETTI 156

TORTELLINI 161

TORTELLONI 165

GARGANELLI 172

GNOCCHI 197

BAKED SEMOLINA GNOCCHI   199

SHRIMP BROCHETTES   227

SQUID   229

FILLETING A CHICKEN BREAST   313

PREPARING AN ARTICHOKE   339 TO 341

JERUSALEM ARTICHOKES   351

FINOCCHIO   376

POTATO CROQUETTES WITH CRISP-FRIED NOODLES   386

SWISS CHARD   414

INSALATA RUSSA   419

SWEET PASTRY FRITTERS   434

ZUCCOTTO   439

MONTE BIANCO   442

THE NAPOLETANA   456

THE MOKA   456

Acknowledgments

It is impossible for cooks ever to give a full account of their debts. Our skills, our tastes, our discoveries, all rest upon the compressed layers of experience of family, friends, chance acquaintances, other cooks, and the long ranks of the generations that have preceded us.

I regret that time and an ungrateful memory have blurred the identity of some of my benefactors. Among them are a deft and patient woman in the vegetable market at the foot of the Quirinale hill, turning from her work to give me the best artichoke-trimming demonstration I have ever seen, and a perfect recipe for making artichokes *alla romana*. The fishermen of my home town, making their dinner on the cobblestone dock after unloading and selling their catch, broiling their fish to absolute perfection. The maids of my youth, working in my father's and my uncle's houses, from whose superb, natural skills I was learning how to cook, unawares, as I discovered many years later.

Fortunately, not all my creditors need to remain anonymous. First, and most important among them, are my family. My father's mother, Nonna Polini, whose handmade pasta remains the paragon to which I must compare every other. My father, Fin, who was skilled and true in everything he put his hand to. My mother, Maria Leonelli, who is still the best cook in the family, my aunt Licia Conconi, who taught me how to make *polenta*, and my cousin Armando Sabbadini. I am grateful too to my mother-in-law, Julia Hazan, through whom I discovered a remarkable new world of cooking.

I should also like to express my debt to Ada Boni, whose *Talismano della Felicità* was indeed a happy talisman in the early period of my marriage, when I first faced alone the mysteries of the kitchen and the expectations of a food-loving husband.

I am further indebted for recipes and assistance to Ginesio Albonetti of La Griglia D'Oro, Cesenatico; "Zia" Ines Anzuoni; Maria Bartoli; Evio Battellani, creator of the Scrigno di Venere and master of Al Cantunzein, Bologna's temple of pasta; Vittorio Boldrini, of Cesenatico's Pesce Spada; Stella Donati, of Star food products; Claudia Fioravanti; Marchese Giuseppe Gavotti, chancellor of the Accademia Italiana della Cucina, sage and witty gentleman of Italian gastronomy; Lorenza Magnani; Roberto Moglia; Pietro Molesini, owner-chef of Al Caminetto, Padriciano (Trieste); Pietro Piromallo of Bologna; Cavaliere Renato Ramponi, chef de cuisine of Florence's Grand Hotel; Silvano Renna of L'Osteriaccia at Cusercoli; Vittorio Rocchi of the non-pareil Rocca di Bazzano restaurant; Bruna Saglio; Valeria and Maria Luisa Simili of Bologna's great bakery; and Bruno Tasselli, of Bologna's Pappagallo.

To Lucia Parini, for her irreplaceable and skillful assistance, I owe special thanks.

I am also particularly grateful to Grace Chu, from whom I learned about teaching cooking; to my students, whose experiences have contributed so much to this book; and to Craig Claiborne, whose warm interest has been chiefly responsible for my cooking having come to public notice.

As for the making of the book, my gratitude forever goes to my editor and publisher, Peter Mollman, for his generous and never-flagging support, to Jane Mollman for her saintly patience and her sensitive, informed reading of the manuscript, and to George Koizumi, for the liveliest and clearest illustrations with which a cookbook author has ever had her recipes illuminated.

Preface

Nothing significant exists under Italy's sun that is not touched by art. Its food is twice blessed because it is the product of two arts, the art of cooking and the art of eating. While each nourishes the other, they are in no way identical accomplishments. The art of cooking produces the dishes, but it is the art of eating that transforms them into a meal.

Through the art of eating, an Italian meal becomes a precisely orchestrated event, where the products of the season, the traditions of place, the intuitions of the cook, and the knowledgeable joy of the participants are combined into one of the most satisfying experiences of which our senses are capable.

I hope that these pages will reward those looking for new dishes with which to please themselves and their friends. But I have tried to put something more here. In my classes I attempt to demonstrate not only how to make dishes but how to make meals. I hope that this book can be used to that same end, and that it will help its readers discover some of the happiness and beauty of the total Italian food experience.

M.H.

New York City
December, 1972

The Classic Italian
Cook Book

INTRODUCTION

ITALIAN COOKING:

WHERE DOES IT COME FROM?

THE first useful thing to know about Italian cooking is that, as
such, it actually doesn't exist. "Italian cooking" is an expression of convenience rarely used by Italians. The cooking of Italy is
really the cooking of its regions, regions that until 1861 were separate, independent, and usually hostile states. They submitted to
different rulers, they were protected by sovereign armies and navies,
and they developed their own cultural traditions and, of course,
their own special and distinct approaches to food.

The unique features of each region and of the individual towns
and cities within it can still be easily observed when one travels
through Italy today. These are living differences that appear in the
physical cast of the people, in their temperament, in their spoken
language, and, most clearly, in their cooking.

The cooking of Venice, for example, is so distant from that of
Naples, although they are both Italian cities specializing in seafood,
that not a single authentic dish from the one is to be found on the

other's table. There are unbridgeable differences between Bologna
and Florence, each the capital of its own region, yet only sixty miles
apart. There are also subtle but substantial distinctions to be made
between the cooking of Bologna and of other cities in its region,
such as Cesena, fifty-two miles away, Parma, fifty-six miles, or
Modena, just twenty-three miles to the north.

It isn't only from the inconstant contours of political geography
that cooking in Italy has taken its many forms. Even more significant
has been the forceful shaping it has received from the two dominant
elements of the Italian landscape—the mountains and the sea.

Italy is a peninsula shaped like a full-length boot that has stepped
into the Mediterranean and Adriatic seas up to its thigh. There it
is fastened to the rest of Europe by an uninterrupted chain of the
tallest mountains on the continent, the Alps. At the base of the Alps
spreads Italy's only extensive plain, which reaches from Venice on
the Adriatic coast westward through Lombardy and into Piedmont.
This is the dairy zone of Italy, and the best-irrigated land. The
cooking fat is butter, almost exclusively, and rice or corn mush
(polenta) are the staples. Up to a few years ago, when thousands
of workers from the south came north to find jobs in Turin and
Milan, macaroni was virtually unknown here.

The northern plain gives out just before touching the Mediterranean shore, where it reaches the foothills of the other great mountain chain of Italy, the Apennines. This chain extends from north to
south for the whole length of the country like the massive, protruding spine of some immense beast. It is composed of gentle, softly
rounded hills sloping toward the seas on the eastern and western
flanks and, in the central crest, of tall, forbidding stone peaks.
Huddled within the links of this chain are countless valleys, isolated
from each other until modern times like so many Shangri-las, giving
birth to men, cultures, and cooking styles profoundly different in
character.

To a certain extent, the Apennine range helps determine that
variety of climates which has also favored diversity in cooking.
Turin, the capital of Piedmont, standing in the open plain at the
foot of the Alps, has winters more severe than Copenhagen. The

Ligurian coast, just a few miles to the west, nestles against the Apennines, which intercept the cold Alpine winds and allow the soft Mediterranean breezes to create that mild, pleasant climate which has made the Riviera famous. Here flowers abound, the olive begins to flourish, and the fragrance of fresh herbs invades nearly every dish.

On the eastern side of the same Apennines that hug the Riviera coast lies the richest gastronomic region in Italy, Emilia-Romagna. Its capital, Bologna, is probably the only city in all Italy whose name is instantly associated in the Italian mind not with monuments, not with artists, not with heroes, but with food.

Emilia-Romagna is almost evenly divided between mountainous land and flat, with the Apennines at its back and at its feet the last remaining corner of the northern plain rolling out to the Adriatic. This Emilian plain is extraordinarily fertile land enriched by the alluvial deposits of the countless Apennine torrents that have run through it toward the sea. It leads all Italy in the production of wheat, which perhaps explains why here it is almost heresy to sit down to a meal that doesn't include a dish of homemade pasta. The vegetables of Emilia-Romagna may well be the tastiest in the world, surpassing even the quality of French produce. The fruit from its perfumed orchards is so remarkable in flavor that local consumers must compete with foreign markets for it. Italy's best hams and sausages are made here and also some of its richest dairy products, among which is the greatest Italian cheese, Parmesan.

In Emilia-Romagna the sea has been as bountiful as the land. The Adriatic, perhaps because it contains less salt than the Mediterranean, perhaps because it is constantly purified by fresh waters from Alpine streams, produces fish famous in all Italy for its fine delicate flesh. When a restaurant in any part of Italy offers fish from the Adriatic it makes sure its patrons know it. Since the quality of the fish is so fine it requires little enhancement in the kitchen, and Adriatic fish cookery has become the essence of masterful simplicity. Nowhere else except perhaps in Japan is fish fried or broiled so simply and well.

In crossing Emilia-Romagna's southern border into Tuscany every aspect of cooking seems to have turned over and, like an embossed coin, landed on its reverse side. Tuscany's whole approach to the preparation of food is in such sharp contrast to that of Bologna that their differences seem to sum up two main and contrary manifestations of Italian character.

Out of the abundance of the Bolognese kitchen comes cooking that is exuberant, prodigal with precious ingredients, and wholly baroque in its restless exploration of every agreeable combination of texture and flavor. The Florentine, careful and calculating, is a man who knows the measure of all things, and his cooking is an austerely composed play upon essential and unadorned themes.

Bologna will sauté veal in butter, stuff it with the finest mountain ham, coat it with aged Parmesan, simmer it in sauce, and smother it with the costliest truffles. Florence takes a T-bone steak of noble size and grills it quickly over a blazing fire, adding nothing but the aroma of freshly ground pepper and olive oil. Both are triumphs.

From Tuscany down, the Apennines and their foothills in their southward march spread nearly from coast to coast so that the rest of Italy is almost entirely mountainous. As a result, two major changes take place in cooking. First, as it is cheaper and simpler on a hillside to cultivate a grove of olive trees than to raise a herd of dairy cows, olive oil supplants butter as the dominant cooking fat. Second, as we get farther away from the rich wheat fields of Emilia-Romagna, soft, homemade egg and flour pasta gives way to the more economical, mass-produced, eggless hard macaroni, the staple of the south.

From Naples south the climate becomes considerably warmer. A harsher sun bakes the land, inflames the temper of the inhabitants, and ignites their sauces. At the toe-tip of the peninsula and in the heart of Sicily there is little rainfall, and most of that only in the winter months. The lands are parched by harsh, burning winds and the temperatures are sometimes higher than in southern Florida and Texas. The food is as extreme as the climate. The colors of the vegetables are intense and violent, the pastas are so pungent that they often need no topping of cheese, and the sweets are of the most overpowering richness.

There is no need here and certainly there is no room to examine in greater detail all the richly varied forms that history and geography have pressed upon the cooking of Italy. What is important is to be aware that these differences exist and that behind the screen of the too-familiar term "Italian cooking" lies concealed, waiting to be discovered, a multitude of riches.

THE ITALIAN ART OF EATING

Not everyone in Italy may know how to cook, but nearly everyone knows how to eat. Eating in Italy is one more manifestation of the Italian's age-old gift of making art out of life.

The Italian art of eating is sustained by a life measured in nature's rhythms, a life that falls in with the slow wheelings of the seasons, a life in which, until very recently, produce and fish reached the table not many hours after having been taken from the soil or the sea.

It is an art that has also been abetted by the custom of shutting down the whole country at midday for two hours or more. Fathers come home from work and children from school, and there is sufficient time for the whole family to celebrate, not just the most important meal, but more likely also the most important event of the day.

There probably has been no influence, not even religion, so effective in creating a rich family life, in maintaining a civilized link between the generations, as this daily sharing of a common joy. Eating in Italy is essentially a family art, practiced for and by the family. The finest accomplishments of the home cook are not reserved like the good silver and china for special occasions or for impressing guests, but are offered daily for the pleasure and happiness of the family group.

The best cooking in Italy is not, as in France, to be found in restaurants, but in the home. One of the reasons that Italian restaurants here are generally so poor is that they do not have Italian home cooking with which to compete. The finest restaurants in Italy are not those glittering establishments known to every traveler, but the very small, family-run *trattorie* of ten or twelve tables that offer home cooking only slightly revised by commercial adaptations. Here the menus are unnecessary, sometimes non-existent, and almost always illegible. Patrons know exactly what they want, and in ordering a meal they are evoking patterns established countless times at home.

Italian food may be a midnight spaghetti snack after the theater, a pizza and a glass of wine, a cool salad on a sultry summer noon. But an Italian *meal* is something else entirely; it is a many-layered experience far richer and more complete than this.

Out of the potentially infinite combinations of first and second courses, of side dishes, of sauces and seasonings, an Italian meal, whether it is set out at home for the entire family or consumed in solitary communion in a restaurant, emerges as a complex composition free of discordant notes. Its elements may vary according to the season and the unique desires of the moment, but their relationships are governed by a harmonious and nearly invariable arrangement.

There is no main course to an Italian meal. With some very rare exceptions, such as *ossobuco* with *risotto*, the concept of a single dominant course is entirely foreign to the Italian way of eating. There are, at a minimum, two principal courses, which are never, never brought to the table at the same time.

The first course may be pasta either in broth or with sauce, or it can be a risotto or a soup. *Minestra*, which is the Italian for "soup," is also used to mean the first course whether it is a soup or not. This is because, to the Italian mind, the first course, even when it is sauced pasta or *risotto*, is still a soup in the sense that it is served in a deep dish and that it always precedes and never accompanies the meat, fowl, or fish course.

After there has been sufficient time to relish and consume the first course, to salute its passing with some wine, and to regroup the taste buds for the next encounter, the second course comes to the table. The choice of the second course is usually a development of the theme established by the first. The reverse may also be true, when the first course is chosen in anticipation of what the second will be. If the second course is going to be beef braised in wine, you will not preface it with spaghetti in clam sauce or with a dish of *lasagne* heavily laced with meat. You might prefer a *risotto* with asparagus, with zucchini, or with plain Parmesan cheese. Or a dish of green *gnocchi*. Or a light potato soup. If you are going to start with *tagliatelle alla bolognese* (homemade noodles with meat sauce), you might want to give your palate some relief by following with a simple roast of veal or chicken. On the other hand, you would not choose a second course so bland, such as steamed fish, that it could not stand up to the impact of the first.

The second course is often attended by one or two vegetable side dishes, which sometimes may develop into a full course of their own. The special pleasures of the Italian table are never keener or more apparent than in this moment when the vegetables appear. In Italian menus the word for a vegetable side dish is *contorno*, which can be translated literally as "contour." This reveals exactly what role vegetables play, because it is the choice of vegetables that defines the meal, that gives it shape, that encircles it with the flavors, textures, and colors of the season.

The sober winter taste, the austere whites and gray-greens of artichokes, cardoons, celery, cauliflower; the sweetness and the tender hues of spring in the first asparagus, the earliest peas, baby carrots, young fava beans; the voluptuous gifts of summer: the luscious eggplant, the glossy green pepper, the sun-reddened tomato, the succulent zucchini; the tart and scented taste of autumn in leeks, finocchio, fresh spinach, red cabbage; these do more than quiet our hunger. Through their presence the act of eating becomes a way of sharing our life with nature. And this is precisely what is at the heart of the Italian art of eating.

An Italian meal is a story told from nature, taking its rhythms, its humors, its bounty and turning them into episodes for the senses. As nature is not a one-act play, so an Italian meal cannot rest on a single dish. It is instead a lively sequence of events, alternating the crisp with the soft and yielding, the pungent with the bland, the variable with the staple, the elaborate with the simple.

It takes a theme such as "fish," states it very gently in a simple antipasto of tender, boiled young squid delicately seasoned with olive oil, parsley, and lemon, contrasts it with a rich and creamy shrimp risotto, and restates it with a superbly broiled bass that sums up every pure and natural quality with which fish has been endowed. All this subsides in a tart salad of seasonal greens and closes on the sweet, liquid note of fresh sliced fruit in wine.

This book has been organized in the same sequence as an Italian meal: first courses first, second courses second, side dishes. Antipasti lead the procession, salads and dessert close it. Recipes for one course carry suggestions on how to choose a course to follow or precede it. The most suitable vegetable accompaniment is suggested with the second course. Through this constant reminder of those patterns which form the Italian way of eating I hope the reader will discover that there is something more significant to an Italian meal than a single overpowering dish oozing sauce and melted cheese.

In the relationships of its varied parts an Italian meal develops something very close to the essence of civilized life itself. No dish overwhelms another, either in quantity or flavor, each leaves room for new appeals to the eye and palate, each fresh sensation of taste, color, and texture interlaces a lingering recollection of the last.

Of course, no one expects that the Italian way of eating can be wholly absorbed into everyday American life. Even in Italy it is succumbing to the onrushing uniformity of an industrial society. In Blake's phrase, man's brain is making the world unlivable for man's spirit. Yet, it is possible even from the tumultuous center of the busiest city life to summon up the life-enhancing magic of the Italian art of eating. What it requires is generosity. You must give liberally of time, of patience, of the best raw materials. What it returns is worth all you have to give.

INGREDIENTS

The character of a cuisine is determined more by basic approach than by ingredients. Ingredients come and go, depending on popular taste and the changing patterns of commerce. It is a picture that emerges more clearly as one steps away from it. It is hard to imagine Italian cooking, and that of Naples in particular, without tomatoes. And Venetians would go into shock if they were deprived of *polenta*. But tomatoes and corn are both fairly recent newcomers to the two venerable cuisines. In the recipes of this book I have introduced shallots, which, although they are an ancient Mediterranean commodity, are not generally available in Italy. Yet they adapt themselves with perfect grace to Italian cooking, and in many instances are preferable to onions.

This is not said to encourage indifference to a precise choice of ingredients but rather to discourage an exaggerated dependence on them. A heavy hand with the garlic or the tomato sauce does not make Italian cooking. There is no question that there are certain components without which it would be impossible to reproduce the taste of Italian cooking as we know it today. Fortunately, these are all available here in some form. In the following list, some of the most important ones are briefly considered.

Alloro

BAY LEAVES

Bay leaves go very nicely with roasts of meat and chicken. Adding them to the fire when broiling fish over charcoal is also a nice touch. Buy them whole from Greek or Italian grocers and store them in a tightly closed glass jar in a cool cupboard.

Brodo

BROTH

Broth is almost as necessary to Italian cooking as stock is to French cooking, although Italian broth is much thinner and less concentrated in flavor than stock. All you need for broth is a few vegetables, some beef, veal, and chicken bones, and, ideally, some good scraps of meat and chicken. If you are doing *ossobuco* (Braised Veal Shanks, Milan Style, page 256) have the butcher saw the bony ends off the shanks, and save them for a broth. Do the same when boning a breast of chicken. If you are not ready to cook these scraps immediately, store them in the freezer and make your broth when you have a nice assortment of bones and meat trimmings. A broth keeps indefinitely in the refrigerator if you boil it for 15 minutes every 3 or 4 days. Or you may freeze it for longer periods. You should always have some on hand.

HOMEMADE MEAT BROTH

Makes about 1½ quarts of broth

1 teaspoon salt	1 canned Italian tomato
1 carrot, peeled	1 small potato, peeled
1 small yellow onion, peeled	6 to 8 cups assorted bones and
1 stalk celery	meat scraps
¼ sweet green pepper	

Put all the ingredients in a stockpot and cover with cold water by 2 inches. Set the cover askew and bring to a boil. When boiling, regulate the heat so that the liquid cooks at the barest simmer. From time to time, but especially during the first few minutes, skim off the scum that rises to the surface. Cook for 2 to 3 hours, without ever letting the liquid come to a steady boil. Strain the broth into a glass or porcelain container and allow to cool uncovered. When cool, store, uncovered, in the refrigerator. When the fat on the surface has hardened, remove it.

If you have not used it up after 4 days, bring the broth to a boil for 10 minutes, allow it to cool, and refrigerate again. If in the meantime you have accumulated other good scraps of meat and bones, add them to the broth, add more vegetables (all but the tomato), add enough water to cover by about 2 inches, and repeat the whole cooking process. In this manner you will never be without good homemade broth.

NOTE
Do not use lamb or pork bones unless you need a particularly strong-tasting broth.

LUGANEGA SAUSAGE

One of the most serious shortcoming of Italian food stores is their lack of good fresh sausages. I have tried every variety of so-called Italian sausages without ever finding any that were acceptable. The only exception is a sausage available in long, continuous coils, not separated into links, called *luganega*. Even this is a qualified exception, because pork butchers here do not make *luganega* as they do in Italy, with pork shoulder and Parmesan cheese. However, it is milder and more honest in taste than all other local Italian sausages, and you can expect very satisfactory results from it.

MORTADELLA

Mortadella is Bologna's most famous pork product, and many Italians consider it the finest sausage in Italy. A well-made *mortadella* is very smooth in texture and possesses a subtle and delicate savoriness. It consists of various cuts of pork finely ground, boiled, and larded. It is delicious in a sandwich, excellent in a plate of mixed cold cuts, and necessary to the cooking of many Bolognese dishes. *Mortadella* is the largest of sausages, in Bologna often reaching a girth of 18 inches or more. Here it is less than half that size. Unfortunately, local mortadella is, at best, an only partially satisfactory imitation of the original product. We must be content that it is available at all, and make use of it. When buying it, do not let your grocer slice it too thin. It should be cut at least ⅛ inch thick.

Funghi secchi

DRIED WILD MUSHROOMS

In the fall and spring one of the most thrilling sights in Italian markets is that of mountains of orange, cream-colored, and nut-brown wild mushrooms fresh from the woods. Ah, the haunting aroma of giant mushroom caps, sautéed with oil, garlic, and parsley! Alas, we are well protected from such temptations here. But while we cannot buy fresh wild mushrooms, their woodsy fragrance has been captured in the dried variety. Drying deprives the mushroom of its succulence but compensates for this by concentrating its flavor. Dried mushrooms can no longer be used as a vegetable, but they are a marvelous seasoning for sauces, *risotto*, meat, and chicken. They are available in Italian groceries, and sometimes at the supermarket. When buying them, look for large, creamy-brown sections. Avoid the dark brown, crumbly kind. Choice mushrooms are expensive, but a little goes a long way. If stored in a tightly closed metal box, they will keep indefinitely.

The water in which dried mushrooms are reconstituted is full of flavor and should never be discarded. Wherever dried mushrooms are called for, the recipe will indicate how the water is to be used.

Olio d'oliva

OLIVE OIL

In the center and south of Italy, in the islands, and along both coasts, olive oil is the fundamental cooking fat. Unlike peanut oil or other vegetable oils, olive oil has a decided taste, which should not be used indiscriminately. The recipes in this book reflect the current trend of Italian cooking by using olive oil only where its presence is essential. In those circumstances where its flavor would be obtrusive and unnecessary to the harmony of a dish it has been supplanted by vegetable oil. However, where raw oil is required, as in salads, the use of anything but olive oil is inconceivable.

Most olive oil packed for export has been so highly refined that it has only the faintest suggestion of olives. This is true of nearly all the widely distributed brands. A recipe calling for olive oil will not be entirely successful with such thin, impalpable oil. Good olive oil should have both the color and taste of the green olive, and that is what you should look for. You are most likely to find it in the green, fruity oils from Sicily, such as Madre Sicilia or Due Sicilie.

After you open the can, decant the oil into a large glass bottle or ceramic jug and leave it uncorked. It will keep indefinitely.

PANCETTA

Pancetta is exactly the same cut of pork as bacon, except that it is not smoked. Instead, it is cured in salt and spices. It comes tightly rolled up in a salami shape, and it is sliced to order. The convenient way to buy it is to get ¼ to ½ pound in thin slices and an equal amount in a single slice. For some recipes you will use the slices just as they are, while for others you will cut the larger piece into cubes or strips. *Pancetta* keeps up to three weeks in the refrigerator, if carefully sealed in plastic wrap.

When it is of good quality, *pancetta* can be eaten as it is, like prosciutto or any other cold cut. In Italian cooking it is used as a flavoring agent in sauces, pasta fillings, vegetables, and roasts. When used next to veal it bastes it as it cooks, and keeps it from drying.

There are no exact substitutes for *pancetta*, but if it is not obtainable you can replace it with prosciutto or unsmoked ham. As far as I know, *pancetta* is available only in Italian food stores.

Parmigiano-Reggiano

PARMESAN CHEESE

This precious cheese, which is an inseparable part of much Italian cooking, is produced by just five small provinces in the old Duchy of Parma, now absorbed into Emilia. It is made only during the mild months of the year, from spring through fall, when the cows can amble out and feed upon the richest pasture in Italy. It is aged at least two years, but good food shops in Italy carry Parmesan that is three or four years old, and even older.

Parmesan is straw yellow in color and has a mellow, rounded, slightly salty taste. It is the finest cheese for cooking because it melts without running and without disintegrating into a rubbery tangle. It has no peer, of course, for grating over pasta, and when it is freshly cut it deserves to be eaten as it is, accompanied by the best red wine you can afford.

When buying Parmesan cheese, ask to look at it and taste it before it is cut for you. If it is whitish and dry, and leaves a bitter aftertaste, do not buy it or, if you must, buy as little as you can get away with. If it is pale yellow, slightly moist on the tongue, and pleasantly salty, invest in a good-sized piece. A three-pound piece of properly wrapped Parmesan will keep for a few weeks in the refrigerator.

How to Store Parmesan

To maintain the freshness of Parmesan cheese you must prevent its moisture from escaping. As soon as you get it home, wrap the cheese in a double or triple thickness of aluminum foil. Make sure the foil is not torn at any point and that it is tightly sealed. Keep it on the bottom shelf of the refrigerator.

Parmesan is usually sold with some of its crust. When cutting off a piece, always cut it with part of the crust attached, because the cheese left next to the crust tends to dry faster. Do not discard the crust. Wrap it and store it like the cheese and save it to use in soups. Do not grate much more cheese than you need. Grated cheese does not keep.

After you have had the cheese a while, you may notice that it has become drier and whiter. If this happens, moisten a piece of cheesecloth and twist it until it is no more than damp. Wrap it around the cheese, then wrap and seal with aluminum foil. Refrigerate overnight. The following day remove the cheesecloth and rewrap with just aluminum foil.

The recipes in this book call for freshly grated Parmesan cheese. Do not under any circumstances use ready-grated cheese sold in jars. Even if this commercially grated cheese were of good quality, which it is not, it would have lost all its flavor long before getting to the market. It is of no interest whatever to Italian cooking.

Prezzemolo

PARSLEY

All Italian vegetable stores, and now many supermarkets, carry Italian parsley. It has a larger, less curly leaf than regular parsley, and a better developed, yet less pungent fragrance. The stem is milder than the leaf, and can sometimes be substituted for the leaves for a more toned-down flavor. For Italian cooking you really should use Italian parsley, but if it is not available don't let it worry you. The other variety is quite satisfactory.

Pepe

PEPPER

Ready-ground pepper is one of those modern conveniences that keep giving progress a bad name. Why it exists I do not know. It is certainly no more work to twist a pepper mill than to brandish a shaker, but there is an enormous difference in the result. The aroma of pepper is short-lived. All that you get with ready-ground pepper is some of its pungency.

Black pepper is the whole fruit of the pepper plant. White pepper is simply black pepper stripped of its shell. White pepper is stronger, but black pepper is used more frequently in Italian cooking because it is more aromatic. Unless you are addicted to pepper, do not buy a large amount at one time. Its flavor is perishable.

Riso

RICE

Italian rice is thicker and shorter than American rice. It takes a little longer to cook, but it has more "tooth" and body. It is ideal for *risotto* because the grains adhere creamily to each other without surrendering their individual firmness. It is excellent also for all Italian soups.

"Arborio" is the generic name of the most commonly imported variety of Italian rice. It is available here under more than one brand name, and can be obtained not only from Italian groceries but also from the food shops of many department stores.

RICOTTA

Ricotta is a soft, bland, white milk product made from whey, that watery part of the milk which separates from the curd when this is made into cheese. Large use of it is made in Emilia, where it is put into delicate fillings for pasta. Also famous are the ricotta cheesecakes of the south. Fresh, true ricotta can be obtained at a few Italian food stores. It is extremely perishable, and even under refrigeration it should be used within 24 to 48 hours. A passable substitute is the more long-lived whole-milk ricotta readily available at most supermarkets.

Perhaps because they are so similar in appearance, some authors suggest that ricotta and cottage cheese are interchangeable. This is a most grievous error. Cottage cheese is completely un-Italian in taste, and should not be contemplated as a replacement for ricotta.

Pecorino romano

ROMANO CHEESE

Romano is Italy's oldest cheese, whose beginnings probably coincide with those of Rome. It is a hard grating cheese made from sheep's milk, hence also called *pecorino*. It is very much sharper than Parmesan and, when grated, breaks down into smaller, more powdery granules. It is not to be considered a zestier alternative to Parmesan. The aggressiveness of Romano enhances such spicy dishes as Bucatini with Pancetta, Tomatoes, and Hot Pepper (page 105), but it would be out of character and strike a jarring note in Tuscan soups, delicate Bolognese pastas, or the *risotti* of the north.

Romano does not make an agreeable table cheese.

Rosmarino

ROSEMARY

This herb is so frequently used to flavor roasted meat or chicken that in Italy the fragrance of rosemary in the house almost invariably means that there is a roast in progress in the kitchen. It is an easy herb to grow in a window box. In the spring, many plant stores will sell you a well-started pot of rosemary that will continue to grow and furnish you with fresh branches for years. Lacking this, you can use dried whole leaves, but avoid the powder.

Salvia

SAGE

The gray-green furry leaves of the sage plant are an excellent flavoring for meat and chicken and have a particular affinity for veal cooked with white wine. If you can grow your own sage or buy it fresh, it is preferable to the dried variety. But dried whole sage leaves can be quite satisfactory. Buy them in branches from Italian or Greek grocers. They will keep almost indefinitely when stored in a tightly closed glass jar or a plastic bag in a cool cupboard. Do not buy powdered sage—it is perfectly useless.

Semolino

SEMOLINA

Farina or semolina, known in Italian as *semolino*, is the coarse-grained particles of durum wheat, the same wheat from which spaghetti and other macaroni is made. Imported Italian *semolino* can be ordered from Italian groceries, and if you are fond of semolina *gnocchi* you'd be well advised to buy a substantial quantity that you can keep on hand. Italian *semolino* has more body and color than the American variety and it gives markedly superior results. Do not confuse *semolino* with quick-cooking breakfast farina.

Maggiorana e origano

SWEET MARJORAM AND ORÉGANO

Marjoram and orégano are closely related plants. Marjoram is considerably milder than orégano, and is used on occasion in northern and central cooking, in soups and braised meats. Orégano is virtually never used outside of southern cooking, where it appears frequently in tomato sauces, and sometimes with fish or salads.

Acqua

WATER

Water is the phantom ingredient in much Italian cooking. One of my students once protested, "When you add water, you add nothing!" But that is precisely why we use it. Italian cooking is the art of giving expression to the undisguised flavors of its ingredients. In many circumstances, an overindulgence in stock, wine, or other flavored liquids would tinge the complexion of a dish with an artificial glow. That is why some recipes will direct that if the quantity of broth used is not sufficient, you should continue cooking with water, as needed. We sometimes use water for deglazing, because it lasts just long enough to help scrape loose the cooking residues stuck to the pan, and then evaporates without a trace. Whenever broth or wine has a part in developing the flavor of a dish, it is in the recipe. Otherwise use water.

La Batteria di cucina

SOME NOTES ON KITCHEN EQUIPMENT

This is not a full-scale discussion of kitchen equipment, a subject that has been handled very competently in many other cook books. It is principally a list of those tools that are particularly necessary to Italian cooking and are sometimes missing from otherwise well-furnished kitchens.

I tegami

POTS AND PANS

The traditional pan of Italian peasant kitchens is made of earthenware. It is unsurpassed for cooking beans and all vegetables, to which aluminum sometimes imparts a harsh, metallic taste. Earthenware is excellent also for stews, fricassees, and slow-simmered sauces. The drawback to earthenware, aside from its fragility, is that it is porous and absorbs some of the cooking fat. If used frequently, it need not cause any concern. If used at long intervals, however, the fat may turn rancid and give off a disagreeable odor.

The best all-purpose cooking ware is heavy, enameled cast iron. It transmits and retains heat magnificently, it is suited to all foods, it is both oven-safe and flameproof, and you can usually serve directly from it at the table. It is also very easy to clean. Have several sizes and shapes available. Little ones are perfect for making a small amount of sauce. Oval casseroles with lids are all but indispensable for long, narrow roasts. Low, open baking pans are what you need for gratinéing vegetables. Two rectangular pans, 2½ to 3 inches high, in different lengths and widths, can be used for *lasagne*.

Absolutely necessary for Italian cooking is a series of heavy frying pans or skillets. You should have at least three—small, medium, and large. They should have very solid, thick bottoms, to help prevent scorching. There are some aluminum alloys that give you thickness without excessive weight. It is also useful to have at least one heavy cast-iron skillet, excellent for all high-temperature frying and for pan-broiling steaks.

For cooking pasta, you need a pot that will comfortably contain at least four quarts of water plus the pasta.

An asparagus cooker makes it considerably simpler to cook asparagus perfectly, and it is useful for other purposes, such as making broth. If you do not have one, you can use a fish poacher, which is indispensable for poaching fish whole. Do not use the poacher for high-temperature cooking, because it is usually made of thin-gauge metal.

Per tagliare

CUTTING TOOLS

In addition to the usual assortment of knives (which should include, incidentally, two or three well-honed paring knives), you need one with a large, flat, well-balanced blade for cutting pasta. A Chinese cleaver is perfect.

A sharp, efficient peeler, because, for Italian dishes, vegetables and fruit frequently require peeling.

A straight pastry wheel for cutting *tortelloni* and other pasta, and a fluted wheel for *pappardelle* noodles.

A half-moon for effortless chopping of vegetables.

Pasta-cutting tools: knife and fluted pastry wheel
and half-moon for all-purpose chopping.

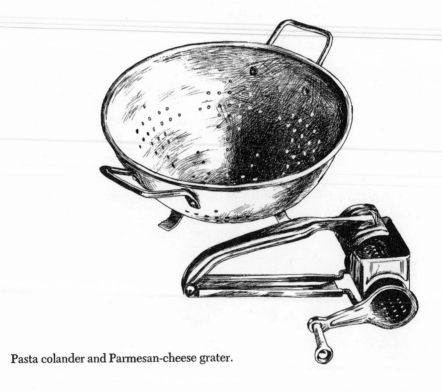

Pasta colander and Parmesan-cheese grater.

Aggegi vari

ODDS AND ENDS

A meat pounder for flattening *scaloppine* and cutlets.

One or more large hardwood chopping boards.

Several wooden spoons with handles of varying lengths.

A large ladle for soups, and a small one for degreasing sauces.

A long-handled fork for turning frying food without getting too close to the pan.

A slotted spatula and a slotted spoon for retrieving food from cooking fat.

A deep slotted spoon for retrieving *gnocchi* and other pasta. The Chinese stores have lovely ones made of bamboo and wire.

A large pasta colander with handles which you can stand in the basin when draining pasta.

A three-footed ring which will fit into any pan and convert it into the bottom half of a double boiler.

A food mill with three different disks. (A blender is not a satisfactory substitute because it flattens out textures to a greater degree than is desirable for Italian dishes.)

Whisks in different sizes.

A rotary grater for Parmesan cheese.

A four-sided grater for vegetables, mozzarella, nutmeg, and so on.

An Italian rolling pin for pasta (see page 112).

A pepper mill.

Italian coffeepots in two-, four-, and six-cup sizes.

Le Salse

SAUCES

THIS is the briefest chapter in the book because, outside of pasta dishes, sauces are used infrequently in Italian cooking. Most fish, meat, and fowl courses stand or fall on their own merits, with no more sauce to enhance their appeal than can be gleaned from loosening the residues or thickening the cooking juices they leave in the pan. Unlike classic French cuisine, Italian cooking has no basic central sauces, branching off and spreading their network throughout the repertory.

The most important Italian sauces are those used for pasta. In Italian, however, they are not even called *salsa* (the Italian for sauce). The correct term is *sugo*, for which there is no accurate English equivalent. There is an infinite number of them, but for an Italian cook, they do not have an independent existence of their own; they are a natural outgrowth of the dish in which they appear. For this reason, and to help steer the reader away from unsuccessful pairings, pasta and its sauces are taken up together in the chapter on first courses. Here you will find just four recipes: mayonnaise, béchamel, piquant green sauce, and red sauce.

There is no need to discuss the uses of mayonnaise, which go well beyond the boundaries of any cuisine. In Italy it is used with many cold dishes, especially cold poached fish. It is indispensable in the preparation of the tuna sauce that is part of one of the most splendid of all cold meat dishes, *vitello tonnato*, Sliced Cold Veal with Tuna Sauce (page 276).

Béchamel, despite its name, is a thoroughly Italian sauce. It is a key element in many pasta and vegetable dishes. The technique for béchamel given here produces a particularly fine, silken white sauce that you might want to use even for non-Italian recipes.

The piquant sauce and the red sauce are traditionally served with Mixed Boiled Meats (page 322), but they are very nice, too, with simple pan-broiled steaks or breaded veal cutlets. The piquant sauce is also an excellent sauce for fish, such as a fine cold, poached striped bass.

Maionese
MAYONNAISE

I can't imagine anyone with a serious interest in food using anything but homemade mayonnaise. Once you've had a little practice, it becomes one of the easiest and quickest sauces you can make. You can even prepare it two or three days ahead of time, storing it in the refrigerator in a small bowl tightly sealed with plastic wrap. Let it return to room temperature before using it. Mayonnaise can make or break any recipe of which it is a part. The commercial variety is so sugary and watery that it is beneath discussion.

You can make mayonnaise with olive oil or vegetable oil. It is lighter and more delicate with vegetable oil, but with fish olive oil is best. Use a pale yellow-green olive oil, such as the oil from Lucca or the Riviera. The deeper-green variety from the south of Italy or from Spain gives mayonnaise a somewhat bitter taste.

A most important point to remember when making mayonnaise is to have all the ingredients at room temperature. The bowl in which the eggs will be beaten and the blades of the electric beater should also be warmed up by dipping them in hot water and drying them quickly.

Makes over 1 cup.

2 egg yolks
Salt
1 to 1⅓ cups olive oil or
    vegetable oil (see note
    below)

2 tablespoons lemon juice,
    approximately

1. In a round-bottomed bowl, and using an electric beater set at medium speed, beat the egg yolks together with ¼ teaspoon salt until the yolks are very pale yellow and the consistency of thick cream. (Until you acquire more confidence in making mayonnaise, you might want to use the low setting on the beater.)

2. Add oil, drop by drop, while beating constantly. Stop pouring oil every few seconds, while you continue beating, until you see that all the oil you've added has been absorbed by the egg yolks and there is none floating free. Continue dribbling in oil and beating until the sauce has become quite thick. Add a teaspoon or less of lemon juice and continue beating. This will thin out the sauce a little. Add more oil, at a slightly faster pace than before, stopping from time to time while you continue beating to allow the egg yolks to absorb the oil completely. When the sauce becomes too thick add more lemon juice, until you've added the full 2 tablespoons. When you have finished adding all the oil, the mayonnaise is done.

3. Taste for salt, which it will surely need, and lemon. If the sauce is to be used for fish you will want it a bit on the tart side. Mix in any addition of salt or lemon with the beater.

REMEMBER:

· all ingredients must be at room temperature.

· the egg yolks must be beaten until they are pale yellow and creamy before adding oil.

· the oil must be added drop by drop until the sauce thickens.

And finally, *note*: Don't exceed ⅔ cup of oil per egg yolk. If you have no experience with making mayonnaise do not use more than *½ cup of oil per egg yolk* the first few times.

Salsa balsamella

BÉCHAMEL SAUCE

Long before the French christened it "béchamel," a sauce of flour and milk cooked in butter, called *balsamella*, was a part of the cooking of Romagna. It is essential to many of its pastas and vegetables, and such an unquestionably native dish as *lasagne* could not exist without it.

Balsamella is possibly the simplest and most quickly made of sauces. The only problem it poses is the formation of lumps. If you add the milk as directed, a little bit at a time, off the heat, beating the sauce constantly with a wooden spoon, you should have absolutely no difficulty in producing a perfectly smooth *balsamella* every time.

Makes 1⅔ cups medium-thick sauce

2 cups milk	3 tablespoons all-purpose flour
4 tablespoons butter	¼ teaspoon salt

1. In a small pan, heat the milk until it comes to the very edge of a boil.

2. While you are heating the milk, melt the butter over low heat in a heavy enameled iron saucepan of 4 to 6 cups' capacity.

3. When the butter is melted, add all the flour, stirring constantly with a wooden spoon. Let the flour and butter bubble for 2 minutes, without ceasing to stir. Do not let the flour become colored.

4. Turn off the heat and add the hot milk 2 tablespoons at a time, stirring it constantly into the flour-and-butter mixture. As soon as the first 2 tablespoons have been incorporated into the mixture, add another 2 tablespoons, always stirring with your trusty spoon. When you have added ½ cup of milk to the mixture, you can start adding ¼ cup at a time, until you have added it all. (Never add more than ¼ cup at one time.)

5. When all the milk has been incorporated, turn on the heat to low, add the salt, and stir-cook until the sauce is as dense as thick

cream. If you need it thicker, cook and stir a little while longer. If you need it thinner, cook a little less.

NOTE

When the sauce cools, it sets, and you will not be able to spread it. Therefore, inasmuch as it takes so little time to prepare, it is best to make it just before you are ready to use it. If you must make it in advance, reheat it slowly, stirring constantly until it is the right consistency again. Béchamel sauce can also be refrigerated.

Salsa verde
PIQUANT GREEN SAUCE

This is a tart green sauce that is always served with boiled meats (page 322) and often with boiled or steamed fish. If you are making it for meat, use vinegar; if for fish, lemon juice. You may vary the proportions according to taste, increasing the vinegar or lemon if you like it tarter, and adding salt when necessary.

For 4 servings

2½ tablespoons finely chopped parsley

2 tablespoons finely chopped capers

6 flat anchovy fillets, mashed in a mortar or bowl, OR 1 tablespoon anchovy paste

½ teaspoon very finely chopped garlic

½ teaspoon strong mustard, Dijon or German

½ teaspoon red wine vinegar (approximately), if the sauce will be used on meat OR 1 tablespoon strained lemon juice (approximately), if the sauce is for fish

½ cup olive oil

Salt, if necessary

1. Put the parsley, capers, mashed anchovy fillets, garlic, and mustard in a bowl and stir, mixing thoroughly. Add the vinegar or lemon juice and stir again. Add the olive oil, beating it vigorously into the other ingredients.

2. Taste for salt and for piquancy. (Add vinegar or lemon juice if you want it tarter, but add very small amounts at a time.)

NOTE

This sauce can be refrigerated for up to a week. Stir it well again before serving. It can also be used as dressing for Hard-Boiled Eggs with Piquant Sauce (page 45), but in that case you must hold back some of the oil.

Salsa rossa

RED SAUCE

This is an alternative to green sauce as an accompaniment to boiled meats. It is mellower, and it is served warm. Also excellent with Breaded Veal Cutlets, Milan Style (page 270) and with broiled steaks, it can be prepared ahead of time and refrigerated up to two weeks, but it must always be warmed up before serving.

For 4 servings

5 medium yellow onions, peeled and sliced thin	2 cups canned Italian tomatoes, with their juice
¼ cup vegetable oil	A pinch of chopped hot red pepper
2 green peppers	½ teaspoon salt

1. Cook the sliced onions in a saucepan with the oil over moderate heat until wilted and soft but not brown.

2. Remove the inner core and seeds from the green peppers. Peel the peppers with a potato peeler, and cut into ½-inch slices. Add to the wilted onions in the saucepan and continue cooking over moderate heat.

3. When the onions and peppers have been reduced by half in bulk, add the tomatoes, the hot pepper, and the salt. Continue cooking over low to moderate heat for 25 to 30 minutes, or until the tomatoes and oil separate. Taste for salt. Warm and stir just before serving.

ANTIPASTI

ANTIPASTI are the rogues of the Italian table. Nothing in all gastronomy plays so boldly upon the eye to excite the palate and set gastric juices in motion. The most appropriate place for antipasti is in a restaurant, where they are usually strategically displayed so that they can cast their spell on every arriving patron.

They are far less frequently a part of the home meal. When served at home, antipasti usually consist of one or more of the wonderful Italian pork products: prosciutto, *mortadella, coppa,* mountain salami, dried sausages. Prosciutto is sometimes served with fruit. There can be no finer antipasto than sweet prosciutto with ripe figs or cantaloupe.

What is an antipasto on one occasion is not necessarily that on another. You will see more antipasti in the index than you will find in this chapter. This is because of the flexibility of many Italian dishes. For example, such an elegant antipasto as Cold Sliced Veal with Tuna Sauce (page 276) can be an excellent second course, and it is among the second courses that you will find it.

All together, there are not as many antipasti here as in other books, perhaps, or as are offered by some restaurants. There are, however, a few more than are customarily prepared in an Italian home. Too much emphasis on antipasti puts a slightly commercial stress on an Italian meal. Use antipasti liberally for parties and buffets. But in the intimacy of a family meal use them wisely—which is to say, sparingly.

Ostriche alla moda di Taranto
BAKED OYSTERS WITH OIL AND PARSLEY

For 6 persons

Rock salt or well-washed pebbles

36 oysters, thoroughly washed and scrubbed, shucked, and each placed on a half shell

1½ tablespoons fine, dry unflavored bread crumbs

Freshly ground pepper, a twist of the mill for each oyster

¼ cup olive oil

Lemon juice

1. Preheat the oven to 500°.

2. Choose enough bake-and-serve pans to accommodate the oysters in one layer. Spread the rock salt or pebbles—the pebbles sold by Japanese stores can be very decorative—on the bottom of the pans. (The salt or pebbles serve both to keep the oysters from tipping and to retain heat.)

3. Arrange the oysters side by side in one layer in the pans. Top each oyster with a sprinkling of bread crumbs, a grinding of pepper, and a few drops of olive oil.

4. Place the oysters in the uppermost level of the preheated oven for 3 minutes. Before serving, moisten each oyster with a few drops of lemon juice.

Ostriche alla parmigiana
BAKED OYSTERS WITH PARMESAN CHEESE

For 6 persons

Rock salt or well-washed
pebbles

36 oysters, thoroughly washed
and scrubbed, shucked,
and each placed on a half
shell

6 tablespoons freshly grated
Parmesan cheese

1 tablespoon fine, dry unflavored bread crumbs

Freshly ground pepper, a
twist of the mill for each
oyster

2½ tablespoons butter

1. Preheat the oven to 500°.

2. Spread the rock salt or pebbles on the bottom of enough bake-and-serve pans to accommodate the oysters in one layer. (See explanation in Step 2 of preceding recipe.)

3. Arrange the oysters side by side in the pans. Top each oyster with ½ teaspoon of grated cheese, a tiny pinch of bread crumbs, a grinding of pepper, and a dot of butter.

4. Place in the uppermost level of the preheated oven for 5 minutes. Serve piping hot.

Spuma fredda di salmone
COLD SALMON FOAM

For 6 persons

15 ounces canned salmon

¼ cup olive oil

2 tablespoons lemon juice

A pinch of salt

Freshly ground pepper,
about 6 twists of the mill

1½ cups very cold whipping
cream

1. Drain the salmon and look it over carefully for bones and bits of skin. Using a fork, crumble it in a mixing bowl. Add the oil, lemon

juice, a little pinch of salt, and the pepper and beat them into the salmon until you've obtained a smooth, evenly blended mixture.

2. In a cold mixing bowl, whip the cream with a whisk or electric beater until it is stiff. Delicately fold the cream into the salmon mixture until it is completely incorporated. Refrigerate for at least 2 hours, but preferably not more than 24.

NOTE

One attractive way of presenting this is to spoon each individual serving onto a lettuce leaf, making a small, rounded mound. Garnish it then by placing a black olive (not the sharp Greek variety) on the mound's peak, and standing a tomato slice and a lemon slice at divergent angles on either side of it. You can use this as a spread for canapés with cocktails or serve it as antipasto.

Cozze e vongole passate ai ferri
BROILED MUSSELS AND CLAMS ON THE HALF SHELL

For 4 to 6 persons

2 dozen littleneck clams, the tiniest you can find, cleaned as directed on page 53	⅓ cup olive oil
	½ cup fine, dry unflavored bread crumbs
2 dozen mussels, cleaned as directed on page 56	1 canned Italian tomato, drained and cut into 2 dozen small strips
3 tablespoons finely chopped parsley	Lemon wedges
½ teaspoon finely chopped garlic	

1. Put the clams and mussels in separate covered pots over high heat until they open their shells. Bear in mind that mussels open up much faster than clams, and take care to remove both mussels and clams from the heat as soon as they are open, or they will become tough. Detach the clams and mussels from their shells, setting aside half the clam shells and half the mussel shells. Rinse off the clams one by one in their own juice to remove all traces of sand.

2. Preheat the broiler.

3. Put the parsley, garlic, olive oil, and bread crumbs in a mixing bowl and add the clams and mussels. Mix well until both clams and mussels are thoroughly coated and let stand at least 20 minutes. (If you feel you will have trouble later distinguishing the clams from the mussels, divide the marinating ingredients into two parts and use two separate bowls.)

4. Wash the clam and mussel shells. In each half shell place one of its respective mollusks. Distribute the leftover marinade in the mixing bowl among all the clams and mussels and top each clam with a sliver of tomato. Place on the broiling pan and run under the hot broiler for just a few minutes, until a light crust forms. Serve hot, with wedges of lemon on the side.

Acciughe

ANCHOVIES

The heady fragrance of anchovies carries into the cooking of every Italian region, from Piedmont to Sicily. Southerners may use them with more abandon than central or northern Italians, but there is no good kitchen in Italy that gets along entirely without anchovies. The best anchovies you can use are those you fillet at home. Canned fillets or paste are a blessed convenience when you have nothing else available, but they cannot come close to the fuller, mellower flavor of homemade fillets. Fillets are made from whole, salt-cured anchovies, and, if you have access to a Greek grocer, that is the ideal place to buy them, although you can find them also at some Italian and other ethnic groceries. They are sold loose, by weight, out of a large can. If the can has been started recently, you are in luck, because the anchovies in the upper half of the can are always the best. The others tend to be saltier and drier. You should fillet the anchovies and steep them in oil as soon as possible, and no later than 24 hours after buying them, otherwise they will dry.

(continued)

ANCHOVIES IN OIL

Whole salt-cured anchovies
(½ pound whole anchovies will yield about 4 servings of fillets)
Olive oil

1. Although all anchovies are not equally salty, it is best to begin by rinsing them quickly in cold running water to remove excess salt. Wipe dry with paper towels.

2. Spread some waxed paper or a flattened brown paper bag on the work counter. Lay the anchovies on the paper, and, grasping each by the tail, gently scrape off its skin with a knife. Remove the dorsal fin and the bones attached to it.

3. Using the knife, separate the anchovy into two halves and remove the spine. Place the fillets in a shallow rectangular dish. As soon as you have a full layer of fillets, cover with olive oil. You can build up several layers in the same dish, but make sure that they are all completely covered by oil. If you are not going to use them immediately, refrigerate them. They will keep for 10 days to 2 weeks.

NOTE
When the oil congeals in the refrigerator it turns into a yellowish-green solid. This doesn't mean it has gone bad. When it reaches room temperature again, it will return to a liquid.

MENU SUGGESTIONS

Aside from their many uses in cooking, anchovy fillets make a marvelous antipasto, the irresistible aroma of which will move the most indolent appetite. You may use them on canapés, of course, just as you would use canned fillets. But these homemade fillets are perfect just by themselves. Serve them with sweet butter, and slices of good crusty French or Italian bread. Follow with a substantial dish that won't be thrown off balance by the rather overwhelming flavor of the anchovies. Two suggestions: Bucatini with Pancetta, Tomatoes, and Hot Pepper (page 105), or Thin Spaghetti with Eggplant (page 98).

Peperoni e acciughe

PEPPERS AND ANCHOVIES

Here broiled sweet peppers and anchovies are steeped together in oil until they soften and there is an exchange of flavors. The peppers acquire pungency, while letting the anchovies share in their sweetness. The result is most appetizing, especially as a prelude to a robust meal.

Approximately 8 servings

8 medium sweet peppers, green, yellow, or red	Freshly ground pepper Orégano
16 large or 20 medium flat anchovy fillets, preferably the home-prepared variety (preceding page)	3 tablespoons capers 4 cloves garlic, lightly crushed with a heavy knife handle and peeled
Salt	Olive oil

1. Place the peppers under a hot broiler. When the skin swells and is partially charred on one side, turn another side toward the flame. When all the skin is blistered and slightly charred, remove the peppers, and peel them while still hot.

2. Cut the peeled peppers lengthwise into strips 1½ to 2 inches wide, removing all the seeds and the pulpy inner core. Pat the strips dry with a cloth or paper towels.

3. Choose a serving dish that will hold the peppers in 4 layers. Arrange a layer of peppers on the bottom. Place 4 to 5 anchovies over the peppers. Add a tiny pinch of salt, a liberal grinding of pepper, a small pinch of orégano, a few capers, and one crushed garlic clove. Repeat until you have used up all the peppers and anchovies. Add enough olive oil to cover the top layer.

4. Put the dish in the refrigerator for 4 hours or more, then bring to room temperature before serving. If you are preparing these peppers several days ahead of time, remove the garlic after 24 hours.

Pomodori ripieni di tonno

TOMATOES STUFFED WITH TUNA AND CAPERS

For 6 persons

6 large, ripe, round, meaty
tomatoes
Salt
2 seven-ounce cans Italian
tuna, packed in olive oil
Mayonnaise (page 26) made
using 1 large egg yolk,
½ cup olive oil, and 2
tablespoons lemon juice

2 teaspoons strong mustard,
Dijon or German
1½ tablepsoons capers, the tinier
the better
Garnishes as suggested below

1. Slice off the tops of the tomatoes. Remove all the seeds and some of the dividing walls, leaving just three or four large sections. Salt lightly and put the tomatoes open end down on a platter, allowing their liquid to drain away.

2. In a bowl, mash the tuna to a pulp with a fork. Add the mayonnaise, holding back 1 or 2 tablespoons, add the mustard and the capers. Mix with a fork to a uniform consistency. Taste and correct for salt.

3. Shake off the excess liquid from the tomatoes, but don't squeeze them. Stuff to the very top with the tuna mixture. Seal the tops with the remaining mayonnaise, and garnish with an olive slice, a strip of green or red pepper, a ring of capers, or parsley leaves. Serve at room temperature or slightly chilled.

Pomodori coi gamberetti
TOMATOES STUFFED WITH SHRIMP

For 6 persons

6 large, ripe, round, meaty
tomatoes

¾ pound small shrimps

1 tablespoon red wine vinegar

Salt

Mayonnaise (page 26) made
with 1 large egg yolk, ½
cup olive oil, and 2½ to 3
tablespoons lemon juice

1½ tablespoons capers, the
tinier the better

1 teaspoon strong mustard,
Dijon or German

Parsley

1. Prepare the tomatoes as indicated on the preceding page.

2. Rinse the shrimps in cold water. Bring 2 quarts of water with the 1 tablespoon of vinegar and 1 tablespoon of salt to a boil. Drop in the shrimps and cook for just 2 minutes after the water returns to a boil. Drain, peel, and devein the shrimps and set aside to cool.

3. Pick out six of the best-looking, best-shaped shrimps and set aside. Chop the rest of the shrimps roughly. Put them in a bowl and mix the chopped shrimps with the mayonnaise, capers, and mustard.

4. Shake off the excess liquid from the tomatoes, but don't squeeze them. Stuff to the top with the shrimp-and-mayonnaise mixture. Garnish each tomato with a shrimp and one or two parsley leaves. Serve at cool room temperature or slightly chilled.

Gamberetti all'olio e limone
SHRIMPS WITH OIL AND LEMON

In Italy, very tiny fresh-caught shrimps are used to prepare this simple but sublime antipasto. The shrimps are boiled very briefly with vegetables, then steeped in olive oil and lemon juice. There is nothing more to it than that, but I've known people whose memories turn to *gamberetti all'olio e limone* with keener joy than they feel toward anything else they had in Italy. Although our ocean shrimps do not have the same sweetness as the tiny shrimps of the Adriatic, they can be very good all the same. For this recipe you should try to use the smallest fresh shrimps you can find.

For 6 persons

1 stalk celery	½ cup olive oil
1 carrot, peeled	¼ cup lemon juice
2 tablespoons red wine vinegar	Freshly ground pepper to
Salt	taste (optional)
1½ pounds small fresh shrimps, washed in cold water but left unpeeled	

1. Put the celery, carrot, vinegar, and 1 tablespoon of salt in a saucepan with 2 to 3 quarts of water and bring to a rapid boil.

2. Add the unpeeled shrimps. If very small, not over ½ inch in diameter, they will be cooked shortly after the water returns to a boil; medium shrimp cook in about 2 to 3 minutes.

3. When cooked, drain the shrimps, peel, and devein. Put them in a shallow bowl and add the oil, lemon juice, 1 teaspoon salt (or more to taste), and optional pepper while the shrimps are still warm. Mix well and let them steep in the seasonings at room temperature for 1 to 1½ hours before serving. Serve with crusty French or Italian bread or with thinly sliced, good-quality white bread, lightly toasted.

NOTE

This dish is far better if never chilled, but if necessary it can be prepared a day ahead of time and kept in the refrigerator under plastic wrap. Always return it to room temperature before serving, however.

Bastoncini di carota marinati
TASTY CARROT STICKS

For 4 persons

¼ pound carrots
1 small clove garlic, lightly
   crushed with a heavy knife
   handle and peeled

Salt and freshly ground
   pepper to taste
¼ teaspoon orégano
1 tablespoon red wine vinegar
Olive oil, enough to cover

1. Peel the carrots, cut them in 2-inch lengths, and cook them in boiling salted water for about 10 or 12 minutes. (Cooking time varies according to the thickness and freshness of the carrots. In order to cook the carrots uniformly put the thickest parts into the water first, then the thinner, tapered ends. You want the carrots tender but quite firm for this recipe because the marinade will continue to soften them.)

2. Drain the cooked carrots, and cut lengthwise into small sticks about ¼ inch thick. Place in a small, deep serving dish.

3. Bury the garlic in the carrots. Add salt and pepper to taste, the orégano and vinegar and enough olive oil to just cover the carrots.

4. Refrigerate and allow to marinate at least overnight, removing the garlic after 24 hours. Serve at room temperature.

MENU SUGGESTIONS

This is a tangy and rustic appetizer. It can be part of an antipasto composed of such other dishes as Anchovies in Oil (page 36), Peppers and Anchovies (page 37), and Tuna and Beans Salad (page 417).

Bagna caôda
HOT ANCHOVY-FLAVORED DIP FOR VEGETABLES

One of the most frequent observations on Italian food is that it is based mainly on peasant cooking. Like many of the commonly held beliefs about Italian cooking, this is not entirely true, but it is a fact that some of the glories of the Italian table were first created in peasant kitchens. Typical of these is *bagna caôda,* a hot dip for raw vegetables. It is a perfect illustration of the gastronomic genius of the Italian peasant. The materials are only those most easily available to him: oil, butter, garlic, a few anchovies in brine, and his own vegetables. The preparation is quick and direct: the garlic is sautéed for the briefest of moments, the anchovies are cooked just long enough to dissolve them, and the vegetables to be dipped into the sauce are raw. The result is a heartening, restorative dish of immensely satisfying flavor.

Eating *bagna caôda* is a two-handed affair. One hand takes a vegetable, the other bread, dipping them alternately in the sauce. The only interruption in this resolute rhythm is for long, slaking swallows of young, lively wine.

In peasant kitchens, *bagna caôda* is prepared in an earthenware pot, kept warm over drowsily glowing coals while everyone gathers around and dips. When the vegetables are finished, the fire is stirred up and eggs are broken into the pot and scrambled with the rest of the sauce. Today in the smart *trattorie* of Piedmont, *bagna caôda* is served in individual earthenware chafing dishes with built-in candle warmers. At home I prefer to make and serve *bagna caôda* in a single pot. It is both better for the sauce and more fun. But however you do it, it is important that the dip be kept warm the entire time that one is eating. The heat should be kept at a minimum, at no more than candle-warmer intensity, because the dip must not continue to cook after it is prepared. An earthenware pot is all but indispensable for *bagna caôda.* If you don't already have one, this is the best of reasons for getting one.

For 6 to 8 persons

¾ cup olive oil

3 tablespoons butter

2 teaspoons finely chopped
  garlic

8 to 10 flat anchovy fillets,
  chopped

1 teaspoon salt

Heat the oil and butter until the butter is thoroughly liquefied and barely begins to foam. (Don't wait for the foam to subside or the butter will be too hot.) Add the garlic and sauté very briefly. It must not take on any color. Add the anchovies and cook over very low heat, stirring frequently, until the anchovies dissolve into a paste. Add the salt, stir, and bring to the table along with raw vegetables, as prepared below.

THE VEGETABLES

cardoons   The traditional vegetable for *bagna caôda* is a very tender, sweet, dwarf cardoon found in many sections of Piedmont. The large cardoon available here in Italian vegetable markets is tougher and often bitter. You might try using just the heart, however, which can be quite nice at times. Wash it thoroughly and cut into four sections, like a celery heart. Rub the cut parts with a little lemon juice or the cardoon will discolor.

artichokes   You don't need to trim artichokes for *bagna caôda* as you do for recipes where they are cooked. Rinse the artichoke in cold water and serve it whole. One pulls off a leaf at a time, dips it, and bites off just the tender part.

broccoli   Cut off the florets and put aside for use in any recipe for cooked broccoli. Serve just the stalks, after peeling the tough outer skin.

spinach   Use only young, crisp spinach. Wash very thoroughly and at length in several changes of cold water until the water shows no trace of soil. Serve with the stems on because they provide a hold for dipping.

zucchini   Only very fresh, small, young, glossy-skinned zucchini are suitable. Wash thoroughly in cold water, lightly scraping the skin to remove any embedded soil. Cut lengthwise into sections 1 inch thick.

sweet peppers   Wash in cold water and cut into quarter sections. Remove the seeds and the pulpy inner core.

celery   Discard any bruised or tough outer stalks. Wash very carefully in cold water.

carrots   Scrape or peel clean and cut lengthwise into sections ½ inch thick.

radishes   Cut off the root tips, wash in cold water, and serve with stems and leaves, attractive and helpful for dipping, left on.

asparagus   This is a vegetable you will never see served with *bagna caôda* in Piedmont. The very thought scandalizes my Piedmontese friends. *Bagna caôda* is a winter dish, asparagus is a spring vegetable, and never the twain, et cetera. It is a pity for them, because I have never tasted any better vegetable with this dip. Use the freshest asparagus you can find, with the crispest stalks and tightest buds. Trim it and peel it as directed on page 354. Wash it with cold water and add a generous quantity of it to the vegetable bowl because it will be very popular.

This is not necessarily a definitive list of vegetables suitable for *bagna caôda*. You should feel free to make your own discoveries. Remember, though, this is a dip for vegetables freshly picked at the peak of their development. Use only the youngest, sweetest vegetables available, and serve as wide a variety of them as possible. And before serving pat all the vegetables dry with a towel.

MENU SUGGESTIONS

Depending on the variety and quantity of vegetables you use, *bagna caôda* can be practically a meal on its own, and would need nothing more to complete it than an Open-Faced Italian Omelet with Cheese (page 327) or with Tomatoes, Onions, and Basil (page 331). If you would like to work it into a fuller meal, however, follow it with Beef Braised in Red Wine Sauce (page 242), Casserole-Roasted Lamb with Juniper Berries (page 280), Baby Lamb Chops Fried in Parmesan Cheese Batter (page 283), Charcoal-Broiled Chicken Marinated in Pepper, Oil, and Lemon (page 307), or Broiled Pork Wrapped in Caul Fat (page 302). A perfect alternative to all these is a magnificent American roast beef.

Uova sode in salsa verde

HARD-BOILED EGGS WITH PIQUANT SAUCE

For 6 persons

6 eggs (U.S. Large)	¼ teaspoon finely chopped
2 tablespoons olive oil	garlic
½ tablespoon chopped capers	¼ teaspoon strong mustard,
1 tablespoon chopped parsley	Dijon or German
1 teaspoon anchovy paste	A small pinch of salt
	12 small strips of pimento

1. Put the eggs in cold water and bring to a boil. Boil slowly for 10 minutes, then set aside to cool. When cool, remove the shells, and cut the eggs in half lengthwise. Carefully remove the yolks without damaging the whites. Set aside the whites.

2. Combine the egg yolks and the remaining ingredients, except for the pimento and the reserved egg whites, in a bowl. Using a fork, mash to a creamy, uniform consistency. Divide into 12 equal parts and spoon into the cavities of the reserved egg whites. Garnish each with a strip of pimento.

NOTE
These can be prepared ahead of time and refrigerated, but serve at room temperature.

Funghi ripieni

STUFFED MUSHROOMS WITH BÉCHAMEL SAUCE

For 6 persons

12 large mushrooms
2½ tablespoons butter
1 tablespoon finely chopped shallots or yellow onion
3 tablespoons chopped prosciutto or cooked ham
Salt
Freshly ground pepper, about 4 twists of the mill

A thick Béchamel Sauce made with: 1½ tablespoons flour, 1½ tablespoons butter, ¼ teaspoon salt, and 1 cup milk (page 28)
3 tablespoons freshly grated Parmesan cheese
Fine, dry unflavored bread crumbs

1. Slice off the ends of the mushroom stems. Wipe the mushrooms clean with a damp cloth. If there are still traces of soil, wash each mushroom carefully under cold running water, working quickly. Dry well with a towel. Detach the stems and chop them fine.

2. Preheat the oven to 500°.

3. In a skillet, sauté the chopped shallots or onion in 2½ tablespoons butter over medium-high heat until pale gold in color. Add the chopped prosciutto and sauté for about a minute. Add the finely chopped mushroom stems, salt, and pepper and cook, stirring, for 2 to 3 minutes. Tilt the skillet and draw off all the fat with a spoon.

4. In a bowl, mix the contents of the skillet with the warm béchamel. Add the grated Parmesan and mix again.

5. Place the mushroom caps, bottoms up, in a butter-smeared baking dish. Sprinkle lightly with salt, fill with the béchamel stuffing, sprinkle with bread crumbs, and dot each cap with butter. Place in the upper third of the preheated oven and bake for 15 minutes, or until a slight crust has formed. Allow to settle for about 10 minutes before serving.

Insalata di funghi e formaggio
MUSHROOM AND CHEESE SALAD

In October and November, when the wild mushrooms are ga-
thered in the woods at the foothills of the Alps, the choicest, firmest
mushrooms go into delicious and wildly expensive salads with white
truffles and cheese. We don't have white truffles here, and wild mushrooms are virtually never seen in the markets, but we have a limitless
supply of excellent cultivated mushrooms and Swiss cheese. This
is not a replica of the Italian original, but it can stand on its own
merits as a very appealing antipasto.

For 4 persons

½ pound very crisp, white fresh
    mushrooms
Juice of ½ lemon
⅔ cup Swiss cheese cut into
    strips 1 inch long, ¼ inch
    wide, and ⅛ inch thick

3 tablespoons olive oil
Salt to taste
Freshly ground pepper, a
    liberal quantity, to taste

1. Detach the mushroom stems from the caps. Save the stems for
another recipe. Wipe the caps clean with a damp cloth, then cut
into slices ⅛ inch thick. Put the slices in a salad bowl and moisten
them with some lemon juice to keep them from discoloring. (You
can prepare these as much as 30 to 45 minutes ahead of time.)

2. When ready to serve, add the strips of Swiss cheese to the bowl
and toss with the olive oil, salt, and pepper.

BRESAOLA

Bresaola is a specialty of the Valtellina, a fertile valley at the
northernmost edge of Lombardy. It is a whole beef filet, cured in
salt and air-dried, a little tarter yet more delicate than prosciutto.
Sliced thin it is one of the finest and most elegant of antipasti. It
can precede any meal, whether hearty or light.

Although Valtellina *bresaola* is not available here, many specialty food shops carry a nearly identical product, Switzerland's Grison. Grison is compressed into a rectangular loaf, while *bresaola* maintains the original round, tapered shape of the filet. This makes Grison somewhat drier than *bresaola*, but otherwise it is a completely acceptable substitute.

It should be served as quickly as possible after it is sliced, at most within 24 hours, or else it will become dry and turn sharp.

Serve it with olive oil, enough to moisten each slice, a few drops of lemon juice, and freshly ground pepper.

Bocconcini fritti

FRIED MORTADELLA, PANCETTA, AND CHEESE TIDBITS

This is a savory hot antipasto that can also be served before meals with an apéritif, or as part of a buffet. In Bologna and its province it is often a prelude to the *grande fritto misto*, the great platter of mixed fried meats and vegetables, found on page 333.

For 6 persons

¼ pound Swiss cheese, in one piece

¼ pound *mortadella*, in one piece

¼ pound *pancetta*, thinly sliced

1 cup all-purpose flour spread on a dish or on waxed paper

2 eggs, lightly beaten, in a bowl

1 cup fine, dry unflavored bread crumbs, spread on a dish or on waxed paper

Vegetable oil, enough to come at least 1 inch up the side of the skillet

1. Cut one-third of the cheese into 1-inch cubes and the rest into ½-inch cubes. Set aside.

2. Cut two-thirds of the *mortadella* into cubes whose sides are as wide as the slice is thick. Cut the rest of the slice into thin strips 2 inches long and about ½ inch wide.

3. Cut the *pancetta* into strips as close as possible in size to the *mortadella* strips.

4. Wrap part of the smaller cheese cubes with strips of *pancetta,* and the others with strips of *mortadella.* Fasten with toothpicks. You now have four kinds of tidbits ready to coat and fry: cheese wrapped in *pancetta,* cheese wrapped in *mortadella,* cheese cubes, and *mortadella* cubes.

5. Roll the tidbits in flour, dip them in egg, then roll them in bread crumbs. (You can prepare them up to this point 3 or 4 hours ahead of time, if you like.)

6. Choose not too large a skillet, so as not to waste oil, then pour in enough oil to come at least 1 inch up the sides of the pan. Heat the oil over high heat.

7. When the oil is very hot, slip in as many of the tidbits as will fit loosely in the pan. Fry until golden brown on both sides, then transfer to paper towels to drain. Continue until you've fried all the tidbits. (Caution: handle them with tongs, not with a fork. The prongs of a fork might puncture the crust on the cheese and it will run out.)

Bruschetta
ROMAN GARLIC BREAD

Although here it is known as garlic bread, the most important ingredient in *bruschetta* is not garlic but olive oil. The origin of *bruschetta* in Italy is probably nearly as old as that of olive oil itself. Each winter in ancient Rome one's first taste of the freshly pressed, dense, green olive oil was most likely an oil-soaked piece of bread that may or may not have been rubbed with garlic. In modern times *bruschetta* became a staple of the poor man's *trattoria,* where it went a long way in making up for the frugality of the fare. When eating in *trattorie* became the fashionable thing to do, *bruschetta* found its way into polite society. The name *bruschetta* comes from *bruscare,* which means "to roast over coals," the original and still the best way of toasting the bread.

(*continued*)

For 6 persons

12 slices Italian whole-wheat
   bread (*pane integrale*),
   1½ inches thick, 3 to 4
   inches wide
4 to 5 cloves garlic, lightly
   crushed with a heavy knife
   handle and peeled

½ cup olive oil, as green and
   dense as you can find,
   preferably Sicilian olive oil
Salt and freshly ground
   pepper to taste

1. Preheat the broiler.

2. Toast the bread on both sides to a golden brown under the hot broiler.

3. Rub one side of the toast while still hot with garlic. Discard the garlic as it dries up and take a fresh clove. Put the toast on a platter, garlic-rubbed side facing up, and pour a thin stream of olive oil over it. Not a few drops, but enough to soak each slice very lightly. Add a sprinkling of salt and a healthy twist or two of freshly ground pepper per slice. The toast is best served while still warm.

I Primi

FIRST COURSES

T HE first course in an Italian meal is almost always a pasta, a
risotto, or a soup. Occasionally, but not frequently, a vegetable, an antipasto, or a fish course may become the first course, but
no pasta or soup is ever turned into a side dish or second course.
Sometimes one finds *risotto* incorporated into the second course,
as when Risotto Milan Style (page 184) is combined with *ossobuco*
(Braised Veal Shanks, Milan Style, page 256). But these instances
are very rare.

First courses are, justifiably, the best-known feature of Italian
cooking. Into them, Italians have poured most of their culinary
genius and inventiveness. Although the temptation is strong to give
as many as possible of these incredibly varied and attractive dishes,
it will not be done here. Rather than take a breathless junket through
the whole landscape of Italian first courses, I thought it would be
more profitable for those with a more than casual interest in good
cooking to tarry over a few selected areas and explore them in depth.

Italy's most original and important contribution to cooking is the
vast repertory of homemade pasta. However, every treatment I have
seen of it has been cursory, inadequate, or, even worse, misleading.
Here, with the first fully detailed exposition of the subject in English,
I have tried to give even the most inexperienced cook easy access

to the techniques and the inexhaustible satisfactions of homemade pasta. The step-by-step analysis of both handmade and machine-made egg pasta should guide any willing beginner safely past the early difficulties toward a well-grounded proficiency in making pasta at home. Once you have mastered the fundamentally simple mechanics of rolling out a thin sheet of egg-pasta dough, you can move on to execute any one of dozens of delicious variations on the pasta theme.

Risotto, another uniquely Italian preparation that approaches pasta in variety and importance, is also examined in detail. The basic *risotto* technique is clearly set down, and you are shown how it can be developed into nine different *risotti.* With taste and ingenuity you can expand this, as Italian families do, into your own personal *risotto* repertory.

You will also find recipes for three varieties of *gnocchi*—potato, semolina, and spinach and ricotta—along with seven different ways of serving them.

In this chapter, too, are some of the heroic country soups of Tuscany, as well as several other traditional soups, including an unusual clam soup and a little-known sauerkraut soup from Trieste.

Macaroni pasta deserves and has been given whole volumes. I have given here fresh versions of some of the best-known sauces as well as several less familiar ones. There are six different tomato sauces and, altogether, twenty-seven different sauces for both home-made and macaroni pasta.

I wish there had been room for more. Perhaps you will be encouraged by what you find here to discover other dishes at their source. But even if you never go beyond the material in this chapter, you will still possess a larger variety of first courses than do most regional Italian cooks.

Zuppa di vongole

CLAM SOUP

Clams, unlike oysters and most mussels, often contain some sand. There are methods for eliminating the sand, such as allowing the clams to stand for long periods in cold water so that they can open up and disgorge it or trapping the sand by straining the cooked clam juices. In terms of flavor, however, when clams are to be served in their shells, as in this soup, neither method is as satisfactory as letting the clams release their juices directly into the sauce. There may be a little sand, but this quickly settles to the bottom of the pot, and with a little care in lifting out the clams and spooning the sauce into the soup plates it will all be left behind.

For 4 persons

3 dozen littleneck clams in their shells, the tiniest you can find

1½ tablespoons finely chopped shallots or yellow onion

½ cup olive oil

2 teaspoons finely chopped garlic

2 tablespoons finely chopped parsley

¼ teaspoon cornstarch dissolved in ⅔ cup dry white wine

Toasted Italian whole-wheat bread (*pane integrale*), 1 slice per serving

1. Set the clams in a large basin or sink filled with cold water. Let stand for 5 minutes, then drain and refill the basin with clean water. Scrub the clams vigorously with a coarse, stiff brush or by rubbing them one against the other. When they are all scrubbed, drain and fill basin again with clean water. Repeat these steps for 20 or 30 minutes, until you see that the water in the basin remains clear. Transfer the cleaned clams to a bowl.

2. Choose a heavy casserole large enough to contain the clams later. (Remember that they more than double in volume when open.) Over medium heat sauté the shallots in the olive oil until translucent. Add the garlic. When it has colored lightly add the

parsley and stir two or three times. Add the cornstarch and wine, turn the heat to high, and cook briskly for 2 minutes.

3. Drop in the clams. Stir, basting them lightly, and cover tightly. Continue cooking over high heat and stir the clams from time to time so that they all cook evenly. When their shells open, they will release their juices, and they will be done.

4. Place a slice of bread in each individual soup plate. Ladle the clams and sauce over the bread, taking care not to scoop up the liquid from the bottom of the pot because it probably contains sand.

NOTE
In Italy we bring the pot to the table and serve the clams a few at a time so that they don't get cold.

MENU SUGGESTIONS

This is an all-purpose first course that can be followed by any fish course, giving the preference, however, to robust rather than delicate flavors. It goes well with Poached Halibut with Parsley Sauce (page 214), Fish Broiled the Adriatic Way (page 224), Stuffed Squid Braised in White Wine (page 232), or Stewed Squid (page 230).

Zuppa di vongole vellutata
VELVETY CLAM SOUP WITH MUSHROOMS

This clam soup from the northern Adriatic coast is a considerable departure from traditional Italian methods of doing shellfish. The clam broth is enriched with eggs, milk, and butter, and completely eschews garlic. You can think of it as a sort of chowder with a special Italian taste.

For 4 persons

3 dozen littleneck clams, the tiniest you can find	3 tablespoons butter
2 tablespoons olive oil	½ pound mushrooms, thinly sliced
1 tablespoon finely chopped shallots or yellow onion	⅛ teaspoon salt
	3 to 4 twists of the pepper mill

3 egg yolks
⅓ cup milk

1 cup chicken broth, homemade
or canned
1 tablespoon cornstarch dissolved in 1 cup warm water

1. Follow the directions for washing and scrubbing clams (page 53).

2. Heat the clams with the olive oil in a covered saucepan over medium-high heat until they open their shells. Give them a vigorous shake or turn them so that they will all heat evenly (some clams are more obstinate than others about opening). When most of them have opened up, it would be best to remove the open clams while waiting for the stubborn ones; otherwise they will become tough as they linger in the pan. Remove the clams from their shells and rinse off any sand on the meat by dipping them briefly one at a time in their own juice. Unless the clams are exceptionally small, cut them up into two or more pieces and set aside. Strain the clam juices through a sieve lined with paper towels and set aside.

3. In a skillet, sauté the shallots in 1½ tablespoons of the butter over medium-high heat. When the shallots have turned pale gold, add the sliced mushrooms, salt, pepper, and sauté briskly for about 3 minutes. Remove from the heat and set aside.

4. In a small bowl mash the remaining 1½ tablespoons of butter until soft and creamy. Set aside.

5. Put the egg yolks in a serving bowl or soup tureen and beat them lightly with a fork or whisk, gradually adding the milk. Swirl in the softened butter.

6. In a medium-sized stockpot or casserole bring the chicken broth to a boil. Mix in the dissolved cornstarch, a little bit at a time. Add the strained clam juices, the contents of the skillet, and the clams. Pour the hot soup, in tiny quantities at first, into the bowl or tureen containing the egg-yolk mixture. Beat rapidly with the whisk as you pour, gradually increasing the quantities of soup until it has all been added to the bowl. Serve immediately with *crostini* made from two to three slices of bread (Fried Bread Squares for Soup, page 88).

Follow this soup with a fish course having a crisp, straightforward taste, such as Shrimp Brochettes, Adriatic Style (page 226), Fish Broiled the Adriatic Way (page 224), or Fried Squid (page 234).

Zuppa di cozze
MUSSEL SOUP

The two most important things to know about the proper preparation of mussels are, first, that you must take your time to clean them, and, second, that it takes virtually no time at all to cook them.

To get mussels clean you must scrub them thoroughly under cold running water with a coarse, stiff brush or rub them one against another until you have removed all traces of dirt and slime. It takes rather a long time because there is a surprising amount of obstinate slime on each mussel, but once you are past this tedious part the rest of the work goes quickly and the result is completely rewarding. Discard all the mussels that are not tightly closed and any that feel much lighter or heavier than the rest. With a sharp paring knife, cut off the tough, ropelike tufts that protrude from the shells. The mussels are now clean and ready.

There are cooks who let the mussels stand for a long time in a bucket of water. Inasmuch as fine, fresh mussels very rarely contain sand, this step is wholly unnecessary. Not only that, but in allowing the mussels to unclench their shells in water you lose much of their precious, tasty juice.

For 4 persons

1½ teaspoons chopped garlic	1 cup canned Italian tomatoes,
⅓ cup olive oil	drained and cut up
1 tablespoon coarsely chopped parsley	⅛ teaspoon chopped hot red pepper

2 pounds fresh mussels,
cleaned and scrubbed as
directed above

4 slices Italian whole-wheat
bread (*pane integrale*),
toasted and (optional)
rubbed with garlic

1. Choose a casserole large enough to contain the mussels later. Sauté the garlic in the oil over moderate heat until it has colored lightly. Add the parsley, stir once or twice, then add the cut-up tomatoes and the chopped hot pepper. Cook, uncovered, at a gentle simmer for about 25 minutes, or until the tomatoes and oil separate.

2. Add the mussels, cover the casserole, raise the heat to high, and cook until the mussels open their shells, about 3 to 5 minutes. To get all the mussels to cook evenly, grasp the casserole with both hands, holding the cover down tight, and jerk it two or three times.

3. Put the 4 slices of toasted bread in 4 soup dishes and ladle the mussels, with all their sauce, over the bread. Serve piping hot.

MENU SUGGESTIONS

There is as much joy for the eye as for the palate here in the delicate, amber mussel within its glossy jet-black shell balanced against the exuberance of the tomato sauce. As a first course, this can precede any fish course that is not sauced with tomato. Broiled or fried fish would be my first choice, but an excellent second course could also be Pan-Roasted Mackerel with Rosemary and Garlic (page 216). If you want to precede it with an antipasto, try Peppers and Anchovies (page 37).

Minestrina tricolore

CREAMY POTATO SOUP WITH CARROTS AND CELERY

This lovely soup is a study in delicate contrasts. The name, *minestrina tricolore,* or "tricolor" soup, comes from the creamed potato, the orange flecks of carrot, and the parsley, which recall the colors of the Italian flag. Its character comes from the interruption of its smooth, velvety consistency by the crisp specks of sautéed carrot and celery. It is quite artless and good.

For 4 to 6 persons

1½ pounds potatoes, peeled and and roughly diced

3 tablespoons finely chopped yellow onion

2 tablespoons butter

3 tablespoons vegetable oil

3 tablespoons finely chopped carrot

3 tablespoons finely chopped celery

5 tablespoons freshly grated Parmesan cheese

1 cup milk

2 cups Homemade Meat Broth (page 10) OR ½ cup canned beef broth mixed with 1½ cups water

Salt to taste

2 tablespoons chopped parsley

1. Put the potatoes and just enough cold water to cover in a stockpot. Cover, bring to a boil, and cook at a moderate boil until the potatoes are tender. Purée the potatoes, with their liquid, through a food mill back into the pot. Set aside.

2. In a skillet sauté the chopped onion, with all the butter and oil, over medium heat until pale gold in color. Add the chopped carrot and celery and cook for about 2 minutes, but not long enough to let the vegetables become soft, since you want them to be crunchy in the soup.

3. Add the entire contents of the skillet to the puréed potatoes in the pot. Turn on the heat to medium and add the grated Parmesan cheese, the milk, and the broth. Stir and cook at a steady simmer for a few minutes, until the cooking fat floating on the surface

is dispersed throughout the soup and the consistency of the soup is that of liquid cream. Add salt to taste. (Bear in mind that this soup will thicken as it cools in the plate. If the soup is too dense, simply add equal parts of broth and milk, as required.) When done, mix in the parsley off the heat. Serve in warm soup plates, with *crostini* (Fried Bread Squares for Soup, page 88) and additional freshly grated Parmesan cheese on the side.

MENU SUGGESTIONS

This is a very pleasant soup that gets along well with virtually any meat or fowl second course. Avoid dishes with cream or milk, and very sharp tomato sauces, however. A nice combination would be with Breaded Veal Cutlets (page 270), Chicken Fricassee with Dried Mushrooms (page 310), or any of the simple roasts.

Zuppa di patate e cipolle
POTATO AND ONION SOUP

For 6 persons

1½ pounds yellow onions, peeled and very thinly sliced
3 tablespoons butter
3 tablespoons vegetable oil
Salt
2 pounds boiling potatoes, peeled and diced into ¼-inch cubes

3½ cups Homemade Meat Broth (page 10) (approximately) OR 3 cups water (approximately) plus ½ cup canned beef bouillon
3 tablespoons freshly grated Parmesan cheese

1. In an uncovered skillet, cook the onion, with all the butter and oil and a dash of salt, over moderate heat. Cook gently and slowly, allowing the onion gradually to wilt. Cook until it turns light brown. Turn off the heat and set aside. Do not remove the onion from the skillet.

2. Boil the diced potato in 3 cups of the homemade broth or 3

cups of water. Add a little salt. Do not boil too rapidly.

3. When the potato is tender add all the onion from the skillet, together with its cooking fat. Loosen any of the cooking residue from the bottom of the skillet with some of the hot liquid in which the potatoes have cooked and add it to the soup.

4. Add the remaining ½ cup homemade broth or ½ cup canned bouillon and bring to a gentle boil. With a wooden spoon mash part of the potatoes against the side of the pot and mix into the boiling liquid. Continue cooking for 8 to 10 minutes. Check the soup for density. If at this point it is too thick (it's supposed to be a soup, not a purée), add homemade broth or water as required.

5. Turn off the heat. Add the grated Parmesan cheese, stirring it into the soup. Taste and correct for salt. Serve with a small bowl of freshly grated Parmesan cheese on the side.

MENU SUGGESTIONS

This soup goes well with meat courses that have a hearty country character. Try it with Meat Loaf Braised in White Wine with Dried Wild Mushrooms (page 249), either of the veal stews on pages 273–274, Roast Pork with Bay Leaves (page 286), or Fried Calf's Brains (page 299).

Risi e bisi
RICE AND PEAS

No one else in Italy cooks rice in so many different ways as the Venetians. They have at least several dozen basic dishes, not counting individual variations, where rice is combined with every likely vegetable, meat, fowl, or fish. Of all of them, the one Venetians have always loved the best has been *risi e bisi*. In the days of the Republic of Venice, *risi e bisi* was the first dish served at the dinner given by the doges each April 25 in honor of Saint Mark. Those, of course, were the earliest, youngest peas of the season, which are the best to use for *risi e bisi*. But one can also make it with later, larger peas, the ones Venetians call *senatori*. You may use frozen peas, if you must, and this recipe shows you how, but until you've made it with choice fresh peas your *risi e bisi* will be a tolerable but slightly blurred copy of the original.

Risi e bisi is not *risotto* with peas. It is a soup, although a very thick one. Some cooks make it thick enough to eat with a fork, but it is at its best when it is fairly runny, with just enough liquid to require a spoon.

For 4 persons

2 tablespoons chopped yellow onion

¼ cup butter

2 pounds fresh peas (unshelled weight) OR 1 ten-ounce package frozen peas, thawed

Salt

3½ cups Homemade Meat Broth (page 10) for fresh peas, 3 cups for frozen (see note below)

1 cup raw rice, preferably Italian Arborio rice

2 tablespoons chopped parsley

½ cup freshly grated Parmesan cheese

NOTE

This is one of those dishes that really demand the flavor and delicacy of homemade broth. If you absolutely must use store-bought broth, use canned chicken broth in the following proportions: *for fresh peas,* 1 cup broth mixed with 2½ cups water; *for frozen peas,* 1 cup broth mixed with 2 cups water.

1. Put the onion in a stockpot with the butter and sauté over medium heat until pale gold.

2. *If you are using fresh peas,* add the peas and 1 teaspoon salt, and sauté for 2 minutes, stirring frequently. Add 3 cups of broth, cover, and cook at a very moderate boil for 10 minutes. Add the rice, parsley, and the remaining ½ cup broth, stir, cover, and cook at a slow boil for 15 minutes, or until the rice is tender but *al dente,* firm to the bite. Stir from time to time while cooking, and taste and correct for salt.

If you are using thawed frozen peas, add the peas and 1 teaspoon salt and sauté for 2 minutes, stirring frequently. Add the broth and bring to a boil. Add the rice and parsley, stir, cover, and cook at a slow boil for 15 minutes, or until the rice is tender but *al dente,* firm to the bite. Stir from time to time while cooking and taste and correct for salt.

3. Just before serving, add the grated cheese, mixing it into the soup.

MENU SUGGESTIONS

The ideal coupling for *risi e bisi* is that other well-known Venetian specialty, Sautéed Calf's Liver with Onions, Venetian Style (page 296). It can also precede Fish Broiled the Adriatic Way (page 224), Shrimp Brochettes, Adriatic Style (page 226), or Sautéed Chicken Breast Fillets with Lemon and Parsley (page 314). Otherwise, it will go well with any meat or fowl dish, saving those, of course, that incorporate peas.

Minestra di sedano e riso
RICE AND CELERY SOUP

For 4 persons

2 cups diced celery stalks (see Step 1 below)	2 cups Homemade Meat Broth (page 10) OR 1 cup canned beef broth mixed with 1 cup water
⅓ cup olive oil	
1 teaspoon salt	
2 tablespoons finely chopped yellow onion	3 tablespoons freshly grated Parmesan cheese
2 tablespoons butter	2 tablespoons chopped parsley
1 cup raw rice, preferably Italian Arborio rice	

1. Wash the celery stalks well, strip them of most of their strings with a vegetable peeler, and dice. Put the diced celery, olive oil, and salt in a saucepan and add enough water to cover. Bring to a steady simmer, cover, and cook until the celery is tender but not soft. Turn off the heat but do not drain.

2. Put the chopped onion in another saucepan or stockpot with the butter and sauté over medium heat until pale gold but not browned.

3. Add half the celery to the saucepan with the onion, using a

slotted spoon. Sauté the celery for 2 or 3 minutes, then add the rice and stir it until it is well coated. Add all the broth.

4. Purée the rest of the celery, with all its cooking liquid, through a food mill directly into the saucepan containing the rice. Bring to a steady simmer, cover, and cook until the rice is tender but firm to the bite, about 15 to 20 minutes.

5. Swirl in the grated cheese, turn off the heat, add the chopped parsley, and mix. Serve promptly, before the rice becomes too soft.

MENU SUGGESTIONS

This tasty but not overwhelming soup would be a good choice if you are going to follow with Meat Balls (page 247), Black-Eyed Peas and Sausages with Tomato Sauce (page 289), Honeycomb Tripe with Parmesan Cheese (page 293), or Oxtail Braised with Wine and Vegetables (page 291), which has a delicious touch of celery of its own.

Zuppa di scarola e riso
ESCAROLE AND RICE SOUP

Scarola is a broad-leafed salad green from the chicory family. It is marvelous in soup as well as in salads. There are probably as many ways to cook it as there are leaves in a head of escarole, but many make it either too bland and retiring or else too aggressively flavored. This version, where the escarole is first briefly sautéed in butter with lightly browned onions, stays at a happy distance from the two extremes.

For 4 persons

1 head of escarole (¾ to 1 pound)	3½ cups Homemade Meat Broth, (page 10) OR 1 cup canned chicken broth mixed with 2½ cups water, OR 2 chicken bouillon cubes dissolved in 3½ cups water
2 tablespoons finely chopped yellow onion	
¼ cup butter	
Salt	

(continued)

½ cup raw rice, preferably
Italian Arborio rice

3 tablespoons freshly grated
Parmesan cheese

1. Detach all the escarole leaves from the head and discard any that are bruised, wilted, or discolored. Wash all the rest in various changes of cold water until thoroughly clean. Cut into ribbons ½ inch wide and set aside.

2. In a stockpot sauté the chopped onion in the butter over medium heat until nicely browned. Add the escarole and a light sprinkling of salt. Briefly sauté the escarole, stirring it once or twice, then add ½ cup of the broth, cover the pot, and cook over very low heat until the escarole is tender—from 25 minutes to more than three-quarters of an hour, depending on the freshness and tenderness of the escarole.

3. When the escarole is tender, add the rest of the broth, raise the heat slightly, and cover. When the broth comes to a boil, add the rice and cover. Cook for 15 to 20 minutes, stirring from time to time, until the rice is *al dente,* firm to the bite. Off the heat, mix in the Parmesan cheese. Taste and correct for salt, spoon into soup plates, and serve.

NOTE

Don't cook the soup ahead of time with the rice in it. The rice will become mushy. If you must do it ahead of time, stop at the end of step 2. About 25 minutes before serving, add the 3 cups of broth to the escarole, bring to a boil, and finish cooking as in step 3.

MENU SUGGESTIONS

Follow the suggestions for Rice and Celery Soup (page 63). This can also precede Casserole-Roasted Lamb with Juniper Berries (page 280).

Minestrina di spinaci
SPINACH SOUP

For 5 or 6 persons

2 ten-ounce packages frozen
   leaf spinach, thawed, OR
   2 pounds fresh spinach
4 tablespoons butter
2 cups Homemade Meat Broth
   (page 10) OR 1 cup canned
   chicken broth mixed with
   1 cup water

2 cups milk
¼ teaspoon nutmeg
5 tablespoons freshly grated
   Parmesan cheese
Salt, if necessary

1. Cook, squeeze dry, and chop the spinach as directed on page 153.

2. Put the chopped, cooked spinach and the butter in a stockpot. Sauté the spinach over medium heat for 2 to 3 minutes.

3. Add the broth, milk, and nutmeg. Bring to a simmer, stirring frequently.

4. Add the Parmesan cheese and cook for 1 more minute, stirring two to three times. Taste for salt. Serve immediately, with *crostini*, Fried Bread Squares for Soup (page 88) on the side.

MENU SUGGESTIONS

This soup can precede any meat or fowl. It goes particularly well with any of the roasts of lamb on pages 278–281, Baby Lamb Chops Fried in Parmesan Cheese Batter (page 283), Fried Calf's Brains (page 299), or Fried Breaded Calf's Liver (page 298).

Minestrone di Romagna
VEGETABLE SOUP

A vegetable soup will tell you where you are in Italy almost as precisely as a map. There are the soups of the south, leaning heavily on tomato, garlic, and oil, sometimes containing pasta; there are those of the center, heavily fortified with beans; the soups of the north, with rice; those of the Riviera, with fresh herbs; and there are nearly as many variations in between as there are local cooks. In Romagna, very little is put into *minestrone* beyond a variety of seasonal vegetables, whose separate characteristics give way and intermingle through very slow cooking in broth. The result is a soup of mellow, dense flavor that recalls no vegetable in particular but all of them at once.

It is not necessary to prepare all the vegetables ahead of time although you may do so if it suits you. The vegetables don't go into the pot all at once, but in the sequence indicated, and while one vegetable is slowly cooking in oil and butter you can peel and cut another. I find this method more efficient and less tedious than preparing all the vegetables at one time, and somehow it produces a better-tasting soup. In any event, cook each vegetable 2 or 3 minutes, at least, before adding the next.

For 6 to 8 persons

½ cup olive oil

3 tablespoons butter

1 cup thinly sliced yellow onion

1 cup diced carrots

1 cup diced celery

2 cups peeled, diced potatoes

1½ cups fresh white beans, if available, OR 1½ cups canned *cannellini* beans or Great Northern beans OR ¾ cup dried white beans, cooked as directed on page 78

2 cups diced zucchini (about 2 medium zucchini) (see note below)

1 cup diced green beans
3 cups shredded cabbage,
    preferably Savoy cabbage
6 cups Homemade Meat Broth
    (page 10) OR 2 cups
    canned beef broth mixed
    with 4 cups water

The crust from a 1- or
    2-pound piece of Parmesan
    cheese, carefully scraped
    clean (optional)
⅔ cup canned Italian tomatoes,
    with their juice
⅓ cup freshly grated Parmesan
    cheese

1. Choose a stockpot large enough for all the ingredients. Put in the oil, butter, and sliced onion and cook over medium-low heat until the onion wilts and is pale gold in color but not browned. Add the diced carrots and cook for 2 to 3 minutes, stirring once or twice. Repeat this procedure with the celery, potatoes, white beans (if you are using the fresh beans), zucchini, and green beans, cooking each one a few minutes and stirring. Then add the shredded cabbage and cook for about 6 minutes, giving the pot an occasional stir.

2. Add the broth, the cheese crust, the tomatoes and their juice, and a little bit of salt. (Go easy on the salt, especially if you are using canned broth. You can correct the seasoning later.) Cover and cook at a very slow boil for at least 3 hours. If necessary, you can stop the cooking at any time and resume it later on. (*Minestrone* must never be thin and watery, so cook until it is soupy thick. If you should find that the soup is becoming *too* thick, you can add another cup of homemade broth or water. Do not add more canned broth.)

3. Fifteen minutes before the soup is done, add the canned or cooked dry beans (if you are not using fresh ones). Just before turning off the heat, remove the cheese crust, swirl in the grated cheese, then taste and correct for salt.

NOTE

Before dicing the zucchini, scrub it thoroughly in cold water to remove all soil—and if still in doubt, peel it.

Minestrone, unlike most cooked vegetable dishes, is even better when warmed up the next day. It keeps up to a week in the refrigerator.

Minestrone goes very well with roasts of all kinds, particularly lamb. You can safely follow it with any meat course that doesn't include any vegetables.

Minestrone freddo alla milanese
COLD VEGETABLE SOUP WITH RICE, MILAN STYLE

One of the few consolations of a hot Milan summer is this basil-scented cold *minestrone*. The *trattorie* make it fresh every morning, fill the soup plates, and set them out along with the rest of the day's specialties displayed near the entrance: fresh-picked vegetables, a poached fish, mountain prosciutto, sweet melons. By noontime the *minestrone* is precisely the right temperature and consistency, and shortly thereafter it is all snapped up.

This is the most beautiful way in which one can revive leftover *minestrone*, and, of course, not only can it be made ahead of time, it *must* be made ahead of time.

For 4 persons

2 cups leftover Vegetable Soup (page 66)	Freshly ground pepper, about 8 twists of the mill
2 cups water	¼ cup freshly grated Parmesan cheese
½ cup raw rice, preferably Italian Arborio rice	8 good-sized fresh basil leaves, cut into 4 or 5 strips each
1 teaspoon salt	

1. In a stockpot, bring the soup and 2 cups of water to a boil. Add the rice, stirring it with a wooden spoon. When the soup returns to a boil, add the salt and pepper, cover the pot, and turn the heat down to medium low. Stir from time to time. Test the rice after 10

to 12 minutes. It should be very firm, because it will continue to soften as it cools in the plate. Taste and correct for salt.

2. When the rice is done, ladle the soup into four individual soup plates, add the grated cheese and the basil, mix well, and allow to cool. Serve at room temperature.

NOTE
Never refrigerate the soup; always serve it the same day it is made.

MENU SUGGESTIONS

Bear in mind that this is a warm-weather dish. The second course could be a cold boiled fish with mayonnaise, Cold Sliced Veal with Tuna Sauce (page 276), Sautéed Veal Scaloppine with Lemon Sauce (page 262).

MINESTRONE, COLD OR HOT, WITH PESTO

COLD MINESTRONE (COLD VEGETABLE SOUP WITH RICE, MILAN STYLE, PRECEDING PAGE):

When the rice is done, at the end of Step 1, swirl in 1 tablespoon of *pesto* (page 139). Ladle into individual soup plates, omitting the basil in Step 2.

HOT MINESTRONE (VEGETABLE SOUP, PAGE 66):

Add 1½ to 2 tablespoons of *pesto* (page 139) at the end of Step 3. If you are making the soup ahead of time, add the *pesto* when reheating, just before serving.

PASSATELLI

Passatelli consists of eggs, Parmesan cheese, and bread crumbs formed into short, thick, cylindrical strands by pressing the mixture through a special tool. The strands are then boiled very briefly in homemade meat broth. The original tool can be replaced by a food mill, but the homemade broth is absolutely essential and cannot be replaced by canned bouillon.

This soup is native only to the Romagna section of Emilia, a nar-

Drop the *passatelli* directly into the boiling broth.

row strip of territory east of Bologna, bordering on the Adriatic Sea. The *romagnoli* want their food to be satisfying but simple and delicate in taste. This soup is all these things and, moreover, extremely quick to prepare.

For 6 persons

7 cups broth from Mixed Boiled Meats (page 322) or Homemade Meat Broth (page 10)	⅓ cup fine, dry unflavored bread crumbs
¾ cup freshly grated Parmesan cheese	¼ teaspoon nutmeg (see note below)
	2 eggs

1. Bring the broth to a steady, moderate boil in an uncovered pot. While the broth is coming to a boil, combine the grated Parmesan, the bread crumbs, and the nutmeg on a pastry board or large cutting block. Make a mound with a well in the center. Break the eggs open into the well and knead all the ingredients together. It should have the tender, granular consistency of cooked cornmeal mush (*polenta*). (If, as sometimes happens, the eggs are a bit on the large side, you may have to add a little more Parmesan and bread crumbs.)

2. Put the disk with the largest holes into your food mill. When the broth boils, press the Parmesan-bread-crumb-and-egg mixture through the mill directly into the boiling broth. Cook at a slow boil for a minute or two at the most. Turn off the heat and allow to rest for 4 to 5 minutes, then ladle into warm soup plates and serve with a bowl of freshly grated Parmesan on the side.

NOTE

The nutmeg can be increased slightly, according to taste, but the flavor of nutmeg should never be more than hinted at.

MENU SUGGESTIONS

The natural second course for *passatelli* is Mixed Boiled Meats (page 322), which should have produced the broth for the soup. If you are making *passatelli* with other broth, you can follow it with any simple roasted meat or fowl.

Zuppa di piselli secchi e patate
SPLIT GREEN PEA AND POTATO SOUP

This is a good, simple soup. It requires so little looking after that I usually make it on the side while I am cooking other things. When it is done, I put it away in the refrigerator, where it keeps perfectly for several days, and then I have a marvelous soup on hand, all ready to heat up at a moment's notice. There is something comforting about having a robust soup like this one to fall back on, especially on a blustery winter evening. The only thing to look out for when reheating is that the soup should not become too thick. If it does, just add some more broth or water.

For 6 persons

½ one-pound package of split green peas, washed and drained

2 medium potatoes, peeled and roughly cut up

5 cups Homemade Meat Broth (page 10) OR 1 cup canned beef broth mixed with 4 cups water OR 1 bouillon cube dissolved in 5 cups water

2 tablespoons chopped yellow onion

3 tablespoons olive oil

3 tablespoons butter

3 tablespoons freshly grated Parmesan cheese

Salt

1. Cook the split peas and potatoes at a moderate boil in 3 cups of the broth until both are quite tender. Then purée the peas and potatoes, with their cooking liquid, through a food mill and into a stockpot.

2. Put the onion in a small skillet along with the oil and butter and sauté over medium-high heat until a rich golden color.

3. Add all the contents of the skillet to the stockpot; then add the remaining 2 cups of broth and bring to a moderate boil. Cook, stirring occasionally, until the oil and butter are dissolved in the

broth. Just before turning off the heat, mix in the grated cheese, then taste and correct for salt. Serve with additional grated cheese and *crostini* (Fried Bread Squares for Soup, page 88) on the side.

NOTE

If you are doing the soup in advance, add the cheese only when you reheat it. Allow the soup to cool thoroughly before refrigerating.

MENU SUGGESTIONS

Any roasted meat or fowl would make an excellent second course. Other possibilities are Left-Over Boiled Beef with Sautéed Onions (page 244), Meat Balls (page 247), Little Veal "Bundles" with Anchovies and Cheese (page 267), Veal Stew with Sage and White Wine (page 273), Boiled Cotechino Sausage, if you are not serving it with lentils (page 287), Stewed Rabbit with White Wine (page 320), or Fried Breaded Calf's Liver (page 298).

Zuppa di lenticchie

LENTIL SOUP

For 4 persons

2 tablespoons finely chopped yellow onion

3 tablespoons olive oil

3 tablespoons butter

2 tablespoons finely chopped celery

2 tablespoons finely chopped carrot

⅓ cup shredded *pancetta*, prosciutto, or unsmoked ham

1 cup canned Italian tomatoes, cut up, with their juice

½ one-pound package of dried lentils, washed and drained

4 cups Homemade Meat Broth (page 10) OR 1 cup canned beef broth mixed with 3 cups water

Salt, if necessary

Freshly ground pepper, 4 to 6 twists of the mill

3 tablespoons freshly grated Parmesan cheese

(continued)

1. Put the onion in a stockpot with the oil and 2 tablespoons of the butter and sauté over medium-high heat until a light golden brown.

2. Add the celery and carrot and continue sautéing for 2 to 3 minutes, stirring from time to time.

3. Add the shredded *pancetta,* and sauté for 1 more minute.

4. Add the cut-up tomatoes and their juice, and adjust the heat so that they cook at a gentle simmer for 25 minutes, uncovered. Stir from time to time with a wooden spoon.

5. Add the lentils, stirring and turning them two or three times, then add the broth, salt (easy on the salt if you are using canned broth), and pepper. Cover and cook, at a steady simmer, until the lentils are tender. (Cooking time is about 45 minutes, but it varies greatly from lentils to lentils, so that the only reliable method is to taste them. Note, too, that some lentils absorb a surprising amount of liquid. If this happens add more homemade broth or water to keep the soup from getting too thick.)

6. When the lentils are cooked, correct for salt; then, off the heat, swirl in the remaining tablespoon of butter and the grated cheese. Serve with additional freshly grated cheese on the side.

MENU SUGGESTIONS

This sturdy soup can precede any meat dish that does not have a strong tomato presence. Good choices would be Beef Braised in Red Wine Sauce (page 242), Left-Over Boiled Beef with Sautéed Onions (page 244), Veal Stew with Sage and White Wine (page 273), Roast Spring Lamb with White Wine (page 278), Pork Loin Braised in Milk (page 284), Roast Pork with Bay Leaves (page 286), any of the roasted, broiled, or fricasseed chickens (except the one with tomatoes), and Sautéed Calf's Liver with Onions, Venetian Style (page 296).

Zuppa di lenticchie e riso
RICE AND LENTIL SOUP

Lentil soup can be made in large batches and frozen. When reheating it, you can vary the basic formula through the simple and pleasant addition of rice.

For 6 persons

Lentil Soup (page 73)
1½ cups Homemade Meat Broth
(page 10) OR ½ cup
canned beef broth mixed
with 1 cup water

½ cup raw rice, preferably
Italian Arborio rice
Salt, if necessary

Bring the soup to a boil, then add the broth. When the soup comes to a boil again, add the rice and stir with a wooden spoon. Cook at a moderate boil until the rice is tender but firm to the bite, about 15 minutes. (If the rice you are using absorbs too much liquid, add more homemade broth or water.) Taste and correct for salt. Serve with freshly grated Parmesan cheese on the side.

MENU SUGGESTIONS

Follow the ones for Lentil Soup (preceding page).

La Jota
BEANS AND SAUERKRAUT SOUP

Trieste has long been the most passionately Italian of cities, but this stout bean soup of hers with potatoes, sauerkraut, and bacon speaks with an unmistakable accent from her Austro-Hungarian past.

An important step in the preparation of the soup is the slow stewing of the sauerkraut to blunt its sharpness. Although *Jota* requires much slow cooking, it can be done at your convenience because the soup should be served at least a day later to give its flavors time for full development. If you must, you can even interrupt its preparation at the end of any step, allow the soup to cool, refrigerate it, and the following day resume cooking where you left off.

When completed, *Jota* is enriched with a final flavoring called *pestà*. Although the components differ—this *pestà* contains salt pork so finely chopped that it is nearly reduced to a paste, hence the name—this procedure strongly recalls the addition of flavored oil in Tuscan bean soups.

For 8 persons

2 pounds fresh cranberry beans (unshelled weight) (see note, page 81)	¾ pound pork's head or pork rind
¼ pound bacon, in 1-inch strips	1 cup peeled, coarsely diced potato (1 medium potato)
1 pound sauerkraut, drained	1 teaspoon salt
½ teaspoon cumin	3 tablespoons cornmeal

THE PESTÀ:

¼ cup finely chopped salt pork	1 teaspoon chopped garlic
1 tablespoon chopped yellow onion	2 teaspoons salt
	3 teaspoons all-purpose flour

1. Shell the beans, rinse them in cold water, and put them in a pot with 3 cups of water. Bring to a boil, then cover and adjust the heat so that they cook at a very slow boil. Cook until tender, about 45 minutes, depending on the beans. When done, set them aside in their own liquid.

2. While the beans are cooking, sauté the bacon in a medium saucepan over moderate heat for 2 to 3 minutes. Add the drained sauerkraut and the ½ teaspoon cumin, mix with the bacon, and cook in the bacon fat for about 2 minutes. Then add 1 cup water, cover the pan, and cook at very low heat for 1 hour. At the end of an

hour the sauerkraut should be very much reduced in volume and there should be no liquid in the pan. If there is still some left, uncover the pan and allow the liquid to evaporate over medium heat.

3. While the beans are cooking and the sauerkraut is stewing, put the pork's head or pork rind in a stockpot with 1 quart of water and bring to a boil. After it has boiled for 5 minutes, drain, discarding the cooking liquid, and cut the head or rind into ¾- to 1-inch-wide strips. (Do not be alarmed if it is very tough. It will soften away to a creamy consistency in later cooking.)

4. Return the cut-up pork to the stockpot. Add the diced potato, 3 cups of water, and 1 teaspoon salt. Cover and cook at a slow but steady boil for 1 hour.

5. Add the beans with their cooking liquid, cover, and cook at a very slow, quiet boil for 30 minutes.

6. Add the sauerkraut. cover, and cook, always at a very slow boil, for 1 hour.

7. Add the cornmeal in a thin stream, stirring it thoroughly into the soup, add 2 cups of water, cover, and cook at the same slow boil for 1 hour. Stir from time to time.

8. When the soup is nearing completion, prepare the *pestà*. Put the chopped salt pork and the onion in a small saucepan and sauté over medium heat until the onion is pale gold. Add the garlic and sauté it until it is nicely colored. Then add 2 teaspoons salt and the flour, 1 tablespoon at a time, stirring it thoroughly and cooking it until it, too, is a rich, blond color.

9. Add the *pestà* to the soup, stirring thoroughly, and simmer for 20 minutes more before serving.

MENU SUGGESTIONS

This is a "heavyweight" among soups and should be balanced in the second course by broiled or roasted meat or fowl. A substantial but suitable meat course with a congenial Triestine flavor is Braised Veal Shanks, Trieste Style (page 257).

COOKING DRIED BEANS

When fresh beans are not available, most Italian cooks use dried beans rather than canned, precooked beans. Dried beans are not only much more economical than canned beans, but, when properly cooked, they have better texture than the generally mushy canned variety. You can buy packed dried beans in all supermarkets, but in many cities there are Greek and other stores that sell them loose, by weight. These are a still better buy than the prepacked beans, and usually offer a far broader selection.

Dried beans should always be soaked before cooking, otherwise their skins will burst before the beans become tender. There are many techniques for cooking dried beans. The following has given consistently successful results, especially with Great Northern beans or kidney beans, which are the closest to the white beans that usually go into Italian soups.

1. Put the desired quantity of beans in a bowl and cover them by 2 inches with cold water. Let them soak overnight in a warm place, such as over the pilot flame of a gas stove. (In this instance, be careful not to use a plastic bowl!)

2. The following day, preheat the oven to 325°.

3. Rinse and drain the beans, put them in a flameproof casserole, and cover with cold water by 2 inches.

4. Bring the beans to a moderate boil on top of the stove, then cover the pot and place in the middle level of the preheated oven. Cook until tender, about 40 to 60 minutes, depending on the beans. Keep them in their liquid until you are ready to use them.

Zuppa di cannellini con aglio e prezzemolo
BEAN SOUP WITH PARSLEY AND GARLIC

This is indeed a bean lover's bean soup. It is virtually all beans, with very little liquid, and just a whiff of garlic. It is thick enough to be served as a side dish next to a good roast. If you like it thinner all you have to do is add a little more broth or water.

For 4 to 6 persons

1 teaspoon chopped garlic
½ cup olive oil
2 tablespoons chopped parsley
2 cups dried white kidney beans or other white beans, cooked as directed on page 78 and drained, OR 2 twenty-ounce cans white kidney beans or other white beans, drained

Salt
Freshly ground pepper, about 8 twists of the mill
1 cup Homemade Meat Broth (page 10), OR canned chicken broth, or water
Toasted Italian bread

1. Put the garlic in a stockpot with the olive oil and sauté over medium heat until just lightly colored.

2. Add the parsley, stir two or three times, then add the drained, cooked beans, ½ teaspoon salt, and pepper. Cover and simmer gently for about 6 minutes.

3. Put about ½ cup of beans from the pot into a food mill and purée them back into the pot, together with the broth or water. Simmer for another 6 minutes, then taste and correct for salt. Serve over slices of toasted Italian bread.

MENU SUGGESTIONS

This needs to be balanced by a fairly substantial, forthright second course. Serve it before any roasted meat or fowl, or before Honeycomb Tripe with Parmesan Cheese (page 293) or Sautéed Calf's Liver with Onions (page 296).

Pasta e fagioli

BEANS AND PASTA SOUP

For 6 persons

2 tablespoons chopped yellow
onion
¼ cup olive oil (slightly less if
there is much fat on the
pork you are using)
3 tablespoons chopped carrot
3 tablespoons chopped celery
3 or 4 pork ribs or a ham bone
with some meat on them
OR 2 small pork chops
⅔ cup canned Italian tomatoes,
cut up, with their juice
2 pounds fresh cranberry beans
(unshelled weight) (see
note below)

3 cups Homemade Meat Broth
(page 10) (approximately)
OR 1 cup canned beef broth
mixed with 2 cups water
(approximately)
Salt
Freshly ground pepper, about
6 twists of the mill
Maltagliati (page 121), made
with 1 egg and ¾ cup all-
purpose flour (basic pasta
recipe, page 113), OR 6
ounces small, tubular
macaroni
2 tablespoons freshly grated
Parmesan cheese

1. Put the onion in a stockpot with the oil and sauté over medium heat until pale gold.

2. Add the carrot, celery, and pork and sauté for about 10 minutes, stirring the vegetables and turning the pork from time to time.

3. Add the chopped tomatoes and their juice, turn the heat down to medium low, and cook for 10 minutes.

4. If you are using fresh cranberry beans, shell the beans, rinse them in cold water, and add to the pot. Stir two or three times, then add the broth. Cover the pot, adjust the heat so that the liquid is bubbling at a very moderate boil, but at a bit more than a simmer, and cook for 45 minutes to 1 hour, or until the beans are tender. (If you are using precooked beans, cook the tomatoes for 20 minutes instead of 10, as in Step 3, then add the drained beans. Let the

beans cook in the tomatoes for 5 minutes, stirring thoroughly, then add the broth and bring to a moderate boil.)

5. Scoop up about ½ cup of beans and mash them through a food mill back into the pot.

6. Add salt and pepper. (If you are using canned broth, taste carefully for salt, because some canned bouillon can be very salty.)

7. Check the soup for density; add more homemade broth or water if needed, and bring the liquid to a steady boil. Add the pasta. If you are using fresh egg pasta, stop the cooking 1 minute after you've dropped it in. If you are using dried pasta or macaroni, taste for doneness and stop the cooking when the pasta is very firm to the bite. (The soup should rest for about 10 minutes before serving, so if you do not stop the cooking when the pasta is very firm it will be quite mushy by the time it gets to the table.) Just before serving, swirl in the grated cheese.

NOTE

Cranberry beans are pink-and-white marbled beans, and they add a wonderful flavor to this soup. If they are not available use 1 cup dried Great Northern beans, cooked as directed on page 78, or 1 twenty-ounce can white kidney beans or other white beans, drained.

The soup can be prepared entirely ahead of time up to, but not including, Step 7. Add the pasta only when you are going to serve the soup.

MENU SUGGESTIONS

This fine, comforting soup can precede any substantial dish of meat or fowl. Particularly nice would be Pan-Broiled Steak with Marsala and Hot Pepper Sauce (page 239), Braised Veal Shanks, Trieste Style (page 257), Roast Spring Lamb with White Wine (page 278), Roast Pork with Bay Leaves (page 286), Chicken Fricassee with Dried Wild Mushrooms (page 310), Stewed Rabbit with White Wine (page 320), or Sautéed Calf's Liver with Onions, Venetian Style (page 296).

Zuppa di cavolo nero
RED CABBAGE SOUP

This is as much a pork-and-beans dish as it is a cabbage soup, and, along with *cassoulet*, it has an honored place in that robust family of Mediterranean dishes using beans and pork or beans and lamb. It is a Tuscan specialty, as are so many bean dishes in Italy, and every Tuscan cook has a personal version of it. A constant element of this and many other Tuscan soups is the garlic- and rosemary-flavored hot oil that is added to the soup just before serving.

You should not hesitate to take some freedom with the basic recipe, varying its proportions of sausage, beans, and cabbage according to taste. In the recipe as given here, soup, meat course, and vegetable are combined in one hearty dish that is a meal in itself. It can be made even heartier by increasing the quantity of sausage. On the other hand, you can eliminate the sausage altogether, substituting for it any piece of pork on a bone, and increase the quantity of broth to make a true soup that will fit as a first course into a substantial country menu.

This dish develops even better flavor when warmed up one or two days later, which means that you can prepare it entirely in advance at the most convenient time on your schedule.

For 6 persons

¼ pound fresh pork rind
½ teaspoon chopped garlic
2 tablespoons chopped yellow
    onion
2 tablespoons thinly shredded
    pancetta
¼ cup olive oil
1 pound red cabbage, coarsely
    shredded
⅓ cup chopped celery

3 tablespoons canned Italian
    tomato, drained and
    coarsely chopped
A tiny pinch of thyme
3 cups Homemade Meat Broth
    (page 10) (approximately)
    OR 1 cup canned beef broth
    mixed with 2 cups water
    (approximately)
Salt

Freshly ground pepper, 6 to
8 twists of the mill
½ pound *luganega* sausage or
other mild sausage

1 cup dried Great Northern
beans or other white beans,
cooked as directed on page
78 and drained, OR 1
twenty-ounce can white
kidney beans, *cannellini*, or
other white beans, drained

FOR THE FLAVORED OIL:

2 large or 3 medium cloves
garlic, lightly crushed with
a heavy knife handle and
peeled

¼ cup olive oil
½ teaspoon chopped rosemary
leaves

1. Put the pork rind in a small saucepan, cover by about 1 inch with cold water, and bring to a boil. After it has boiled for 1 minute, drain and allow to cool. Cut into strips about ½ inch wide and 2 to 3 inches long and set aside.

2. Put the garlic, onion, and *pancetta* in a stockpot with the oil and sauté over medium heat until the onion and garlic are very lightly colored.

3. Add the shredded cabbage, the chopped celery, the pork rind, the tomato, and a tiny pinch of thyme. Cook over medium-low heat until the cabbage has completely wilted. Stir thoroughly from time to time.

4. When the cabbage has become soft, add the broth, 2 teaspoons salt, and pepper, cover the pot, and cook at very low heat for 2 to 2½ hours. This cooking may be done at various stages, spread over two or three days. In fact the soup acquires even better flavor when reheated in this manner.

5. Off the heat, uncover the pot, tilt it slightly, and draw off as much as possible of the fat that rises to the surface.

6. Brown the sausage in a small pan for 6 to 8 minutes over medium-low heat. They need no other fat than that which they throw off, which you will discard after they are browned on all sides.

(*continued*)

7. Return the pot to the burner and bring to a simmer. Add the browned sausages, drained of their fat. Purée half the cooked beans into the pot, and stir well. Cover and simmer for 15 minutes.

8. Add the remaining whole beans and correct for desired thickness by adding more homemade broth or water. Taste and correct for salt. Cover and simmer for 10 more minutes. (The soup may be prepared entirely ahead of time up to and including this point. Always return it to a simmer before proceeding with the next step.)

9. Put the crushed garlic cloves and the oil in a small pan and sauté over lively heat until the garlic is nicely browned. Add the chopped rosemary, turn off the heat, and stir two or three times. Pour the oil through a sieve into the soup pot, cover, and simmer for 15 minutes more. Serve with good, crusty Italian or French bread.

MENU SUGGESTIONS

If you are using this as a meal-in-itself dish, you might still precede it with either of the baked oyster dishes on pages 32-33, Broiled Mussels and Clams on the Half Shell (page 34), Peppers and Anchovies (page 37), Mushroom and Cheese Salad (page 47), or a platter of assorted cold cuts. If you decide to omit the sausages and use this as soup, it can precede any roast of meat or fowl, and would also go well with Meat Loaf Braised in White Wine with Dried Wild Mushrooms (page 249), Fried Breaded Calf's Liver (page 298), or Broiled Pork Liver Wrapped in Caul Fat (page 302). This would make a good, stout weekend dinner in the country, with the possibility of a long walk later to work it off.

Zuppa di ceci
CHICK-PEA SOUP

This savory soup can be made entirely ahead of time, refrigerated for as long as ten days, and it will lose none of its taste or aroma when warmed up. Many like to purée the whole soup through a food mill, in which case it may become necessary to add a little more broth until the soup has the consistency of cream. It is served then with *crostini* (Fried Bread Squares for Soup, page 88). If you try this soup and like it, make more than you need the next time. You will then be able to use it again as the base for Chick-pea and Pasta Soup (page 87) or Chick-pea and Rice Soup (page 86).

For 4 to 6 persons

¾ cup dried chick-peas OR 2 sixteen-ounce cans chick-peas

4 whole cloves garlic, peeled

⅓ cup olive oil

1½ teaspoons finely crushed rosemary leaves, almost powder fine

⅔ cup canned Italian tomatoes, roughly chopped, with their juice

1 cup Homemade Meat Broth (page 10) OR 1 bouillon cube dissolved in 1 cup water

Salt, if necessary

Freshly ground pepper, about 4 twists of the mill

1. If you are using dried chick-peas you must first soak them overnight. Put them in a large enough bowl, add water to cover by 2 inches, and let them soak all night in a warm corner of the kitchen. (Over the gas pilot would be an excellent place, but do not use a plastic bowl.)

2. The following morning preheat the oven to 325°. Discard the water in which the chick-peas have soaked, put them in a medium-sized stockpot, add enough water to come up 1 inch above

the chick-peas (do *not* add salt), and bring them to a boil on top of the stove. Cover tightly and cook in the middle level of the oven for 1½ hours, or until the chick-peas are tender. (At this stage they are almost exactly equivalent to the canned variety, except that they are not salted and have slightly better texture. Canned chick-peas are very convenient, but they are also considerably more expensive. Which ones to use will have to be your decision. It doesn't matter to the soup.) I always peel chick-peas before using them in soup, but it is a chore, and if you'd rather put up with the peels than with the chore you can omit it.

3. Sauté the garlic cloves in the olive oil in a heavy casserole over medium-high heat. When the garlic is well browned remove it. Add the crushed rosemary leaves to the oil, stir, then add the chopped tomatoes with their juice. Cook over medium heat for about 20 to 25 minutes, or until the tomatoes separate from the oil.

4. Add the drained chick-peas and cook for 5 minutes, turning them in the sauce. Add the broth or the dissolved bouillon cube, bring to a boil, cover, and keep at a steady, moderate boil for 15 minutes. Taste and correct for salt, add freshly ground pepper, and allow to boil about 1 minute more, uncovered. Serve hot.

NOTE:
If you are making the soup ahead of time, add the salt and pepper when you warm it up.

Zuppa di ceci e riso

CHICK-PEAS AND RICE SOUP

For 8 persons

Chick-pea Soup (page 85)
3 cups Homemade Meat Broth (page 10) (approximately) OR 2 bouillon cubes dissolved in 3 cups water (approximately)

1 cup raw rice
Salt, if necessary

1. Purée the basic chick-pea soup through a food mill into a stockpot. Add the broth and bring to a boil. Add the rice, stir, cover the pot, and cook at a steady but moderate boil. Stir from time to time, and after 10 or 12 minutes check to see if more broth is required. (Some types of rice absorb more liquid than others, and the soup must be fairly liquid or it isn't a soup.)

2. The soup is done when the rice is tender but firm, from 15 to more than 20 minutes, according to the type of rice you are using. Taste and correct for salt. Allow to rest for a minute or two, then spoon into soup plates and serve.

NOTE

This soup, or any other that contains rice, cannot be prepared ahead of time because the rice will become mushy.

Zuppa di ceci e maltagliati
CHICK-PEAS AND PASTA

For 8 persons

Chick-pea Soup (page 85)
2 cups Homemade Meat Broth (page 10) (approximately) OR 2 bouillon cubes dissolved in 2 cups water (approximately)
Maltagliati (page 121), made with 1 egg and ¾ cup of flour (basic pasta recipe, page 113), or ½ pound small macaroni
Salt, if necessary
2 to 3 tablespoons freshly grated Parmesan cheese

1. Purée about one-third of the basic soup through a food mill into a stockpot. Add the rest of the soup and all the broth and bring to a boil. Add the pasta, stir, cover the pot, and cook at a steady but moderate boil. If you are using freshly made pasta, watch it carefully because it cooks very rapidly, in a minute or less. Whatever pasta you may be using, stop the cooking when it is very firm to the bite, because the pasta continues to soften even after the heat is turned off. With store-bought macaroni you may have to add some liquid while cooking, if the soup becomes too thick.

(*continued*)

2. Taste and correct for salt. Allow the soup to bubble for a few brief moments after you add the salt, then turn off the heat and mix in the grated cheese. (Remember that Parmesan cheese is salty, so regulate the amount you add by the saltiness of the soup.) Allow to rest for a minute or two, spoon into soup plates, and serve.

NOTE

This soup cannot be prepared ahead of time because the pasta would become too soft.

MENU SUGGESTIONS

These chick-pea soups, like all the bean soups, call for a substantial meat course to follow. Any of the lamb roasts on pages 278-281, or the Roast Pork with Bay Leaves (page 286), would be perfect. Broiled steak would be excellent too.

Crostini di pane per minestra

FRIED BREAD SQUARES FOR SOUP

For 4 persons

4 slices firm-bodied, good-quality white bread	**Vegetable oil, enough to come ½ inch up the side of the pan**

1. Cut away the crusts from the bread and cut the slices into ½-inch squares.

2. Choose a medium-sized skillet. (Inasmuch as you need oil to a depth of ½ inch, it is wasteful to choose too broad a skillet. If the bread doesn't fit in all at one time, it doesn't matter. Bread browns very rapidly and it can be done a few pieces at a time.) Heat the oil in the skillet over moderately high heat. It should become hot enough so that the bread sizzles when it goes in. Test it first with one square. When the oil is hot, put in as much bread as will fit loosely in a single layer. Turn the heat down, because bread

will burn quickly if the oil gets too hot, move the squares around in the pan, and as soon as they turn a light-gold color transfer them with a slotted spoon or spatula to paper towels to drain. Finish doing all the squares, adjusting the heat as necessary so that the bread will brown lightly without burning.

NOTE

Crostini can be prepared several hours ahead of time. After more than a day, however, they take on a stale, rancid taste.

HOW TO COOK PASTA

There is probably no single cooking process in any of the world's cuisines simpler than the boiling of pasta. This very simplicity appears to have had an unsettling effect on some writers, to judge from the curiously elaborate and often misleading procedures described in many Italian cook books. One book tells you to drop pasta into boiling water a little bit at a time. Another counsels you to lift it painstakingly strand by strand when draining it. A third suggests you can keep pasta warm in a 200° oven until you are ready to sauce it. Ah, pasta, what sins have been committed in thy name! Here is the way it is really done.

Water It is important to cook pasta in abundant water, but it is not necessary to drown it. Italians calculate 1 liter of water per 100 grams of pasta. This works out to slightly more than 4 quarts for 1 pound of pasta. Stick to just 4 quarts of water for every pound of pasta. It will be quite sufficient.

Salt When the water comes to a boil, add 1½ heaping tablespoons of salt for every 4 quarts of water. If the sauce you are going to be using is very bland, you may put in an additional ½ tablespoon of salt.

When and how to put in the pasta Put in the pasta when the salted water has come to a rapid boil. Add all the pasta at once. When you put it in a little at a time, it cannot all cook evenly. If you are cooking long pasta, such as spaghetti or *perciatelli,* after dropping it in the pot you must bend it in the middle with a wooden spoon to force the strands entirely under water. Never, never break spaghetti in two. Stir the pasta with a wooden spoon to keep it from sticking together. Cover the pot after you put in the pasta to accelerate the water's return to a boil. Watch it, lest it boil over. When it returns to a boil, uncover, and cook at a lively but not too fierce a boil, until it is *al dente.*

Al dente *Al dente* means "firm to the bite," and that is how Italians eat pasta. Unfortunately, they are the only ones who do. Of course, it is not easy to switch to firm pasta when one is used to having it soft and mushy, and it is very tempting to ingratiate oneself with one's readers by not pressing the issue. The whole point of pasta, however, is its texture and consistency, and overcooking destroys these. Soft pasta is no more fit to eat than a limp and soggy slice of bread.

In the course of civilization's long and erratic march, no other discovery has done more than, or possibly as much as, pasta has to promote man's happiness. It is therefore well worth learning how to turn it out at its best.

No foolproof cooking times can be given, but you can begin by ignoring those on the box. They are invariably excessive. There are so many variables, such as the type and make of pasta, the hardness and quantity of water, the heat source, even the altitude (it is impossible to make good pasta at over 4,500 feet above sea level), that the only dependable procedure is to taste the pasta frequently while it boils. As soon as pasta begins to lose its stiffness and becomes just tender enough so that you can bite through without snapping it, it is done. You should try at first to stop the cooking when you think the pasta is still a little underdone. Do not be afraid to stop too early. It is probably already overcooked, and, in any case, it will continue to soften until it is served. Once you have learned to cook and eat pasta *al dente*, you'll accept it no other way.

Draining, saucing, and serving pasta The instant pasta is done you must stop its cooking and drain it. Adding a glass of cold water to the pot as you turn off the heat is helpful, but it is not necessary if you are very quick about emptying the pot into the pasta colander. Give the colander a few vigorous sideways and up-and-down jerks to drain the pasta of all its water. Transfer the pasta without delay to a warm serving bowl. If grated cheese is called for, add it at this point and mix it into the pasta. The pasta's heat will melt it partially so that it will blend creamily with the sauce. Add the sauce and toss the pasta rapidly with two forks or a fork and spoon, coating it thoroughly with sauce. Add a thick pat of butter, unless you are using a sauce dominated by olive oil, toss briefly, and bring to the table immediately, serving it in warm soup plates. *Note*: There are two important points to remember in this whole operation:

1. The instant pasta is done, drain it, sauce it, and serve it with the briefest interval possible, because pasta continues to soften at every stage from the colander to the table.

2. Sauce the pasta thoroughly, but avoid prolonged tossings and exaggerated liftings of strands into the air, because there is one thing worse than soft pasta and that is cold pasta.

Reheating As a rule, pasta cannot be reheated, but some kinds of leftover pasta, such as *rigatoni* or *ziti*, can be turned into a very successful dish when baked (page 110).

Choosing pasta shapes Although all macaroni pasta is made from the same, identical dough, the end result is determined by shape and size. Spaghetti is probably the most successful vehicle for the greatest variety of sauces. Thin spaghetti (spaghettini) is best for seafood sauces and for any sauce whose principal fat is olive oil. Regular spaghetti is ideal for butter-based white sauces or tomato sauces. The one sauce that somehow doesn't work very well with spaghetti is meat sauce. With meat sauce you ought to choose a substantial, stubby cut of pasta, such as *rigatoni*. Try it also with shells (*conchiglie*); their openings will trap little bits of meat. *Fusilli* and *rotelle* are splendid with dense, spicy cream and meat sauces, such as the sausage sauce on page 109, which cling deliciously to all their twists and curls. There are hundreds of pasta shapes, of which a dozen or more are easily available. You ought to experiment with all the ones you find, and develop your own favorite liaisons of pasta and sauce.

I strongly recommend that you try imported Italian pasta. It is vastly superior to domestic pasta because it really cooks to and holds that absolutely perfect degree of toothy tenderness which deserves to be called *al dente*. It also swells considerably in the cooking, which means that pound for pound it will go farther than American-made pasta. Such excellent brands as De Cecco and Carmine Russo are easily available at all well-stocked Italian groceries, in a broad variety of shapes and cuts.

Sughi di pomodoro

FIVE TOMATO SAUCES FOR SPAGHETTI AND OTHER PASTA

We have all heard about the decline of the fresh tomato. To judge by the plastic-wrapped examples in the supermarkets not even the worst reports are exaggerated. The poor tomato is picked half ripe, gassed, shuttled great distances, and artificially quickened back to life. One who has never tasted a tomato honestly ripened on the vine by the heat of the summer sun cannot possibly believe that this is one of agricultural man's greatest triumphs, one of the most glorious products he has ever grown.

The situation is difficult, but not entirely hopeless. It is still possible to make a good sauce from fresh tomatoes, and it is something that everyone should experience before real tomatoes disappear altogether. You will have to limit yourself, in making these sauces, to those few weeks of the year when the tomatoes on the market are likely to be locally grown. The best tomatoes for this purpose, and those on which the recipes here are based, are the long, narrow plum tomatoes. They should feel reasonably firm, but yielding, not wooden to the touch. And they should be an even, intense red. If you use other varieties of tomatoes, you may have to increase the quantities, depending on how watery they are.

When choice, ripe, fresh tomatoes are not available, a good tomato sauce can be made with canned imported Italian plum tomatoes. I find the tomatoes of San Marzano superior to all others, especially the ones packed by Luigi Vitelli, which are sweet and full-flavored. At the foot of each of the following five recipes there are instructions on how to substitute canned tomatoes for fresh.

TOMATO SAUCE I

Of the three basic tomato sauces given here, this is the most concentrated and the most strongly flavored. It goes well with all macaroni pasta.

For 6 servings

2 pounds fresh, ripe plum tomatoes	⅓ cup finely chopped carrot
½ cup olive oil	⅓ cup finely chopped celery
⅓ cup finely chopped yellow onion	2 teaspoons salt
	¼ teaspoon granulated sugar

1. Wash the tomatoes in cold water. Cut them in half, lengthwise. Cook in a covered saucepan or stockpot at a steady simmer for 10 minutes. Uncover and simmer gently for 1½ hours more.

2. Purée the tomatoes through a food mill into a bowl. Discard the seeds and skin.

3. Rinse and dry the saucepan. Put in the olive oil, then add the chopped onion, and lightly sauté over medium heat until just

translucent, not browned. Add the carrot and celery and sauté for another minute. Add the puréed tomato, the salt, and the sugar, and cook at a gentle simmer, uncovered, for 20 minutes. Stir from time to time while cooking.

If using canned tomatoes: use 2 cups tomatoes with their juice, omit Steps 1 and 2, and simmer 45 minutes instead of 20.

TOMATO SAUCE II

Although this sauce is made with the same ingredients as Tomato Sauce I, it has a fresher, more delicate flavor. There are two reasons for this. First, the tomato is cooked much less, just enough to concentrate it, but not so long that its garden-sweet taste is altered. Second, the vegetables are cooked right along with the tomato instead of undergoing a preliminary sautéing in oil. It is an excellent all-purpose sauce for every kind of pasta, from spaghettini to such thicker, stubby cuts as *penne* or *ziti*.

For 6 servings

2 pounds fresh, ripe plum tomatoes	⅔ cup chopped onion
	Salt
⅔ cup chopped carrot	¼ teaspoon granulated sugar
⅔ cup chopped celery	½ cup olive oil

1. Wash the tomatoes in cold water. Cut them in half, lengthwise. Cook in a covered stockpot or saucepan over medium heat for 10 minutes.

2. Add the carrot, celery, onion, 2 teaspoons salt, and sugar and cook at a steady simmer, uncovered, for 30 minutes.

3. Purée everything through a food mill, return to the pan, add the olive oil, and cook at a steady simmer, uncovered, for 15 minutes more. Taste and correct for salt.

If using canned tomatoes: Use 2 cups tomatoes and their juice. Start the recipe at Step 2, cooking the tomatoes with the vegetables as directed.

TOMATO SAUCE III

This is the simplest and freshest of all tomato sauces. It has no vegetables, except an onion. The onion is not sautéed, it is not chopped, it is only cut in two and cooked together with the tomato. Except for salt and a tiny amount of sugar, the sauce has no seasonings. It has no olive oil, only butter. What does it have? Pure, sweet tomato taste, at its most appealing. It is an unsurpassed sauce for potato *gnocchi*, and it is excellent with spaghetti, *penne*, and *ziti*.

For 6 servings

2 pounds fresh, ripe plum tomatoes	1 medium yellow onion, peeled and halved
¼ pound butter	Salt
	¼ teaspoon granulated sugar

1. Wash the tomatoes in cold water. Cut them in half, lengthwise. Cook in a covered stockpot or saucepan until they have simmered for 10 minutes.

2. Purée the tomatoes through a food mill back into the pot. Add the butter, onion, 1½ teaspoons salt, and sugar and cook at a slow but steady simmer, uncovered, for 45 minutes. Taste and correct for salt. Discard the onion.

If using canned tomatoes: Use 2 cups tomatoes and their juice, and start the recipe at Step 2.

TOMATO SAUCE WITH MARJORAM AND CHEESE

The fragrance of marjoram and the slight piquancy of Romano cheese make this a particularly appetizing sauce for summer. It is excellent with *perciatelli* and spaghetti.

(continued)

For 6 servings

Tomato Sauce II (page 94)

2 teaspoons marjoram

2 tablespoons freshly grated
Parmesan cheese

2 tablespoons freshly grated
Romano *pecorino* cheese

1 tablespoon olive oil

1. Bring the tomato sauce to a simmer. Add the marjoram, stir, and simmer for 8 to 10 minutes.

2. When the pasta is ready to be seasoned, mix both grated cheeses and the olive oil into the sauce, off the heat. Stir thoroughly but rapidly and pour over the pasta. Serve the pasta with additional grated Parmesan cheese on the side.

TOMATO SAUCE WITH ROSEMARY AND PANCETTA

This savory sauce is particularly good with stubby cuts of macaroni, such as *maccheroncini, ziti,* or *penne.* It is also excellent with *spaghettini.*

For 6 to 8 servings

All the ingredients of Tomato
Sauce II (page 94)

2 teaspoons finely chopped
dried rosemary leaves

½ cup thin strips of rolled
pancetta, ⅛ inch wide by
2 inches long

1. Make Tomato Sauce II, up to and including puréeing the cooked tomatoes and vegetables. Then proceed as follows.

2. Heat up the olive oil in a small skillet over medium-high heat. When hot, add the chopped rosemary and the *pancetta* strips. Sauté for 1 minute, stirring constantly. Transfer all the contents of the skillet to a saucepan, together with the puréed tomatoes, and cook at a steady simmer, uncovered, for 15 minutes. Taste and correct for salt.

Spaghettini alla carrettiera

THIN SPAGHETTI WITH FRESH BASIL
AND TOMATO SAUCE

Carretti were hand- or mule-driven carts in which wine and produce were brought into Rome from the surrounding hills. The *carrettieri*, the cart drivers, were notoriously underpaid and had to improvise inexpensive but satisfying meals that could be quickly prepared in the intervals between treks to and from the city.

There are many versions of *spaghettini alla carrettiera*. This is evidently a spring and summer version, because it calls for a large quantity of fresh basil. It has a very fresh, unlabored taste. Don't be put off by the amount of garlic required. It simmers in the sauce without browning so that its flavor comes through very gently. In Rome, one would use very ripe, small sauce tomatoes called *casalini*, which thicken quickly in cooking. For our purposes, a good-quality canned Italian plum tomato is best.

For 4 persons

1 large bunch fresh basil, preferably with the smallest possible leaves

2 cups canned Italian plum tomatoes, seeded, drained, and coarsely chopped

5 large cloves garlic, peeled and chopped fine

⅓ cup olive oil, more if desired

Salt

Freshly ground pepper, about 6 twists of the mill

1 pound *spaghettini*

1. Pull off all the basil leaves from the stalks, rinse them briefly in cold water, and roughly chop them. The yield should be about 1½ to 2 cups.

2. Put the chopped basil, tomatoes, garlic, the ⅓ cup olive oil, 1 teaspoon salt, and pepper in an uncovered saucepan and cook over medium-high heat for 15 minutes. Taste and correct for salt.

(continued)

3. Drop the *spaghettini* in 4 quarts of boiling salted water. Since thin spaghetti cook very rapidly, begin testing them early for doneness. They should be truly *al dente*, very firm to the bite.

4. Drain the *spaghettini* in a large colander, giving the colander two or three vigorous upward jerks to make all the water run off, and transfer quickly to a large hot bowl. Add the sauce, mixing it thoroughly into the *spaghettini*. You may, if you wish, add a few drops of raw olive oil. Serve immediately.

NOTE

No grated cheese is called for.

MENU SUGGESTIONS

If you want to precede this with an antipasto, try either some cold Sautéed Mushrooms with Garlic and Parsley (page 379), or Peppers and Anchovies (page 37). As a second course, serve Pan Roast of Veal (page 252), Roast Pork with Bay Leaves (page 286), or Chicken Fricassee with Dried Wild Mushrooms (page 310), Avoid any second course with tomatoes.

Spaghettini con le melanzane

THIN SPAGHETTI WITH EGGPLANT

For 4 persons

1 medium eggplant (about 1 pound)
1½ teaspoons finely chopped garlic
3 tablespoons olive oil
2 tablespoons finely chopped parsley

1¾ cups canned Italian tomatoes
⅛ teaspoon finely chopped hot red pepper or less, to taste
Salt
1 pound *spaghettini*

1. Trim, slice, salt, and fry the eggplant according to the instruc-

tions for Fried Eggplant (page 372). Set aside to drain on paper towels.

2. In a medium-sized saucepan sauté the garlic in olive oil over moderate heat just until the garlic begins to color lightly. Stirring rapidly, add the parsley, tomatoes, chopped hot pepper, and ¼ teaspoon salt. Cook, uncovered, for about 25 minutes, or until the tomatoes have separated from the oil and turned to sauce.

3. Cut the fried eggplant slices into slivers about ½ inch wide. When the sauce is ready, add the eggplant slivers and cook for 2 or 3 minutes more. Taste for salt. (You can prepare the sauce three or four days in advance if you like.)

4. Drop the *spaghettini* into 4 quarts of boiling salted water. Since thin spaghetti cook very rapidly and continue to soften even after draining, you must be ready to stop the cooking when the *spaghettini* are still quite firm.

5. Put a small quantity of the sauce in a warm serving bowl. Add the drained *spaghettini*, mix, add the rest of the sauce quickly, mix again, and serve immediately.

NOTE
This dish does not call for a topping of grated cheese.

MENU SUGGESTIONS

This can precede the peppery Pan-Broiled Steak (page 239), Braised Veal Shanks, Trieste Style (page 257), any roast of lamb (pages 278-281), Roast Chicken with Rosemary (page 306), or Broiled Pork Liver Wrapped in Caul Fat (page 302). If you want an appetizer, try Mushroom and Cheese Salad (page 47).

Spaghettini alle vongole
THIN SPAGHETTI WITH RED CLAM SAUCE

For 4 persons

1 dozen littleneck clams, the
tiniest you can find
1½ teaspoons finely chopped
garlic
3 tablespoons olive oil
1 teaspoon chopped anchovy
fillets or anchovy paste
1½ tablespoons finely chopped
parsley

2 cups canned Italian tomatoes,
coarsely chopped, with
their juice
Salt
Freshly ground pepper, about
6 twists of the mill
1 pound *spaghettini*

1. Wash and scrub the clams thoroughly as directed on page 53. Heat them over high heat in a covered pan until they open their shells. Detach the clams from the shells and rinse off any sand on the meat by dipping them briefly one at a time in their own juice. Unless the clams are exceptionally small, cut them up into two or more pieces and set aside. Strain the clam juices through a sieve lined with paper towels and set aside.

2. In a saucepan, sauté the garlic in the olive oil over medium heat. When the garlic has colored lightly, add the chopped anchovies or paste and stir. Add the chopped parsley, stir, then add the chopped tomatoes with their juice and the strained clam juices. Cook, uncovered, at a gentle simmer for about 25 minutes, or until the tomatoes and oil separate. Taste and correct for salt, then add the pepper. Off the heat, mix in the chopped clams. (If you are preparing the sauce ahead of time, hold back the clams until after you've warmed up the sauce; otherwise they will become tough and rubbery. Film them with a little olive oil to keep them moist.)

3. Drop the *spaghettini* into 4 quarts of boiling salted water and cook until *al dente*, firm to the bite. (*Spaghettini* cook very rapidly and should be eaten even slightly more *al dente* than other

pasta.) Drain the pasta immediately when cooked. Transfer to a warm bowl and mix in the sauce, thoroughly seasoning all the strands. Serve right away.

NOTE

No grated cheese is called for in this recipe.

MENU SUGGESTIONS

For an antipasto: Shrimps with Oil and Lemon (page 39), or Broiled Mussels and Clams on the Half Shell (page 34). As a second course, Fish Broiled the Adriatic Way (page 224) would be perfect, and so would Fried Squid (page 234) or, if you've skipped the shrimp antipasto, Shrimp Brochettes, Adriatic Style (page 226), or Poached Halibut with Parsley Sauce (page 214).

Spaghettini al sugo di pomodoro e acciughe

THIN SPAGHETTI WITH ANCHOVY AND TOMATO SAUCE

For 4 persons

1 teaspoon chopped garlic	1½ cups canned Italian tomatoes,
⅓ cup olive oil	chopped, with their juice
4 flat anchovy fillets, coarsely	Salt
chopped	Freshly ground pepper, 6 to
2 tablespoons chopped parsley	8 twists of the mill
	1 pound *spaghettini*

1. Put the garlic in a small saucepan with the oil and sauté over medium heat until it has colored lightly.

2. Add the chopped anchovies and parsley and sauté for another 30 seconds, stirring constantly.

3. Add the tomatoes, ½ teaspoon salt, and pepper. Stir, and adjust the heat so that the sauce cooks at a gentle but steady simmer for 25 minutes. Stir frequently. Taste and correct for salt.

(continued)

4. Bring 4 quarts of water to a boil, add 1½ tablespoons salt, drop in the *spaghettini*, and cook until *al dente*, firm to the bite. Drain, transfer promptly to a warm bowl, mix thoroughly with the sauce, and serve at once.

NOTE

Although the sauce takes only slightly more time to do than does cooking the pasta, it may be prepared in advance, and reheated before using.

MENU SUGGESTIONS

Follow those given for Thin Spaghetti with Red Clam Sauce (page 101).

Spaghetti al tonno
SPAGHETTI WITH TUNA SAUCE

For 4 or 5 persons

½ teaspoon finely chopped garlic	10 ounces Italian tuna or domestic tuna packed in oil, drained
5 tablespoons olive oil	
3 tablespoons finely chopped parsley	Salt
	Freshly ground pepper, about 6 twists of the mill
1½ cups canned Italian tomatoes, coarsely chopped, with their juice	3 tablespoons butter
	1 pound spaghetti

1. In a skillet, sauté the garlic, with all the olive oil, over medium heat until it has colored lightly. Add the chopped parsley, stir, and cook for another half minute. Add the chopped tomatoes and their juice, stir well, lower the heat, and cook at a steady, gentle simmer, uncovered, for about 25 minutes, or until the tomatoes separate from the oil.

2. While the tomato sauce is simmering, drain the tuna and break it up into small pieces with a fork. When the tomato sauce

is done, add the tuna to it, mixing it well into the sauce. Add just a light sprinkling of salt, bearing in mind that the tuna is already salty, add pepper, and cook at a gentle simmer, uncovered, for 5 minutes. Taste and correct for salt, turn off the heat, and swirl in the butter.

3. Drop the spaghetti into 4 quarts of boiling salted water and cook until *al dente,* very firm to the bite. Drain and transfer immediately to a warm serving bowl. Mix in all the sauce and serve immediately.

NOTE

The sauce may be prepared entirely ahead of time and refrigerated for one or two days. Add the butter, however, only after it has been reheated. No grated cheese is called for with this sauce.

MENU SUGGESTIONS

Antipasto: Broiled Mussels and Clams on the Half Shell (page 34). Second course: Pan-Roasted Mackerel with Rosemary and Garlic (page 216), Shrimp Brochettes, Adriatic Style (page 226), or Fish Broiled the Adriatic Way (page 224). Avoid tomato or cream sauces.

Spaghetti "ajo e ojo"
SPAGHETTI WITH GARLIC AND OIL

This is one of the easiest, quickest, and tastiest pasta dishes you can prepare. Its humble origins are in the shanty towns of Rome, but it is now a universal favorite, especially among Rome's chic insomniacs, who depend upon a wee hours' *spaghettata* to see them through the night until their early-morning bedtime.

In most versions, crushed garlic cloves are sautéed in olive oil until they are nearly black. They are then discarded and the spaghetti is seasoned with the flavored oil. In this recipe the garlic is chopped, sautéed lightly, and left in the oil to be added to the spaghetti. The result is a fuller yet milder taste of garlic, with no trace of bitterness.

(continued)

For 4 persons

½ cup plus 1 tablespoon olive oil	1 pound spaghetti or *spaghettini*
2 teaspoons very finely chopped garlic	Freshly ground pepper, 6 to 8 twists of the mill
Salt	2 tablespoons chopped parsley

1. The sauce can be prepared in the time it takes to bring the water for the spaghetti to a boil. When you've turned on the heat under the water, put the ½ cup oil, the garlic, and 2 teaspoons of salt in a very small saucepan. Sauté the garlic over very low heat, stirring frequently, until it slowly becomes a rich, golden color.

2. Drop the spaghetti into the boiling salted water and cook until tender but *al dente*, very firm to the bite. Drain immediately, transfer to a warm bowl, and add the oil and garlic sauce. Toss rapidly, coating all the strands, adding pepper and parsley. Mix the remaining tablespoon of olive oil into the spaghetti and serve.

MENU SUGGESTIONS

Aside from its *dolce vita* standing as a late-night snack, Spaghetti with Garlic and Oil is an easy introduction to any plain but hearty second course, whether it is fish, meat, or fowl. Avoid following it with dishes that have a bold garlic taste, which would be monotonous, or a delicate sauce, which would be lost on the palate after the brashness of the spaghetti. Specially recommended would be Thin Pan-Broiled Steaks with Tomatoes and Olives (page 241), Beef Patties with Anchovies and Mozzarella (page 245), Meat Balls (page 247), or Veal Scaloppine with Tomatoes (page 264).

Bucatini all'Amatriciana

BUCATINI WITH PANCETTA, TOMATOES, AND HOT PEPPER

For 4 persons

1 medium yellow onion,
  chopped fine
2 tablespoons butter
3 tablespoons vegetable oil
1 slice rolled *pancetta,* ¼ inch
  thick, cut into strips ½ inch
  wide and 1 inch long
1½ cups canned Italian tomatoes
½ to 1 small dried hot red
  pepper, chopped fine

Salt
1 pound *bucatini* or *perciatelli*
  (thick, hollow spaghetti)
3 tablespoons freshly grated
  Parmesan cheese
1 tablespoon freshly grated
  Romano *pecorino* cheese,
  more if desired

1. Sauté the onion in a saucepan with all the butter and oil until it is pale gold. Add the strips of *pancetta* and sauté for about a minute. Add the tomatoes, chopped hot pepper, and 1½ teaspoons salt. Cook over medium heat, uncovered. The sauce is done when the tomatoes and the cooking fats separate, about 25 minutes. Turn off the heat and taste for salt.

2. Drop the *bucatini* into 4 quarts boiling salted water. Stop the cooking when very firm, very *al dente,* and drain immediately. (Although large in diameter, the *bucatini* are hollow and have very thin sides, and they quickly turn from firm to soft. They will continue to soften as they are being seasoned and while they rest in the serving bowl.)

3. Transfer the cooked *bucatini* to a warm serving bowl, add the sauce, and mix. Add the Parmesan and the Romano and mix very thoroughly. Taste for salt and spiciness. If you like it somewhat sharper you can add a little more Romano, but not so much as to overwhelm the other flavors.

(continued)

MENU SUGGESTIONS

Antipasto: ideally, good Italian salami, if you can find it. Or the Braised Artichokes with Mortadella Stuffing (page 343). A perfect second course would be Casserole-Roasted Lamb with Juniper Berries (page 280). Other suggestions: Roast Chicken with Rosemary (page 306), Meat Loaf Braised in White Wine with Dried Wild Mushrooms (page 249), or Sautéed Calf's Liver with Onions, Venetian Style (page 296).

Fusilli alla pappone
FUSILLI WITH CREAMY ZUCCHINI AND BASIL SAUCE

For 4 persons

1 pound zucchini	⅔ cup roughly chopped fresh
Vegetable oil, enough to come	basil
½ inch up the side of a	1 egg yolk, beaten lightly with
medium skillet	a fork
1 pound *fusilli* (spiral spaghetti)	½ cup freshly grated Parmesan
3 tablespoons butter	cheese
3 tablespoons olive oil	¼ cup freshly grated Romano
1 teaspoon all-purpose flour	*pecorino* cheese (see note
dissolved in ⅓ cup milk	below)
Salt	

1. Wash the zucchini as directed on page 392 and cut into sticks about 3 inches long and ⅛ inch thick.

2. Heat the vegetable oil in a skillet over medium-high heat. Fry the zucchini sticks, a few at a time, so that they are not crowded. Fry them until they are a light-brown color, not too dark, turning them occasionally. As each batch is done, transfer to paper towels to drain.

3. Drop the *fusilli* into 4 quarts of boiling salted water, stirring with a wooden spoon. It will cook while you prepare the sauce.

4. In another skillet, melt half the butter and add all the olive oil. When the butter begins to foam, turn the heat down to medium low, and stir in the flour-and-milk mixture, a little bit at a time. Cook, stirring constantly, for 30 seconds. Add the fried zucchini sticks, turning them two or three times, then add ¼ teaspoon salt and the chopped basil. Cook long enough to turn everything once or twice. Off the heat, swirl in the remaining butter. Rapidly mix in the egg yolk, then all the grated cheese. Taste and correct for salt.

5. Cook the *fusilli* until *al dente*, firm to the bite. Drain, transfer to a warm serving bowl, toss with all the sauce, and serve immediately.

NOTE

You may increase the quantity of Romano and decrease the Parmesan if you prefer a more piquant cheese flavor.

MENU SUGGESTIONS

Antipasti: none is required. This is a rather rich sauce, and the palate should be kept limber enough to deal with it. Second courses: Pan-Broiled Steak with Marsala and Hot Pepper Sauce (page 239), Veal Stew with Sage and White Wine (page 273), Baby Lamb Chops Fried in Parmesan Cheese Batter (page 283), or Pan-Roasted Chicken with Garlic, Rosemary, and White Wine (page 304).

Penne al sugo di pomodoro e funghi secchi
PENNE WITH A SAUCE OF TOMATOES AND DRIED WILD MUSHROOMS

For 4 persons

1 ounce dried wild mushrooms
2 tablespoons finely chopped shallots or yellow onion
1 tablespoon vegetable oil
4 tablespoons butter
2 tablespoons ¼-inch-wide strips of *pancetta*, prosciutto, or unsmoked ham

1½ cups canned Italian tomatoes, cut up, with their juice
Salt
Freshly ground pepper, about 4 twists of the mill
1 pound *penne* or other short tubular pasta, such as *mezzani* or *ziti*

1. Put the mushrooms to soak in 1 cup lukewarm water for about 30 minutes. When they have finished soaking, lift out the mushrooms but do not discard the water. Rinse the mushrooms in several changes of cold water and set aside. Strain the water from the soak through a sieve lined with paper towels and set aside.

2. Put the shallots in· a small saucepan with the oil and butter and sauté over medium heat until pale gold.

3. Add the *pancetta*, and continue sautéing for another minute or two, stirring several times.

4. Add the cut-up tomatoes and their juice, the mushrooms, the strained liquid from the mushroom soak, ¼ teaspoon salt, and pepper, and cook, uncovered, at a gentle simmer for 45 minutes. Stir with a wooden spoon from time to time.

5. Drop the pasta into boiling salted water and cook until tender but *al dente*, firm to the bite. Drain, giving the colander a few vigorous up-and-down shakes to let all the water run off. Transfer to a warm serving bowl, pour all the sauce over the pasta, and mix thoroughly but rapidly. Serve immediately, with a bowl of freshly grated Parmesan cheese on the side.

MENU SUGGESTIONS

You can follow this with any second course of meat or fowl that does not contain tomatoes or mushrooms. Particularly good choices would be broiled steak, Pan Roast of Veal (page 252), Roast Spring Lamb with White Wine (page 278), Charcoal-Broiled Chicken Marinated in Pepper, Oil, and Lemon (page 307), or the Broiled Pork Liver Wrapped in Caul Fat (page 302).

Conchiglie con il sugo per la gramigna
CONCHIGLIE WITH SAUSAGE AND CREAM SAUCE

Gramigna is both a kind of crab grass and a thin, short tubular macaroni with which one usually serves this sauce. *Gramigna,* to my knowledge, is not available here, but this creamy, tasty sauce is every bit as delectable with *conchiglie, fusilli,* or *rotelle*: any pasta whose twists or cavities can trap little morsels of sausage and cream. Use a mild, sweet sausage. Avoid any sausage containing hot peppers, fennel seeds, or other pungent spices. *Luganega* is best, but you may substitute other sweet sausages if you can't find *luganega.* Breakfast sausage or German bratwurst are acceptable alternatives.

For 4 persons

6 to 8 ounces *luganega* sausage	Freshly ground pepper, about
1½ tablespoons chopped shallots or yellow onion	4 twists of the mill
	⅔ cup heavy cream
2 tablespoons butter	Salt
2 tablespoons vegetable oil	1 pound *conchiglie, fusilli,* or *rotelle*

1. Skin the sausage and crumble it as fine as possible.

2. Put the shallots in a small saucepan with the butter and oil and sauté until pale gold.

(continued)

3. Add the crumbled sausage meat and sauté it for 10 minutes, stirring frequently.

4. Add the pepper and the cream, turn up the heat to medium high, and cook until the cream has thickened. Stir frequently while cooking. Taste and correct for salt.

5. Drop the *conchiglie* into 4 quarts of boiling salted water and stir with a wooden spoon. When *al dente,* firm to the bite, drain, giving the colander a few vigorous up-and-down jerks to shake all the water out of the *conchiglie*'s cavities. Transfer to a warm serving bowl, toss with all the sauce, and serve immediately, with a little freshly grated Parmesan cheese on the side.

MENU SUGGESTIONS

No antipasti are recommended. Suitable second courses could be the Beef Braised in Red Wine Sauce (page 242), the Roast Spring Lamb with White Wine (page 278), the Breaded Veal Cutlets (page 270), or the Charcoal-Broiled Chicken Marinated in Pepper, Oil, and Lemon (page 307).

Rigatoni al forno col ragù
BAKED RIGATONI WITH MEAT SAUCE

For 6 persons

1 pound *rigatoni* or similar-cut pasta, such as *mezzani, ziti,* or *penne*	A medium-thick Béchamel Sauce (page 28)
Salt	6 tablespoons freshly grated Parmesan cheese
2 cups Meat Sauce, Bolognese Style (page 127)	2 tablespoons butter

1. Preheat the oven to 400°.

2. Drop the pasta into 4 quarts of boiling salted water and cook until just *al dente,* firm to the bite. (It should be a shade firmer than

you would ordinarily cook it because it will soften more as it bakes in the oven.) Drain and transfer to a large mixing bowl.

3. Add the meat sauce, the béchamel sauce, and 4 tablespoons of the grated cheese to the pasta. Mix thoroughly. Transfer to a butter-smeared bake-and-serve dish. Level the top with a spatula, sprinkle it with the remaining 2 tablespoons grated cheese, and dot with butter. Place in the uppermost level of the oven and bake for 10 minutes. Allow to settle a few minutes before serving.

MENU SUGGESTIONS

Follow this with Rolled Stuffed Breast of Veal (page 254), Sautéed Veal Chops with Sage and White Wine (page 272), Pork Loin Braised in Milk (page 284), Stewed Rabbit with White Wine (page 320), or Pan-Roasted Squab (page 319).

La Sfoglia
(Pasta all'uovo fatta in casa)
HOMEMADE EGG PASTA

Macaroni pasta is factory made with flour and water. In home-made pasta, eggs take the place of water and hands replace machines. Although egg pasta is now produced in almost every Italian province, it is the specialty of Emilia-Romagna, and even today the pasta produced there is incontestably the finest in Italy. Until comparatively recent times, spaghetti and other macaroni were nearly unknown to the Emilian table. The only pasta consumed was homemade pasta, and it was made fresh every day in virtually every home. My grandmother, who died at ninety-three, made pasta for us daily until the last few years of her life. At the end, when, instead of homemade pasta, an occasional dish of macaroni would appear on our table, she would be saddened and perplexed by our declining taste.

There is no denying that, for a beginner, making pasta at home takes time, patience, and a considerable amount of physical effort. The rewards are such, however, that you should be persuaded to make the attempt. When you have mastered basic pasta dough you will have immediate access to some of the most miraculous creations in all gastronomy: *fettuccine, tagliatelle, tortellini, cappelletti, cappellacci, tortelloni, cannelloni, lasagne, garganelli,* and all their glorious variations. As you become skillful, you will discover, too, that the fresh egg pasta you are making at home is not only vastly better than what you can buy in any store, but that it is also superior to what you are likely to eat in any restaurant this side of the Alps.

WHAT YOU NEED TO MAKE PASTA

• A steady surface on which to work, 24 inches deep, 36 inches wide, preferably unvarnished wood, but it can well be formica. Marble is not too satisfactory.

• A rolling pin, 1½ inches in diameter, 32 inches long. This is the ideal size for pasta. You will probably not find it in any store, but you can easily have one cut for you from hardwood at a good lumber supply house. Make sure the ends are sanded and smooth.

Before using a new rolling pin, wash it with soap and water and rinse. Dry thoroughly with a soft towel and let dry further in the warmth of the kitchen. Then dampen a cloth in olive oil or lightly grease your hands and rub oil over the entire surface of the pin. Do not overgrease. When the oil has been absorbed, lightly rub some flour over the pin. This procedure should be repeated every dozen or so times that the rolling pin is used.

• A broad-bladed, well-balanced knife. A Chinese cleaver is excellent.

• A place protected from draughts and not overheated. Pasta dough must not dry out too quickly while you are working on it.

THE INGREDIENTS

Although no one making pasta in Italy ever really measures out flour, the traditionally accepted formula corresponds to 1 level cup of flour for every egg. I have experimented with this, as well as with other proportions, and I have found that, with American flour, the best results are obtained using ¾ cup of flour for every U.S. Large egg. This must not be considered an inflexible rule, however, because eggs vary in size, and in flour-absorption qualities. Start with ¾ cup of flour per egg. If you find that the egg will take a little more flour, add it. It is easier for beginners to work with less than with more flour, because the dough stays softer and easier to handle. If you keep it too soft, however, it may also become a problem, because very soft dough is likely to stick and tear. Until you develop a feel for the right consistency, you are safest with these recommended proportions:

3 or 4 persons*	5 or 6 persons*	7 or 8 persons*
2 eggs	3 eggs	4 eggs
1½ cups all-purpose flour	2¼ cups all-purpose flour	3 cups all-purpose flour

* These servings for flat pasta only. Stuffed pasta goes further. See individual recipes for yield.

For stuffed pasta, such as *tortellini*, add 1 teaspoon of milk for each egg used. This is to make the pasta easier to seal. In Emilia-Romagna we never add oil, water, or salt to pasta dough.

HANDMADE EGG PASTA (BASIC RECIPE)*

There are four steps in making a sheet of egg-pasta dough from eggs and flour. In the first step the eggs are combined with as much flour as they will take without becoming stiff and dry. In the

* See also page 122 for homemade pasta made on the pasta machine.

Beat the eggs, and mix them with the flour drawn from
the inside wall of the well.

Knead the dough, pressing it with the heel of your palm . . .

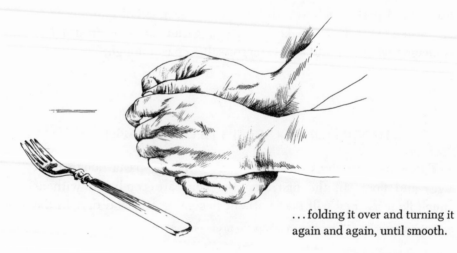

. . . folding it over and turning it
again and again, until smooth.

second, the eggs and flour are kneaded to a smooth, elastic consistency. In the third, the dough is opened out with the rolling pin to a circular sheet about ⅛ inch thick. In the last step the sheet is wrapped around the pin and stretched again and again until it is almost paper thin and transparent. All together, it should take a reasonably skillful person less than 25 minutes. Here is a detailed description of each step:

1. Pour out the flour on the working surface, shape it into a mound, and make a well in the center of the mound. Put the whole eggs in the well. If you are making stuffed pasta, and the recipe calls for milk, add the milk. Beat the eggs lightly with your fingers or with a fork, for a minute or two. Start mixing flour into the eggs with a circular motion, drawing the flour from the inside wall of the well. Use one hand for mixing, the other for supporting the outside wall of the well, lest it collapse and let the eggs run through. When the eggs cease to be runny, tumble the rest of the flour over them, and, working with palms and fingertips, push and squeeze the eggs and flour until they are a well-combined but somewhat crumbly paste. If the eggs were very large, or had exceptional flour-absorption qualities, the mass may be on the moist and sticky side. Add as much flour as the mass will absorb without becoming stiff and dry, but do not exceed 1 cup of flour per egg.

2. Set the egg and flour mass to one side and scrape off every last crumb of caked flour from the working surface and from your hands. Wash and dry your hands. Knead the mass, pressing against it with the heel of your palm, folding it over and turning it again and again. After 8 to 10 minutes it should be a smooth, compact, and elastic ball of dough. Pat it into a flattish bunlike shape. (If you are making a lot of pasta and using more than 2 eggs, divide the mass in two and keep one half covered between 2 soup plates while you roll out and thin the other half. When you've become more experienced, you can try doing the entire mass at one time.)

(continued)

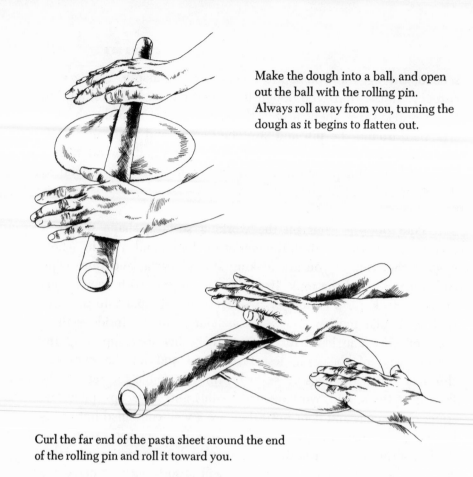

Make the dough into a ball, and open
out the ball with the rolling pin.
Always roll away from you, turning the
dough as it begins to flatten out.

Curl the far end of the pasta sheet around the end
of the rolling pin and roll it toward you.

Giving the pasta sheet a final
thinning out: move hands back
and forth, quickly and lightly,
over the length of the rolling
pin. At the same time roll the
pin backward and forward to
thin the sheet evenly.

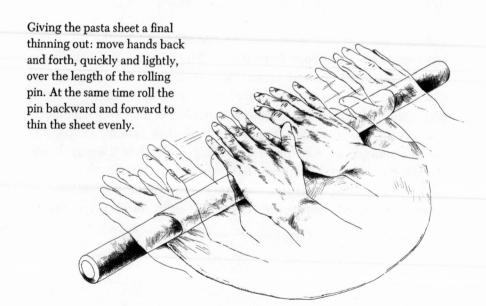

3. Dust the work surface lightly with flour. Open out the ball of dough with the rolling pin, starting to roll at about one-third of the way in on the ball, rolling forward, away from you. Rotate the dough one quarter turn after every roll so that it opens out into an even, circular shape. As it begins to flatten out, gradually lessen the degree of rotation after each roll, but don't lose control of the shape. It must stay as round as possible. Don't press the dough *against* the work surface. Roll it *out and away*, without putting weight on it. Stop when you have rolled out a sheet ⅛ inch thick.

4. This last step is the hardest one for beginners to learn. But it doesn't require particular skills; it is all a question of getting the right motion. Once you have it you have mastered pasta, and you will never again give it a second thought. The objective is to give the pasta sheet its final thinning out by stretching it with a sideways pressure of your hands as you wrap it around the rolling pin. Here is how you do it. Curl the far end of the pasta sheet around the center of the rolling pin, and roll it toward you, with both your palms cupped over the center of the pin. When you have rolled up about a quarter of the sheet, don't roll up any more. Quickly roll the pin backward and forward, and *at the same time* slide the palms of your hands away from each other and toward the ends of the rolling pin, dragging them against the surface of the pasta. Roll up some more of the sheet, quickly roll backward and forward while repeating the same stretching motion with the palms of your hands. By the time the sheet is completely rolled up, you should have repeated the stretching motion 12 to 14 times in 8 seconds or less. Unroll the pasta, turning the pin slightly so that the sheet doesn't open out to exactly the place where you rolled it up before. Flatten out any bumps or creases, and even off the edges with the rolling pin. If the dough is a little sticky, dust very lightly with flour from time to time. Repeat the same rolling up and stretching operation several times, until the pasta is almost paper thin and transparent. The entire step must be carried out in not much more than 8 minutes, otherwise the pasta will dry, lose its elasticity, and become impossible to thin.

(continued)

Repeat the rolling-up-and-stretching operation until
the pasta is almost paper-thin and transparent.

For *tagliatelle, fettuccine,* and
maltagliati: Hold the roll loosely
with one hand, and with the other
hold the knife so that the flat
part of the blade leans against
your knuckles.

Open out the noodles, and let dry
for 5 minutes before cooking.

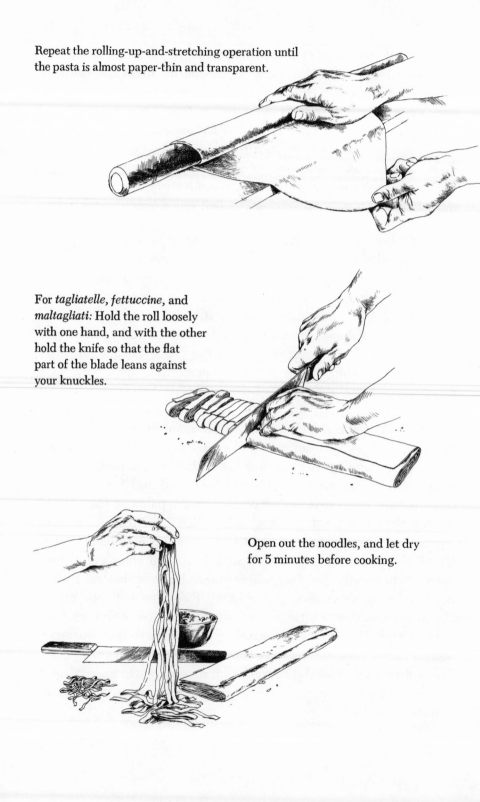

For stuffed pasta, do not allow the dough to dry. Omit the next step and proceed immediately to cut and stuff it as directed in the individual recipes. If you are making more than one sheet of pasta, cut and stuff the first sheet before rolling out the second.

For *tagliatelle, fettuccine,* and *maltagliati* (pages 120–123), proceed as follows:

5. Roll up the sheet of pasta on your rolling pin. Lay a clean, dry towel on a table. Unroll the pasta on the towel, letting about a third of the sheet hang over the edge of the table. After about 10 minutes, turn it, letting another third hang over the edge. Turn it again after another 10 minutes. Pasta for noodles must be dried out so that the noodle ribbons, when cut, do not stick together. It must not be overdried, however. Before cutting, it must be folded into a flat roll, so it has to stay soft and pliable enough to fold without cracking. When the surface of the pasta begins to take on a leathery look it is ready for folding and cutting. This drying process usually takes about 30 minutes but in a very hot room it can take as little as 15 or 20 minutes.

6. Roll up the pasta on the rolling pin and unroll it on the work surface. Fold it over and over into a flat roll about 3 inches wide. Place one hand on the roll, with fingertips partly drawn back under your knuckles. Hold the knife with your other hand, crosswise to the roll, leaning the flat part of the blade against your knuckles. Cut the pasta to the width desired, pulling back your knuckles after each cut and following them with the flat side of the blade. Keep your knuckles high and don't lift the knife above them. (This method gives you perfect control of the knife and is almost completely accident-proof.) When you have cut the entire roll, open out the noodles on a clean, dry towel and allow them to firm up for 5 minutes. They are then ready to cook. Gather them up with the towel and let them slide into the boiling water.

FLAT PASTA
TAGLIATELLE, AND OTHER NOODLES

There are two broad categories of egg pasta. There is stuffed pasta, such as *tortellini, tortelloni, cannelloni,* and *lasagne,* and there is non-stuffed pasta, which includes all varieties of noodles. We refer to this last category as flat pasta, and here are the most important shapes in which it is cut.

All of the following shapes are cut from a rolled-up sheet of home-made pasta dough. (See Step 6, preceding page.)

TAGLIATELLE

Tagliatelle are the long, narrow noodles, and it is probably the best-known cut of all. This is the uncontested specialty of Bologna. Of all their many contributions to civilized life, there is probably none for which the Bolognese have any higher regard or greater affection than *tagliatelle.* Just as at the International Bureau of Weights and Measures in Paris the standard of the meter is deposited in the form of a platinum bar, in Bologna, at the Chamber of Commerce, there is a sealed glass case wherein the ideal width and thickness of *tagliatelle* are embodied in a solid gold noodle. According to the Accademia Italiana della Cucina (Italian Academy of Cooking), the correct dimensions of raw *tagliatelle* are: thickness, 1 millimeter (slightly more than $\frac{1}{32}$ inch), and width, 6 millimeters (slightly less than $\frac{1}{4}$ inch). This sort of precision deserves our wonder and admiration, but, inasmuch as we are not making yardsticks, we are only making noodles, we can permit ourselves some elasticity.

The most desirable width, in terms of wrapping-around-the-sauce ability and of plumpness in the plate, hovers around $\frac{1}{4}$ inch. No need to worry, however, if you exceed it slightly. The thickness is simply that of the thinnest pasta dough you are able to produce. If you are using the pasta machine, this entire discussion is academic because the cutting blades and the rollers predetermine width and thickness.

Tagliatelle is best served Bolognese fashion, with Meat Sauce, Bolognese Style (page 127).

FETTUCCINE

This is the term Romans use for noodles, and it is commonly assumed that they are precisely the same as *tagliatelle*, except for the name. The fact is, however, that *fettuccine*, as Romans are accustomed to eat them, are somewhat narrower and thicker than *tagliatelle*. I find this slightly stouter noodle ideally suited to carry sauces in which heavy cream is an essential ingredient.

For *fettuccine*, keep your pasta dough not quite paper thin, and cut it into noodles about ⅛ inch wide.

TAGLIOLINI, TAGLIARINI

These are very thin noodles, best suited for use in soups, with chicken or meat broths. The dough should be as thin as possible, and cut into noodles $\frac{1}{16}$ inch wide. The narrow blades on the pasta machine are perfect for *tagliolini*.

When even narrower, *tagliolini* are called *capellini* or *capelli d'angelo*. *Capello* means hair and *capelli d'angelo*, angel hair. They are indeed hair thin. In fact, they are too thin for most people to cut by hand, so they are usually store bought.

PAPPARDELLE

These are the broadest of noodles. They are cut to a width of ⅝ inch with a fluted pastry wheel, which gives them their characteristic crimped edge. *Pappardelle*, unlike all other noodles, are cut directly from a flat, open sheet of pasta. Allow the dough to dry about half as long as for other noodles, then divide the pasta sheet in half before cutting it into *pappardelle*. In Tuscany, *pappardelle* are served with a sauce made from hare, whose rich, gamy taste goes well with the broadness of the noodle. Another excellent sauce for *pappardelle* is the chicken-liver sauce given on page 137.

MALTAGLIATI

Maltagliati are used exclusively for soups, especially soups with beans or chick-peas. *Maltagliati* literally means "badly cut." Instead of cutting the pasta roll straight across as you would for other noodles,

Pappardelle are cut with a fluted pastry wheel, which gives them their characteristic crimpled edge.

Maltagliati are produced by cutting off both corners of the pasta roll and then cutting straight across.

cut it on the bias, first cutting off one corner, then the other. This leaves the pasta roll coming to a point in the center. Cut it straight across, thus giving the roll a straight edge again, then cut off the corners once more as before. At its broadest point, *maltagliati* should be about ½ inch wide or less, but precision, as the name indicates, is not terribly important.

There is no bean soup calling for pasta that is not immensely improved when you use homemade *maltagliati* instead of commercial macaroni. Like all noodles, maltagliati easily keeps for a month without refrigeration, so that you can always have a supply on hand.

QUADRUCCI

The name means "little squares," and that is exactly what they are. They are made by first cutting the pasta into *tagliatelle* noodles, then cutting the still-folded ribbons crosswise into squares. It makes a fine, delicate pasta for use with a good, clear meat or chicken broth.

HOMEMADE PASTA USING THE PASTA MACHINE

The pasta machine kneads and thins out pasta and cuts it, if you wish, into two different noodle widths. It is truly effortless, but, unfortunately, machine pasta is not really as fine as the handmade kind. Something happens to its composition as it goes through the steel rollers that gives the dough an ever so slightly slippery texture. Moreover, the machine gives you only one degree of thinness, whereas for *fettuccine,* for example, you might want the pasta a little thicker, or for stuffed pasta a little thinner. These considerations aside, however, machine pasta can be quite good; it is certainly superior to the commercial variety, and it is far better than having no homemade pasta at all.

1. Combine the eggs and flour exactly as in Step 1 of the handmade pasta recipe (page 115).

2. The smooth steel rollers at one end of the machine knead, roll out, and thin the dough. The first setting, at which the rollers are

Some varieties of cut pasta, drawn to their actual size.

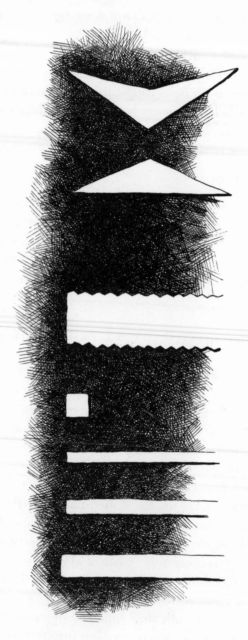

maltagliati

pappardelle

quadrucci

tagliolini

fettuccine

tagliatelle

widest apart, is for kneading. Pull off a piece of the egg and flour mass about the size of a lemon, keeping the rest of the mass covered between two soup plates. Feed the mass through the rollers 8 to 10 times, until it is smooth and elastic. Each time after you knead it, fold it over and turn it before feeding it through the rollers again, so that it will be kneaded evenly.

3. Shift the rollers to the next setting and pass the kneaded dough through. Do not fold the dough. Lower the setting again, and feed through once more. Go down all the settings, feeding the dough once through each setting until it is thoroughly thinned out. If the dough is sticky, dust it lightly with flour.

4. If you are making stuffed pasta, proceed immediately to cut the dough and stuff it as directed in the recipes. For noodles, allow the pasta to dry on a clean towel for at least 15 minutes. Before cutting, trim the dough to a workable length, no more than 24 inches.

5. For *tagliatelle* (page 120), feed the dough through the broad cutting blades. The narrow blades are suitable only for making the *tagliolini*, very thin noodles, best served in broth. For *fettuccine* or *maltagliati*, fold the dough into a flat roll and cut it by hand, as directed in Step 6 of the handmade pasta recipe (page 119).

KEEPING HOMEMADE PASTA

Uncooked flat noodle pasta, such as *tagliatelle, fettuccine, tagliolini, maltagliati*, and so on, keeps a very long time, even as long as a month or more, without refrigeration. Allow the opened-out noodles to dry thoroughly. When dry transfer to a platter or large soup bowl. (Handle carefully, because pasta is very brittle at this stage and breaks easily.) Put away, uncovered, in a dry, cool cupboard. Use exactly as you would fresh pasta, except that it will take somewhat longer to cook.

Although stuffed pasta can also be made ahead of time, it does not keep as long as noodle pasta. How long it keeps depends on the stuffing. Follow the suggestions at the end of each recipe.

COOKING HOMEMADE PASTA

Follow the same procedure as for macaroni pasta. If the pasta is to be seasoned with a very delicate sauce, add a bit more salt to the water in which it boils.

People who are doing it for the first time are always astonished to see how quickly fresh egg pasta cooks. As a general rule, fresh flat pasta is done within 5 to 10 *seconds* after the water in which it has been dropped returns to a boil. Stuffed pasta takes a while longer, and all dried pasta takes much longer, several minutes at least. Taste it frequently as it boils to avoid overcooking.

Always stir pasta with a wooden spoon immediately after dropping it in the pot, or it may stick together.

Pasta verde
SPINACH PASTA

Spinach is added to pasta dough to color it and to make it slightly softer and creamier. It doesn't significantly alter its flavor. You can use green pasta exactly as you would yellow pasta. It is found most frequently in the form of *lasagne* (page 143) or *tagliatelle* (page 129), but *cappelletti* (page 155), *tortelloni* (page 164), and *garganelli* (page 170) can also be very successful when made with spinach pasta. Green pasta is particularly attractive when served with Tomato and Cream Sauce (page 163), or any sauce in which the white of cream and béchamel or the red of tomato predominates.

Spinach pasta is made with precisely the same technique used for yellow pasta.

½ ten-ounce package frozen leaf spinach, thawed, or ½ pound fresh spinach

¼ teaspoon salt

2 eggs

1½ cups all-purpose flour, approximately

1. If you are using frozen spinach, cook it with ¼ teaspoon salt in

a covered pan over medium heat for 5 minutes. Drain and let cool.

If you are using fresh spinach, try to choose young, tender spinach. Remove all the stems, and discard any leaves that are not perfectly green and crisp. Wash it in a basin of cold water, changing the water several times until it shows no traces of soil. Cook it with ¼ teaspoon of salt in a covered pan over medium heat with just the water that clings to the leaves. Cook until tender, 15 minutes or more, then drain and allow to cool.

Squeeze the cooked spinach with your hands as dry as you can, then chop it very fine.

2. Pour the flour on the work surface, shape it into a mound, and make a well in the center. Put the whole eggs and the chopped spinach in the well, and lightly beat the eggs and the spinach together, using your fingers or a fork. Add flour gradually to the egg and spinach mixture, drawing it in from the inside wall of the well. Since it is impossible to estimate in advance exactly how much flour the egg and spinach will absorb, simply work it into the egg and spinach mixture gradually until the mixture has incorporated as much flour as possible without becoming stiff and dry. When the mass is ready for kneading, proceed exactly as though it were yellow pasta. Refer to Step 2 of the basic pasta recipe (page 115), or knead it and thin it out in the pasta machine (page 123).

NOTE

If you are making stuffed pasta, do *not* add milk to spinach pasta. It is soft enough to seal well without it. Cooking times for spinach pasta are slightly shorter than for yellow pasta.

Ragù

MEAT SAUCE, BOLOGNESE STYLE

Ragù is not to be confused with *ragoût*. A *ragoût* is a French meat stew, while *ragù* is Bologna's meat sauce for seasoning its homemade pasta. The only thing they share is a common and justified origin in the verb *ragoûter*, which means "to excite the appetite."

A properly made *ragù* clinging to the folds of homemade noodles is one of the most satisfying experiences accessible to the sense of taste. It is no doubt one of the great attractions of the enchanting city of Bologna, and the Bolognese claim one cannot make a true *ragù* anywhere else. This may be so, but with a little care, we can come very close to it. There are three essential points you must remember to make a successful *ragù*:

• The meat must be sautéed just barely long enough to lose its raw color. It must not brown or it will lose delicacy.

• It must be cooked in milk *before* the tomatoes are added. This keeps the meat creamier and sweeter tasting.

• It must cook at the merest simmer for a long, long time. The minimum is 3½ hours; 5 is better.

The union of *tagliatelle* and *ragù* (following page) is a marriage made in heaven, but *ragù* is also very good with *tortellini*, it is indispensable in *lasagne*, and it is excellent with such macaroni as *rigatoni*, *ziti*, *conchiglie*, and *rotelle*. Whenever a menu lists pasta *alla bolognese*, that means it is served with *ragù*.

For 6 servings, or 2¼ to 2½ cups

2 tablespoons chopped yellow onion	Salt
3 tablespoons olive oil	1 cup dry white wine
3 tablespoons butter	½ cup milk
2 tablespoons chopped celery	⅛ teaspoon nutmeg
2 tablespoons chopped carrot	2 cups canned Italian tomatoes, roughly chopped, with their juice
¾ pound ground lean beef, preferably chuck or the meat from the neck	

1. An earthenware pot should be your first choice for making *ragù*. If you don't have one available, use a heavy, enameled cast-iron casserole, the deepest one you have (to keep the *ragù* from reducing too quickly). Put in the chopped onion, with all the oil and butter, and sauté briefly over medium heat until just translucent. Add the celery and carrot and cook gently for 2 minutes.

2. Add the ground beef, crumbling it in the pot with a fork. Add 1

teaspoon salt, stir, and cook only until the meat has lost its raw, red color. Add the wine, turn the heat up to medium high, and cook, stirring occasionally, until all the wine has evaporated.

3. Turn the heat down to medium, add the milk and the nutmeg, and cook until the milk has evaporated. Stir frequently.

4. When the milk has evaporated, add the tomatoes and stir thoroughly. When the tomatoes have started to bubble, turn the heat down until the sauce cooks at the laziest simmer, just an occasional bubble. Cook, uncovered, for a minimum of 3½ to 4 hours, stirring occasionally. Taste and correct for salt. (If you cannot watch the sauce for such a long stretch, you can turn off the heat and resume cooking it later on. But do finish cooking it in one day.)

NOTE

Ragù can be kept in the refrigerator for up to 5 days, or frozen. Reheat until it simmers for about 15 minutes before using.

Tagliatelle alla bolognese
TAGLIATELLE WITH BOLOGNESE
MEAT SAUCE

For 6 persons

2 to 2½ cups Meat Sauce, Bolognese Style (previous page)

Tagliatelle (page 120), made with 3 eggs and 2¼ cups

all-purpose flour (basic pasta recipe, page 113)

1½ tablespoons salt

1 tablespoon butter

½ cup freshly grated Parmesan cheese

1. Heat 4 to 5 quarts of water and, while it is coming to a boil, bring the sauce to a very gentle simmer, stirring it well.

2. When the water boils, add the salt, then all the noodles, and stir with a wooden spoon. If the pasta is fresh, it will be done within 5 to 10 *seconds* after the water returns to a boil. Drain immediately and shake the colander well.

(*continued*)

3. Spoon a little bit of hot sauce onto the bottom of a warm serving platter, add the noodles, pour the rest of the sauce over them, and toss the noodles with the sauce, the butter, and the grated cheese. Serve without delay, with additional freshly grated cheese on the side.

MENU SUGGESTIONS

For an authentic Bolognese meal, follow with Sautéed Turkey Breast Fillets with Ham, Cheese, and White Truffles (page 316), Other second courses could be Pan Roast of Veal (page 252), Roast Spring Lamb with White Wine (page 278), Pan-Roasted Chicken with Garlic, Rosemary, and White Wine (page 304), or Stewed Rabbit with White Wine (page 320).

Fettuccine all'Alfredo

FETTUCCINE TOSSED IN CREAM AND BUTTER

There actually was an Alfredo, in whose Roman restaurant this lovely dish became famous. Alfredo had a gold fork and spoon with which he gave a final toss to each serving of *fettuccine* before it was sent to the table. Despite its southern origin, this dish has now become a fixture of those Italian restaurants abroad specializing in northern cuisine. Although it is astonishingly simple, it isn't often that one finds it done well. Its essential requirements are homemade —better yet handmade—pasta cooked very firm, and good-quality fresh heavy cream.

For 5 or 6 persons

1 cup heavy cream
3 tablespoons butter
Salt
Fettuccine (page 121), made with 3 eggs and 2¼ cups all-purpose flour (basic pasta recipe, page 113)

⅔ cup freshly grated Parmesan cheese
Freshly ground pepper, 4 to 6 twists of the mill
A very tiny grating of nutmeg

1. Choose an enameled cast-iron pan, or other flameproof cook-and-serve ware, that can later accommodate all the cooked *fettuccine* comfortably. Put in ⅔ cup of the cream and all the butter and simmer over medium heat for less than a minute, until the butter and cream have thickened. Turn off the heat.

2. Bring 4 quarts of water to a boil. Add 2 tablespoons of salt, then drop in the *fettuccine* and cover the pot until the water returns to a boil. If the *fettuccine* are fresh, they will be done a few seconds after the water returns to a boil. If dry, they will take a little longer. (Cook the *fettuccine* even firmer than usual, because they will be cooked some more in the pan.) Drain immediately and thoroughly when done, and transfer to the pan containing the butter and cream.

3. Turn on the heat under the pan to low, and toss the *fettuccine*, coating them with sauce. Add the rest of the cream, all the grated cheese, ½ teaspoon salt, the pepper, and nutmeg. Toss briefly until the cream has thickened and the *fettuccine* are well coated. Taste and correct for salt. Serve immediately from the pan, with a bowl of additional grated cheese on the side.

MENU SUGGESTIONS

For an elegant dinner you can precede this with an antipasto of Baked Stuffed Zucchini Boats (page 395) or Mushroom and Cheese Salad (page 47). The second course may be Beef Braised in Red Wine Sauce (page 242), Sautéed Veal Chops with Sage and White Wine (page 272), Sautéed Veal Scaloppine with Marsala (page 261), Braised Sweetbreads with Tomatoes and Peas (page 295), Sautéed Chicken Livers with Sage (page 303), or any roast in this book, *except* for pork braised in milk.

Paglia e fieno alla ghiotta

YELLOW AND GREEN NOODLES WITH CREAM, HAM, AND MUSHROOM SAUCE

Paglia e fieno, "straw and hay," is the bucolic, but self-effacing name of one of the most exquisite of pasta dishes. It is a combination of narrow yellow and spinach noodles, served with a cream sauce. Sautéed tiny fresh peas are usually a part of the sauce, but a less common version, using mushrooms, is given here. I think it would be a pity to limit one's enjoyment of this elegant dish to those rare occasions when very young, freshly picked peas appear on the market, and in this sauce, I much prefer the lovely, rounded taste of good mushrooms to the indifferent presence of frozen, canned, or mealy middle-aged peas. You may substitute prosciutto for the ham, but it will give you a somewhat sharper flavor and coarser texture.

For 6 to 8 persons

¾ pound crisp, white mushrooms	¾ cup heavy cream
2 tablespoons finely chopped shallots or yellow onion	*Fettuccine* (page 121), made with 2 eggs and 1½ cups all-purpose flour (basic pasta recipe, page 113)
6 tablespoons butter	
Salt	
Freshly ground pepper, about 6 twists of the mill	Spinach Pasta (page 126), cut into *fettuccine*
6 ounces unsmoked ham, shredded	½ cup freshly grated Parmesan cheese

1. Slice off the ends of the mushroom stems. Wipe the mushrooms clean with a damp cloth. If there are still traces of soil, wash very rapidly in cold running water and dry thoroughly with a towel. Dice into ¼-inch cubes and set aside.

2. Choose a skillet that can later accommodate the mushrooms loosely. Put in the chopped shallots and half the butter and sauté over medium heat until the shallots have turned pale gold in color. Turn the heat up to high and add the diced mushrooms. When the mushrooms have absorbed all the butter, briefly turn the heat down

to low, add 1 teaspoon salt and the pepper, and shake the pan, moving and tossing the mushrooms. As soon as the mushroom juices come to the surface, which happens quickly, turn the heat up to high and cook the mushrooms for about 3 minutes, stirring frequently. Turn the heat down to medium, add the ham, and cook it for less than a minute, stirring as it cooks. Add half the heavy cream, and cook just long enough for the cream to thicken slightly. Taste and correct for salt. Turn off the heat and set aside.

3. Choose an enameled iron pan or other flameproof serving dish that can later accommodate all the noodles without piling them too high. Put in the rest of the butter and the cream and turn on the heat to low. When the butter is melted and incorporated into the cream, turn off the heat and proceed to boil the pasta.

4. Spinach pasta cooks faster than yellow pasta, so the two pastas must be boiled in separate pots. Bring 4 quarts of water in each pot to a boil and add 1 tablespoon of salt to each. First drop the yellow noodles in one pot, and stir them with a wooden spoon. Immediately after, drop the spinach noodles in the other pot and stir them with the spoon. Taste the spinach noodles for doneness 5 seconds or so after the water returns to a boil. They should be quite, quite firm because they will continue to soften up while cooking with the sauce. Drain well and transfer to the waiting pan. Immediately after, drain the yellow noodles and transfer them to the same pan. (Be very sure not to overcook the noodles. It is safer to err on the side of underdone than overdone.)

5. Turn on the heat to low and start tossing the noodles, coating them with butter and cream. Add half the mushroom sauce, mixing it well with the noodle strands. Add the grated cheese and mix it into the noodles. (This entire step should not take more than a minute.) Turn off the heat. Make a slight depression in the center of the mound of noodles and pour in the rest of the mushroom sauce. Serve immediately, with a bowl of additional grated cheese on the side.

MENU SUGGESTIONS

Follow the suggestions given for Fettuccine Tossed in Cream and Butter (page 131).

Fettuccine al gorgonzola

FETTUCCINE WITH GORGONZOLA SAUCE

This sauce is both creamy and piquant, two qualities that are seldom combined in Italian cooking. Its mild piquancy comes from gorgonzola, Italy's incomparable blue cheese. The sauce works best when the gorgonzola is creamy and mellow. Look for cheese that is warm white in color, soft, and, preferably, recently cut. Avoid dry, crumbly, or yellowish cheese. You can try substituting domestic gorgonzola or other blue cheeses, if you are so inclined, but you will never achieve the perfectly balanced texture and flavor of this sauce with any cheese but choice Italian gorgonzola.

Besides *fettuccine, garganelli* (Homemade Macaroni, page 170) and Potato Gnocchi (page 195) are absolutely lovely with gorgonzola sauce.

For 6 persons

4 ounces gorgonzola	¼ cup heavy cream
⅓ cup milk	⅓ cup freshly grated Parmesan
3 tablespoons butter	cheese
Salt	
Fettuccine (page 121) made with 3 eggs and 2½ cups all-purpose flour (basic pasta recipe, page 113)	

1. Choose a shallow enameled iron pan, or other flameproof serving dish, that can later accommodate all the pasta. Put in the gorgonzola, milk, butter, and 2 teaspoons salt and turn on the heat to low. Mash the gorgonzola with a wooden spoon, and stir to incorporate it into the milk and butter. Cook for about 1 minute, until the sauce has a dense, creamy consistency. Turn off the heat and set aside until you are almost ready to add the pasta.

2. Bring 4 quarts of water to a boil. Add 2 tablespoons of salt, then drop in the *fettuccine* and cover the pot until the water returns to

a boil. If the *fettuccine* are fresh, they will be done a few seconds after the water returns to a boil. If dry, they will take a little longer.

3. Just seconds before the pasta is done, turn on the heat under the sauce to low, and stir in the heavy cream. Add the drained, cooked pasta (if you are doing *gnocchi*, add each batch as it is done) and toss it with the sauce. Add all the grated cheese and mix it into the pasta. Serve immediately, directly from the pan, with a bowl of additional grated cheese on the side.

MENU SUGGESTIONS

It would be a pity to cancel out this marvelous sauce by following it with another highly flavored dish. A good choice for the second course would be the Pan Roast of Veal (page 252), Breaded Veal Cutlets (page 270), the Baby Lamb Chops Fried in Parmesan Cheese Batter (page 283), or the Sautéed Chicken Breast Fillets with Lemon and Parsley (page 314).

Fettuccine al sugo di vongole bianco
FETTUCCINE WITH WHITE CLAM SAUCE

This is a tomato-less sauce that includes two ingredients rarely used in Italian clam sauces: butter and cheese. But this departure from tradition is justified and successful because it adds smoothness and delicacy to the sauce. On the Adriatic, where I first came across it, this sauce is served with the clams still in their shells. The size of full-grown Adriatic clams, however, is little more than a thumbnail. If you tried it with husky American ocean clams, you might have difficulty in accommodating the pasta in the same dish.

For 4 persons

2 dozen littleneck clams, the tiniest you can find	1 teaspoon chopped garlic
1 tablespoon chopped shallots or yellow onion	2 tablespoons chopped parsley
½ cup olive oil	¼ teaspoon chopped dried hot red pepper
	¼ cup white wine

(*continued*)

1 tablespoon butter

2 tablespoons freshly grated
    Parmesan cheese

Salt

Fettuccine (page 121), made
    with 2 eggs and 1½ cups
    all-purpose flour (basic
    pasta recipe, page 113)

1. Wash and scrub the clams as directed on page 53, then put in a covered saucepan over high heat. As the clams open up, shuck them and put them in a small bowl. When all the clams have been shucked, pour the juices from the pan over them and set aside.

2. Put the shallots in a small saucepan with the oil and sauté over medium-high heat until translucent.

3. Add the garlic and sauté until lightly colored.

4. Add the parsley and hot pepper, stir three or four times, then add the wine. Allow the wine to boil until it has evaporated by half, then turn off the heat. (The sauce may be prepared several hours ahead of time up to this point.)

5. Rinse the clams one by one in their own juice and chop into small pieces.

6. Filter the clam juices through a sieve lined with paper towels. You should have about ⅔ cup of liquid. If there is more, discard it. Add the liquid to the sauce and boil until it is reduced by half.

7. Add the clams, turn them quickly in the hot sauce, and turn off the heat. Add the butter and cheese, mixing thoroughly. Taste and correct for salt. (No salt at all may be required, especially in the summer, when clams seem to be saltier.)

8. Add 1½ teaspoons salt to 4 quarts rapidly boiling water, then drop in the pasta and drain as soon as it is tender but *al dente,* firm to the bite. (If you are using freshly made pasta, remember that it is done a few seconds after the water returns to a boil.)

9. The moment the pasta is drained, transfer it to a warm serving bowl, add the sauce (previously reheated if no longer hot), toss thoroughly but rapidly, and serve immediately. Additional grated cheese may be served on the side if desired.

NOTE

The sauce is also excellent with spaghetti or with *garganelli* (Homemade Macaroni, page 170).

This can be preceded by Shrimps with Oil and Lemon (page 39), the Herb-Flavored Seafood Salad (page 421), or Cold Sautéed Trout in Orange Marinade (page 220). The second course could be Fish Broiled the Adriatic Way (page 224) or the Baked Striped Bass and Shellfish Sealed in Foil (page 212).

Pappardelle con il ragù di fegatini

PAPPARDELLE WITH
CHICKEN-LIVER SAUCE

Pappardelle are the broadest of the long noodles. In Tuscany and elsewhere they are often served with a sauce made from stewed hare. Another good condiment for *pappardelle* is this magnificent sauce of chicken livers. The same sauce is also quite good with regular noodles (*tagliatelle*, page 120). In the Molded Risotto with Parmesan Cheese and Chicken-Liver Sauce (page 183), it makes a very elegant and delicious first course.

For 4 persons

½ pound chicken livers

2 tablespoons chopped shallots or yellow onion

3 tablespoons olive oil

2 tablespoons butter

¼ teaspoon finely chopped garlic

3 tablespoons diced *pancetta*, prosciutto, or unsmoked ham

1½ teaspoons chopped sage

¼ pound ground lean beef

Salt

Freshly ground pepper, 6 to 8 twists of the mill

1 teaspoon tomato paste dissolved in ¼ cup dry white vermouth

Pappardelle (page 121), made with 2 eggs and 1½ cups all-purpose flour (basic pasta recipe, page 113)

1. Clean the chicken livers of any greenish spots and particles of

fat, then wash them, cut them each up into 3 or 4 pieces, and dry them thoroughly on paper towels. Set aside.

2. Put the shallots in a small saucepan with the oil and butter, and sauté lightly over medium heat until translucent.

3. Add the garlic, but do not allow it to become colored. Stir two or three times, then add the diced *pancetta* and the chopped sage leaves. Sauté for about half a minute and stir.

4. Add the ground meat, crumbling it with a fork, and cook until it has completely lost its raw red color.

5. Add 1 teaspoon salt and the pepper and turn the heat up to medium high. Add the chicken livers and stir and cook until they have lost their raw color.

6. Add the tomato paste and vermouth mixture, stir well, and cook for about 8 to 10 minutes. Taste and correct for salt.

7. When the sauce is nearly done, drop the pasta into 4 quarts of boiling water that contains 1 tablespoon salt. Drain as soon as it is tender but *al dente*, firm to the bite. (If you are using fresh, moist pasta, remember that it is done just a few seconds after the water returns to a boil.)

8. The moment the pasta is drained, transfer it to a warm platter, add the sauce, toss thoroughly but rapidly, and serve immediately, with grated Parmesan cheese on the side, if desired.

NOTE

You should time the preparation of this sauce so that it is ready to use the moment the pasta is cooked. If it has been prepared a bit ahead of time and has cooled, it should be reheated very gently. On no account should it be prepared long in advance or refrigerated, because the chicken livers would stiffen, lose delicacy, and acquire sharpness.

MENU SUGGESTIONS

The second course should be a fine meat dish, not strongly seasoned. It can be broiled steak, Beef Braised with Red Wine Sauce (page 242), Pan Roast of Veal (page 252), Breaded Veal Cutlets (page 270), Roast Spring Lamb with White Wine (page 278), or Baby Lamb Chops Fried in Parmesan Cheese Batter (page 283).

Pesto

GENOESE BASIL SAUCE FOR
PASTA AND SOUP

If the definition of poetry allowed that it could be composed with the products of the field as well as with words, *pesto* would be in every anthology. Like much good poetry, *pesto* is made of simple stuff. It is simply fresh basil, garlic, cheese, and olive oil hand ground into sauce. There is nothing more to it than that, but every spoonful is loaded with the magic fragrances of the Riviera.

The Genoese, who invented it, insist that authentic *pesto* cannot be made without their own small-leaved basil and a marble mortar. This is true and it isn't. It is true that Genoese basil is particularly fragrant, partly because of the soil but, even more important, because of the very salty Mediterranean breezes that bathe it as it grows. It is also true that grinding the basil into the marble of the mortar somehow releases more of its flavor than other methods. But, with all this, *pesto* is such an inspired invention that it survives almost anything, including our minty, large-leafed basil and the electric blender.

Two recipes are given here, one for the blender and one for the mortar. The ingredients are identical, the difference is one of procedure. You should try, at least once, to make pesto in a mortar, because of the greater character of its texture and its indubitably richer flavor. But blender *pesto* is still so good that we should enjoy it with a clear conscience whenever we don't have the time or the patience for the mortar. Also, since fresh basil has a brief season, and *pesto* keeps quite well in the freezer, the blender is absolutely invaluable for making a large supply to keep on hand.

In Genoa, they use equal quantities of Parmesan cheese and of a special, mildly tangy Sardinian cheese made of sheep's milk. The Romano *pecorino* cheese available here is considerably sharper than Sardo *pecorino*. You must therefore increase the proportion of Parmesan to *pecorino,* or you will throw the fine equilibrium of flavors in *pesto* out of balance. The proportion I suggest is 4 parts Parmesan to 1 part Romano. As you become familiar with *pesto* you can adjust this to taste. A well-rounded *pesto* is *never* made with all Parmesan or all *pecorino.*

The old, traditional recipes do not mention pine nuts or butter. But modern *pesto* invariably includes them, and so does this recipe.

Potato Gnocchi (page 195) are delicious with *pesto,* and so is spaghetti. The Genoese use it with *fettuccine,* which they call *trenette* (page 142), and it can be a spectacular addition to cold or hot *minestrone* (page 69).

BLENDER PESTO

Enough for about 6 servings of pasta

2 cups fresh basil leaves (see note below)
½ cup olive oil
2 tablespoons pine nuts
2 cloves garlic, lightly crushed with a heavy knife handle and peeled

1 teaspoon salt
½ cup freshly grated Parmesan cheese
2 tablespoons freshly grated Romano *pecorino* cheese
3 tablespoons butter, softened to room temperature

1. Put the basil, olive oil, pine nuts, garlic cloves, and salt in the blender and mix at high speed. Stop from time to time and scrape the ingredients down toward the bottom of the blender cup with a rubber spatula.

2. When the ingredients are evenly blended, pour into a bowl and beat in the two grated cheeses by hand. (This is not much work, and it results in more interesting texture and better flavor than you get when you mix in the cheese in the blender.) When the cheese has been evenly incorporated into the other ingredients, beat in the softened butter.

3. Before spooning the *pesto* over pasta, add to it a tablespoon or so of the hot water in which the pasta has boiled.

NOTE

The quantity of basil in most recipes is given in terms of whole leaves. American basil, however, varies greatly in leaf sizes. There are small, medium, and very large leaves, and they all pack differently in the measuring cup. For the sake of accurate measurement, I suggest that you tear all but the tiniest leaves into two or more small pieces. Be gentle, so as not to crush the basil. This would discolor it and waste the first, fresh droplets of juice.

MORTAR PESTO

Same yield as blender pesto

2 cups fresh basil leaves (see note above)

2 tablespoons pine nuts

2 cloves garlic, lightly crushed with a heavy knife handle and peeled

A pinch of coarse salt

½ cup freshly grated Parmesan cheese

2 tablespoons freshly grated Romano *pecorino* cheese

½ cup olive oil

3 tablespoons butter, softened to room temperature

1. Choose a large marble mortar with a hardwood pestle. Put the basil, pine nuts, garlic, and coarse salt in the mortar. Without pounding, but using a rotary movement and grinding the ingredients against the sides of the mortar, crush all the ingredients with the pestle.

2. When the ingredients in the mortar have been ground into a paste, add both grated cheeses, continuing to grind with the pestle until the mixture is evenly blended.

3. Put aside the pestle. Add the olive oil, a few drops at a time at first, beating it into the mixture with a wooden spoon. Then, when all the oil has been added, beat in the butter with the spoon.

4. As with blender *pesto*, add 1 or 2 tablespoons of hot water from the pasta pot before using.

MAKING PESTO FOR THE FREEZER

1. Mix all the ingredients in the blender as directed in Step 1 of blender *pesto*. Do *not* add the cheese or butter. Spoon the contents of the blender cup into a jar. If you are doubling or tripling the recipe, divide it into as many jars. Seal tightly and freeze.

2. Before using, thaw overnight in the refrigerator. When completely thawed, beat in the grated cheeses and the butter as in Step 2 of blender *pesto*. Adding the cheese at this time, rather than before freezing, is no more work and it gives the sauce a much fresher flavor.

In Genoa, *pesto* is traditionally served with *fettuccine*, which the Genoese call *trenette*. *Trenette* are cooked and served together with boiled, sliced potatoes. Here is how to make them:

Trenette col pesto
TRENETTE WITH POTATOES AND PESTO

For 6 persons

1½ tablespoons salt	all-purpose flour (basic
3 medium potatoes, peeled and	pasta recipe, page 113)
thinly sliced	Genoese Basil Sauce for
Fettuccine (page 121), made	Pasta and Soup (previous
with 2 eggs and 1½ cups	page)

1. In 4 to 5 quarts water, to which 1½ tablespoons salt have been added, boil the sliced potatoes until nearly tender.

2. Add the *fettuccine*. If the pasta is fresh, it will be done 5 to 10 seconds after the water returns to a boil. Drain both *fettuccine* and potatoes, transfer to a warm platter, and toss the *fettuccine* with the *pesto*. Serve immediately.

MENU SUGGESTIONS FOR TRENETTE, GNOCCHI, AND SPAGHETTI
WITH PESTO

Pesto is compatible with fish, and any pasta seasoned with *pesto* can be followed by Fish Broiled the Adriatic Way (page 224), or

Shrimp Brochettes, Adriatic Style (page 226). Other suitable second courses are Little Veal "Bundles" with Anchovies and Cheese (page 267), the Rolled Breast of Chicken Fillets Stuffed with Pork (page 315), the Baby Lamb Chops Fried in Parmesan Cheese Batter (page 283), Fried Calf's Brains (page 299), and Fried Breaded Calf's Liver (page 298).

Lasagne verdi al forno
BAKED GREEN LASAGNE WITH MEAT SAUCE

Although this classic *lasagne* as we make it in Romagna is richly laced with meat sauce and béchamel, it is almost austere compared to the southern variety that is popular here. In the expatriate southern style, *lasagne* spills over with sausages, meat balls, ricotta, mozzarella, hard-boiled eggs, and anything else personal inclination may suggest. *Lasagne* in Romagna is not intended as a catchall. While acting as a vehicle for a moderate amount of meat sauce, the pasta maintains its own clearly established character. The béchamel that is added should be no more than is necessary to bind the layers and maintain moistness during baking.

It is extremely important to avoid overcooking *lasagne*. Mushy *lasagne* is an abomination. And do not use boxed macaroni *lasagne* for this recipe. *Lasagne* is never, but simply never, made with anything but homemade pasta dough.

For 6 persons

2¼ cups Meat Sauce Bolognese Style (page 127)

Béchamel Sauce (page 28), made with 3 cups milk, 6 tablespoons butter, 4½ tablespoons all-purpose flour, and ¼ teaspoon salt. It should be fairly thin, with the consistency of sour cream.

A sheet of Spinach Pasta (page 126)

1 tablespoon salt

⅔ cup freshly grated Parmesan cheese

2 tablespoons butter

(continued)

1. Prepare the meat sauce and béchamel and set aside.

2. If you are making the pasta by hand, roll out a sheet that is not quite paper thin. Cut the dough into rectangular strips about 4½ inches wide and 11 inches long. Do not allow it to dry any longer than it takes to bring 4 quarts of water to a boil. While the water is coming to a boil, lay some clean, dry towels flat on the work counter and set a bowl of cold water near you at the range. When the water boils, add the salt, then drop in 4 of the pasta strips. Stir with a wooden spoon. Cook for just 10 seconds after the water returns to a boil, then retrieve the pasta with a large slotted spoon, dip it in the bowl, and rinse it with cold water. Wring each strip very gently by hand and lay it flat on the towel. Cook all the pasta in the same manner, including the trimmings. When it is all laid out on the towel, pat it dry on top with another towel.

3. Preheat the oven to 450°.

4. Choose a 14-inch bake-and-serve *lasagne* pan. Smear the bottom with a little bit of meat sauce, skimming it from the top, where there is more fat. Place a single layer of pasta in the pan, overlapping the strips, if necessary, no more than ¼ inch. (Do not prop up the edges of the pasta along the sides of the pan. It will become dry and tough there.) Spread enough sauce on the pasta to dot it with meat, then spread béchamel over the meat sauce. Before sprinkling cheese, taste the béchamel and meat sauce coating. If it is on the salty side, sprinkle the grated cheese sparsely. If it is rather bland, sprinkle the cheese freely. Add another layer of pasta and coat it as before. (Do not make more than 6 thin layers of pasta at the maximum, since *lasagne* shouldn't be too thick, and do not build up the layers any higher than ½ inch from the top of the pan.) Use the trimmings to plug up any gaps in the layers. Coat the top layer with béchamel, sprinkle with cheese, and dot lightly with butter.

5. Bake on the uppermost rack of the oven for 10 to 15 minutes, until a light, golden crust forms on top. Do not bake for more than 15 minutes. If after 10 minutes' baking you see that no crust is beginning to form, raise the oven temperature for the next 5 minutes.

6. Allow *lasagne* to settle 5 to 8 minutes before serving. Serve directly from the pan.

MENU SUGGESTIONS

A very nice preliminary to green *lasagne* is sweet prosciutto, served with a slice of ripe cantaloupe. A suitable second course would be Rolled Stuffed Breast of Veal (page 254), Roast Spring Lamb with White Wine (page 278), Sautéed Lamb Kidneys with White Wine (page 300), Roast Chicken with Rosemary (page 306), or Stewed Rabbit with White Wine (page 320).

Lo scrigno di Venere
YELLOW PASTA SHELLS STUFFED WITH SPINACH FETTUCCINE

This breathtakingly beautiful dish is a bonus for those of you who have learned to make pasta by hand. The large sheet of yellow pasta required cannot be turned out by machine. The sheet is used to form individual shells of yellow pasta to be filled with spinach *fettuccine* seasoned with a sauce of ham, béchamel, and dried wild mushrooms, then sealed and baked. It calls for quite a bit of work, but the weight of your efforts will drop from your shoulders at the joyous surprise your family and friends will show as they unwrap their individual pasta shells.

It is very important to understand the rhythm of the recipe. Read it carefully and do not start on it until you feel you know exactly how the work is to be organized, so that everything will fall into the right place at the right time.

For 6 persons

3 ounces dried wild mushrooms
1 cup Béchamel Sauce (page 28) (see Step 2, below)
    Spinach pasta (page 126), cut by hand into *fettuccine* (page 121)

2 tablespoons chopped shallots or yellow onion
4½ tablespoons butter
    Salt
⅔ cup unsmoked ham, cut into ¼-inch strips

(continued)

1 cup heavy cream

A sheet of homemade pasta dough (page 113), made with 3 eggs and 2¼ cups flour

⅓ cup freshly grated Parmesan cheese

6 gratin pans, about 4½ inches in diameter

1. Put the dried mushrooms in a small bowl with 1½ cups lukewarm water. They must soak at least 30 minutes.

2. Make the thin béchamel sauce (keeping it thin by cooking it little; it should have the consistency of thin sour cream). Set aside off the heat, over a pan filled with hot water.

3. Prepare the spinach pasta, rolling it out either by hand or by machine, but cutting it into *fettuccine* by hand.

4. Remove the mushrooms from their soak, but do not discard the water. Strain the water through a sieve lined with paper towels and set aside. Rinse the mushrooms in cold running water, chop each into two or three pieces, and set aside.

5. Put shallots in a saucepan with 3 tablespoons of the butter and sauté over medium heat until pale gold.

6. Add the mushrooms, their water, and 1½ teaspoons salt. Cook at a simmer until their liquid has evaporated.

7. Add the ham, stir three or four times, and add the heavy cream. Cook briefly until the cream thickens slightly; then turn off the heat and set aside.

8. Prepare the sheet of yellow pasta, rolling it out as thin as possible by hand. Let the dough dry for 10 minutes.

9. Choose a pot cover 8 inches in diameter. Lay the sheet of pasta flat and cut it into 6 disks with the pot cover. (The leftover pasta can be cut up, dried, and used in a soup.)

10. Bring 4 quarts of water to a boil, add 1 tablespoon salt, and drop in the pasta disks, cooking them two at a time. While the water is coming to a boil, lay some clean, dry towels flat on your work counter and set a bowl of cold water near the stove. Cook the pasta for 20 to 30 seconds after the water returns to a boil, then retrieve it with a slotted spoon, dip it in the bowl, rinsing with cold water, wring it out gently by hand, and open it up flat on a towel.

Scrigno di Venere: Pick up
the disk of pasta dough and
close it over the *fettuccine* . . .

. . . gathering it in regular,
pleatlike folds.

Twist the top together and
fasten it with a toothpick.
Wrap a single *fettuccina* around
the toothpick.

11. Bring another 4 to 5 quarts of water to a boil, add 1 tablespoon salt, and drop in the spinach *fettuccine*.

12. While the water is coming to a boil, warm up the ham and mushroom sauce. When it has simmered for a minute or so, turn the heat down to very low and add all the grated cheese, mixing it thoroughly into the sauce. Turn off the heat.

13. Keep an eye on the spinach *fettuccine*. It will be done a few seconds after the water returns to a boil. When done, drain and season immediately with the ham and mushroom sauce. Set aside 6 single strands of *fettuccine,* and divide the rest of the *fettuccine* into 6 portions.

14. Preheat the oven to 450°.

15. Take the gratin pans and smear the remaining butter on the bottom of each; then, working on a large, flat platter, coat a pasta disk on both sides with some of the béchamel sauce. Place the disk in one of the pans, centering it, and letting its edges hang over the sides. Put one of the portions of *fettuccine* in the center of the disk. Make sure it has its share of sauce. Keep the *fettuccine* fairly loose— do not press them down. Pick up the disk at the edges and close it by folding the edges toward the center. Fasten the folds at the top with a toothpick, then wrap one of the single strands of *fettuccine* around the toothpick as decoratively as you can. Repeat the operation until you have filled and sealed all 6 pasta disks. (You can prepare the shells up to this point in the morning for the evening, if you like.)

16. Put the pans with the shells in the uppermost level of the preheated oven. Bake for 5 to 8 minutes, or until a light brown crust forms on the edges of the folds.

17. Transfer each shell from its pan to a soup plate, lifting it carefully with two metal spatulas. Remove the toothpick without disturbing the decorative *fettuccina*. Serve at once.

MENU SUGGESTIONS

This magnificent presentation should be followed by a simple but elegant second course. My first choice would be Pan-Roasted Squab (page 319). Other possibilities are Sautéed Breaded Veal Chops (page 268), Sautéed Veal Chops with Sage and White Wine (page 272), Sautéed Chicken Breast Fillets with Lemon and Parsley (page 314), or a fine whole roasted chicken. If you want to precede the shells with an antipasto, serve Baked Oysters with Oil and Parsley (page 32), Cold Salmon Foam (page 33), or Bresaola (page 47).

Cannelloni
MEAT-STUFFED PASTA ROLLS

This is among the few homemade egg pasta dishes that is not native to Emilia-Romagna. It may have originated in Piedmont. *Cannelloni* is one of the most elegant of pastas, but although a number of ingredients and several different steps are involved, it is not a difficult dish to produce. In fact, it is probably the easiest of all stuffed pastas to make.

The pasta for *cannelloni* is given the briefest of boils before being stuffed. It is then seasoned with a simplified meat sauce and topped with a thin béchamel sauce. The second and final cooking takes place in the oven.

For 6 persons

> Béchamel Sauce (page 28),
>   made with 2 cups milk,
>   ¼ cup butter, 3 tablespoons
>   all-purpose flour, and ¼
>   teaspoon salt

THE STUFFING:

1½ tablespoons finely chopped
    yellow onion
2 tablespoons olive oil
6 ounces lean ground beef
    Salt
½ cup chopped *mortadella* or
    unsmoked ham

1 egg yolk
½ teaspoon nutmeg
1½ cups freshly grated Parmesan
    cheese
1¼ cups fresh ricotta

(continued)

THE MEAT SAUCE:

1 tablespoon finely chopped
   yellow onion
2 tablespoons olive oil

6 ounces lean ground beef
1 teaspoon salt
½ cup canned Italian tomatoes,
   chopped, with their juice

A sheet of homemade pasta
   dough (page 113), using
   2 eggs and 1½ cups all-
   purpose flour

1 tablespoon salt
⅓ cup freshly grated Parmesan
   cheese
¼ cup butter

1. Make the béchamel sauce. It should be rather thin, with a consistency similar to that of sour cream. Set aside.

2. To make the stuffing, put the chopped onion in a saucepan or a skillet with the olive oil and cook over medium heat until translucent but not colored. Add the ground beef, turn the heat down to medium low, and cook it without letting it brown. Crumble the meat with a fork as it cooks. When it loses its raw red color, cook it for 1 minute more without browning. Transfer the meat with a perforated ladle or colander to a mixing bowl, carrying with it as little of the cooking fat as possible. Add 1½ teaspoons salt, chopped *mortadella*, egg yolk, nutmeg, grated cheese, ricotta, and ¼ cup of the béchamel sauce. Mix thoroughly. Taste and correct for salt and set aside.

3. To make the meat sauce, put the chopped onion in a saucepan with the olive oil and sauté over medium heat until very pale gold in color. Add the meat, turn the heat down to medium low, and cook without browning, exactly as you did for the stuffing. Add the salt and the chopped tomatoes and their juice and cook at the barest simmer for 45 minutes. Set aside.

4. Prepare the pasta dough, and, if you are making it by hand, make it as thin as possible. (The pasta machine has only one setting for thinness.) Cut the pasta into rectangles 3 inches by 4 inches. Do not allow it to dry any longer than it takes to bring 4 quarts of water to a boil. While the water is coming to a boil, lay one or more clean, dry towels open flat on the work counter, and set a bowl of

cold water not far from the stove. When the water comes to a boil, add the salt, then drop in 5 of the pasta strips. Stir with a wooden spoon. When the water returns to a boil, wait 20 seconds, then retrieve the pasta with a large slotted spoon, dip it and rinse it in the cold water, then spread it on the dry towel. Cook all the pasta strips, no more than 5 at a time, in the same manner. When all the pasta is laid out on the towel, pat it dry with another towel.

5. Preheat the oven to 400°.

6. Take a bake-and-serve pan 9 inches by 14 inches and butter the bottom. To stuff the pasta, I find a wood cutting block very comfortable to work on, but a large platter or any clean, flat surface will do. Lay a pasta strip flat and spread a tablespoon of stuffing on it, covering the whole strip except for a ½-inch border all around. Roll the strip up on its narrow side, keeping it somewhat loose. Lay it in the baking pan with its folded-over edge facing down. Proceed until you've used up either all the pasta or all the stuffing. (Somehow it's hard to make them come out exactly even.) Squeeze the *cannelloni* in tightly, if you have to, but don't overlap them.

7. Spread the meat sauce over the *cannelloni*, coating them evenly with sauce. Spread the béchamel sauce over this. Sprinkle with the grated cheese and dot with the butter. Bake on the next-to-highest rack in the oven for 15 minutes, or until a very light, golden crust forms. (Do not in any case exceed 20 minutes, or it will be overcooked.) Allow to settle for about 10 to 15 minutes, then serve. Although the *cannelloni* are already richly seasoned, you might have some extra grated cheese available at the table.

MENU SUGGESTIONS

Bresaola (page 47) would be a fine antipasto with which to precede *cannelloni*. As a second course you could follow with Beef Braised in Red Wine Sauce (page 242), Rolled Stuffed Breast of Veal (page 254), Hothouse Lamb, Roman Style (page 281), or Pan-Roasted Squab (page 319).

Il rotolo di pasta

SLICED PASTA ROLL WITH SPINACH FILLING

In this dish an entire sheet of pasta dough is rolled up with spinach stuffing, wrapped in cheesecloth, and boiled. When cool it is sliced like a roast, seasoned with a béchamel and tomato sauce, and baked very briefly in a very hot oven. It is a delicious change of pace from all the familiar pasta dishes, and it lends itself to a very attractive presentation.

For 6 persons

½ recipe Tomato Sauce III (page 95)

2 ten-ounce packages frozen leaf spinach, thawed, OR 2 pounds fresh spinach

Salt

2 tablespoons finely chopped yellow onion

6 tablespoons butter

A sheet of homemade pasta dough (page 113), made with 2 eggs and 1½ cups all-purpose flour

3½ to 4 tablespoons chopped prosciutto, unsmoked ham, or *mortadella*

1 heaping cup fresh whole-milk ricotta

1 cup freshly grated Parmesan cheese

¼ teaspoon nutmeg

1 egg yolk

Medium-thick Béchamel Sauce (page 28), made with 1 cup milk, 2 tablespoons butter, 1½ tablespoons all-purpose flour, and ⅛ teaspoon salt

⅓ cup freshly grated Parmesan cheese

1. Prepare the tomato sauce and set aside.

2. If you are using frozen spinach, cook the thawed spinach in a covered pan with ½ teaspoon of salt for 5 minutes.

If you are using fresh spinach, discard any wilted or discolored leaves and all the stems. Wash in a basin in several changes of cold water until the water shows no trace of soil. Cook with just the water that clings to the leaves in a covered pan with ½ teaspoon of salt for 15 minutes, or until tender.

Drain the spinach, squeeze lightly to remove most of its moisture, and chop roughly. Set aside.

3. In a skillet, sauté the onion, with ¼ cup butter, over medium heat. When the onion turns pale gold in color, add the chopped prosciutto and sauté for about 30 seconds more. Then add the chopped, cooked spinach and sauté it for 2 to 3 minutes. You will find that all the butter has been absorbed.

4. Transfer the contents of the skillet to a mixing bowl, and add the ricotta, 1 cup grated Parmesan cheese, nutmeg, and, last of all, the egg yolk. Mix all the ingredients with a fork until they are well combined. Taste and correct for salt.

5. Make the pasta as directed in the basic recipe, then roll out as thin a sheet of pasta as you can and lay it flat in front of you. Spread the filling over the pasta, starting about 3 inches in from the edge near you. The filling should cover all but a ¼-inch border all around the sheet, and the 3-inch border near you. Fold this 3-inch border over the filling, and continue to fold until you've rolled up all the pasta. Wrap the pasta roll tightly in a cheesecloth, tying the two

Sliced Pasta Roll with Spinach Filling: Arrange the slices in the dish slightly overlapping, like shingles.

ends securely with string. (If you are using the pasta machine, follow exactly the same stuffing procedure, except that you will have to make several short rolls instead of one long one. Each roll must be wrapped in cheesecloth separately.)

6. If you've made a single long roll you will need a fish poacher or other long, deep pan that can accommodate the pasta and 3 to 4 quarts of water. If you have several short rolls, a large stockpot or kettle will do. Bring the water to a boil, add 1 tablespoon of salt, then put in the pasta roll or rolls and cook at a gentle but steady boil for 20 minutes. Lift out the pasta. If it is a single long roll use the fish retriever in the poacher or two slotted spoons or spatulas, to make sure it doesn't split in the middle. Unwrap the pasta while it is hot and set aside to cool.

7. Preheat the oven to 400°.

8. While the pasta cools, prepare the béchamel, and when ready mix it with the already prepared tomato sauce. When the pasta is cool, cut it like a roast into slices about ¾ inch thick.

9. Choose a bake-and-serve dish that can accommodate the pasta slices in a single layer. Lightly smear the bottom of the dish with 2 to 3 tablespoons of sauce. Arrange the slices in the dish slightly overlapping, like shingles. Pour the rest of the sauce over the pasta, then sprinkle ⅓ cup grated Parmesan cheese over the sauce and dot lightly with the remaining 2 tablespoons butter. Bake on the uppermost rack of the oven for 15 minutes. Allow to settle 6 to 8 minutes, then serve from the baking dish.

NOTE

After this dish has been entirely assembled it can wait several hours (but not overnight) at room temperature before going into the oven.

MENU SUGGESTIONS

An excellent choice for a second course would be any of the three lamb roasts on pages 278-281. Also suitable would be Pan-Roasted Chicken with Garlic, Rosemary, and White Wine (page 304), Roast Chicken with Rosemary (page 306), or Stewed Rabbit with White Wine (page 320). Avoid any dish that has a decided tomato presence.

Cappelletti

CAPPELLETTI FILLED WITH MEAT AND CHEESE

In the Romagna section of Emilia-Romagna, *cappelletti* served in capon broth is the traditional dish for Christmas and New Year's Day. We usually prepare all the *cappelletti* for both occasions at one time, on Christmas Eve. Since this means a production of several hundred *cappelletti*, everyone in the family, children included, moves into the kitchen to stuff and wrap dumplings. Children, in fact, are ideal for the job because their narrow, tapered fingers permit them to wrap the tightest, smallest dumplings. When you set out to make *cappelletti*, try to make a family event out of it. The work goes quickly, it is fun, and it engenders respect for quality and beauty in food.

If you travel out of Romagna a dozen miles or less into the province of Bologna, the word *cappelletti* has little meaning. But the Bolognese have a virtually identical product called *tortellini*. The stuffings will vary, but then no two families make stuffing exactly the same way. The basic difference is one of shape. While the pasta for *tortellini* is cut into disks, that for *cappelletti* is cut into squares. This gives *cappelletti* its characteristic resemblance to little peaked hats, which is precisely what its name means.

Makes about 200 cappelletti (*see note below*)

2 tablespoons butter
¼ pound lean pork loin, diced
    into ½-inch cubes
    Salt and freshly ground
    pepper
5½ ounces chicken breast, boned,
    trimmed of all fat, and
    diced into ½-inch cubes
3 tablespoons *mortadella*, finely
    chopped

1¼ cups fresh ricotta
1 egg yolk
1 cup freshly grated Parmesan
    cheese
½ teaspoon nutmeg
    Homemade pasta dough
    (page 113) made with 4
    eggs, 3 cups all-purpose
    flour, and 1 tablespoon
    milk

(continued)

Cappelletti: On 1½-inch squares of dough, put about ¼ teaspoon of filling. Fold each square diagonally, with the edges not quite meeting. Press down firmly to seal the edges.

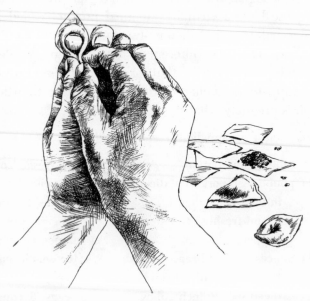

Bend a *cappelletto* around the finger and press one corner over the other.

1. Melt the butter in a skillet over medium heat. Just as the foam begins to subside, add the pork, seasoning it with ½ teaspoon salt and 3 or 4 twists of the pepper mill. Cook gently for about 10 minutes, browning it on all sides. Remove from the skillet with a slotted spoon and set aside to cool. Add the chicken to the skillet, seasoning it with ½ teaspoon salt and another 3 or 4 twists of the pepper mill. Brown it on all sides, remembering that chicken breast cooks very rapidly, in about 2 to 3 minutes, depending on the thickness. Remove from the skillet with a slotted spoon and set aside to cool, together with the pork.

2. When the pork and chicken are cool, chop them by hand as fine as possible. (Do not "blender" them or machine-grind them. The filling should not be so homogenized that the character and texture of the meat do not come through.) Put the chopped meat into a bowl and combine it with the *mortadella*, fresh ricotta, egg yolk, grated cheese, and nutmeg. Mix thoroughly until all the ingredients are evenly amalgamated. Taste and correct for salt.

3. Prepare the dough as directed in the basic recipe. If you are rolling and stretching it by hand, divide the kneaded mass in two, rolling out one half while keeping the other half covered between two soup plates. (Pasta for dumplings needs no drying; on the contrary, it should be quite soft.) As soon as you've rolled out the first half of the mass into as thin a sheet of dough as possible, cut and stuff the dough as directed below. Then roll out the other half of the mass. (If you are using the pasta machine, cut and stuff each strip of dough as soon as it is thinned out.)

4. Fold the sheet of pasta dough loosely two or three times, leaving a few inches of it not rolled up. Keeping the rest of the dough under a towel, cut a continuous strip 1½ inches wide from the unfolded part. Trim the strip so that it is perfectly straight. (You can let the trimmings dry and use them on another occasion in soup.) If you are making machine pasta, cut the dough into similar 1½-inch strips. You can adjust the width of the strip about ¼ inch either way so you won't have too much to trim away.

5. Cut the strip into 1½-inch squares. Put about ¼ teaspoon of the filling in the center of each square. Fold the square in half, diag-

onally across, forming a triangle. The upper edges should not quite meet the lower, but should stop about ⅛ inch short. Press down firmly to seal the sides. Pick up the triangle at one end of its long base, holding it between your thumb and index finger with the tip of the triangle pointing upward. Grasp the other end of the base with the other hand and wrap the base around the index finger of the first hand until the two ends meet. Press them firmly together. As you are folding the dumpling around your finger, make sure the peaked part doesn't hang down. Force it to fold toward you so that, as you close the dumpling, its peak points in the same direction as your fingertip.

6. As you make the dumplings, set them out in neat rows on a dry clean towel. If you are not using the *cappelletti* immediately, turn them every couple of hours until they are uniformly dry. When dry they will keep for at least a week. In Italy we keep them in a dry, cool cupboard, but, if you prefer, you can refrigerate them in an open container. Make sure they are quite dry, however, or they will stick to each other.

NOTE

Calculate 16 to 18 a person if served in broth, 2 dozen or more apiece if served with sauce.

Cappelletti in brodo

CAPPELLETTI IN BROTH

For 6 persons

2½ quarts Homemade Meat Broth (page 10) (see note below)	100 *cappelletti* (page 155), approximately

Bring the broth to a boil. Drop in the *cappelletti* and stir gently from time to time with a wooden spoon. Fresh *cappelletti* cook very much faster than the dry ones; so, if fresh, taste for doneness 5 minutes after the broth returns to a boil. If dry, it may take more than three times as long. (For cooking dry *cappelletti*, it is advisable to increase the amount of broth by ½ cup, because some is lost through evaporation.) When the *cappelletti* are done—they should be firm but thoroughly cooked—ladle them into individual soup plates along with the broth. Serve immediately, with a bowl of grated Parmesan cheese on the side.

NOTE

2½ quarts of the broth is the amount you need for cooking the pasta. If any is left over, it can be refrigerated or frozen and used again.

MENU SUGGESTIONS

You can precede *cappelletti* in broth with good-quality mixed cold cuts such as prosciutto, *mortadella*, and Tuscan-type salami. Or you can make your own Fried Mortadella, Pancetta, and Cheese Tidbits (page 48). An obviously suitable second course is Mixed Boiled Meats (page 322), but they also go well with Beef Braised in Red Wine Sauce (page 242), Sautéed Turkey Breast Fillets with Ham, Cheese, and White Truffles (page 316), Pork Loin Braised in Milk (page 284), or Chicken Fricassee with Dried Wild Mushrooms (page 310).

Cappelletti con la panna
CAPPELLETTI WITH BUTTER AND HEAVY CREAM

For 6 persons

1 tablespoon olive oil	3 tablespoons butter
2 tablespoons salt	½ cup freshly grated Parmesan
150 *cappelletti* (page 155)	cheese
⅔ cup heavy cream	

1. Bring 4 quarts of water, containing 1 tablespoon of olive oil, to a boil. Add 2 tablespoons of salt, then drop in the *cappelletti*.

(continued)

2. While the *cappelletti* are cooking, choose an enameled cast-iron or other flameproof cook-and-serve pan that will later accommodate all the *cappelletti* without stacking them too high. Put in half the cream and all the butter and simmer over moderate heat for less than a minute, until the cream and butter have thickened. Turn off the heat.

3. Fresh *cappelletti* are done within 5 minutes after the water returns to a boil, while dry *cappelletti* may take 15 to 20 minutes. When done—they should be firm, but cooked throughout—transfer them with a large slotted spoon or colander to the pan containing the cream and butter and turn the heat on to low. Turn the *cappelletti* to coat them all with the cream and butter sauce. Add the rest of the cream and all the grated cheese, and continue turning the *cappelletti* until they are evenly coated and all the cream has thickened. Serve immediately from the same pan, with a bowl of additional grated cheese on the side.

MENU SUGGESTIONS

See the ones for Fettuccine Tossed in Cream and Butter (page 131).

TORTELLINI

Some people prefer the rounder, more compact shape of *tortellini*. If you would like to make *tortellini alla panna* or *tortellini in brodo*, follow every direction in the above recipes except for cutting the pasta. Instead of cutting the pasta into squares, cut it into 2-inch disks, using juice glass, cookie cutter, or any circular instrument with that diameter. The disks are stuffed, folded, wrapped, and sealed exactly as the squares are.

Tortellini begin as circles. When stuffed and folded over, the edges do not come exactly together.

Bend around the finger and press one corner over the other.

Tortellini di prezzemolo
TORTELLINI FILLED WITH PARSLEY AND RICOTTA

For 4 to 6 persons

⅓ cup finely chopped parsley,
  preferably Italian parsley
1¼ cups fresh ricotta
1 cup freshly grated Parmesan
  cheese
Salt
1 egg yolk

¼ teaspoon nutmeg
A sheet of homemade pasta
  dough (page 113), made
  with 3 eggs, 2¼ cups all-
  purpose flour, and 1
  tablespoon milk

1. Combine all the filling ingredients—parsley, ricotta, grated Parmesan cheese, ½ teaspoon salt, egg yolk, and nutmeg—in a mixing bowl and mix well with a fork. Taste and correct for salt, then set aside.

2. Prepare the pasta as directed in the basic recipe and roll out the thinnest sheet of pasta dough you can (if you are doing it by hand). Thereafter, follow all the cutting, stuffing, and wrapping directions for *cappelletti* (pages 157–158). There is only one difference, and that is that the pasta is cut into disks instead of squares. This recipe calls for *tortellini* slightly larger than the meat-filled variety, which means the disks should be between 2¼ and 2½ inches in diameter. (If you have no cutter quite that size, you should be able to find a glass that will do.)

NOTE

Parsley-and-ricotta filling will not keep, so you should plan to cook the *tortellini* the same day you make them. The best way to serve these delicate dumplings is with cream and butter. Follow exactly the same method given for Cappelletti with Butter and Heavy Cream (page 159). Or for a soft touch of color and a bit more flavor, try the lovely, pale Tomato and Cream Sauce given below.

MENU SUGGESTIONS

Follow those given for Fettuccine Tossed in Cream and Butter (page 131).

Sugo di pomodoro e panna
TOMATO AND CREAM SAUCE

For 6 servings

¼ pound butter
3 tablespoons finely chopped
    yellow onion
3 tablespoons finely chopped
    carrot
3 tablespoons finely chopped
    celery

2½ cups canned Italian tomatoes,
    with their juice
2 teaspoons salt, more if
    necessary
¼ teaspoon granulated sugar
½ cup heavy cream

1. Put all the ingredients except the heavy cream in a saucepan and cook at the merest simmer for 1 hour, uncovered. Stir from time to time with a wooden spoon.

2. Purée the contents of the pan through a food mill (you can prepare the sauce up to this point ahead of time, and refrigerate it for a few days or freeze it) into a saucepan and bring to a simmer, stirring with a wooden spoon. Add the heavy cream and stir-cook for 1 minute more. Taste and correct for salt. Use immediately.

MENU SUGGESTIONS

In addition to Tortellini Filled with Parsley and Ricotta, this sauce is excellent with *cappelletti* (page 155), Tortelloni Filled with Swiss Chard (page 164), and Green Gnocchi (page 200). It is not disagreeable with macaroni pasta, but it is perhaps too delicate. Second courses following pasta seasoned with this sauce could be Pan Roast of Veal (page 252), Sautéed Veal Chops with Sage and White Wine (page 272), Breaded Veal Cutlets (page 270), Roast Spring Lamb with White Wine (page 278), and any of the chicken dishes that do not contain tomato.

Tortelloni di biete

TORTELLONI FILLED WITH SWISS CHARD

For 5 or 6 persons

2 large bunches Swiss chard (see note below)	1 egg yolk
Salt	⅔ cup freshly grated Parmesan cheese
2½ tablespoons finely chopped yellow onion	¼ to ½ teaspoon nutmeg
3½ tablespoons prosciutto, rolled *pancetta*, or unsmoked ham	A sheet of homemade pasta dough (page 113) made with 2 eggs, 1½ cups all-purpose flour, and 2 teaspoons milk
¼ cup butter	
1 cup fresh ricotta	

1. Pull the Swiss chard leaves from the stalks, discarding any bruised or discolored leaves. If the chard is mature and the stalks are large and white, save them to make Swiss Chard Stalks with Parmesan Cheese (page 370). Wash the leaves in a basin in several changes of cold water until the water shows no soil deposit. Lift up the leaves and transfer them to a saucepan or stockpot without shaking them. (The water that clings to the leaves is all the water they need for cooking.) Add ¼ teaspoon salt, cover the pot, and cook over medium heat until tender, approximately 15 minutes, depending on the freshness of the chard. Drain, squeeze out all the moisture you can, and chop the chard very fine. Set aside.

2. In a small skillet, sauté the chopped onion and prosciutto, in the butter, over medium heat. After less than a minute, add the chopped, cooked Swiss chard leaves and a small pinch of salt, and cook for 2 to 3 minutes more, until all the butter has been absorbed.

3. Transfer the contents of the skillet to a mixing bowl. Add the ricotta, egg yolk, grated Parmesan cheese, and nutmeg, and mix thoroughly with a fork until all the ingredients have been well combined. Taste and correct for salt and nutmeg.

(*continued*)

Tortelloni are laid out on a sheet of pasta by the shallow teaspoonful. The edge of the pasta is folded over...

...and cut into squares with a fluted pastry wheel.

4. If you are hand-making the pasta, roll out the thinnest sheet of dough you can. Do not allow it to dry. Fold the sheet loosely two or three times, leaving about 5 inches of it extended away from you and keeping the near, folded part covered with a towel. Trim the farthest edge of the sheet so that it is perfectly straight. Dot the pasta with shallow teaspoonfuls of filling, spacing them 1½ inches apart, and setting them in a straight row 2¼ inches from the trimmed edge of the sheet. Pick up the edge and fold it toward you over the stuffing, which should then remain enclosed in the middle of a long tube. Detach this folded-over part from the pasta sheet, using a pastry cutter. Then divide it into squares, cutting straight across between each bulge of filling. Each square will have 3 cut edges. Press them firmly together, moistening them if necessary, to make sure they are tightly sealed. (If you are making machine pasta, stuff and cut each strip of dough as it is thinned out by the machine before kneading and thinning out more pasta.) Repeat the operation until you've run out of pasta or stuffing. (It is virtually impossible to make them come out exactly the same, but leftover pasta can be cut into *maltagliati* (page 121) and used in soup. Leftover stuffing makes a tasty sandwich spread.) For cooking instructions, see following recipe.

The flavor of all cooked leaf vegetables is noticeably impaired by any attempt at conservation; therefore you must use this pasta the same day you make it.

NOTE

Although Swiss chard has a sweeter, more delicate taste than spinach, it is not always as readily available. In case you can't find chard, spinach makes a very satisfactory substitute. Use either 2 ten-ounce packages of frozen leaf spinach or 2 pounds fresh spinach.

For frozen spinach, first thaw the spinach, then cook it slowly in a covered pan for 5 minutes with ¼ teaspoon salt.

For fresh spinach, remove the stems and discard any wilted leaves. Wash in a basin in several changes of cold water until the water shows no trace of soil. Cook in a covered saucepan with ¼ teaspoon salt and whatever water clings to the leaves for 15 to 20 minutes or until tender.

Drain the cooked spinach, squeeze most of the moisture out of it, chop it very fine, and use it exactly as directed for Swiss chard.

Tortelloni al burro e formaggio
TORTELLONI WITH BUTTER AND CHEESE

This is the simplest way pasta is served in Italy, and it is marvelously well suited to the delicate taste of *tortelloni*. It is also an excellent way to serve spaghetti.

For 5 or 6 persons

1 tablespoon olive oil	¼ pound butter
2 tablespoons salt	1 cup freshly grated Parmesan
Tortelloni Filled with Swiss	cheese
Chard (page 164)	

1. Bring 4 quarts water containing 1 tablespoon oil to a boil. Add 2 tablespoons salt, then the *tortelloni*. Cover until the water returns to a boil.

2. While the *tortelloni* are cooking, cut 1 stick (¼ pound) butter into thin strips and put in a very warm serving bowl.

3. As soon as the *tortelloni* are cooked *al dente*, firm to the bite, about 5 minutes after the water returns to a boil, transfer them with a large slotted spoon or colander to the bowl containing the butter. Add the grated cheese and toss, coating all the *tortelloni* with butter and cheese. Serve immediately, with a bowl of additional grated cheese on the side.

MENU SUGGESTIONS

There is really no meat course that is incompatible with a butter-and-cheese-seasoned pasta. The chard filling is quite delicate, however, and deserves a not-too-pungent successor. I would avoid anything with sharp tomato and orégano flavoring.

TORTELLONI WITH BUTTER AND HEAVY CREAM

Use the same method given for Cappelletti with Butter and Heavy Cream (page 159).

TORTELLONI WITH TOMATO AND CREAM SAUCE

Cook the *tortelloni* as directed above for the butter-and-cheese sauce, but season with Tomato and Cream Sauce (page 163).

Cappellacci del Nuovo Mondo
CAPPELLACCI FILLED WITH SWEET POTATOES AND PARSLEY

One of the pleasantest memories of my university days in Ferrara is of the leisurely hours spent at the dinner table with friends, where food and talk gave us release from the pressures of exams and the anxieties of impending adulthood. Often these meals started with a dish of *cappellacci di zucca,* pasta dumplings filled with pumpkin. This is a specialty of Ferrara that is not made elsewhere in Italy, or even in Emilia-Romagna, except in the homes or *trattorie* of expatriate Ferrarese.

The pumpkin used in Ferrara looks very much like American pumpkin. It is yellow, flat, and broad, with a diameter of about 16 inches. It has a unique, beautifully rounded taste that is difficult to describe. It is sweet, but savory, not cloying. I have tried to make *cappellacci* here using pumpkin, Hubbard squash, acorn squash, and any other variety of squash I could find, but I have always found the taste flat and disappointing. Some time ago, at a Thanksgiving dinner, with my thoughts far from home, a biteful of sweet potatoes suddenly brought back to me Ferrara and its *cappellacci*. The following day my long-suffering family was trying out a new dish under the sun, Italian egg pasta with American sweet potato filling. It went over well then, and has since become our favorite dish to spring on unsuspecting newly arrived Italian guests.

It is not, of course, Ferrara's *cappellacci,* but it makes good use of the same idea, that of combining pasta with a sweet vegetable filling. It may also encourage you to give expression to your own inventiveness and special tastes through the traditional techniques of homemade pasta.

For 5 or 6 persons

1¾ pounds sweet potatoes (not yams)

1¼ cups freshly grated Parmesan cheese

3 tablespoons finely chopped parsley

2 tablespoons chopped *mortadella,* prosciutto, or unsmoked ham

1 egg yolk

½ teaspoon nutmeg

½ teaspoon salt

A sheet of homemade pasta dough (page 113), made with 2 eggs, 1½ cups all-purpose flour, and 2 teaspoons milk

1. Preheat the oven to 450°.

2. Put the potatoes to bake in the middle level of the oven. After 20 minutes turn the thermostat down to 400°. Cook for another 35 to 40 minutes, or until the potatoes are very tender when pierced with a fork.

3. Turn off the oven. Remove the potatoes and split them in half, lengthwise. Return the potatoes to the oven, cut side facing up, and leave the oven door slightly ajar. Remove the potatoes after 10 minutes.

4. Peel the potatoes and purée them through a food mill into a bowl. Add all the other ingredients, except of course the pasta, and mix thoroughly with a fork until the mixture is smooth and evenly blended. Taste and correct for salt.

5. Prepare the pasta as directed in the basic recipe and proceed to cut it and stuff it exactly as directed in Step 4 of Tortelloni Filled with Swiss Chard on page 166.

CAPPELLACCI WITH BUTTER AND CHEESE

Follow the directions for Tortelloni with Butter and Cheese (page 167).

CAPPELLACCI WITH MEAT SAUCE

Cappellacci are also very good with Meat Sauce, Bolognese Style (page 127). Calculate about 2 cups sauce for this quantity of pasta.

MENU SUGGESTIONS

Antipasti: Bresaola (page 47), Fried Mortadella, Pancetta, and Cheese Tidbits (page 48), or mixed Italian cold cuts. If you want to turn this into an Italian Thanksgiving dinner, roast turkey makes an excellent second course. Otherwise, all the other roasts of veal, lamb, pork, or chicken given here are good choices. Also suitable is Broiled Pork Liver Wrapped in Caul Fat (page 302), or Lamb Kidneys with White Wine (page 300).

Garganelli
HOMEMADE MACARONI

Garganelli is macaroni made by hand from egg pasta. Looking somewhat like a grooved version of *penne* or *ziti*, it is native to that section of Emilia called Romagna, and it demonstrates that for the *romagnoli*, even when it comes to macaroni, there is no pasta like homemade egg pasta. I can't justify *garganelli* to anyone who measures the advantages of a dish by the speed with which it can be prepared. But I do recommend it to those who do not regret the time spent in producing pasta whose superb texture and lovely hand-turned shape cannot be duplicated by anything bought in a box.

If you have a long, rainy afternoon on your hands, or if you have friends helping you, make a large amount of dough. *Garganelli* will keep for weeks after it dries, and you can make enough to have a supply on hand.

For 6 to 8 persons

Homemade pasta dough   1 tablespoon salt
(page 113), using 4 eggs and
3 cups all-purpose flour

1. Roll out the thinnest sheet of pasta that you can, if you are making it by hand. Fold the sheet into a loose roll and cover it, leaving just a few inches exposed. Cut this exposed part into 1½-inch squares. (If you are machine-making the pasta, cut each thinned-out strip of dough into squares and roll into *garganelli,* as directed below, before kneading and rolling out more dough.)

2. Have ready a dowel or smooth, round pencil, ¼ inch in diameter and 6 to 7 inches long. Take a large, absolutely clean comb, with teeth at least 1½ inches long (the closest equivalent to the original wooden tool, which is, in fact, called *pettine,* or "comb") and lay it flat on the table, with the teeth pointing away from you. Lay a pasta square diagonally on the comb, so that one corner points in the same direction as the teeth, another toward you. Place the dowel on the square and parallel to the comb. Curl the corner of the square facing you around the dowel and, with a gentle downward pressure, push the dowel away from you and off the comb. Curled around the dowel you will have a single macaroni with a lightly ridged surface. Tip the dowel on its end and the macaroni will slide off. Proceed until all the dough has been cut and rolled into macaroni.

3. *Garganelli* are boiled like all other pasta, then served with your choice of sauce (see note below). Boil up to 6 servings of *garganelli* in 4 quarts of water with 1 tablespoon of salt. Add more water for more servings, as needed. *Garganelli,* like all other egg pasta, will cook much faster when fresh and soft than when dry, so, if fresh, start tasting them for doneness 20 to 30 seconds after the water returns to a boil. (Do not overcook. It would be a pity to have gone to all the trouble of making *garganelli* and then ruin them by overcooking.)

(continued)

Garganelli are made by rolling pasta squares over a comb.
Il pettine (shown at top) is the Italian tool for *garganelli*.

NOTE

The ideal sauces for *garganelli* are without a doubt Meat Sauce, Bolognese Style (page 127), and Gorgonzola Sauce (page 134). Another excellent sauce is the white clam sauce on page 135. I also find *garganelli* particularly good with Broccoli and Anchovy Sauce for Orecchiette and Other Pasta (page 174). This sauce is unknown in Romagna, just as *garganelli* is unknown in Apulia, where the sauce comes from. But the two hit it off beautifully together.

MENU SUGGESTIONS

If you are using meat sauce, Braised Veal Shanks, Trieste Style (page 257), Little Veal "Bundles" with Anchovies and Cheese (page 267), any of the three lamb roasts on pages 278–281, or Chicken Fricassee with Dried Wild Mushrooms (page 310) are good choices for the second course. If you are using the Broccoli and Anchovy Sauce, see the suggestions under that recipe (page 175). If white clam sauce, see the suggestions under the recipe for Fettuccine with White Clam Sauce (page 137).

Orecchiette

HOMEMADE PASTA FROM APULIA

The territory of Apulia extends over the entire heel and half the instep of the Italian boot. It is a region of glorious coastlines, of bleached, agonizingly beautiful towns, and a tough, ancient race of shepherds and fishermen. They say of Bari, their principal port, that if Paris had had the sea it would have been a little Bari. There is a similar lack of understatement in Apulian food. The favorite Apulian vegetables are cabbage, cauliflower, peppers, and broccoli. Hot pepper is used freely, anchovies appear in nearly every variety of dish short of dessert, everything is cooked in dense, fruity Apulian olive oil, and a hard, piquant ricotta is grated for seasoning pasta.

Apulia, like Emilia-Romagna, has a strong tradition of homemade pasta. It is made without eggs, just hard durum wheat flour and water, which makes a firmer, chewier, less delicate dough than the Emilian *sfoglia*. It is better suited, however, to its native, highly flavored sauces. Like all pasta, it comes in many shapes. The best known outside Apulia is *'recchie*, in Italian *orecchiette*, or "little ears." These are small disks of pasta given their earlike shape by a rotary pressure of the thumb. The broccoli and anchovy sauce that follows this recipe is an ideal sauce for *orecchiette*.

For 6 persons

1 cup semolina, preferably the imported Italian kind called *semolino*	½ teaspoon salt
	Up to 1 cup of lukewarm water, as required
2 cups all-purpose flour	

1. Combine the semolina, flour, and salt and pour them on your work surface, making a mound with a well in the center. Add a few tablespoons of water at a time, incorporating it with the flour until the flour has absorbed as much water as possible without becoming stiff and dry. (The consistency should not be sticky, but it should be somewhat softer than that of egg pasta.) Knead the mass until it is smooth and elastic.

2. Keeping the rest of the dough covered with a cloth or a soup bowl, pull off a ball about the size of a lemon from the kneaded dough. Roll the ball into a sausagelike cylinder about ¾ inch thick. Slice it into disks ¹⁄₁₆ inch thick. Place a disk in the cupped palm of one hand and, with a rotary pressure of the thumb of the other hand, make a depression in the center slightly broadening the disks to a width of about 1 to 1¼ inches. The shape should be that of a very shallow mushroom cap, with edges slightly thicker than the center. Repeat the procedure until you've used up all the dough.

NOTE

Orecchiette can be used fresh or allowed to dry and kept a month or more in a dry cupboard. This pasta takes considerably longer than egg pasta to cook, but it is cooked in exactly the same manner, in abundant salted boiling water.

Sugo di broccoli e acciughe
BROCCOLI AND ANCHOVY SAUCE FOR
ORECCHIETTE AND OTHER PASTA

For 4 servings

2 cups fresh broccoli florets	Freshly ground pepper, 8 to
Salt	10 twists of the mill
6 tablespoons olive oil OR ¼	1 tablespoon butter
cup olive oil plus 2 table-	6 tablespoons freshly grated
spoons butter (see note	Parmesan cheese
below)	6 tablespoons freshly grated
6 large or 8 medium flat anchovy	Romano *pecorino* cheese
fillets, chopped	

1. Wash the broccoli florets in cold water. Bring 2 quarts of water to a boil, add ¼ teaspoon salt and florets. Cover and cook at a moderate boil until tender, about 7 to 8 minutes. Drain and set aside.

2. Put ¼ cup oil (if you are adding butter later) or all the oil (if

you are using no butter) in a skillet with the chopped anchovies. Cook over medium heat, mashing the anchovies with a wooden spoon until they dissolve into a paste. Add the broccoli florets, the pepper, and, if you are using it, the 2 tablespoons butter. Turn the broccoli in the anchovy sauce as you sauté it lightly for 4 to 5 minutes. Taste and correct for salt. (If the anchovies were very salty, none may be needed.)

3. Add the sauce to the cooked pasta, plus 1 tablespoon of butter and the two grated cheeses. Mix the grated cheese thoroughly into the hot pasta. Serve immediately. No additional cheese is required at the table.

NOTE

The *pugliesi*, who invented this sauce, use only olive oil. I find that a little bit of butter makes the sauce creamier and smoother.

MENU SUGGESTIONS

A fish antipasto has a natural affinity with this sauce. Try Broiled Mussels and Clams on the Half Shell (page 34), or Shrimps with Oil and Lemon (page 39). For a second course, any of the three lamb roasts on pages 278–281 or Roast Pork with Bay Leaves (page 286) would be suitable.

Crespelle
ITALIAN PANCAKES

Italians make very thin pancakes that they use as they would use *cannelloni*, stuffing them with a variety of fillings and transforming them into yet another series of pasta dishes.

Two traditional fillings are given here, one with spinach and prosciutto, and another with meat sauce. Once you have tried them and acquired experience and self-confidence, you should experiment with your own formulas, using other vegetables, such as thinly sliced artichoke hearts, or other meat ingredients, such as chicken livers.

(continued)

Remember that the fillings must always be completely cooked before the *crespelle* are stuffed, and that you need a certain amount of béchamel sauce for creamy liaison.

Makes 16 to 18 crespelle

THE BATTER:

1 cup milk	2 eggs
Generous ¾ cup all-purpose flour	⅛ teaspoon salt

FOR COOKING THE CRESPELLE:

1 to 2 tablespoons butter

1. Put the milk in a bowl and add the flour gradually, sifting it through a sieve. Beat with a fork or whisk until all the flour and milk are evenly blended. Add the two eggs and salt, beating them until they are thoroughly incorporated into the mixture.

2. Put ½ teaspoon butter in a heavy 8-inch skillet, melting it over medium-low heat. Rotate the pan so that the bottom is evenly coated with butter.

3. When the butter is fully melted but not brown, pour 2 tablespoons of batter over the center of the pan. Quickly lift the pan away from the burner and tip it in several directions with a seesaw motion so that the batter covers the whole bottom.

4. Return the skillet to the fire. Cook until the pancake has set and turned a pale-brown color on one side. Turn it with a spatula and brown it very lightly on the other side; then transfer it to a platter.

5. Coat the bottom of the skillet with a tiny amount of butter, half what you used at first, and proceed as above until all the pancake batter is used up.

NOTE

In order to pour the batter all at once into the pan without scooping it up tablespoon by tablespoon, mark off 2 tablespoons with tape on a small measuring cup or juice glass and fill it in advance, refilling it while you do the pancakes.

Crespelle may be made hours, or even days, in advance, if refrigerated and interleaved with plastic wrap or waxed paper. They may even be frozen.

Crespelle alla fiorentina
ITALIAN PANCAKES FILLED WITH SPINACH

For 4 persons

1 pound fresh spinach OR 1 ten-ounce package frozen leaf spinach, thawed

3 tablespoons finely chopped yellow onion

4 tablespoons butter

½ cup chopped prosciutto, *mortadella,* or unsmoked ham

1¼ cups freshly grated Parmesan cheese

¼ teaspoon nutmeg

1 cup plus 5 tablespoons Béchamel Sauce (page 28)

Salt

Crespelle (Italian Pancakes, previous page)

1. Cook, drain, squeeze most of the moisture out of the spinach and chop as directed in Sliced Pasta Roll with Spinach Filling (page 152).

2. Put the chopped onion in a small skillet with 2 tablespoons of the butter and sauté over medium heat until pale gold.

3. Add the chopped prosciutto, stir, and sauté lightly for less than a minute.

4. Add the chopped spinach and cook for 2 to 3 minutes, stirring constantly, until it has completely absorbed all the butter.

5. Transfer the contents of the skillet to a mixing bowl, and combine with 1 cup of the grated cheese, the nutmeg, the 5 tablespoons béchamel, and ¼ teaspoon salt. Mix thoroughly, then taste and correct for salt.

6. Preheat the oven to 450°.

7. Lightly smear the bottom of a flameproof bake-and-serve dish with butter. Lay one of the *crespelle* on a flat, clean work surface and spread a skimpy tablespoon of filling over it, leaving a ½-inch border uncovered. Roll up the *crespella,* keeping it loose and rather

flat. Place it in the bottom of the dish, with its folded-over end facing down. Proceed until you have filled and rolled up all the *crespelle,* arranging them in a single layer in the baking dish and keeping them not too tightly packed.

8. Spread the remaining 1 cup of béchamel sauce over the *crespelle.* Make sure the ends of the *crespelle* rolls are well covered, and that there is some béchamel in between them. Sprinkle with ¼ cup grated cheese and dot lightly with butter.

9. Place in the uppermost level of the preheated oven for 5 minutes, then run under the broiler for less than a minute, until a light crust has formed. Allow to settle for a minute or so, then serve from the same dish.

MENU SUGGESTIONS

This can precede any meat or fowl, execpt those very boldly seasoned.

Crespelle con il ragù
ITALIAN PANCAKES FILLED WITH MEAT SAUCE

For 4 persons

1½ cups Meat Sauce, Bolognese
    Style (page 127)
½ cup plus 2 tablespoons
    Béchamel Sauce (page
    28)
¼ teaspoon nutmeg

Crespelle (Italian Pancakes,
    page 175)
⅓ cup freshly grated Parmesan
    cheese
2 tablespoons butter

1. Draw off all the fat that floats to the surface of the meat sauce, then combine 1 cup of the meat sauce with 2 tablespoons of the béchamel and the nutmeg in a bowl.

2. Preheat the oven to 450°.

3. Stuff the *crespelle* and arrange them in a lightly buttered flame-

proof bake-and-serve dish, following the directions in Step 7 of the preceding recipe.

4. Mix the remaining ½ cup meat sauce with the ½ cup béchamel and spread it over the *crespelle*. Sprinkle with the grated cheese, dot lightly with butter, and place in the uppermost level of the pre-heated oven for 5 minutes, then run under the broiler for less than a minute, until a light crust has formed. Allow to settle for a minute or so, then serve from the same dish.

MENU SUGGESTIONS

Follow the suggestions given for Meat-Stuffed Pasta Rolls (page 149).

RISOTTO

Risotto is a uniquely Italian technique for cooking rice. There are so many things you can do with *risotto* that it is almost a cuisine all by itself. Unfortunately, it is the most misunderstood of all the well-known Italian dishes. The French seem to believe it is the same thing as rice pilaf. Others think it is just rice boiled in broth with seasonings. If you have never had it except in restaurants, you have very likely never had a true *risotto*. Restaurant *risotto*, even in Italy, is usually precooked rice pilaf that is given a *risotto* treatment before serving. It can even be reasonably good sometimes, but genuine *risotto* is quite another thing.

Risotto can be made with almost any ingredient added to the rice: shellfish, game, chicken livers, sausages, vegetables, herbs, cheese. The variations are inexhaustible, yet they are all produced through this one basic technique.

THE BASIC RISOTTO TECHNIQUE

In making *risotto*, the objective is to cause rice to absorb, a little at a time, enough hot broth until it swells and forms a creamy union of tender, yet firm grains. The following outline can be used as a guide for all *risotto* recipes.

1. Sauté chopped onion in butter and oil until the onion is very lightly colored.

2. Add rice, and sauté it for 1 to 2 minutes. Stir to coat it well with cooking fat.

3. Add ½ cup of simmering broth and stir while cooking, until the rice absorbs the liquid and wipes the sides of the pot as you stir. When the rice dries out, add another ½ cup of simmering broth and continue to stir-cook. You must be steadfast and tireless in your stirring, always loosening the rice from the entire bottom surface of the pot; otherwise it will stick. Add liquid as the rice dries out, but don't "drown" the rice. Remember, *risotto* is not boiled rice.

4. Correct heat is very important in making *risotto*. It should be very lively, but if the liquid evaporates too rapidly the rice cannot cook evenly. It will be soft outside and chalky inside. If the heat is too slow, the rice becomes gluey, which is even worse. Regulate the heat so that, if you are using Italian rice, it will cook in about 30 minutes' time. The *risotto* is done when the rice is tender but *al dente*, firm to the bite. You must be able to judge when the rice is close to doneness, so that as it finishes cooking you won't swamp it with excess liquid. Until you acquire experience with *risotto*, it is safer, after 20 minutes' cooking, to reduce the dose of broth to ¼ cup at a time, at frequent intervals. When cooked, the rice should be creamily bound together, neither dry nor runny.

PREPARING IT AHEAD OF TIME

Once *risotto* is made it must be served. It cannot be warmed up. If absolutely necessary, however, you can partially cook it several hours ahead of time. This is an unorthodox method, but it works.

1. Cook the rice to the halfway point, when the outside is almost tender but the inside is quite hard. Allow it to dry out before removing it from the heat, being careful that it doesn't stick. Spread it very thinly on a large cold platter.

2. A quarter of an hour or so before serving, melt 1 tablespoon of butter in a casserole. Add the rice and stir, coating it well with butter. Add ½ cup of simmering broth and resume cooking it in the normal manner until done.

HOW MUCH BROTH TO USE

The quantity of liquid given in the following recipes for *risotto* should be considered an approximate amount. You may end using less or slightly more than indicated, but this is not significant. There are too many variables involved to be able to establish a "correct" amount of liquid. What is important is never to cook *risotto* with too much liquid *at one time,* and to bring it to its final tender but firm-to-the-bite stage so that it is creamy but not saturated.

Risotto alla parmigiana
RISOTTO WITH PARMESAN CHEESE

This is the purest and perhaps the finest of all *risotti.* The only major ingredient added to the rice and broth is Parmesan cheese. In Italian cooking, you should never use anything except good-quality, freshly grated Parmesan cheese, but for this particular *risotto* you should make a special effort to obtain authentic, aged, Italian *parmigiano-reggiano* from the best supplier you know.

During the truffle season in Italy, the *risotto* is crowned at the table with thinly sliced fresh white truffles. Fresh truffles are sometimes available here for a few days in late November or early December. If you should have a chance at a nice large truffle, do get it for this *risotto.* It is going to set you back a considerable amount, but you are not likely to regret it.

(continued)

4 servings

5 cups Homemade Meat Broth (page 10) or 1 cup canned chicken broth mixed with 4 cups water	3 tablespoons butter
	2 tablespoons vegetable oil
	1½ cups raw Italian Arborio rice
	½ heaping cup freshly grated Parmesan cheese
2 tablespoons finely chopped shallots or yellow onion	Salt, if necessary

1. Bring the broth to a slow, steady simmer.

2. Put the shallots in a heavy-bottomed casserole with 2 tablespoons of the butter and all the oil and sauté over medium-high heat until translucent but not browned.

3. Add the rice and stir until it is well coated. Sauté lightly, then add ½ cup of the simmering broth. Proceed according to the basic directions for making *risotto* (page 180), adding ½ cup of simmering broth as the rice dries out, and stirring it very frequently to prevent it from sticking. (If you run out of broth, continue with water.)

4. When you estimate that the rice is about 5 minutes away from being done, add all the grated cheese and the remaining tablespoon of butter. Mix well. Taste and correct for salt. Remember, when the cooking nears the end, not to add too much broth at one time. The *risotto* should be creamy but not runny. Serve immediately, with additional grated cheese, if desired, on the side.

MENU SUGGESTIONS

There is virtually no second course of meat, fowl, or variety meats that cannot follow this *risotto*. It can complement a delicate dish such as Sautéed Veal Scaloppine with Marsala (page 261), or hold its own before something as earthy as Oxtail Braised with Wine and Vegetables (page 291). It goes especially well before Sweetbreads Braised with Tomatoes and Peas (page 295), or Sautéed Chicken Livers with Sage (page 303). Do avoid any dishes with cheese. It would create monotony.

Anello di risotto alla parmigiana con il ragù di fegatini

MOLDED RISOTTO WITH PARMESAN CHEESE AND CHICKEN-LIVER SAUCE

In this elegant combination of a creamy white *risotto* with a dark and lovely sauce you have what Italians would call *un boccone da cardinale*, "a morsel fit for a cardinal." In Italy the church has always been known for its patronage of the arts.

For 4 or 5 persons

Risotto with Parmesan Cheese (page 181), made with 2 tablespoons butter and 1 tablespoon oil and omitting the butter at the end

Chicken-liver sauce (page 137), made with only 2 tablespoons olive oil and 1 tablespoon butter

Lightly butter a 6-cup ring mold. When the *risotto* is done, spoon it all into the ring mold and tamp it down. Invert the mold over a serving platter and lift it away, leaving a ring of *risotto* on the platter. Pour all the sauce in the center of the ring, and serve immediately.

MENU SUGGESTIONS

Follow the ones given for Pappardelle with Chicken-Liver Sauce (page 138).

Risotto alla milanese

RISOTTO, MILAN STYLE

For 6 persons

1 quart Homemade Meat Broth (page 10) OR 1 cup canned chicken broth mixed with 3 cups of water

2 tablespoons diced beef marrow, *pancetta*, or prosciutto

2 tablespoons finely chopped shallots or yellow onion

5 tablespoons butter

2 tablespoons vegetable oil

2 cups raw Italian Arborio rice

⅓ teaspoon powdered saffron OR ½ teaspoon chopped whole saffron, dissolved in 1½ cups hot broth or water

Salt, if necessary

Freshly ground pepper, about 4 twists of the mill or more to taste

¼ cup freshly grated Parmesan cheese

1. Bring the broth to a slow, steady simmer.

2. In a heavy-bottomed casserole, over medium-high heat, sauté the beef marrow and shallots in 3 tablespoons of the butter and all the oil. As soon as the shallots become translucent, add the rice and stir until it is well coated. Sauté lightly for a few moments and then add ½ cup of the simmering broth, about a ladleful. Proceed according to the basic directions for making *risotto* (page 180), adding a ladleful of hot broth as the rice dries out, and stirring it very frequently to prevent it from sticking. After 15 minutes add half the dissolved saffron. When the rice has dried out, add the rest of the saffron. (The later you add the saffron, the stronger the taste and aroma of saffron will be at the end. Herbs that call too much attention to themselves are a rude intrusion upon the general harmony of a dish, but if you like a stronger saffron presence wait another 5 to 8 minutes before adding the diluted saffron. But be careful it doesn't upstage your *risotto*.) When the saffron liquid has been absorbed, finish cooking the *risotto* with hot broth. (If you run out of broth, add water.)

3. When the rice is done, tender but *al dente,* firm to the bite, taste for salt. (If the broth was salty, you might not need any. Consider, too, the saltiness of the cheese you will be adding.) Add a few twists of pepper to taste, and turn off the heat. Add 2 tablespoons of butter and all the cheese and mix thoroughly. Spoon into a hot platter and serve with a bowl of freshly grated cheese on the side.

MENU SUGGESTIONS

Risotto Milan Style is traditionally served with Braised Veal Shanks, Milan Style (page 256), one of the rare instances when a first course is served together with the meat course in an Italian menu. It is a well-justified exception, because the two dishes are an ideal complement to each other. This *risotto* can also be served as a regular first course when the second course is a roasted or braised meat or fowl.

Risotto coi funghi secchi

RISOTTO WITH DRIED WILD MUSHROOMS

For 6 persons

1 ounce imported dried wild
 mushrooms
1 quart Homemade Meat Broth
 (page 10) OR 1 cup canned
 chicken broth mixed with
 3 cups of water
2 tablespoons finely chopped
 shallots or yellow onion
4 tablespoons butter

3 tablespoons vegetable oil
2 cups raw Italian
 Arborio rice
¼ cup freshly grated Parmesan
 cheese
Salt, if necessary
Freshly grated pepper, about
 4 twists of the mill

1. Soak the mushrooms in 2 cups of lukewarm water for at least 30 minutes before cooking. After the liquid turns very dark strain it through a sieve lined with paper towels and set aside. Continue

soaking and rinsing the mushrooms in frequent changes of water until the mushrooms are soft and thoroughly free of soil.

2. Bring the broth or the canned broth and water to a slow, steady simmer.

3. In a heavy-bottomed casserole, over medium-high heat, sauté the chopped shallots or onion in half the butter and all the oil until translucent but not brown. Add the rice and stir until it is well coated. Sauté lightly for a few moments and then add a ladleful, ½ cup, of the simmering broth. Proceed according to the basic directions for making *risotto* (page 180), adding 1 ladleful of hot liquid as the rice dries out, and stirring it very frequently to prevent it from sticking. When the rice has cooked for 10 to 12 minutes add the mushrooms and ½ cup of the strained mushroom liquid. As it becomes absorbed, add more of the mushroom liquid, ½ cup at a time. After you've used up the mushroom liquid finish cooking the rice with hot broth. (If you run out of broth, add water.)

4. When the rice is done, turn off the heat and mix in the grated Parmesan and the rest of the butter. Taste and correct for salt. (If the broth was very salty, you may not need any salt at all.) Add a few twists of pepper and mix. Spoon the rice into a hot serving platter and serve immediately with a bowl of freshly grated cheese on the side.

MENU SUGGESTIONS

It is perhaps easier to say what second courses to avoid than to indicate which ones to choose. Stay away from any dish with mushrooms, of course, and also from other sharply competitive flavors, such as the Thin Pan-Broiled Steaks with Tomatoes and Olives (page 241) and Veal Scaloppine with Tomatoes (page 264) or Casserole-Roasted Lamb with Juniper Berries (page 280). Otherwise, all roasts, stews, and fricassees of meat and fowl are good choices. Particularly good are all the sautéed veal dishes.

Risotto col ragù
RISOTTO WITH MEAT SAUCE

For 4 persons

5 cups Homemade Meat Broth (page 10) OR 1 cup canned chicken broth mixed with 4 cups water

1 cup Meat Sauce, Bolognese Style (page 127)

1½ cups raw Italian Arborio rice

Salt, if necessary

3 tablespoons freshly grated Parmesan cheese

1 tablespoon butter

1. Bring the broth to a slow, steady simmer.

2. Heat the meat sauce in a heavy, open casserole over medium heat. When it is hot and simmering, add the rice and stir until it is thoroughly mixed into the meat sauce. Cook for a few moments longer, then add a ladleful, ½ cup, of simmering broth. Proceed according to the basic directions for making *risotto* (page 180), adding a ladleful of simmering broth as the rice dries out, and stirring it very frequently to prevent it from sticking. (If you run out of broth, continue with water.) When the rice is done, tender yet *al dente*, firm to the bite, taste for salt. If you find it is on the salty side, reduce or omit the grated cheese. Turn off the heat and swirl in 1 tablespoon of butter. Transfer to a hot platter and serve.

MENU SUGGESTIONS

The meat sauce makes this a very substantial *risotto*. Choose a lighter second course, such as Sautéed Veal Scaloppine with Lemon Sauce (page 262) or with Marsala (page 261). The Charcoal-Broiled Chicken Marinated in Pepper, Oil, and Lemon (page 307) would also be a good choice.

Risotto con la luganega
RISOTTO WITH LUGANEGA SAUSAGE

For 6 persons

5 cups Homemade Meat Broth
  (page 10) OR 1 cup canned
  chicken broth mixed with
  4 cups water
2 tablespoons finely chopped
  shallots or yellow onion
3 tablespoons butter
2 tablespoons vegetable oil

2 cups raw Italian Arborio rice
¾ pound *luganega* sausage
¼ cup dry white wine
Salt, if necessary
Freshly ground pepper, about
  5 or 6 twists of the mill
3 tablespoons freshly grated
  Parmesan cheese

1. Bring the broth to a slow, steady simmer.

2. In a heavy-bottomed casserole, over medium-high heat, sauté the chopped shallots with 2 tablespoons of butter and all the oil. When translucent, add the rice and stir until it is well coated. Sauté lightly for a few moments, then add a ladleful, ½ cup, of the simmering broth. Proceed according to the basic instructions for making *risotto* (page 180), adding a ladleful of hot broth as the rice dries out, and stirring it very frequently to prevent it from sticking.

3. While the rice is cooking, cut the *luganega* into 2-inch lengths and cook it in a skillet over medium-high heat with the wine. After the wine has evaporated, continue browning the sausage in its own fat for 12 to 15 minutes. Remove and set aside, but do not discard the juices in the skillet.

4. When the rice is done, tender, but *al dente,* firm to the bite, taste for salt. (You might not need any if the broth was salty. Consider too the saltiness of the cheese you will be adding.) Add a few twists of pepper to taste and turn off the heat. Add the tablespoon of butter and all the cheese and mix thoroughly. Spoon into a hot platter.

5. Tip the skillet in which the sausage was cooked and draw off

all but 2 tablespoons of the fat. Add 2 tablespoons of water, turn the heat to high, and while the water boils away scrape up and loosen any residue stuck to the pan. Return the sausages to the pan for a few moments, turning them as they warm up. Make a slight depression in the center of the mound of *risotto* on the platter, and on it place the sausages and their sauce. Serve immediately.

NOTE

Additional grated cheese is not usually called for with this *risotto*, but it is best to have some in a bowl at the table to suit individual taste.

MENU SUGGESTIONS

This *risotto* can precede any roasted or braised meat except pork. It is also good before chicken, if simply roasted or broiled, such as in the Charcoal-Broiled Chicken Marinated in Pepper, Oil, and Lemon (page 307).

Risotto con gli asparagi

RISOTTO WITH ASPARAGUS

For 6 persons

1 pound fresh asparagus
    Homemade Meat Broth (page 10) OR 1 cup canned chicken broth mixed with water, sufficient to come to 5 cups liquid when added to the water in which the asparagus has cooked (see Step 3)
2 tablespoons finely chopped shallots or yellow onion

5 tablespoons butter
3 tablespoons vegetable oil
2 cups raw Italian Arborio rice
    Salt, if necessary
    Freshly ground pepper, about 4 twists of the mill
¼ cup freshly grated Parmesan cheese
1 tablespoon finely chopped parsley

1. Trim, wash, and boil the asparagus, following the instructions for cooking asparagus on page 354. Drain, reserving the cooking liquid, and set aside to cool.

(continued)

2. When the asparagus is cool, cut into ½-inch pieces, utilizing as much of the stalk as possible. If the very bottom of the stalk is tough and stringy, keep just the tender inner core, scraping it up with a knife.

3. Add the broth to the water in which the asparagus cooked and bring to a slow, steady simmer.

4. In a heavy-bottomed casserole, over medium-high heat, sauté the shallots in 3 tablespoons of the butter and all the oil until translucent. Add the cut-up asparagus and sauté lightly for 2 minutes, stirring frequently. Add the rice and stir until it is thoroughly coated. Sauté lightly for a few moments, then add a ladleful, ½ cup, of the simmering broth. Proceed according to the basic directions for making *risotto* (page 180), adding a ladleful of hot broth as the rice dries out, and stirring it very frequently to prevent it from sticking. (If you should run out of broth, continue with water.)

5. When the rice reaches the proper consistency, tender but *al dente*, firm to the bite, taste it to see if it requires salt. Add a few twists of freshly ground pepper to taste. Turn off the heat and mix in the remaining 2 tablespoons of butter and all the grated cheese. Add the chopped parsley and mix. Spoon the rice onto a hot serving platter and serve. At the table it can be topped with a little more freshly grated Parmesan cheese.

MENU SUGGESTIONS

Follow the suggestions for Risotto with Zucchini, page 192. Of course you won't accompany the second course with any side dish of asparagus.

Risotto con le zucchine
RISOTTO WITH ZUCCHINI

For 4 persons

4 medium zucchini or 6 small
    ones (see note below)
3 tablespoons coarsely chopped
    yellow onion
5 tablespoons vegetable oil
½ teaspoon finely chopped
    garlic
    Salt
5 cups Homemade Meat Broth
    (page 10) OR 1 cup canned
    chicken broth mixed with
    4 cups water

3 tablespoons butter
1½ cups raw Italian Arborio rice
    Freshly ground pepper, about
    4 twists of the mill
1 tablespoon finely chopped
    parsley
3 tablespoons freshly grated
    Parmesan cheese

1. Carefully wash or scrape the zucchini clean and slice into disks ½ inch thick. Set aside.

2. In a medium-sized skillet (9-inch) sauté the onion with 3 tablespoons of the oil over medium-high heat. When the onion becomes translucent, àdd the chopped garlic, and as soon as it colors lightly, add the sliced zucchini and turn the heat down to medium low. Add a tiny pinch of salt after 10 or 12 minutes. The zucchini are done when they turn a rich golden color, usually about 30 minutes. (You can prepare them ahead of time, several hours or a few days, if you refrigerate them tightly covered with plastic wrap.)

3. Bring the broth or canned broth and water to a slow, steady simmer. Transfer the zucchini to a heavy-bottomed casserole, leaving behind in the pan as much of the cooking fat as possible. Add 2 tablespoons butter and the remaining 2 tablespoons oil to the casserole and turn the heat to high. When the fat and zucchini begin to bubble, add the rice and stir until it is well coated. Sauté lightly for about 1 minute, then add a ladleful, ½ cup, of the simmer-

ing broth. Proceed according to the basic directions for making *risotto* (page 10), adding 1 ladleful of hot liquid as the rice dries out, and stirring it very frequently to keep it from sticking. (If you run out of broth, add water.)

4. When the rice is done, tender but *al dente,* firm to the bite, taste for salt. (If the broth was very salty, you might not need any. Bear in mind, too, that the Parmesan cheese you will add is salty.) Turn off the heat, add a few twists of pepper, the tablespoon of butter, the chopped parsley, and the grated Parmesan and mix thoroughly. Spoon onto a hot platter and serve immediately, with a bowl of freshly grated cheese on the side.

NOTE

If you've made the zucchini stuffed with meat and cheese on page 397, use the chopped cores of 8 to 10 zucchini.

MENU SUGGESTIONS

Any meat or chicken roast will make a fine second course, as would Sautéed Lamb Kidneys with White Wine (page 300), Fried Breaded Calf's Liver (page 298), and Sautéed Chicken Livers with Sage (page 303). Avoid stews or fricassees containing vegetables, and don't accompany the second course with any side dish of zucchini.

Risotto con le vongole
RISOTTO WITH CLAMS

For 6 persons

3 dozen littleneck clams, the tiniest you can find
1 tablespoon finely chopped yellow onion
5 tablespoons olive oil
2 teaspoons finely chopped garlic

2 tablespoons chopped parsley
2 cups raw Italian Arborio rice
⅓ cup dry white wine
Salt and freshly ground pepper to taste

1. Wash and scrub the clams thoroughly, according to the directions on page 53. Heat them over high heat in a covered pan until they open their shells, giving them a vigorous shake or turning them so that they will heat up more evenly. (Some clams are more stubborn about opening up than others.) When most of them have opened up, it is best to remove them while waiting for the tardy ones; otherwise they will become tough as they linger in the pan. Remove the clams from their shells and rinse off any sand on the meat by dipping them briefly one at a time in their own juice. Unless the clams are exceptionally small, cut them up in two or more pieces and set aside. Strain the clam juices through a sieve lined with paper towels and set aside.

2. Bring 5 cups of water to a slow, steady simmer.

3. In a heavy-bottomed casserole, sauté the chopped onion in the olive oil over medium-high heat. When translucent, add the garlic and sauté until it colors lightly. Add the parsley, stir, then add the rice and stir until it is well coated with oil. Sauté lightly for a few moments and then add the wine. When the wine has evaporated and the rice dries out, add the strained clam juices. As the rice dries out, add a ladleful, ½ cup, of the simmering water. Proceed according to the basic directions for making *risotto* (page 180), adding a ladleful of simmering water as the rice dries out, and stirring it very frequently to prevent it from sticking. After 15 or 20 minutes add salt and pepper to taste.

4. When the rice is done, tender but *al dente*, firm to the bite, taste and correct for salt and pepper. Add the clams, mixing them into the hot rice; then turn off the heat and spoon the rice onto a hot platter. Serve immediately.

NOTE

This *risotto*, as is true of all pastas and soups with a seafood base, does not call for grated cheese.

MENU SUGGESTIONS

For a complete fish dinner, you can start with Baked Oysters with Oil and Parsley (page 32), or Cold Salmon Foam (page 33),

(continued)

as an antipasto. Follow the *risotto* with Fish Broiled the Adriatic Way (page 224). Other second courses could be Stuffed Squid Braised in White Wine (page 232), or the Fillet of Sole with Piquant Tomato Sauce (page 219).

Riso filante con la mozzarella
RICE WITH FRESH BASIL AND MOZZARELLA CHEESE

This is nothing more than boiled rice and fresh basil enmeshed in the fine tangles of melted mozzarella. It is another example of how, in Italian cooking, simple handling of the simplest ingredients results in a dish interesting in texture, lovely to look at, and, best of all, delicious.

For 4 persons

1 tablespoon salt
1½ cups raw rice, preferably
    Italian Arborio rice
6 tablespoons butter, cut up
2 tablespoons shredded fresh
    basil OR 1 tablespoon
    chopped parsley

1¼ cups mozzarella cheese,
    shredded on the largest
    holes of the grater
⅔ cup freshly grated Parmesan
    cheese

1. Bring 3 quarts of water to a boil, add the salt, then the rice, and mix with a wooden spoon. Cover the pot and cook at a moderate but steady boil until the rice is tender but *al dente*, firm to the bite. (Depending on the rice, it should take about 15 to 20 minutes.) While cooking, stir from time to time with a wooden spoon.

2. Drain and transfer the rice to a warm serving bowl. Mix in the cut-up butter; then add the basil (or parsley) and mix.

3. Add the shredded mozzarella and mix quickly and thoroughly. (The heat of the rice unravels the mozzarella, forming a soft, fluffy skein of cheese and rice flecked with basil green.)

4. Add the grated Parmesan cheese, stir two or three times, and serve immediately.

This would be very nice before a second course of Thin Pan-Broiled Steaks with Tomatoes and Olives (page 241), Veal Scaloppine with Tomatoes (page 264), Veal Rolls in Tomato Sauce (page 265), Veal Stew with Tomatoes and Peas (page 274), or Chicken Fricassee with Green Peppers and Tomatoes (page 309). Actually it can precede any kind of meat or fowl—roasted, braised, fried, or sautéed—as long as it isn't made with cheese or milk.

Gnocchi di patate
POTATO GNOCCHI

Most recipes for potato *gnocchi* call for one or more egg yolks. I find that the eggless version produces finer *gnocchi*. Eggs may make them easier to handle, but they also make them tough and rubbery. Eggless *gnocchi* are light, fluffy, and less filling. *Gnocchi* can be seasoned with almost any sauce. Three particularly happy combinations are *gnocchi* with Tomato Sauce III (page 95), with Pesto (page 139), or with Gorgonzola Sauce (page 134).

For 4 to 6 persons

1½ pounds boiling potatoes (not Idaho potatoes or new potatoes)
1 cup all-purpose flour

Tomato Sauce III (page 95), or Pesto (page 139), or Gorgonzola Sauce (page 134)
⅔ cup freshly grated Parmesan cheese, more if necessary

1. Boil the potatoes, unpeeled, in abundant water. (Do not test them too often while cooking by puncturing them with a fork or they will become waterlogged.) When cooked, drain them, and peel as soon as you can handle them. Purée them through a food mill or potato ricer while still warm.

2. Add most of the flour to the mashed potatoes and knead into

a smooth mixture. (Some potatoes take more flour than others, so it is best not to add all the flour at once.) Stop adding flour when the mixture is soft, smooth, and still slightly sticky. Shape it into sausage-like rolls about as thick as your thumb, then cut the rolls into ¾-inch lengths.

3. This step is more complicated to explain than it is to execute. At first, just go through the motions until you feel you've understood the mechanics of the step. Then start on the *gnocchi*—but without losing heart if the first few don't turn out quite right. You will soon acquire the knack and do a whole mess of *gnocchi* in two or three minutes. (And, in working with *gnocchi*, it will make your life much easier if you remember to dust repeatedly with flour the *gnocchi*, your hands, and any surface you are working on.)

Take a fork with long, rounded, slim prongs. Working over a counter, hold the fork sideways—that is, with the prongs pointing from left to right (or right to left) and with the concave side facing you. With the other hand, place a dumpling on the inside curve of the fork just below the points of the prongs and press it against the prongs with the tip of the index finger pointing directly at and perpendicular to the fork. While pressing the dumpling with your finger, flip it away from the prong tips, and toward the handle of the fork. Don't drag it, flip it. As it rolls to the base of the prongs, let it drop to the counter. The dumpling will then be somewhat crescent-shaped, with ridges on one side formed by the prongs, and a deep depression on the other formed by your fingertip. (This is not just a capricious decorative exercise. It serves to thin out the middle section of the dumpling so that it will cook more evenly, and to create little grooved traps in its surface for the sauce to sink into and make the *gnocchi* tastier.)

4. Drop the *gnocchi*, about 2 dozen at a time, into 5 quarts or more of boiling salted water. In a very short time they will float to the surface. Let them cook just 8 or 10 seconds more, then lift them out with a slotted spoon and transfer to a heated platter. Season with a little of the sauce you are using. (If you are using the tomato sauce, add a light sprinkling of grated cheese.) Drop more *gnocchi* in the

Place *gnocchi* on the inside curve of a fork and press against
the prongs with the tip of the index finger, pointing directly at
and perpendicular to the fork. While pressing the dumpling with
your finger, flip it away from the prong tips, toward the fork handle,
and as it rolls let it drop to the counter.

boiling water and repeat the whole process until they are cooked.
When all the *gnocchi* are done, pour the rest of the sauce over them
and mix in all the grated cheese. Serve hot.

MENU SUGGESTIONS

If sauced with *pesto*, see the suggestions for Trenette with Potatoes and Pesto (page 142). If sauced with tomato sauce: Beef
Braised in Red Wine Sauce (page 242), Braised Veal Shanks, Trieste
Style (page 257), Rolled Stuffed Breast of Veal (page 254), Casserole-Roasted Lamb with Juniper Berries (page 280), Sautéed
Calf's Liver with Onions, Venetian Style (page 296), or Rolled
Breast of Chicken Fillets Stuffed with Pork (page 315) are some
suitable second courses. If sauced with gorgonzola, see the suggestions for Fettuccine with Gorgonzola Sauce (page 135).

Gnocchi alla romana

BAKED SEMOLINA GNOCCHI

Although many Romans will maintain that semolina *gnocchi* are not *alla romana*, this dish can be traced back directly to Imperial Rome. Apicius gives a recipe for *gnocchi* made of semolina milk exactly like these, then fried and served with honey. All that has changed substantially since then is the cooking method and the seasoning.

For 4 to 6 persons

1 quart milk	1 cup freshly grated Parmesan
1 heaping cup semolina, prefer-	cheese
ably imported Italian	2 teaspoons salt
semolino. If possible, avoid	2 egg yolks
using quick-cooking break-	7 tablespoons butter
fast farina.	

1. Heat the milk in a heavy saucepan over moderate heat until it is just short of boiling. Lower the heat and add the semolina, pouring it in a thin, slow stream and beating it steadily into the milk with a whisk. Continue beating until it forms a thick mass on the whisk as it turns (about 10 minutes). Remove from the heat.

2. Add ⅔ cup of the grated cheese, salt, the 2 egg yolks, and 2 tablespoons of butter to the semolina. Mix rapidly, to avoid coagulating the egg, until all the ingredients are well bended.

3. Moisten a formica or marble surface with cold water and spoon out the semolina mixture, using a metal spatula or a broad-bladed knife to spread it to a thickness of approximately ⅜ inch. (Dip the spatula or knife into the cold water from time to time.) Let the semolina cool completely, about 30 to 40 minutes.

4. Preheat the oven to 450°.

5. With a 1½-inch biscuit cutter, or with a small glass of approximately the same diameter, cut the semolina mixture into disks, moistening the cutting tool from time to time in cold water to make the cuts easier and neater.

6. Smear the bottom of a rectangular or oval bake-and-serve dish with butter. Lift off the small four-sided sections of semolina in between the disks and lay them on the bottom of the baking dish. Dot with butter and sprinkle with grated Parmesan. Over this arrange all the disks in a single layer, overlapping them like roof tiles. Dot with butter and sprinkle with the remaining grated cheese. Place on the uppermost rack of the oven and bake for 15 minutes or until a light golden crust has formed. If after 15 minutes the crust hasn't formed, turn the oven thermostat up to 500° and bake for 5 more minutes. Allow to settle a few minutes before serving.

NOTE

The entire dish can be prepared up to two days ahead of time before baking if it is refrigerated and covered with plastic wrap.

MENU SUGGESTIONS

This is a dish of uncomplicated taste and texture that can precede any meat dish or fowl. It is a particularly fitting first course when the second course is Hothouse Lamb, Roman Style (page 281). Sweetbreads Braised with Tomatoes and Peas (page 295) or Rolled Breast of Chicken Fillets Stuffed with Pork (page 315) are also excellent choices. For an antipasto you might have the Artichokes, Roman Style (page 337), or the Mushroom and Cheese Salad (page 47).

Baked Semolina Gnocchi

Gnocchi verdi

SPINACH AND RICOTTA GNOCCHI

For 4 persons

1 tablespoon finely chopped yellow onion	Salt
2 tablespoons butter	¾ cup fresh ricotta
2 tablespoons very finely chopped *mortadella*, *pancetta*, or unsmoked ham	⅔ cup all-purpose flour
	2 egg yolks
	1 cup freshly grated Parmesan cheese
1 ten-ounce package frozen leaf spinach, thawed, OR 1 pound fresh spinach, prepared as directed on page 152	¼ teaspoon nutmeg

1. Put the onion in a skillet with the butter and sauté over medium heat until pale gold.

2. Add the chopped *mortadella* and continue sautéing just long enough to stir 3 or 4 times, combining the *mortadella* well with the onion and butter.

3. Add the spinach and ¼ teaspoon salt and sauté for 5 to 6 minutes, stirring frequently. (The spinach will absorb all the butter, but it is not necessary to add any more.)

4. Transfer the entire contents of the skillet to a mixing bowl. Add the ricotta and flour, mixing thoroughly with a wooden spoon. Add the egg yolks, grated cheese, and nutmeg, and incorporate them thoroughly into the mixture with the spoon. Taste and correct for salt.

5. Make small pellets out of the mixture, shaping them quickly in the palm of your hand. Ideally they should be about ½ inch in diameter, but if this size is too small for you to handle, or the job too tedious, you can make them as large as ¾ inch. (The smaller the better, however, because they cook more quickly and stay softer.) When the mixture begins to stick to your hands, dust your hands lightly with flour.

6. Cook the *gnocchi* as indicated in the three recipes that follow.

Gnocchi verdi al burro e formaggio

GREEN GNOCCHI GRATINÉED WITH BUTTER AND CHEESE

For 4 persons

1½ tablespoons salt	4½ tablespoons butter
Spinach and Ricotta Gnocchi	½ cup freshly grated Parmesan
(preceding recipe)	cheese

1. Preheat the oven to 375°.

2. Bring 4 quarts of water to a boil. Add the salt, then drop in the *gnocchi*, a few at one time. Two to three minutes after the water returns to a boil, retrieve the *gnocchi* with a slotted spoon and place in a butter-smeared bake-and-serve dish. Add more *gnocchi* to the boiling water, repeating the above procedure, until all the *gnocchi* are cooked and in the baking dish.

3. Melt the butter in a small pan and pour it over the *gnocchi*.

4. Sprinkle all the grated cheese over the *gnocchi*. Place the dish on the uppermost rack of the oven for about 5 minutes, until the cheese has melted. Allow to settle for a few minutes before serving, then serve directly from the baking dish, with additional grated cheese on the side.

MENU SUGGESTIONS

Follow with any roast: beef, veal, lamb, pork, or fowl. Other excellent choices for the second course would be Beef Braised in Red Wine Sauce (page 242), Veal Rolls in Tomato Sauce (page 265), Chicken Fricassee with Green Peppers and Tomatoes (page 309), Sautéed Calf's Liver with Onions, Venetian Style (page 296), or Fried Breaded Calf's Liver (page 298).

Gnocchi verdi in brodo
GREEN GNOCCHI IN BROTH

If you have very good homemade broth on hand, made from beef, veal, and/or chicken, you can make a delicious and elegant soup with green *gnocchi*. Served as soup, *gnocchi* go quite a bit further, so calculate about 6 ample servings, using the same quantity of *gnocchi* produced with the basic recipe.

For 6 persons

> 2 quarts homemade broth
> Spinach and Ricotta Gnocchi (page 200)

Bring the broth to a boil. Drop in all the *gnocchi* and cook for 3 to 4 minutes after the broth has returned to a boil. Ladle into soup plates and serve with a bowl of freshly grated Parmesan cheese on the side.

MENU SUGGESTIONS

If the broth comes from meat boiled for the occasion, a platter of Mixed Boiled Meats (page 322) would be the ideal second course. Otherwise, follow the suggestions given for Green Gnocchi Gratinéed with Butter and Cheese (page 201). Especially indicated would be a substantial dish, such as Beef Braised in Red Wine Sauce (page 242).

Gnocchi verdi con sugo di pomodoro e panna
GREEN GNOCCHI WITH TOMATO AND CREAM SAUCE

For 4 persons

Tomato and Cream Sauce (page 163)	Spinach and Ricotta Gnocchi (page 200)
2 tablespoons salt	

1. Keep the sauce warm as you prepare the rest of the dish.

2. Bring 4 quarts of water to a boil. Add the salt, then the *gnocchi*, a few at a time. Three to four minutes after the water returns to a boil, retrieve the *gnocchi* with a slotted spoon, and place on a hot serving platter. Season with a little bit of sauce. Add more *gnocchi* to the boiling water, repeating the above procedure, until all the *gnocchi* are cooked and sauced. Pour any remaining sauce over the *gnocchi*, and serve immediately, with a bowl of freshly grated Parmesan cheese on the side.

MENU SUGGESTIONS

The perfect second course would be a roast of veal, either the Pan Roast of Veal (page 252) or the Rolled Stuffed Breast of Veal (page 254). Also suitable is the Pan-Roasted Chicken with Garlic, Rosemary, and White Wine (page 304) or Roast Chicken with Rosemary (page 306). Avoid any second course that is pungent or includes tomatoes.

POLENTA

For the past three centuries *polenta* has been the staff of life in much of Lombardy and all of Venetia, particularly in Friuli, that northern region of Venetia which arches toward Yugoslavia.

To call *polenta* a cornmeal mush is a most indelicate use of language. In country kitchens, *polenta* was more than food, it was a rite. It was made daily in an unlined copper kettle, the *paiolo*, which was always kept hanging at the ready on a hook in the center of the fireplace. The hearth was usually large enough to accommodate a bench on which the family sat, warming itself at the fire, making talk, watching the glittering cornmeal stream into the boiling kettle, encouraging the tireless stirring of the cook. When the *polenta* was done, there was a moment of joy as it was poured out in a steaming, golden circle on the beechwood top of the *madia*, a cupboard where bread and flour was stored. Italy's great nineteenth-century novelist, Alessandro Manzoni, described it as looking like a harvest moon coming out of the mist. The image is almost Japanese.

The uses of *polenta* are infinite, and although it is always listed among the first courses, it cannot be neatly labeled a First Course, Second Course, or Side Dish. It can be any of the three. When piping hot it can be eaten alone, with butter and cheese. Or it can accompany any stewed, braised, or roasted meat or fowl. With game birds it is divine. When it has cooled and hardened, it can be fried, broiled, or sliced and baked with a variety of fillings.

There are two basic types of *polenta* flour. One is fine-grained, the other coarse. The coarse-grained is the one used in these recipes because of its more interesting, robust texture. Some traditional Italian recipes tell you to stir *polenta* for an hour or even more. But with a modern stove this is completely unnecessary. In the method given below, 20 minutes' stirring after all the cornmeal has been added will produce absolutely perfect *polenta*.

BASIC METHOD FOR MAKING POLENTA

1 tablespoon salt	2 cups coarse-grained cornmeal

1. Bring 6½ cups of water to a boil in a large, heavy kettle.
2. Add the salt, turn the heat down to medium low so that the water is just simmering, and add the cornmeal in a very thin stream, stirring with a stout, long wooden spoon. The stream of cornmeal must be so thin that you can see the individual grains. A good way to do it is to let a fistful of cornmeal run through nearly closed fingers. Never stop stirring, and keep the water at a slow, steady simmer.
3. Continue stirring for 20 minutes after all the cornmeal has been added. The *polenta* is done when it tears away from the sides of the pot as you stir.

4. When done, pour the *polenta* onto a large wooden block or a platter. Allow it to cool first if you are going to slice it in preparation for subsequent cooking. Otherwise, serve it piping hot.

NOTE

It may happen that some of the *polenta* sticks to the bottom of the pot. Cover the bottom with water and let it soak for 25 minutes. The *polenta* will then wash away easily.

Polenta con la luganega
POLENTA WITH SAUSAGES

For 4 to 6 persons

2 tablespoons chopped yellow onion

3 tablespoons olive oil

3 tablespoons chopped carrot

3 tablespoons chopped celery

¼ pound sliced *pancetta*, cut into strips ½ inch wide

1 pound *luganega* sausage or other sweet sausage, cut into 3-inch lengths

1 cup canned Italian tomatoes, cut up, with their juice

Polenta (previous page)

1. Put the onion in a saucepan with the oil and sauté over medium heat until pale gold.

2. Add the carrot, celery, and *pancetta*. Sauté for 3 to 4 minutes, stirring frequently.

3. Add the sausages and cook for 10 minutes, always at medium heat, turning them from time to time.

4. Add the tomatoes and their juice and cook at a gentle simmer for 25 minutes, stirring from time to time. Cover the pan and transfer to a 200° oven to stay warm while you prepare the *polenta*.

5. When the *polenta* is done, pour it onto a large platter. Make a depression in the center and pour in the sausages and all their sauce. Serve immediately.

(continued)

This is a second course, but *polenta* takes the place of pasta or rice, so you can omit the first course. It is quite appropriate to precede this with a plate of mixed Italian cold cuts, such as prosciutto, good salami, and *mortadella*. Another excellent antipasto would be Peppers and Anchovies (page 37).

Polenta al burro e formaggio
POLENTA WITH BUTTER AND CHEESE

For 4 to 6 persons

Polenta (page 204), cooked with an additional ½ cup of water to keep it a little thinner	¼ pound butter 6 tablespoons freshly grated Parmesan cheese

Pour the *polenta* onto a warm platter and mix with the butter and cheese. Serve promptly.

In this case *polenta* is served as a first course, and may be followed by any meat or fowl. Particularly suitable are the roasts of lamb, pork, or chicken.

Polenta fritta
FRIED POLENTA

For 4 to 6 persons or more, depending on how it is used

Polenta (page 204)
Vegetable oil, enough to come ¾ inch up the side of a skillet

1. Prepare the *polenta* as directed in the basic recipe and allow it to cool completely and become firm. Divide it into four parts, then cut these into slices ½ inch thick. (The traditional way to cut *polenta* is with a tautly held thread.)

2. Heat the oil in a skillet over high heat. When the oil is very hot, slide in as many slices of *polenta* as will fit comfortably. Fry until a transparent, not colored, crust forms on one side, then turn them and do the other side. Transfer to paper towels to drain.

MENU SUGGESTIONS

Fried *polenta* is ideal as a component of the Mixed Fried Meats, Vegetables, Cheese, Cream, and Fruit (page 333). It can also accompany Sautéed Calf's Liver with Onions, Venetian Style (page 296), or any roasted meat or fowl. In this case, a soup rather than pasta or rice would be preferable as a first course.

Polenta col gorgonzola
POLENTA WITH GORGONZOLA

Polenta prepared in this manner is excellent as an antipasto or as a nourishing snack.

Polenta (page 204), allowed to cool and sliced as in Fried Polenta, above   **Gorgonzola or any ripe, tangy cheese**

1. Preheat the broiler to its maximum setting.

2. Toast the *polenta* slices under the broiler until they are a light, spotty brown on both sides. Spread the cheese on one side of the hot, toasted slices and serve immediately.

Polenta pasticciata

BAKED POLENTA WITH MEAT SAUCE

For 6 persons

Béchamel Sauce (page 28)   2 cups Meat Sauce, Bolognese
(see Step 2, below)   Style (page 127)
Polenta (page 204), allowed   ⅔ cup freshly grated Parmesan
to cool   cheese
                               1 tablespoon butter

1. Preheat the oven to 450°.

2. Make the béchamel, keeping it on the thin side by cooking it less. It should have the consistency of sour cream. Set aside.

3. Slice the cold *polenta* horizontally into 3 layers, each about ½ inch high. Watch both sides of the *polenta* mass as you cut to make sure you are slicing evenly.

4. Lightly butter an 11-inch *lasagne* pan. Cover with a layer of *polenta,* patching where necessary to cover uniformly.

5. Spread béchamel sauce over the *polenta,* then spread the meat sauce and sprinkle with Parmesan cheese. Cover this with another layer of *polenta* and repeat the operation, leaving just enough béchamel, meat sauce, and Parmesan cheese for a light topping over the next and final layer of *polenta.* Dot the top lightly with butter.

6. Bake in the uppermost level of the preheated oven for 10 to 15 minutes, until a light crust has formed on top. Remove from the oven and allow to settle for about 5 minutes before serving.

NOTE
You may prepare this entirely ahead of time up to the point the dish is ready for the oven. It may be refrigerated overnight, but it should be returned to room temperature before baking.

MENU SUGGESTIONS

Follow the ones given for Baked Green Lasagne with Meat Sauce (page 145), which this dish strongly resembles.

I Secondi

SECOND COURSES

WHILE Italian first courses owe their luxuriance to the fertile imagination of the home cook, the austerity of the second courses is the legacy of the hunter and the fisherman. Strike everything broiled or roasted from a list of Italian second courses and you would be left with a very brief list indeed. This should be no cause for regret, however. If the second courses were as exuberant as the pastas, an Italian meal would exhaust both our enjoyment and our digestion.

Next to broiling and roasting, sautéing and frying are the most important cooking methods, and they are all amply represented in this chapter.

The section on fish is relatively brief, which may startle anyone familiar with the excellence and (before polluted waters) the abundance of Italian fish. But while green beans, chicken, and even veal may give roughly the same results here that they do in Italy, there is very little in American waters that resembles Italian fish. Not one of our species of shellfish coincides with an Italian one. No matter what you might read in restaurant menus, there are no *scampi* here. Also missing are other delectable crustaceans such as *mazzancolle, langostini,* and *cannocchie.* Very tiny shrimps do exist but are rarely seen fresh in the markets. We do not have the tiny, peppery clams of the Adriatic, or the sweet succulent ones of the

209

Tyrrhenian. We do not have sea dates or sea truffles, or miniature squid and cuttlefish, or the small red mullet. And we have nothing that can approach the Adriatic sole, the world's finest flat fish.

Some of the varieties of ocean fish, however, do lend themselves to an Italian taste in cooking. The finest local fish in my opinion is the striped bass. There is a beautiful recipe for baked striped bass stuffed with shellfish and sealed in foil that would not turn out any better with any Italian fish. Fresh young halibut and red snapper are other excellent fish for which specific recipes are given. There is a general recipe for broiling fish that will give an Italian flavor to the fish already mentioned, as well as to such other varieties as sea bass, porgy, and pompano. For the adventurous, and for those who already know it and like it, there is a brief section on squid. Local squid is not very different from large Italian squid, and the recipes included here should give very happy results. Fish soup is, by definition, a collection of what fish is available. There is a recipe for it in this chapter that should be successful wherever you might be, as long as it is close to a source of good salt-water fish.

The quality of Italian meat is often, but unjustly, maligned. It is true that beef in the south and certain parts of the north can be perfectly terrible, but in those regions cattle is used first for labor, then for food. For meat the people raise lambs, and the delectable *abbacchi* of Rome or kids of Apulia can make one forget filet mignon. Lamb can be butchered at various ages, and the flavor and cooking methods vary accordingly. There are three substantially different lamb roasts in this chapter. One is for hothouse or baby lamb, which is nearly as young as Roman *abbacchio,* another is for slightly older spring lamb, and the third is for the more mature, generally available standard lamb.

There is superb beef in Italy, and it is found in Tuscany. Beef from Val di Chiana cattle can hold its own with Burgundy's Charolais, Japan's Wadakin, or our own Black Angus. The most famous cut of beef in Italy is Florence's T-bone steak, known as *fiorentina,* whose simple but special cooking method is given here. Piedmont also produces good beef, and the Beef Braised in Red Wine Sauce in this chapter is a Piedmontese specialty.

Piedmont, along with Lombardy, produces marvelous, milky veal. Italy's veal dishes are probably its best-known contribution to meat courses, and in this chapter there are, in fact, more recipes for veal than for any other meat. Veal when cut into *scaloppine* has its own special tempo of cooking. It is done very briefly, and at quick, high heat. Today there is far better veal being marketed in this country than ever before. With care in the buying and cooking, it is now possible to produce veal dishes of a very high order.

Italian chicken dishes have always had a universal appeal. They are uncomplicated, easygoing, and invariably charming. Here there are two simple roasts, a tasty, peppery broiled chicken, and two typically Italian fricassees with vegetables. Chicken and turkey breast fillets are very much an Italian specialty. You will find a clear and detailed explanation of a technique for making fillets that can be adapted for any recipe calling for chicken or turkey breasts. This is followed by three examples of how the technique is used in Italian cooking, including Bologna's famous turkey breast fillets with ham, cheese, and truffles.

Close to the end of the chapter, there is a section on variety meats. Those who already include them in their cooking will find some newly edited classic dishes, and some less familiar ones. Those who do not may look the other way, but they should be encouraged to give one of them a try, at least once.

Italians make an excellent open-faced omelet which is called a *frittata,* but they have kept the secret of it at home. Restaurant *frittata* is more often than not stiff and leathery, which has led travelers to conclude that Italians cannot cook eggs. In the last section of this chapter you will find a full explanation of the method—practically the opposite of that of a French omelet—and six excellent examples of *frittate.* If you follow the instructions carefully, you will find that a *frittata* can be every bit as delectable as an omelet, but with more of a country flavor. With a *frittata* it is easier to serve a number of people than with omelets, which are difficult to make with a large quantity of eggs. If you already know how to make omelets, learn how to make *frittate,* and your repertory will have been doubled.

Branzino al cartoccio con frutti di mare

BAKED STRIPED BASS AND SHELLFISH SEALED IN FOIL

This fish is stuffed with mussels, shrimp, and oysters, sealed in heavy foil, and oven braised. Its flesh remains extraordinarily juicy and becomes delicately flavored with a fresh sea fragrance. The ideal way to prepare it is to completely remove the bones while leaving the fish intact. At the table you'll then be able to cut it into neat, boneless slices, which makes it so much more attractive to serve and agreeable to eat. Here is how you do it:

There is a slit in the fish's belly made by the dealer when he cleans out its intestinal cavity. With a sharp knife extend this slit for the whole length of the fish from head to tail. This will expose the entire backbone, from the upper half of which extend the rib bones imbedded in the belly. Using your fingers and a small knife pry these rib bones loose and detach them. With the same technique, loosen the backbone, separating it from the flesh around it. Now carefully bend the head, snapping off the backbone at that end, then do the same with the tail. At this point you will be able to lift away the entire backbone. If you don't feel up to doing this yourself, you should be able to persuade your fish dealer to do it for you. But make sure he slits open the fish on only one side, the belly side.

If you wish, you can substitute red snapper for the striped bass.

For 6 persons

12 mussels, cleaned as directed on page 56	2 tablespoons thinly sliced yellow onion
6 medium or 12 tiny shrimps	Juice of 1 medium lemon
6 oysters, unshelled	2½ teaspoons salt
2 tablespoons chopped parsley	Freshly ground pepper, 5 or 6 twists of the pepper mill
2 cloves garlic, lightly crushed with a heavy knife handle and peeled	1 striped bass or red snapper (3 to 3½ pounds), boned as directed above
½ cup olive oil	
⅓ cup fine, dry unflavored bread crumbs	

1. Put the mussels in a covered pan over high heat until their shells open, just a few minutes. Detach the mussels from their shells and put them in a mixing bowl large enough to hold all the ingredients except the fish. Strain the juices from the mussels left in the pan into the mixing bowl, using a sieve lined with a thickness of paper towel.

2. Peel and devein the shrimp. Wash them thoroughly in cold water and pat dry. If they are extra large, slice them in half lengthwise. Drop them into the mixing bowl.

3. Shuck the oysters and add them and their juices to the mixing bowl. Add all the other ingredients, except for the fish, to the bowl. Mix thoroughly, but not roughly, so as not to bruise the shellfish.

4. Preheat the oven to 475°.

5. Wash the fish in cold running water inside and out. Pat thoroughly dry with paper towels.

6. Spread a double thickness of heavy-duty aluminum foil on the bottom of a long, shallow baking dish, remembering that the piece of foil must be large enough to close over the fish at all points. Spread some of the liquid from the mixture in the bowl on the bottom of the foil. Place the fish in the center and stuff it with all the ingredients from the bowl, reserving some of the liquid, with which you will now coat the outside of the fish. Fold the foil over the fish and seal it tightly with a double lengthwise fold, making sure the corners are tightly tucked in. Place in the upper third of the oven and bake for about 40 minutes. When cooked the fish will be very tender and soaked in cooking juices.

7. Allow the fish to rest 10 minutes in the sealed foil, then place the whole package on a serving platter. (Unveiling the fish at the table can be very dramatic, but it can also be quite messy. Don't do it unless you have a little serving table on the side. Also, don't lift the fish out of the foil, because it has no bones and will break up.) Cut the foil open and trim it with scissors down to the edge of the platter. Bring the fish to the table whole and slice it as you would a roast.

(*continued*)

MENU SUGGESTIONS

You can build a very fine fish dinner around this dish. For antipasti you can start with the Cold Salmon Foam (page 33), the Herb-Flavored Seafood Salad (page 421), or the Tomatoes Stuffed with Tuna and Capers (page 38). Choose a first course with *pesto*, either Trenette with Potatoes and Pesto (page 142) or Potato Gnocchi (page 195). No vegetable side dish is required. Follow the fish with a green salad, or a Green Bean Salad (page 412).

Pesce da taglio con salsa di prezzemolo
POACHED HALIBUT WITH PARSLEY SAUCE

For 4 persons

THE FISH:

½ medium yellow onion, sliced thin

1 stalk celery

2 or 3 sprigs parsley

1 bay leaf

⅛ teaspoon fennel seeds

1 cup dry white wine

½ teaspoon salt

2 pounds halibut, cut in one slice, bone removed

THE SAUCE:

1 tablespoon finely chopped yellow onion

2½ tablespoons butter

2 tablespoons olive oil

2 tablespoons finely chopped parsley

½ teaspoon finely chopped garlic

1 tablespoon chopped capers

2 teaspoons anchovy paste

2 teaspoons all-purpose flour dissolved in ½ cup broth or, with 1 bouillon cube, in ½ cup hot water

2 tablespoons red wine vinegar

Salt to taste

Freshly ground pepper, about 4 twists of the mill

THE GARNISH:

- 2 hard-boiled eggs, sliced
- 1 lemon, sliced into ¼-inch disks
- Parsley leaves

Gherkins, sliced lengthwise but left whole at one end so they can be fanned out

1. Put the sliced onion, the celery stalk, parsley sprigs, bay leaf, fennel seeds, white wine, salt, and 1 quart water in a deep saucepan. Bring to a boil and let bubble at a moderate pace for about 15 minutes. There must be enough liquid to cover the fish; if you feel it is insufficient, add more water. Meanwhile, wash the fish in cold water and pat dry. When the poaching liquid has bubbled for 15 minutes, add the fish, cover the pan, and cook at a slow simmer for 10 to 12 minutes. Turn off the heat, but don't remove the fish from the pan. Let it sit in the poaching liquid while you prepare the sauce.

2. In a small saucepan sauté the chopped onion, with 1½ tablespoons of the butter and all the oil, over medium heat until translucent but not browned. Add the chopped parsley, garlic, capers, and anchovy paste. Stir well and sauté lightly for a few moments. Add the flour-broth mixture a tablespoon at a time, stirring thoroughly, then add the vinegar. Stir and keep at a moderate boil for 2 minutes. Taste and correct for salt, then add the pepper. Off the heat, swirl in the remaining tablespoon of butter.

3. Remove the fish from the pan, lifting it carefully so that it doesn't break up (try using two metal spatulas), and place it on a warm serving platter. Pour the sauce over it and garnish with hard-boiled egg slices, lemon slices topped with parsley leaves, and fanned-out sliced gherkins. Serve immediately.

MENU SUGGESTIONS

For antipasto, Cold Salmon Foam (page 33) or the Oysters with Parmesan Cheese (page 33). First course, a Risotto with Clams (page 192), or the Fettuccine with White Clam Sauce (page 135). No vegetable side dish, just a green salad after the fish.

Sgomberi in tegame con rosmarino e aglio

PAN-ROASTED MACKEREL WITH ROSEMARY AND GARLIC

In the small fishing towns along the Adriatic coast this is a very popular way of cooking mackerel; the slow cooking in oil keeps its firm flesh tender and juicy and the subdued taste of rosemary and garlic make mackerel's robust flavor gentler and very appealing.

For 4 persons

⅓ cup olive oil
4 cloves garlic, peeled
4 mackerel (about ¾ pound each), cleaned but with heads and tails on
1 three-inch sprig fresh rose-

mary or 1 teaspoon dried rosemary, crumbled
Salt and freshly ground pepper to taste
Juice of ½ lemon
Lemon wedges

1. Wash the mackerel under cold running water and pat dry.
2. Heat the oil in a casserole and lightly sauté the garlic.
3. Add the mackerel and rosemary and lower the heat to medium. Brown the fish well on each side but take care that it doesn't stick to the pan. (Should it stick, be careful as you turn it so it doesn't break up.) Season each side with salt and pepper.
4. When the fish is nicely browned add the lemon juice, cover with a tight-fitting lid, turn the heat down to low, and cook slowly for approximately 15 minutes, or until tender. Serve piping hot, with wedges of lemon on the side.

MENU SUGGESTIONS

As a first course, Clam Soup (page 53), Thin Spaghetti with Red Clam Sauce (page 100), Thin Spaghetti with Anchovy and Tomato Sauce (page 101), or Risotto with Clams (page 192). No vegetables. Follow the fish with Mixed Salad (page 408), or Zucchini Salad (page 415).

Pagello con i funghi trifolati
RED SNAPPER WITH SAUTÉED MUSHROOMS

In this recipe the fish is slowly simmered in wine and broth with a flavor base of sautéed vegetables, anchovy, parsley, and bay leaves. It is then combined with mushrooms sautéed in the classic Italian manner with oil, garlic, and parsley. Although the flavorings in this dish are numerous, they are used in minuscule quantities, and are calculated to set off rather than cloak the delicacy and sweetness of the fish.

For 4 persons

THE SAUTÉED MUSHROOMS:

3 tablespoons olive oil
½ teaspoon chopped garlic
½ pound crisp, fresh mushrooms

3 teaspoons chopped parsley
¼ teaspoon salt

THE FISH:

3 tablespoons olive oil
1 tablespoon butter
2 tablespoons finely chopped yellow onion
2 tablespoons finely chopped carrot
1 large clove garlic, lightly crushed with a heavy knife handle and peeled
1 teaspoon chopped flat anchovy fillet
2 teaspoons chopped parsley
½ bay leaf, crumbled
⅓ cup dry white wine

1 red snapper (2 to 2½ pounds), cleaned, scaled, and washed, but with head and tail left on
1 teaspoon salt
Freshly ground pepper, 4 to 6 twists of the mill
½ cup Homemade Meat Broth (page 10) OR ¼ cup canned beef broth mixed with ¼ cup water OR ½ bouillon cube dissolved in ½ cup warm water

1. Using the ingredients listed above, prepare and cook the mushrooms as directed on page 379. Set aside after cooking.

(*continued*)

2. In a skillet just large enough for the fish, put the olive oil, butter, onion, and carrot. Cook over medium-low heat until the onion is translucent but not browned.

3. Add the garlic and chopped anchovy. Cook, stirring, for a minute or two, until the anchovy has dissolved and the garlic has released some of its fragrance; then add the parsley and cook long enough to stir everything once or twice.

4. Add the bay leaf and the wine. Cook, stirring frequently, until the wine has evaporated by half.

5. Add the red snapper, half the salt and pepper, and all the broth, and put a cover on the skillet, setting it slightly askew. Cook, keeping the heat always at medium low, and after about 10 minutes, slightly longer if the fish is larger, turn the fish over carefully (possibly using two metal spatulas) so that it stays intact, and add the rest of the salt and pepper. After it has cooked another 10 minutes on the second side, add the mushroom mixture, drained of its oil. Cover the pan and let the mushrooms and fish cook together for no more than a minute. Serve piping hot.

MENU SUGGESTIONS

Antipasto to precede this dish could be Baked Oysters with Oil and Parsley (page 32), Cold Salmon Foam (page 33), or Shrimps with Oil and Lemon (page 39). Avoid the ones that are very salty or highly flavored. As a first course after the antipasto, an excellent choice would be Fettuccine with White Clam Sauce (page 135), spaghetti with the same sauce or with Red Clam Sauce (page 100), or Risotto with Clams (page 100). No vegetable accompaniment is required. Follow the fish with Mixed Salad (page 408).

Filetti di sogliola con pomodoro e capperi
FILLET OF SOLE WITH PIQUANT TOMATO SAUCE

I am not very fond of American sole, and the reason is that it isn't really sole, it is flounder. Flounder has none of the firm, compact texture of true sole, and only a trace of its delicate taste. Crisply fried Adriatic sole is simply one of the best things it is possible to eat, but I wouldn't try it with flounder. The best one can do with flounder is to take the edge off its awkwardness through the graces of a seductive sauce. The following version relies on the unabashed charms of a tangy tomato sauce, and, if you are partial to sole, you'll find it works quite well.

For 6 persons

⅔ cup thinly sliced yellow onion

5 tablespoons olive oil

1½ teaspoons finely chopped garlic

1 teaspoon orégano

2 tablespoons very tiny capers, or larger capers roughly chopped

1 cup canned Italian tomatoes, cut up, with their juice

Salt to taste

Freshly ground pepper, about 6 twists of the mill

2 pounds fresh sole fillets, preferably grey sole

1. Put the sliced onion in a skillet with the olive oil and cook over medium heat until soft and pale gold in color. Add the garlic, and when it has colored lightly add the orégano and capers, stirring once or twice. Add the cut-up tomatoes and their juice, salt, and pepper. Stir well and cook at a steady simmer for 15 to 20 minutes, or until the tomatoes and the oil separate.

2. Preheat the oven to 450°.

3. Rinse the fish fillets in cold water and blot dry. The fillets are going to be arranged in a single layer in a baking dish, folded over end to end and slightly overlapping. Choose a bake-and-serve dish just large enough for the job, and smear the bottom with about a table-

spoon of the tomato sauce. Dip each fillet on both sides in the sauce in the skillet, then fold it and arrange it in the baking dish as directed above. Pour the remaining sauce over the fillets, and place the dish in the uppermost level of the oven. Cook for no more than 5 to 8 minutes, depending upon the thickness of the fillets. (Don't overcook, or the fish will become dry.)

4. When you remove the dish from the oven you may find that the fish has thrown off liquid, thinning out the sauce. If this happens, tilt the dish and spoon all the sauce and liquid into a small pan. Boil it rapidly until it is sufficiently concentrated, then pour it back over the fish. Serve immediately.

MENU SUGGESTIONS

The first course could be Risotto with Clams (page 192), Fettuccine with White Clam Sauce (page 135), or Spaghetti with Garlic and Oil (page 103). If you want an antipasto, serve Shrimps with Oil and Lemon (page 39). Follow the fish with Mixed Salad (page 408) or Green Bean Salad (page 412).

Trota marinata all'arancio
COLD SAUTÉED TROUT IN ORANGE MARINADE

Long ago Italian lakes and rivers were busy with trout and other delicious small fish. A day's catch used to result in a large mess of fried fish for dinner, and marinating it was a genial way to cope with the leftovers. Fish treated this way is so remarkably good that soon people started to fry it especially for the purpose of marinating it.

There are many widely different marinades. The one most frequently published is the one in which garlic, vinegar, and herbs are the principal ingredients. It is very popular, but I find it rather aggressive. The marinade given here is elegantly flavored with orange, lemon, and vermouth. It settles fragrantly but gently into the delicate flesh of trout, perch, or other fresh-water fish.

For 6 persons

3 trout, perch, or other fresh-
water fish (about ¾ pound
each), cleaned and scaled,
but with heads and tails
left on

½ cup olive oil

½ cup or less all-purpose
flour, spread on a dish or
on waxed paper

2 tablespoons finely chopped
yellow onion

1 cup dry white Italian
vermouth

2 tablespoons chopped orange
peel

½ cup freshly squeezed orange
juice

Juice of 1 lemon

1 tablespoon salt

Freshly ground black pepper,
about 6 twists of the mill

1½ tablespoons chopped parsley

Unpeeled orange slices
(optional)

1. Wash the trout in cold water and pat dry thoroughly with paper towels.

2. Heat the oil in a skillet over medium heat. When the oil is hot, dip both sides of the trout lightly in flour and slip into the skillet. (If all the trout won't fit into the skillet at one time, dip in flour just the ones you are ready to fry.)

3. Brown the fish well on one side, then on the other, calculating about 5 minutes for the first side and 4 minutes for the other. Transfer the fish to a deep dish large enough to contain them in a single layer. Reserve the oil in the skillet.

4. With a very sharp knife, make two or three small diagonal cuts in the skin on both sides of each fish. Be careful not to tear the skin apart, and do not cut into the flesh.

5. Put the chopped onion in the skillet in which you fried the fish and sauté it in the same oil, over medium heat, until pale gold. Add the vermouth and the orange peel and let the vermouth boil for 15 or 20 seconds. Stir, then add the orange juice, lemon juice, salt, and pepper. Let everything bubble for about 30 seconds, stirring two or three times. Add the chopped parsley, stir again once or twice, then pour the entire contents of the skillet over the trout.

6. Plan to serve the trout no earlier than the following day. Let

the fish soak in the marinade for at least 6 hours at room temperature, then refrigerate. (They will keep in the refrigerator for 3 to
4 days; after that they lose their fresh taste.) Take them out sufficiently ahead of time to serve them at room temperature. If you
like, you may garnish them with unpeeled orange slices.

MENU SUGGESTIONS

This is a fine antipasto for an elegant fish dinner. It can be
followed by Fettuccine with White Clam Sauce (page 135) or
Trenette with Potatoes and Pesto (page 142), and then by Fish
Broiled the Adriatic Way (page 224), or Baked Striped Bass and
Shellfish Sealed in Foil (page 212).

You can also promote the trout to a second course, preceded by
Cold Salmon Foam (page 33), and/or Potato Gnocchi (page 195)
with Genoese Basil Sauce for Pasta and Soup (page 139), or
Velvety Clam Soup with Mushrooms (page 54). Follow with Green
Bean Salad (page 412) or Mixed Salad (page 408).

Salame di tonno

TUNA SALAMI

In this recipe tuna is combined with mashed potatoes and eggs
to form a salami-like roll, which is then slowly simmered with
vegetables, herbs, and white wine. It is served cold, sliced, with a
caper and anchovy mayonnaise. The tuna completely loses its
tinned, salty taste and acquires an elegance of texture and flavor
that is pointed up but not overwhelmed by the seasonings.

For 6 persons

1 medium potato	1 whole egg plus 1 white
2 seven-ounce cans imported Italian tuna packed in olive oil, drained	Freshly ground pepper, about 6 twists of the mill
¼ cup freshly grated Parmesan cheese	Cheesecloth

THE FLAVORED BROTH:

½ medium yellow onion, sliced thin

1 stalk celery

1 carrot

6 parsley sprigs, stems only

Salt

1 cup dry white wine

A MAYONNAISE (PAGE 26) MADE WITH:

1 egg yolk

2 tablespoons lemon juice

⅔ cup olive oil

½ teaspoon salt

WHEN THE MAYONNAISE IS MADE, INCORPORATE THE FOLLOWING:

2 tablespoons chopped capers

¼ teaspoon anchovy paste

Sliced black olives

1. Boil the potato, unpeeled, until it is tender. Drain, peel, and mash through a potato ricer or food mill.

2. Mash the tuna in a bowl. Add the grated cheese, the whole egg plus the egg white, the pepper, and the mashed potato.

3. Moisten a piece of cheesecloth, wring it until it is just damp, and lay it out flat on the work counter. Place the tuna mixture at one end of the cloth, shaping it into a salami-like roll about 2½ inches in diameter. Wrap it in the cheesecloth, covering it with at least two layers. Tie the ends securely with string.

4. Put the sliced onion, celery stalk, carrot, parsley stems, ½ teaspoon salt, and the wine in a saucepan or oval casserole, together with the tuna roll. Add enough water to cover by about 1 inch. Cover the pot and bring to a boil. When it reaches a boil, adjust the heat so that it cooks at the gentlest of simmers. Cook for 45 minutes.

5. When cooked, remove the tuna roll and, as soon as you can handle it, unwrap it gently. Set aside to cool completely.

6. While the tuna loaf is cooling, make a mayonnaise with the egg yolk, lemon juice, olive oil, and ½ teaspoon salt, according to the directions on page 26. Incorporate the chopped capers and anchovy paste.

7. Cut the cold tuna roll into slices ⅜ inch thick. Arrange the slices

on a platter, overlapping them very slightly. Cover the slices with the caper- and anchovy-flavored mayonnaise and garnish with black olive slices running the length of the platter, over the center of each slice of tuna.

MENU SUGGESTIONS

This is a very attractive dish for a buffet. It can also be combined with a salad to make a very light meal for a hot summer day, and it can be presented as a lovely antipasto before Fish Broiled the Adriatic Way (see below).

Pesce ai ferri alla moda dell'Adriatico
FISH BROILED THE ADRIATIC WAY

Broiling fish over a charcoal or wood fire is the favorite way of doing fish along the Adriatic. Before broiling, the fish is steeped in a marinade of olive oil, lemon juice, salt, and bread crumbs for an hour or more. This not only enhances the flavor of the fish, but keeps it from drying out while cooking.

For 4 persons

2½ to 3 pounds fish, either whole,
    with head and tail left on,
    or thick slices of larger fish
2 teaspoons salt
¼ cup olive oil
2 tablespoons lemon juice
6 tablespoons fine, dry
    unflavored bread crumbs

½ teaspoon rosemary (optional;
    for use only on such dark-
    fleshed fish as mackerel
    or bluefish)
1 or 2 bay leaves (optional)
Lemon wedges

1. If you are using a whole fish, scale and clean it, wash it in cold water, and dry it thoroughly on paper towels.

2. Salt the fish on both sides, put it on a platter, and add the olive oil and lemon juice. Turn the fish two or three times to coat it well.

Add the bread crumbs, turning the fish again until it is well coated. If you are preparing a dark-fleshed fish, add the rosemary. Marinate for 1 to 2 hours at room temperature, turning and basting the fish from time to time. Save the marinade.

3. If you are doing the fish in the broiler, preheat it to the maximum at least 15 minutes before cooking. If you are doing the fish over charcoal, the fire must also be ready 15 minutes ahead of time. Throw a bay leaf or two in the fire just before setting the fish on the charcoal grill.

4. Put the fish on the grill at a distance of 4 to 5 inches from the source of heat. Broil on both sides, until done. (Cooking times vary greatly, depending on the thickness of the fish and the intensity of the heat. You must learn to judge it time by time. A 3-pound striped bass, for example, should be done in about 20 minutes. Do not overcook or it will become dry, nor undercook, because partly done fish is most disagreeable. The flesh should come away easily from the bone and show no traces of translucent, raw pink color.) Baste the fish occasionally while it broils with the leftover marinade. Serve piping hot, with lemon wedges.

MENU SUGGESTIONS

You can precede broiled fish with any pasta or rice with a seafood sauce. Other suggestions for a first course: Mussel Soup (page 56), Clam Soup (page 53), or Velvety Clam Soup with Mushrooms (page 54), Cold Vegetable Soup with Rice Milan Style (page 68), Thin Spaghetti with Anchovy and Tomato Sauce (page 101), Spaghetti with Genoese Basil Sauce for Pasta and Soup (page 139), or Trenette with Potatoes and Pesto (page 142), Spaghetti with Garlic and Oil (page 103), or Spaghetti with Tomato Sauce III (page 95). You can accompany it, if you like, with Diced Pan-Roasted Potatoes (page 387), but with no other vegetables. Follow with any raw salad or with the Zucchini Salad (page 415). If you'd like an antipasto, choose among Shrimps with Oil and Lemon (page 39), Herb-Flavored Seafood Salad (page 421), or Baked Oysters with Oil and Parsley (page 32).

Spiedini di gamberi dell'Adriatico

SHRIMP BROCHETTES, ADRIATIC STYLE

I have tasted many versions of this very simple dish in seafood and Italian restaurants here, but I have never come across any that recall the delicate balance of flavors and the juicy texture of the shrimps that fishermen cook all along the Adriatic. You must start, of course, with very good-quality shrimps from a reputable fish market, fresh if possible. Do not try to make do with the bags of frozen shrimps from the supermarket freezer. Aside from the shrimps, however, the success of this dish depends upon how you apply the coating of oil and bread crumbs. There must be just enough oil to coat the shrimps, but not so much as to drench them. There must be enough bread crumbs to retain the oil and to form a light protective covering over the delicate flesh, but not so much as to bury the shrimps under a thick, gross crust. Follow the proportions indicated below, but bear in mind that the quantities are approximate. If you use larger shrimps you will need less oil and crumbs because there is less total surface per pound to be coated. Also, some bread crumbs go further than others, depending upon how absorbent they are. An essential ingredient is your good judgment.

For 6 persons

1½ pounds small shrimps	2 teaspoons finely chopped
3½ tablespoons olive oil	parsley
3½ tablespoons vegetable oil	¾ teaspoon salt
⅔ cup fine, dry unflavored	Freshly ground pepper, 5 or
bread crumbs	6 twists of the mill
½ teaspoon very finely chopped	Lemon wedges
garlic	

1. Preheat the broiler to its maximum setting. (The broiler must be heated at least 15 minutes before the shrimps are to be cooked.)

2. Shell and devein the shrimps. Wash in cold water and pat thoroughly dry with paper towels.

3. Put the shrimps in a comfortably large mixing bowl. Add as much of the two oils (mixed in equal parts) and of the bread crumbs as you need to obtain an even, light, creamy coating on all the shrimps. (Do not add it all at once because it may not be necessary, but if you are working with very tiny shrimps, you may need even more. In that case, always use 1 part olive oil to 1 part vegetable oil.) When the shrimps are well coated, add the chopped garlic, parsley, salt, and pepper and mix well. Allow the shrimps to steep in the marinade for at least 20 minutes at room temperature.

4. Have ready some flat, double-edged skewers. Skewer the shrimps lengthwise, 5 or more shrimps per brochette, depending upon the size. As you skewer each shrimp, curl and bend one end inward so that the skewer goes through the shrimp at three points. This is to make sure that the shrimps won't slip as you turn the skewer.

(continued)

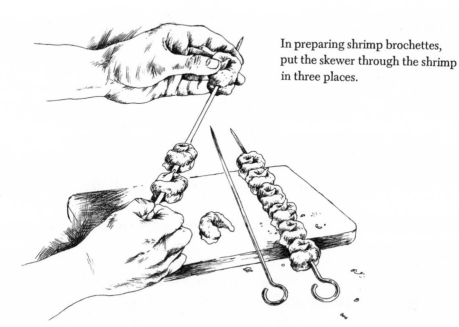

In preparing shrimp brochettes, put the skewer through the shrimp in three places.

5. These shrimps require brisk, rapid cooking. Wait until the broiler has been on for 15 minutes. Cook the shrimps no more than 3 minutes on one side and 2 minutes on the other, and even less if the shrimps are very small. Each side is done as soon as a crisp, golden crust forms.

6. Serve piping hot, on the skewers, with lemon wedges on the side.

MENU SUGGESTIONS

Very tiny shrimps broiled in this manner are a frequent part of Italian "shore dinners," served together with a mixture of broiled and fried fish. American shrimps are frequently sufficiently large to suffice as a course of their own. The dish can be preceded by a Risotto with Clams (page 192), Clam Soup (page 53), Mussel Soup (page 56), or Trenette with Potatoes and Pesto (page 142). Generally no vegetable is served with it, but the Sautéed Mushrooms with Garlic and Parsley (page 379) can be a very agreeable accompaniment. Follow the shrimp with Mixed Salad (page 408).

Calamari

SQUID

It is odd how New Englanders, who consume clams by the ton, dread the thought of eating another excellent mollusk, the squid. Actually, the flesh of the squid, when properly cooked, is far more delicate and tender than most clams. It is no accident that fish-loving countries from Italy to Japan regard the squid and its numerous relatives as one of the sea's most delectable offerings. If you are open minded about experimenting with food, you will be well rewarded by the taste of squid.

The squid most commonly available here corresponds to the large Italian squid, *Calamari* and *calamaroni*. Its sac, exclusive of tentacles, measures from 3½ inches to 6 or 7 inches in length. It is available either fresh or frozen, and both are good. In Italy, freshly caught large squid is kept in the refrigerator one or two days before cooking, to relax its rigid flesh. In this country it is probably already that old before it reaches the market. Use squid only when it is a pure, milky white in color. The tastiest, sweetest squid, whether fresh or frozen, comes to the markets in early spring.

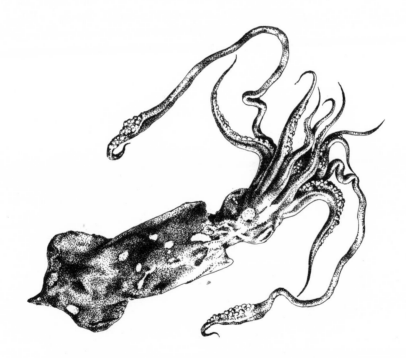

HOW TO CLEAN SQUID

Your dealer will clean squid if you ask him, but he rarely does a thorough job. It is much better to do the whole thing at home rather than to pick up where he has left off.

Hold the sac in one hand, and, with the other, firmly but gently pull off the tentacles. If you are not too abrupt, all the contents of the sac should come away attached to the tentacles. Cut the tentacles above the eyes, reserve the tentacles, and discard everything else from the eyes down.

Remove the quill-like bone from the sac, and thoroughly wash out the inside of the sac, removing anything it may still contain. Peel off the sac's outer skin, which comes off quite easily if the job is done under cold running water. Also under running water, peel off as much of the skin on the tentacles as will come off.

Rinse both sac and tentacles in several changes of cold water, until the water runs clear. Dry thoroughly. The squid is now ready for cooking.

Calamari e piselli alla livornese
STEWED SQUID WITH TOMATOES AND PEAS

For 4 to 6 persons

- 1½ tablespoons finely chopped yellow onion
- 3 tablespoons olive oil
- 1½ teaspoons finely chopped garlic
- 1 tablespoon finely chopped parsley
- ¾ cup canned Italian tomatoes, coarsely chopped, with their juice
- 2 pounds smallest possible squid, cleaned and prepared for cooking as directed above
- Salt and freshly ground pepper to taste
- 2 pounds fresh peas (unshelled weight) or 1 ten-ounce package frozen peas, thawed

1. Put the onion in a flameproof casserole with the olive oil and sauté over medium heat until it begins to turn pale gold. Add the garlic and sauté until it colors lightly but does not brown. Add the parsley, stir once or twice, then add the tomatoes. Cook at a gentle simmer for 10 minutes.

2. Slice the squid sacs into rings about ¾ inch to 1 inch wide. Divide the tentacle cluster into two parts. Add all the squid to the casserole; then add the salt and pepper, stir, cover, and cook at a gentle simmer for 30 minutes.

3. If you are using fresh peas, add them to the casserole at this time. Cover and continue cooking until the squid is tender, about another 20 minutes. (Cooking times, however, vary considerably, depending on the size and toughness of the squid, so test from time to time with a fork. When the squid is easily pierced, it is done.) If you are using thawed frozen peas, add them to the casserole when the squid is practically done, because they need only a few minutes' cooking. Taste and correct for salt and pepper before serving.

NOTE

This stewed squid can be prepared entirely ahead of time and refrigerated up to 2 days. Warm up slowly just before serving.

MENU SUGGESTIONS

Serve Broiled Mussels and Clams on the Half Shell (page 34), Peppers and Anchovies (page 37), or even some Shrimp Brochettes, Adriatic Style (page 226) as an antipasto. Skip the first course, because you will be sopping up lots of bread with the tasty sauce. No vegetables, of course. Follow with Shredded Carrot Salad (page 406).

Calamari ripieni stufati al vino bianco

STUFFED SQUID BRAISED IN WHITE WINE

For 6 persons

> 6 large squid (the sac
> should measure 4½ to 5
> inches, not including the
> tentacles)

THE STUFFING:

> 1 tablespoon olive oil,
> approximately
>
> 2 tablespoons finely chopped
> parsley
>
> ½ teaspoon finely chopped
> garlic, or more to taste
>
> 1 whole egg, lightly beaten

> 2½ tablespoons freshly grated
> Parmesan cheese
>
> ¼ cup fine, dry, unflavored
> bread crumbs
>
> ½ teaspoon salt
> Freshly ground pepper, about
> 6 twists of the pepper mill

THE BRAISING LIQUID:

> Olive oil, enough to come
> ¼ inch up the side of the
> skillet
>
> 4 whole cloves garlic, peeled

> ½ cup canned Italian tomatoes,
> coarsely chopped, with
> their juice
>
> ½ teaspoon finely chopped
> garlic
>
> ¼ cup dry white wine

1. Clean and prepare the squid as directed on page 230.
2. Chop the squid tentacles very fine. In a bowl, mix them with all the stuffing ingredients until you have a smooth, even mixture. There should be just enough olive oil in the mixture to make it slightly glossy. If it doesn't have this light surface gloss, add more olive oil.
3. Divide the stuffing into 6 equal parts and spoon it into the squid

sacs. (Do not overstuff, because the squid shrinks as it cooks and too much stuffing may cause it to burst.) Sew up each opening tightly with darning needle and thread—and be sure to put the needle safely away as soon as you are finished using it or it may disappear into the sauce.

4. Choose a skillet large enough to hold the squid in a single layer and coat the bottom with just enough olive oil to come ¼ inch up the side of the pan. Heat the oil over medium-high heat and sauté the garlic cloves until golden brown. Discard the garlic and put in the stuffed squid. Brown the squid well on all sides, then add the chopped tomatoes with their juice, the chopped garlic, and the wine. Cover tightly and cook over low heat for 30 to 40 minutes. The squid is done when it feels tender at the pricking of a fork.

5. Remove the squid to a cutting board and allow to settle for a few minutes. Slice away just enough from the sewn-up end to remove the thread and cut the rest into slices ½ inch thick. Arrange the slices on a warm serving platter so that each squid sac is recomposed. Warm up the sauce in the skillet, pour over the sliced squid, and serve immediately.

NOTE

This dish can be prepared 4 or 5 days ahead of time and refrigerated. Warm it up as follows: Preheat the oven to 300°. Transfer the squid and the sauce to a bake-and-serve dish, add 2 to 3 tablespoons of water, and place in the middle level of the oven. Turn and baste the slices as they warm up, being careful that they don't break up. Serve when warm.

MENU SUGGESTIONS

If you wish to serve a vegetable side dish with the squid, the most suitable would be steamed potatoes. It is quite sufficient, however, to serve Zucchini Salad (page 415) or mixed greens afterwards. It can be preceded by Fettuccine with White Clam Sauce (page 135), or Risotto with Clams (page 192). I have found that Bresaola (page 47), with its tart, clean taste, makes an ideal prelude to this rather robust dish.

Calamari fritti

FRIED SQUID

One of the most prized delicacies along the Adriatic is very tiny squid, often no more than 1½ inches long, fried whole in hot oil. They are incredibly tender and sweet, and, should you find yourself on the Adriatic coast, do not miss your chance to eat them. Although not quite so tender and delicate, our larger local squid can be very good indeed when fried, but it must first be cut up into rings.

For 4 persons

3 pounds squid	Salt
Vegetable oil, enough to come 1 inch up the side of the pan	Lemon wedges
1 cup all-purpose flour, spread on waxed paper or on a platter	

1. Clean the squid as directed on page 230, drying it thoroughly on paper towels. Cut the squid sacs into rings about ⅜ inch wide and separate the tentacle cluster into two parts. Make sure it is all very thoroughly dried.

2. Heat the oil over high heat.

3. When the oil is very hot, dip the squid in the flour, shake off the excess, and slip into the pan. Do not put in any more at one time than will fit loosely in the skillet. Cover the skillet with a spatter screen, since squid has a tendency to burst while frying.

4. As soon as the squid is fried to a tawny gold on one side, turn it. When both sides are done, transfer to paper towels to drain. Sprinkle with salt and serve with lemon wedges on the side.

Fried squid can be preceded by Broiled Mussels and Clams on the Half Shell (page 34), Herb-Flavored Seafood Salad (page 421), Clam Soup (page 53), or Thin Spaghetti or Fettuccine with White Clam Sauce (page 135), with Red Clam Sauce (page 100), or with Tuna Sauce (page 102). Follow with Mixed Salad (page 408) or Zucchini Salad (page 415).

Il brodetto di papi
MY FATHER'S FISH SOUP

Fish soup is one of the most ancient dishes of the Mediterranean. In Italy, every coast town has its own traditional version. On the Tuscan coast it is called *cacciucco,* on the Adriatic side it is called *brodetto* ("little broth"), and elsewhere simply *zuppa di pesce.* To describe every variety of *cacciucco* or *brodetto* would take a larger volume than this one because it changes not just from town to town but from family to family. One of the best soups I've ever tasted is my father's, for which he acquired a considerable reputation in his lifetime. It has the merit of achieving an over-all hearty flavor without the individual delicacy and character of each fish being overwhelmed. My father would use a large variety of small fish, nine or more different kinds, but in this country we have to make do with a smaller variety of larger fish. Ocean fish is quite different from that of the Adriatic, but this is no cause for despair. The very idea behind fish soup is that it can turn virtually any combination of fish into a succulent and satisfying dish. This particular soup does it as well as any I've ever tried.

You need at least 3 to 4 heads for this recipe, so buy as many small whole fish as you can find; otherwise, your fish dealer can probably supply you with a few heads. The greater the variety, the tastier and more interesting the soup becomes. If you use dark-fleshed, fatty fish such as mackerel, bluefish, or eel, it adds to the flavor of the soup, but use it in small quantities. I have been very successful with porgy, sea bass, red snapper, salmon, halibut, scrod, and striped bass. If you can find it, by all means include sculpin. American sole or flounder adds very little to the soup, and it always has a most disagreeably submissive consistency.

For 6 to 8 persons

3 to 4 pounds assorted fresh fish, cleaned and scaled

½ pound or more shrimps in their shells

1 pound squid, cleaned and prepared for cooking as directed on page 230

½ dozen littleneck clams

½ dozen mussels

3 tablespoons finely chopped yellow onion

6 tablespoons olive oil

1½ teaspoons chopped garlic

3 tablespoons chopped parsley

½ cup dry white wine

1 cup canned Italian tomatoes, cut up, with their juice

Salt

Freshly ground pepper, about 10 twists of the mill

1. Wash all the fish under cold running water. Cut off the heads and set aside. Cut the larger fish into slices 3 to 3½ inches wide and set aside. (Fish no longer than 6½ inches can be kept whole.) Wash the shrimps very thoroughly in cold water, but do not remove the shells. Set aside.

2. Divide the squid's tentacle cluster into 2 or 3 parts. Slice the sacs into rings 1 inch wide. Set aside.

3. Wash and scrub the clams and mussels very thoroughly, according to the directions on pages 53 and 56. Heat the clams and mussels in separate, covered pans over medium-high heat until they open. Remove the clams from their shells, filter their juices through a sieve lined with paper towels, and set aside. Remove the mussels from their shells. Tipping the pan, gently draw off with a spoon all but the bottom, murky part of the mussel juices and set aside.

4. Choose a skillet large enough to contain all the fish later in

one layer. Lightly sauté the onion in the olive oil over medium heat until translucent, then add the chopped garlic and continue sautéing until it colors lightly. Add the chopped parsley and stir two or three times, then add the wine and raise the heat to high. When the wine has boiled briskly for about 30 seconds, add the chopped tomatoes with their juice. Stir, turn the heat down to a gentle simmer, and cook for about 25 minutes, or until the tomatoes and oil separate.

5. Add the fish heads, ½ tablespoon salt and the ground pepper, then cover the pan and cook for 10 to 12 minutes over medium heat, turning the heads over after 5 or 6 minutes. Remove the heads from the pan and pass them through a food mill. Add the puréed heads to the pan, together with the sliced squid and their tentacles. Cover and cook at a slow, steady simmer for 30 or 40 minutes, or until the squid are tender and easily pierced by a fork. Add the fish, holding back the smallest and tenderest pieces for 1 or 2 minutes, then add another ½ tablespoon salt and all the juices from the clams and mussels. Cover and cook over medium heat for 10 minutes, turning and basting the fish once or twice. After 5 minutes' cooking add the whole, unshelled shrimps. Add the clams and mussels at the very last, giving them just enough time to warm up. Taste and correct for salt. Serve hot, with plenty of good country-style Italian bread for dunking into the broth.

NOTE

The ideal pot for *brodetto* is dark red earthenware. It cooks the soup to perfection and is charming to serve from at the table. If your pan is not suitable for serving, transfer the fish with some delicacy (otherwise it will break up into unattractive bits) to a hot, deep serving platter. Spoon all the sauce and shellfish over it.

MENU SUGGESTIONS

This is both soup and second course, a meal in itself. If you want to make more of an event out of it, precede it with Shrimp Brochettes, Adriatic Style (page 226), or Shrimps with Oil and Lemon (page 39), or Mushroom and Cheese Salad (page 47). Follow the soup with Green Bean Salad (page 412), or Zucchini Salad (page 415).

La fiorentina
STEAK BROILED THE FLORENTINE WAY

Beans and beef are Tuscany's most celebrated contributions to the Italian table. Even before the discovery of America, Florence was famous for its T-bone steak, known in Italy simply as a *fiorentina*. Although the particular flavor and texture of a *fiorentina* cannot be duplicated with any other meat but that of Tuscan-raised Val di Chiana beef, a fine American beefsteak, prepared the Florentine way, can be spectacularly good.

Nothing could be more straightforward than the preparation of a *fiorentina*, but it is often misunderstood outside of Tuscany, even by Italians. The error that is made most frequently is to marinate the steak in oil before broiling, which will make even the finest meat taste of tallow. Here is how the Florentines do it.

For 2 persons

½ teaspoon peppercorns, crushed in a mortar or inside a cloth with a heavy blunt object

1 T-bone steak, 1½ inches thick
Salt
Olive oil

1. Rub the peppercorns into both sides of the meat.

2. Broil the steak, over a very hot hardwood or charcoal fire, to the desired doneness. (A *fiorentina* should be very rare.) Salt the steak on the broiled side as you turn it.

3. When the steak is done, but while it is still on the grill, moisten it very lightly on both sides with a few drops of olive oil. Serve immediately.

MENU SUGGESTIONS

A *fiorentina* fits perfectly into any American steak dinner. In an Italian menu it might be preceded by any of the bean or chick-pea soups, by Pappardelle with Chicken-Liver Sauce (page 137),

Risotto with Parmesan Cheese (page 181), or, skipping the first course, by Artichokes Roman Style (page 337), or Fava Beans, Roman Style (page 359). The vegetable accompaniment (if you started with soup or pasta), can be Sautéed Peas with Prosciutto, Florentine Style (page 383), Sautéed Spinach (page 388), or Sliced Zucchini with Garlic and Tomatoes (page 394). In Florence, in the spring, the salad would be Green Bean Salad (page 412).

Bistecca alla diavola
PAN-BROILED STEAK WITH MARSALA AND HOT PEPPER SAUCE

While Italians may have anticipated by a few centuries Americans' predilection for steaks broiled over coals, they have not overlooked the virtues of pan-broiling. It often gives brilliant results, as in this fiery steak whose own cooking juices are turned into a peppery sauce with a little help from such Italian ingredients as Marsala, garlic, fennel seeds, tomato paste, and, of course, *peperoncino rosso*, hot red pepper.

For 4 persons

4 shell steaks or any other good steak cut (about 3 pounds), ¾ inch thick
¼ cup olive oil
Salt and freshly ground pepper to taste
½ cup dry Marsala
½ cup dry red wine
1½ teaspoons finely chopped garlic

1 teaspoon fennel seeds
1 tablespoon tomato paste diluted in 1 tablespoon water
¼ teaspoon chopped hot red pepper (see note below)
2 tablespoons chopped parsley

1. Choose a skillet large enough to accommodate the steaks in a single layer. Put in the olive oil, and tilt the pan in several directions so that the bottom is well coated. Heat the oil over high heat until

a haze forms over it, then put in the meat. Cook the steaks 3 minutes on one side, and 2 to 3 minutes on the other, for rare meat. Regulate the heat to make sure the oil doesn't burn. When done, transfer the steaks to a warm platter, and season with salt and pepper.

2. Tip the pan, and, with a spoon, remove all but 1½ to 2 tablespoons of fat. Turn on the heat again to high and add the Marsala and the red wine. Boil the wine for about 30 seconds, while scraping the pan with a wooden spoon to loosen any cooking residues.

3. Add the garlic, cook just long enough to stir 2 or 3 times, then add the fennel seeds and stir again for a few seconds.

4. Add the diluted tomato paste and the chopped red pepper. Turn the heat down to medium and stir-cook for about 1 minute, until the sauce is thick and syrupy.

5. Return the steaks to the pan, just long enough to turn them in the hot sauce. Transfer steaks and sauce to a hot platter, sprinkle the parsley over the meat, and serve immediately.

NOTE
Don't use the crushed red pepper in jars, unless you absolutely can't find the tiny, dried, whole red peppers. These are available at most Italian, Greek, or Latin American groceries.

MENU SUGGESTIONS

As a first course choose either vegetable *risotto* (pages 189–191), or Risotto with Parmesan Cheese (page 181), or Fusilli with Creamy Zucchini and Basil Sauce (page 106), or any of the stuffed pastas on pages 155–164 as long as they are not sauced with tomato or meat sauce. Or you can have a vegetable first course, such as Artichokes, Roman Style (page 337), or Baked Stuffed Zucchini Boats (page 395). If you are not having pasta, Potato Croquettes with Crisp-Fried Noodles (page 385) are a good accompaniment. Other vegetable suggestions: Zucchini Fried in Flour-and-Water Batter (page 392), Sautéed Green Beans with Butter and Cheese (page 361), and Gratinéed Jerusalem Artichokes (page 353).

Fettine di manzo alla sorrentina

THIN PAN-BROILED STEAKS WITH
TOMATOES AND OLIVES

This tasty southern dish utilizes thin slices of beef and can be quite successful with inexpensive cuts of meat. It takes 25 minutes or less if you start from scratch and no more than 5 minutes if the sauce has been prepared ahead of time.

For 4 persons

½ medium yellow onion, sliced thin

Olive oil, sufficient to come ¼ inch up the side of the pan

2 medium cloves garlic, peeled and diced

⅔ cup canned Italian tomatoes, roughly chopped, with their juice

1 dozen black Greek olives, pitted and quartered

¼ teaspoon orégano

Salt to taste

Freshly ground pepper, 6 to 8 twists of the mill

1 pound beef steaks, preferably chuck or chicken steaks, sliced ¼ inch thick, pounded, and edges notched to keep from curling

1. In a good-sized skillet (the broader the skillet, the faster the sauce will thicken), slowly sauté the sliced onion in the olive oil, letting it wilt gradually. As it takes on a pale gold color, add the diced garlic. Continue sautéing until the garlic has colored lightly, then add the tomatoes, olives, orégano, salt, and pepper. Stir and cook at a lively simmer until the tomatoes and oil separate, about 15 minutes or more. (The sauce may be prepared ahead of time up to this point.) Turn the heat down, keeping the sauce at the barest simmer.

2. Heat up a heavy iron skillet until it is smoking hot. Quickly grease the bottom with an oil-soaked cloth or paper towel. Put in

the beef slices and cook just long enough to brown the meat well on both sides. As you turn the meat, season it with salt and pepper. (Do not overcook or the thinly sliced steaks will become tough.) Transfer the browned meat first to the simmering sauce, turning it quickly and basting it with sauce, then to a hot platter, pouring the sauce over the meat. Serve immediately.

MENU SUGGESTIONS

An excellent first course would be Spaghetti with Garlic and Oil (page 103), or Baked Semolina Gnocchi (page 198). Avoid any pasta with either tomato or cream sauce. Escarole and Rice Soup (page 63), and the Rice and Lentil Soup (page 75) are also good choices for the first course. For the vegetable, Braised Artichokes and Peas (page 347) or Braised Artichokes and Leeks (page 348) would temper nicely the piquancy of the tomatoes and olives.

Stracotto al Barolo
BEEF BRAISED IN RED WINE SAUCE

For 6 persons

Vegetable oil

1 beef roast (4 pounds), preferably chuck

1 tablespoon butter

3 tablespoons coarsely chopped yellow onion

2 tablespoons coarsely chopped carrot

2 tablespoons coarsely chopped celery

1½ cups dry red wine (see note below)

1 cup Homemade Meat Broth (page 10) or canned beef bouillon, more if necessary

1½ tablespoons canned Italian tomatoes, chopped

A pinch of thyme

⅛ teaspoon marjoram

Salt and freshly ground pepper to taste

1. Preheat the oven to 350°.

2. Pour enough oil into a heavy, medium-sized skillet to just cover the bottom. Turn on the heat to moderately high, and when the oil is quite hot slip in the meat. Brown well on all sides. Transfer the meat to a platter and set aside.

3. Choose a casserole, with a tight-fitting lid, just large enough to contain the meat. Put in 2 tablespoons of vegetable oil, the butter, and the chopped vegetables, and over moderate heat sauté the vegetables lightly, stirring from time to time. The vegetables should wilt and color lightly, but should not brown. Turn off the heat and put in the well-browned meat.

4. Tip the skillet, and with a spoon draw off and discard as much of the fat as possible. Add the wine, turn the heat to high, and boil for less than a minute, scraping up and loosening the browning residue stuck to the pan. Add this to the meat in the casserole.

5. Add the broth or canned bouillon to the casserole. It should come two-thirds up the side of the meat; add more if it doesn't. Add the tomatoes, thyme, marjoram, salt, and pepper. Turn the heat to high and bring to a boil, then cover the pot and place it in the middle level of the preheated oven. Braise for about 3 hours, every 20 minutes or so turning the meat and basting it with its liquid, and making sure it is cooking at a steady, slow simmer. (If it is not, regulate the heat accordingly.) At times, either because the cover doesn't fit tightly or because of the texture of the meat, you'll find all the liquid has evaporated or been absorbed. If this happens before the meat is cooked, add 3 or 4 tablespoons of warm water. The meat is cooked when it feels very tender at the pricking of a knife or fork.

6. Remove the meat to a cutting board. If the cooking liquid is too thin and has not reduced to less than ⅔ cup, place the casserole on the stove and boil the liquid over high heat until it has thickened, loosening any residue that may be stuck to the pot. Taste the sauce, adding salt and pepper if necessary. Slice the meat and place on a warm platter, with the slices slightly overlapping. Pour all the sauce over the meat and serve promptly.

(continued)

NOTE

The ideal wine to use is Barbera or Barolo, which have the right amount of acidity combined with full-bodied flavor. If neither is available a good, stout California Pinot Noir will give excellent results.

MENU SUGGESTIONS

Any first course that is not too pungent in flavor, and does not have fish, can precede this substantial beef dish. All three varieties of *gnocchi* (pages 195, 198, and 200) are suitable, as are some of the more delicate pastas, such as Tortelloni Filled with Swiss Chard (page 164) and Fettuccine Tossed in Cream and Butter (page 130). Risotto with Parmesan Cheese (page 183), or either of the vegetable *risotti* (pages 189–191) are excellent. Or try the nice little Creamy Potato Soup with Carrots and Celery (page 58) or Lentil Soup (page 73). For vegetables, any of the butter and cheese ones will do, such as the Swiss Chard Stalks with Parmesan Cheese (page 370), or the fried vegetables, such as Crisp-Fried Whole Artichokes (page 344) or Fried Asparagus (page 358).

Il bollito rifatto con le cipolle
LEFTOVER BOILED BEEF WITH SAUTÉED ONIONS

The art of serving leftovers is not a highly developed one in Italy, perhaps because portions tend to be small and appetites large. An exception is this savory way to refurbish leftover boiled beef. It comes from Florence, where, from the time Florentines have been Florentines, nothing has ever been thrown away.

For 4 persons

3 cups thinly sliced yellow
    onions
¼ cup olive oil

1 pound boiled beef (approximately), cut into slices ⅜ inch thick
Salt

Freshly ground pepper, 4 to 6 twists of the mill

1 bouillon cube dissolved in ½ cup Homemade Meat Broth (page 10) or in ½ cup water

1 or 2 tablespoons leftover juices from any beef or veal roast (optional)

1. Put the sliced onions in a skillet with the olive oil and cook slowly over medium-low heat until a light brown color.

2. Add the sliced beef, 2 teaspoons salt, the pepper, broth, and the optional roasting juices. Cover the pan and cook at a gentle simmer for 10 minutes. Uncover, raise the heat to medium, and cook until the broth has completely evaporated. Taste and correct for salt. Serve piping hot.

NOTE

This method is also successful with leftover broiled steak.

MENU SUGGESTIONS

Precede this with hearty Chick-Pea Soup (page 85), or any of the good country soups such as Bean Soup with Parsley and Garlic (page 79), or Bean and Pasta Soup (page 80). Follow with a salad.

Polpette alla pizzaiola

BEEF PATTIES WITH ANCHOVIES AND MOZZARELLA

Although it is very far from being a national dish, Italians do eat "hamburger." This is particularly true of some areas of the south where the beef is rather tough and it is chopped to make it tender. The following version of "hamburger," in its frank, zesty taste, in the simplicity of its approach, and in its decorative appearance, is undeniably Italian.

(continued)

For 6 persons

1 3-by-3-inch piece white bread, crust removed	¼ cup vegetable oil
3 tablespoons milk	6 canned Italian tomatoes, opened flat, without seeds and juice
1½ pounds lean beef, preferably chuck, ground	1 teaspoon orégano
1 egg	6 slices mozzarella, 4 inches square, ¼ inch thick
Salt	
¾ cup fine, dry unflavored bread crumbs, spread on a dinner plate or on waxed paper	12 flat anchovy fillets

1. Preheat the oven to 400°.

2. In a saucer or small bowl, soak the bread in the milk and mash it to a cream with a fork. Put the meat in a bowl, add the bread and milk mush, the egg, and 1 teaspoon salt, and knead with your hands until all the ingredients are well mixed.

3. Divide the meat mixture into 6 patties 1½ inches high and turn them over in the bread crumbs.

4. Over medium heat, heat the oil in a skillet until the meat sizzles when it is slipped in. Add the meat patties and cook 4 minutes on each side, handling them delicately when you turn them over so they don't break up. When done, transfer to a butter-smeared baking dish.

5. Cover each patty with a flattened tomato, reserving a small strip of each tomato, no larger than ½ inch, to be used for garnish. Season lightly with salt and a pinch of orégano. Over each tomato place a slice of mozzarella, and over the mozzarella place two anchovy fillets in the form of a cross. Where the anchovies meet place the reserved strip of tomato. Put the dish in the upper-most level of the oven and bake for 15 minutes, or until the mozzarella melts.

NOTE

These patties can be prepared several hours ahead of time before they are put in the oven.

MENU SUGGESTIONS

The Split Green Pea and Potato Soup (page 72), Lentil Soup (page 73), Risotto with Parmesan Cheese (page 181), and Spaghetti with Fresh Basil and Tomato Sauce (page 97) are all good choices for the first course. An excellent vegetable accompaniment would be any of the ones sautéed with garlic, such as spinach (page 388), broccoli (page 363), mushrooms (page 379), eggplant (page 374), or Jerusalem artichokes (page 352).

Polpettine

MEATBALLS

For 4 persons

⅓ cup milk	3 tablespoons freshly grated
1 slice firm, fine-quality white	Parmesan cheese
bread, crust removed	Vegetable oil
1 pound lean beef, preferably	Salt
from the neck, ground	Freshly ground pepper, 3 to
1 tablespoon finely chopped	4 twists of the mill
yellow onion	Fine, dry unflavored bread
1 tablespoon chopped parsley	crumbs
1 egg	1 cup canned Italian tomatoes,
A tiny pinch of nutmeg or	cut up, with their juice
marjoram	

1. Put the milk and the bread in a saucepan and bring to a boil. Mash the bread with a fork and blend it uniformly into the milk. Set aside and let cool before proceeding with the next step.

2. In a mixing bowl put the chopped meat, onion, parsley, egg, nutmeg or marjoram, grated Parmesan, 1 tablespoon of oil, the bread and milk mush, 1 teaspoon of salt, and the pepper. Mix everything thoroughly but gently by hand.

3. Gently, without squeezing, shape the mixture into small round

balls about 1 inch in diameter. Roll the meatballs lightly in the bread crumbs.

4. Choose a skillet, large enough to hold all the meatballs in a single layer, with a cover. Pour in oil until it is ¼ inch deep. Turn on the heat to medium high, and when the oil is quite hot slip in the meatballs. (Sliding them in with a broad spatula is a good way of doing it. Dropping them in will splatter hot oil over you and your kitchen floor.) Brown the meatballs on all sides, turning them carefully so that they don't break up or stick to the pan.

5. When well browned turn off the heat, tip the pan slightly, and remove as much of the fat that floats to the surface as you can with a spoon. Turn on the heat to medium, add the chopped tomatoes with their juice and ¼ teaspoon of salt, and turn the meatballs over once or twice with care, so that they don't break up. Cover the skillet and cook until the tomato has thickened into sauce, about 25 minutes. While cooking, turn the meatballs over from time to time, and taste for salt.

NOTE

The meatballs can be prepared entirely ahead of time and refrigerated for several days.

MENU SUGGESTIONS

A Creamy Potato Soup with Carrots and Celery (page 58), Potato and Onion Soup (page 59), Rice and Celery Soup (page 62), or Escarole and Rice Soup (page 63) would be a good first course here. For vegetables serve Sautéed Peas with Prosciutto, Florentine Style (page 383), or any of the fried vegetables (pages 346, 358, 378, and 392).

Polpettone alla toscana

MEAT LOAF BRAISED IN WHITE WINE WITH DRIED WILD MUSHROOMS

This juicy and beautifully flavored meat loaf is from Tuscany, whose Chianina beef is the best in Italy. It should be made with a fine, lean cut of beef, all of whose fat has been removed before chopping. The loaf should be firmly packed, not loose and crumbly, so that when it is cooked it can be cut into thin, elegant, compact slices.

For 4 to 5 persons

1 ounce imported dried wild mushrooms

1 pound lean beef, ground

A 2-by-2-inch square piece good-quality white bread, crust removed

1 tablespoon milk

1 tablespoon finely chopped yellow onion

2 teaspoons salt

Freshly ground pepper, about 6 twists of the mill

2 tablespoons chopped prosciutto, or *pancetta*, or *mortadella*, or if you really can't obtain any of these, unsmoked ham

⅓ cup freshly grated Parmesan cheese

¼ teaspoon finely chopped garlic

1 egg yolk

¾ cup fine, dry unflavored bread crumbs, spread on a platter or waxed paper

1 tablespoon butter

2 tablespoons vegetable oil

⅓ cup dry white wine

2 tablespoons tomato paste

1. Put the dried mushrooms in a small bowl or large tumbler with 1 cup of lukewarm water. Let them soak at least 20 minutes.

2. Put the chopped meat in a bowl, loosening it up with a fork.

3. Put the bread and milk in a small pan. Over medium heat, mash it with a fork until it is creamy. Add it to the meat in the

bowl, along with the chopped onion, salt, pepper, chopped prosciutto, grated cheese, and chopped garlic. Mix gently but thoroughly by hand until all the ingredients have been incorporated into the meat. Add the egg yolk, mixing it into the other ingredients. Shape the meat into a single, firmly packed ball. Place the ball of meat on any flat surface, a cutting block or large platter, and roll it into a compact salami-like loaf about 2½ inches thick. Tap it with the palm of your hand to drive out any air bubbles. Roll the loaf in the bread crumbs until it is evenly coated.

4. Drain the mushrooms, reserving the water in which they have soaked. (Remember that they should have soaked at least 20 minutes.) Strain the dark liquid through a fine sieve lined with paper towels and set aside. Rinse the mushrooms in several changes of clean, cold water. Chop them roughly and set aside.

5. Choose a heavy-bottomed, preferably oval casserole, just large enough for the meat. Over medium heat, heat all the butter and oil. When the butter foam subsides, add the meat loaf and brown it well on all sides, handling the meat carefully at all times lest the loaf break up.

6. When the meat has been evenly browned, add the wine and raise the heat to medium high. Boil the wine briskly until it is reduced by half. Turn the loaf carefully once or twice.

7. Turn the heat down to medium low and add the chopped mushrooms. Warm up the strained mushroom liquid in a small pan and stir the tomato paste into it. When the tomato paste is thoroughly diluted, add to the meat. Cover and cook at a steady simmer, turning and basting the meat once or twice. After 30 minutes, set the cover slightly askew and cook for another 30 minutes, turning the meat at least once.

8. Transfer the meat loaf to a cutting board and allow to settle for a few minutes before cutting into slices about ⅜ inch thick. Meanwhile, if the sauce in the pot is a little too thin, boil it rapidly, uncovered, over high heat until it is sufficiently concentrated. Spoon a little bit of sauce over the bottom of a warm serving platter, arrange the meat loaf slices in the platter, partly overlapping, then pour the rest of the sauce over the meat.

This deserves a robust Tuscan soup as a first course. Choose any of the chick-pea soups (pages 85–87), the Bean Soup with Parsley and Garlic (page 79), the Beans and Pasta Soup (page 80) or Red Cabbage Soup (page 82). Also suitable are Baked Semolina Gnocchi (page 198) or Risotto with Parmesan Cheese (page 181). For a vegetable, accompany with Fried Finocchio (page 378), Zucchini Fried in Flour-and-Water Batter (page 392), or Fried Whole Artichokes (page 344).

Vitello

VEAL

Italy's finest veal comes from entirely milk-fed calves less than three months old. The meat is faintly rosy, nearly white, extraordinarily fine-grained, and almost perfectly lean.

Up to a few years ago, comparable veal was not marketed in this country. Only large, partially grazed or grain-fed animals whose flesh was deep pink and sometimes even lightly marbled with fat, were butchered. This is still a commonly distributed type of veal, but some markets and most of the better butchers now sell meat that approaches, even if it does not quite reach, the quality of northern Italian veal. If you buy it carefully, looking for meat that is very pale pink in color, you can attempt with confidence any of the delicious preparations to which veal lends itself.

Arrosto di vitello

PAN ROAST OF VEAL

If there is any dish in Italy that comes close to being a part of every family's repertory, it is probably this exquisitely simple pan-roasted veal. There is an infinite number of ways of roasting veal more elaborately, but there is none that produces more savory or succulent, tender meat. The success of this method lies in slow, watchful cooking, carefully regulating the amount of liquid so that there is just enough to keep the veal from drying out but not so much as to saturate it and dilute its flavor.

The best-looking roast comes from the top round, which some butchers will prepare for you. Rolled, boned shoulder of veal also makes an excellent and considerably less expensive roast.

For 6 persons

2 pounds roast of veal, boned	2 tablespoons vegetable oil
3 medium cloves garlic, lightly crushed with the handle of a knife and peeled	2 tablespoons butter
	1 teaspoon salt
	⅔ cup dry white wine
1 teaspoon rosemary leaves Freshly ground pepper, about 8 to 10 twists of the mill OR ¼ teaspoon crushed peppercorns	

1. If the roast is to be rolled, spread on it the garlic, rosemary, and pepper while it is flat, then roll and tie it securely. If it is a solid piece, pierce it at several points with a sharp, narrow-bladed knife and insert the rosemary and garlic. (You will season it with pepper later.) Tie it securely.

2. Choose a heavy-bottomed saucepan or casserole, preferably oval, just large enough for the meat. Heat the oil and butter over medium-high heat, and when the butter foam begins to subside add the meat and brown it well on all sides for about 15 minutes.

Sprinkle the meat with salt and, if it was omitted before, pepper.

3. Cook just long enough to turn the roast once and then add the wine. As soon as the wine comes to a boil, lower the heat so that it is barely simmering, set the cover askew, and cook until the meat is tender when pierced by a fork, about 1½ to 2 hours. Turn the roast from time to time, and if the cooking liquid dries up add 1 or 2 tablespoons of warm water.

4. When the roast is done, transfer it to a cutting board. If there is no liquid left in the pan, put in ½ cup of water. Evaporate the water rapidly over high heat while loosening the cooking residues stuck to the pan. All together you should have about a spoonful of sauce per serving, so, if there is too much liquid left, concentrate it quickly over high heat. Cut the roast into slices no more than ¼ inch thick. Arrange them on a warm platter, spoon the sauce over them, and serve immediately.

MENU SUGGESTIONS

This roast really presents no problems over the choice of a first course. I would exclude none, except those with fish or with a very spicy sauce. Particularly nice with roast veal is the Tagliatelle with Bolognese Meat Sauce (page 129). Other pasta suggestions: Thin Spaghetti with Fresh Basil and Tomato (page 97) or Cappellacci Filled with Sweet Potatoes and Parsley (page 168). Most vegetables are also a suitable accompaniment. Sweet and Sour Onions (page 382) would be ideal. Other suggestions: Sautéed Peas with Prosciutto, Florentine Style (page 383), either of the sautéed mushrooms (pages 379–381), Sautéed Spinach (page 388), or any of the vegetables with butter and cheese, such as the carrots on page 365.

Petto di vitello arrotolato

ROLLED STUFFED BREAST OF VEAL

Roast boned breast of veal is an ideal way to enjoy the tenderness and delicate taste of veal without paying its usually steep price. It is an attractive-looking dish, and not at all complicated to prepare. If you are irredeemably opposed to dressing your own cuts of meat, you can have the butcher bone the breast for you. But be sure to take the bones home with you, as they make an excellent veal stock or addition to meat broth. Boning it yourself, however, is quite simple, it keeps the cost down, and it can even be enjoyable.

Lay the piece of breast on the work counter, ribs down, and, slipping the blade of a sharp knife between the meat and the bones, work carefully, detaching all the meat in a single, flat, uninterrupted piece. Remove all gristly bits and loose patches of skin, leaving just the single layer of skin that adheres to and covers the meat.

For 4 to 6 persons

1 piece breast of veal (4½ to 5 pounds with bones, about 1¾ pounds boned), bones removed as directed above

Salt

Freshly ground pepper, about 4 to 6 twists of the mill

¼ pound rolled *pancetta* (see note below)

2 whole cloves garlic, peeled

½ teaspoon dried rosemary leaves

2½ tablespoons butter

1 tablespoon vegetable oil

1 cup dry white wine, approximately

1. Remove the bones from the veal as directed above, then lay the boned meat flat. Sprinkle lightly with salt, add pepper, cover with a layer of sliced *pancetta,* place on it the two garlic cloves spaced apart, and sprinkle the rosemary leaves over all. Roll the meat up tightly, jelly-roll fashion, and fasten securely with string.

2. Heat the butter and oil over medium heat in a heavy-bottomed casserole just large enough to contain the veal. When the butter

foam subsides, add the meat and brown well on all sides. Season lightly with salt, add enough wine to come one-third of the way up the side of the meat, and turn the heat up to high. Let the wine boil briskly for about 10 seconds, turning the meat in it, then turn the heat down to medium low and set the cover on, slightly askew. Cook until tender when pierced by a fork, about 1¾ to 2 hours. Turn and baste the meat from time to time. If it is sticking, add a couple of tablespoons of warm water.

3. Transfer the veal to a carving board. Allow it to settle for a minute or two and then cut into slices ⅜ inch thick. (As you slice, look for the garlic cloves and remove them.) Arrange the slices on a warm platter.

4. Tilt the casserole and remove all but 2 or 3 tablespoons of fat. Add 2 tablespoons of water, turn the heat on to high, and while the water evaporates scrape up and loosen any cooking residue stuck to the pan. Pour over the sliced veal and serve immediately.

NOTE

If *pancetta* is not available, prosciutto or cooked ham are acceptable, although not equally satisfactory, substitutes.

MENU SUGGESTIONS

The same general observations hold true for this roast that were made for the pan roast on page 253. In addition, one should bear in mind that this one has *pancetta* (or prosciutto), so it would be better to avoid any first course or vegetable accompaniment that is thickly laced with either *pancetta* or prosciutto. Particularly ideal first courses here would be Rice and Peas (page 60), Baked Rigatoni with Meat Sauce (page 110), Risotto with Parmesan Cheese (page 181), or either vegetable *risotto* (pages 189–191).

Ossobuco alla milanese (oss bus)

BRAISED VEAL SHANKS, MILAN STYLE

Ossobuco, oss bus in Milanese dialect, literally means "bone with a hole," or hollow bone. It is made with the shanks of milk-fed veal, very slowly braised in broth with vegetables and herbs, and it turns, when done, into one of the most tender morsels of meat one can eat. A properly cooked *ossobuco* needs no knife; it can be broken up with a fork. The hind shanks are better than the front ones for *ossobuco* because they are meatier and more tender. When the butcher prepares your shanks, have him saw off the two ends, which contain mostly bone and little meat (you can use them in a broth). Have him cut the shanks into pieces no more than 2 inches long, the size at which *ossobuco* cooks best, making sure he doesn't remove the skin enveloping the shanks. It helps to hold the *ossobuco* together and it has a delectable, creamy consistency when cooked.

For 6 persons

1 cup finely chopped yellow onion

⅔ cup finely chopped carrot

⅔ cup finely chopped celery

¼ cup butter

1 teaspoon finely chopped garlic

2 strips lemon peel

½ cup vegetable oil

2 shanks of veal, sawed into 8 pieces about 2 inches long, each securely tied around the middle

¾ cup all-purpose flour, spread on a plate or on waxed paper

1 cup dry white wine

1½ cups Homemade Meat Broth (page 10) OR canned beef broth, approximately

1½ cups canned Italian tomatoes coarsely chopped, with their juice

¼ teaspoon dried thyme

4 leaves fresh basil (optional)

2 bay leaves

2 or 3 sprigs parsley

Freshly ground pepper, about 6 twists of the mill

Salt, if necessary

1. Preheat the oven to 350°.

2. Choose a heavy casserole with a tight-fitting lid that is just large enough to contain the veal pieces later in a single layer. (If you do not have a casserole large enough for all the veal, use two small ones, dividing the chopped vegetables and butter in two equal parts, but adding 1 extra tablespoon of butter per casserole.) Put in the onion, carrot, celery, and butter and cook over medium heat for 8 to 10 minutes, until the vegetables soften and wilt. Add the chopped garlic and lemon peel at the end. Remove from the heat.

3. Heat the oil in a skillet over medium-high heat. Turn the trussed pieces of veal in the flour, shaking off any excess. When the oil is quite hot (test it with the corner of one of the pieces of veal: a moderate sizzle means the heat is just right), brown the veal on all sides. (Brown the veal as soon as it has been dipped in flour, otherwise the flour may dampen and the meat won't brown properly.) Stand the pieces of veal side by side on top of the vegetables in the casserole.

4. Tip the skillet and draw off nearly all the fat with a spoon. Add the wine and boil briskly for about 3 minutes, scraping up and loosening any browning residue stuck to the pan. Pour over the pieces of veal in the casserole.

5. In the same skillet, bring the broth to a simmer and pour into the casserole. Add the chopped tomatoes with their juice, the thyme, basil, bay leaves, parsley, pepper, and salt. (Hold off on salt until after cooking if you are using canned beef broth. It is sometimes very salty.) The broth should come up to the top of the veal pieces. If it does not, add more.

6. Bring the contents of the casserole to a simmer on top of the stove. Cover tightly and place in the lower third of the preheated oven. Cook for about 2 hours, carefully turning and basting the veal pieces every 20 minutes. When done, they should be very tender when pricked with a fork, and their sauce should be dense and creamy. (If, while the veal is still cooking, there is not enough liquid in the casserole, you may add up to ⅓ cup of warm water. If the reverse is true, and the sauce is too thin when the veal is done,

remove the meat to a warm platter, place the uncovered casserole on top of the stove, and over high heat briskly boil the sauce until it thickens.) Pour the sauce over the veal and serve piping hot.

NOTE

When transferring the veal pieces to the serving platter, carefully remove the trussing strings without breaking up the shanks.

GREMOLADA

The traditional recipe for *ossobuco* calls for a garnish of herbs, grated lemon peel, and garlic called *gremolada*, which is added to the veal shanks as they finish cooking. Tradition deserves respect, but art demands sincerity, and cooking is, above all else, an art. In the light of modern taste, I find that the *gremolada* overloads with unnecessary pungency a beautifully balanced and richly flavored dish. I never serve *ossobuco* with *gremolada*. If you feel, however, that you absolutely must try it for yourself, here are the recommended ingredients:

1 teaspoon grated lemon peel	1 tablespoon finely chopped
¼ teaspoon very finely chopped garlic	parsley

Some old recipes also include sage and rosemary, but that, I think, is going too far. *Gremolada* is sprinkled over the veal shanks just as they finish cooking.

MENU SUGGESTIONS

The natural accompaniment for *ossobuco* is Risotto, Milan Style (page 184), as was noted under that recipe. It is not served separately, but together with *ossobuco*. If you would just as soon not have *risotto*, you can precede *ossobuco* with Potato Gnocchi (page 195) with Gorgonzola Sauce (page 134), or with Artichokes, Roman Style (page 337). *Ossobuco* can be served without any vegetables on the side, but if you are willing to make the effort, Sautéed Peas with Prosciutto (page 383) make a very happy accompaniment. Follow *ossobuco* with a fine salad. An excellent one would be Jerusalem Artichoke and Spinach Salad (page 406).

Lo "schinco"

BRAISED VEAL SHANKS, TRIESTE STYLE

This is the same cut that in Milan is sawed into 2-inch pieces and called *ossobuco*. In Trieste the shanks are cooked whole and flavored with anchovies, which give the dish a decidedly different texture and character from *ossobuco*, although still every bit as tender. It is served whole, in all its magnificence, and carved at the table.

As in *ossobuco*, the hind shanks are to be preferred because they are more tender. Have the butcher saw off the two joints at the end where there is no meat.

For 6 persons

½ cup chopped yellow onion
3 tablespoons olive oil
3 tablespoons butter
2 veal shanks
2 cloves garlic, crushed lightly with a knife handle and peeled
1 teaspoon salt

Freshly ground pepper, about 6 twists of the mill
⅓ cup dry white wine
4 large or 6 medium flat anchovy fillets
1½ cups Homemade Meat Broth (page 10) OR ½ cup canned beef broth mixed with 1 cup water

1. Preheat the oven to 350°.
2. Choose a heavy casserole, preferably oval, just large enough for the shanks. Put in the onion with the oil and butter, and sauté over medium heat until pale gold.
3. Add the shanks, garlic, salt, pepper, and wine. Simmer the wine for about 1 minute, turning the shanks once or twice. Add the anchovies and the broth, cover, and bring to a boil. Transfer the casserole to the preheated oven and cook for 2 hours, or until the meat is extremely tender. (It should come easily off the bone.) Turn and baste the shanks every 20 minutes. (While the meat is cooking, if you find that the cooking liquids have dried up, you may add ⅓ cup warm water. If, on the contrary, the meat is done but the cook-

ing juices are too thin, return to the stove, uncover, turn on the heat to high and boil until the juices are concentrated.)

NOTE

This dish can be prepared entirely ahead of time, refrigerated, and re-heated like *ossobuco*.

MENU SUGGESTIONS

Another specialty of Trieste is Beans and Sauerkraut Soup (page 75), which makes an ideal choice for a first course here. Also excellent would be Potato Gnocchi (page 195) with Gorgonzola Sauce (page 134) or Risotto with Parmesan Cheese (page 181). Any of the fried vegetables, such as Zucchini Fried in Flour and Water Batter (page 392) or Fried Whole Artichokes (page 344), is a suitable accompaniment, and so is Sweet and Sour Onions (page 382).

SCALOPPINE

The perfect *scaloppina* is cut across the grain from the top round. It is cut a shade more than ¼ inch thick and flattened to a shade less than ¼ inch. It is a solid slice of meat without any muscle separations. The problem lies in finding a butcher to cut it. I have discussed this with many American butchers, and I know exactly the answer yours will give you. With varying degrees of politeness it will be, "That is not the way we do it." One solution is to allow the butcher to cut a thin slice across the entire leg, which you can then divide into its separate muscles. This, however, will give you *scaloppine* of uneven texture and, while acceptable, will not be wholly satisfactory. A better alternative is to look for the kind of butcher who is willing to cooperate with you, and give you what you want—at a price. It may be expensive, but it will save you much heartache.

Once you have found this paragon, make sure not only that he cuts the *scaloppine* from a single muscle but also that he cuts them across the grain. If *scaloppine* are cut any other way, the muscle fibers will contract in the cooking, producing a wavy, shrunken, tough slice of meat.

Scaloppine di vitello al Marsala
SAUTÉED VEAL SCALOPPINE WITH MARSALA

For 4 persons

3 tablespoons vegetable oil

1 pound veal *scaloppine*, very thinly sliced and pounded flat

¾ cup all-purpose flour, spread on a dinner plate or waxed paper

½ teaspoon salt

Freshly ground pepper, 5 to 6 twists of the mill

½ cup dry Marsala

3 tablespoons butter

1. Heat the oil over medium-high heat in a heavy skillet.

2. Dip the veal *scaloppine* in flour, coating them on both sides and shaking off any excess. When the oil is quite hot slip the *scaloppine* into the pan and quickly brown them on both sides, which should take less than a minute for each side if the oil is hot enough. (If you can't get all of them into your skillet at one time, do them a few at a time but dip them in flour only as you are ready to brown them, otherwise the flour will get soggy and the *scaloppine* won't brown properly.) Transfer the browned meat to a warm platter and season with salt and pepper.

3. Tip the skillet and draw off most of the fat with a spoon. Turn the heat on to high, add the Marsala, and boil briskly for less than a minute, scraping up and loosening any cooking residue stuck to the pan. Add the butter and any juices that may have been thrown off by the *scaloppine* in the platter. When the sauce thickens, turn the heat down to low and add the *scaloppine*, turning them and basting them with sauce once or twice. Transfer meat and sauce to a warm platter and serve immediately.

(*continued*)

MENU SUGGESTIONS

An elegant first course would be Italian Pancakes Filled with Spinach (page 177), Meat-Stuffed Pasta Rolls (page 149), or Yellow and Green Noodles with Cream, Ham, and Mushroom Sauce (page 132). Risotto with Parmesan Cheese (page 181) or either vegetable *risotto* (pages 181–191) would also be a good choice. The vegetable: Sautéed Green Beans with Butter and Cheese (page 361) or Sautéed Finocchio with Butter and Cheese (page 377).

Scaloppine di vitello al limone
SAUTÉED VEAL SCALOPPINE WITH LEMON SAUCE

For 4 persons

2 tablespoons vegetable oil	Salt and freshly ground
¼ cup butter	pepper to taste
1 pound veal *scaloppine*, thinly	2 tablespoons lemon juice
sliced and pounded flat	2 tablespoons finely chopped
¾ cup all-purpose flour, spread	parsley
on a dish or on waxed paper	½ lemon, thinly sliced

1. Heat the oil and 2 tablespoons of the butter in a skillet, over medium-high heat. (It should be quite hot. Thinly sliced veal must cook quickly or it will become leathery.)

2. Dip both sides of the *scaloppine* in flour and shake off the excess. Slip the *scaloppine*, no more than will fit comfortably in the skillet at one time, into the pan. If the oil is hot enough the meat should sizzle.

3. Cook the *scaloppine* until they are lightly browned on one side, then turn and brown the other side. (If they are very thin they should be completely cooked in about 1 minute.) When done, transfer to a warm platter and season with salt and pepper.

4. Off the heat, add the lemon juice to the skillet, scraping loose the cooking residue. Swirl in the remaining 2 tablespoons of butter. Add the parsley, stirring it into the sauce.

5. Add the *scaloppine*, turning them in the sauce. Turn on the heat to medium very briefly, just long enough to warm up the sauce and *scaloppine* together—but do not overdo it, because the *scaloppine* are already cooked.

6. Transfer the *scaloppine* to a warm platter, pour the sauce over them, garnish with the lemon slices, and serve immediately.

MENU SUGGESTIONS

These exquisite *scaloppine* should be preceded by a first course that has both delicacy and character. It could be spaghetti with Tomato Sauce III (page 95), Fettuccine Tossed in Cream and Butter (page 130), Tortelloni Filled with Swiss Chard (page 164), with either Butter and Cheese (page 167) or Tomato and Cream Sauce (page 163), Risotto with Asparagus (page 189), Rice and Peas (page 60), or Spinach and Ricotta Gnocchi (page 200), with either of the two sauces recommended. Some of the vegetables that can accompany the *scaloppine* are Fried Artichoke Wedges (page 346), Gratinéed Jerusalem Artichokes (page 353), Sautéed Green Beans with Butter and Cheese (page 361), Cauliflower Gratinéed with Butter and Cheese (page 366), and Zucchini Fried in Flour and Water Batter (page 392).

Scaloppine di vitello alla pizzaiola
VEAL SCALOPPINE WITH TOMATOES

For 4 persons

2½ tablespoons vegetable oil
3 cloves garlic, peeled
1 pound veal *scaloppine*, very thinly sliced and pounded flat
¾ cup all-purpose flour, spread on a dinner plate or waxed paper
Salt

Freshly ground pepper, 4 to 5 twists of the mill
⅓ cup white wine
3 teaspoons tomato paste diluted in ½ cup warm water
1 tablespoon butter
½ teaspoon orégano
2 tablespoons capers

1. In a heavy-bottomed skillet heat the oil over high heat and sauté the garlic cloves. When they are browned, remove them.

2. Dip both sides of the veal *scaloppine* in the flour, shake off the excess, and sauté very rapidly on both sides in the hot oil. (Do not overcook. It is sufficient to brown them lightly, which should take a minute or less each side. And never dip the *scaloppine* in flour until you are just ready to cook them. If you do it ahead of time the flour becomes damp and they won't brown properly.) Transfer the *scaloppine* to a warm platter and season with salt and pepper.

3. Tip the skillet and draw off most of the fat with a spoon. Turn on the heat to moderately high, add the wine, and scrape up and loosen the cooking residue in the pan. Then add the diluted tomato paste, stir, add the butter, stir, and continue cooking for a few minutes, until the liquids thicken into sauce. Add the orégano and the capers, stirring them into the sauce. Cook for another minute, then add the sautéed *scaloppine*, turning them quickly once or twice in the sauce. Transfer to a warm platter, pouring the sauce over the veal, and serve immediately.

This is a zesty but amiable second course that can follow practically any soup or *risotto* and any pasta that does not carry a cream-based sauce or a tomato sauce. It is ideally accompanied by green vegetables sautéed in oil such as the spinach on page 388 or the *finocchio* on page 378.

Rollatini di vitello al pomodoro
VEAL ROLLS IN TOMATO SAUCE

For 4 persons

1 pound veal *scaloppine,* very thinly sliced and pounded flat	2 tablespoons vegetable oil
	Salt to taste
	Freshly ground pepper, about 4 twists of the mill
¼ pound rolled *pancetta,* sliced very thin	½ cup dry white wine
5 tablespoons freshly grated Parmesan cheese	1 tablespoon tomato paste with just enough warm water to dilute it
¼ cup butter	

1. If the *scaloppine* are unusually large, cut them down to about 5 inches in length and 3½ to 4 inches in width. (If some pieces are irregular it doesn't really matter; it is better to use them than to waste them.) Over each *scaloppina* lay enough *pancetta* to cover. Sprinkle with grated cheese and roll up into a tight, compact roll. Fasten each roll with one or two toothpicks. Insert the toothpicks not across the roll, but into it along the length, so that the roll can turn in the pan.

2. In a heavy skillet, heat up 3 tablespoons of butter and all the oil over medium-high heat. When the butter foam subsides, add the veal rolls and brown quickly on all sides. Transfer the veal to a warm platter, remove the toothpicks, and season with salt and pepper.

3. Add the wine to the skillet, turn the heat to high, and boil

briskly for about 2 minutes, scraping up and loosening any browning residue stuck to the pan. Add the diluted tomato paste, stir, turn the heat down to medium, and cook for several minutes, until the tomato separates from the cooking fat. Return the veal rolls to the skillet and warm them up for a minute, turning them in the sauce. Off heat, swirl in the remaining tablespoon of butter. Transfer to a very warm serving platter and serve without delay.

NOTE

This dish can be prepared entirely ahead of time and refrigerated for a few days in its sauce. When making ahead of time, do not remove the toothpicks at the end of Step 2. You will need them to hold the veal rolls together while they warm up.

To reheat, remove the meat from the sauce and allow time to return to room temperature, meanwhile preheating the oven to 325°. Add 1 tablespoon of water to the sauce and bring it to a simmer on the stove. Return the meat to the pan, cover, and warm up in the oven. Turn the rolls once or twice while reheating.

Rollatini take some time to heat up inside. They must be hot through and through before serving. Remove from the oven when they feel quite hot at the touch of a finger.

MENU SUGGESTIONS

First course: Tortelloni with Butter and Cheese (page 167), Italian Pancakes Filled with Spinach (page 177), Trenette with Potatoes and Pesto (page 142), or Rice and Peas (page 60). Choose white vegetables such as Gratinéed Jerusalem Artichokes (page 353), Fried Finocchio (page 378), or Braised and Gratinéed Celery with Parmesan Cheese (page 368).

Fagottini di vitello leccabaffi
LITTLE VEAL "BUNDLES" WITH
ANCHOVIES AND CHEESE

These veal "bundles" are made of very thin *scaloppine* coated with a sauce of anchovies and tomato and a layer of cheese. The cheese should be bland to balance the pungency of the anchovies. The *scaloppine* are then rolled and tightly trussed up and cooked very rapidly over high heat, first with butter, then with a little Marsala.

For 6 persons

5 tablespoons butter

8 large or 10 medium flat anchovy fillets

¼ cup chopped parsley

6 tablespoons canned Italian tomatoes, drained and seeds removed

Freshly ground pepper, about 12 twists of the mill

1½ pounds veal *scaloppine*, very thinly sliced and pounded flat

½ teaspoon salt

8 ounces mozzarella, preferably smoked mozzarella, or Bel Paese cheese, cut into slices ⅛ inch thick or grated on the largest holes of the grater

½ cup all-purpose flour, spread on a dish or on waxed paper

1 cup dry Marsala

1. Put 2 tablespoons of the butter and all the anchovies in a very small saucepan, and, over very low heat, mash the anchovies to a pulp with a fork.

2. Add the chopped parsley, the tomatoes, and the pepper, turn the heat up to medium, and cook, stirring frequently, until the tomato thickens into sauce.

3. Lay the veal *scaloppine* flat, sprinkle them with salt, spread the sauce over them, and cover, except for a ¼-inch edge all around, with a layer of cheese. Roll up the *scaloppine*, push the ends in, and truss tightly, running the string both around the rolls and over the ends.

4. In a skillet that can later accommodate all the bundles without crowding, melt the remaining 3 tablespoons of butter over medium-high heat. When the butter foam begins to subside, roll the *scaloppine* lightly in the flour, shaking off the excess, and slide them into the skillet. Brown on all sides for about 2 minutes. (If a little cheese oozes out of the rolls, it is quite all right. It enriches the sauce, and the floating white shreds of cheese are very attractive.) When the meat is well browned, add the Marsala and turn the heat up to high. While the wine boils, turn the veal rolls, and scrape up any browning residue in the pan. Cook for 2 to 3 minutes, stirring constantly, until the wine and other cooking juices have turned into a creamy sauce. Transfer the meat and sauce to a warm platter and serve immediately.

MENU SUGGESTIONS

This can be part of a meal that starts with a fish antipasto, such as Broiled Mussels and Clams on the Half Shell (page 34), Shrimps with Oil and Lemon (page 39), or Baked Oysters with Oil and Parsley (page 32). The first course can be Spaghetti with Garlic and Oil (page 103) or Trenette with Potatoes and Pesto (page 142). For vegetable: Fried Finocchio (page 378), Sautéed Jerusalem Artichokes (page 352), or Sautéed Diced Eggplant (page 374).

Costolette alla milanese
SAUTÉED BREADED VEAL CHOPS

A breaded veal chop *alla milanese* is, at its best, the most perfect thing that one can do with veal. When skillfully done, the tender, juicy eye of the chop is enveloped by a delectable crust, very thin and very crisp. It is cooked entirely in butter, and the trick one must learn is to keep the butter hot enough long enough to cook the meat all the way through, but not so hot that it will burn.

The greatest problem we have in doing this dish is that of getting the right kind of chop. The only correct cut is the rib chop. In Italy, where veal comes from a very small animal, each rib yields a single chop, which is flattened to make it broad and thin. Only the eye is left on the bone, and a sufficient length of the rib is left on to give the appearance of a handle. American veal is much larger and the meat on a single rib is too thick for one chop. This means that out of one rib you must have the butcher prepare two chops, one with the handle, one without. The tail of the chop should be trimmed away, leaving a clean, round eye. Since you must pay for the trimmings, take them home and use them for broth. The chops should be pounded flat, but, before pounding the one with the bone, the butcher must knock off the corner where the rib meets the backbone.

It will be a rather expensive cut of meat, and it won't be quite a Milanese-looking chop, but you will have a beautiful piece of veal. If you give its preparation the necessary care, the result should amply reward your efforts and expense.

For 6 persons

3 veal rib chops, divided into
    6 chops and pounded flat
2 eggs, lightly beaten with 1
    teaspoon salt, in a soup
    plate

1½ cups fine, dry unflavored
    bread crumbs, spread on
    a dish or on waxed paper
6 tablespoons butter

1. Dip each chop in the beaten eggs, coating both sides, and letting excess egg flow back into the plate as you pull the chop away. Dredge the chops in the bread crumbs, pressing the crumbs with your hands into the surface of both sides of the chops.

2. Choose a skillet that can later contain the chops in a single layer. Put in the butter and melt it over medium-low heat. When the butter foam subsides, slip the chops into the skillet. Cook for 3 minutes on one side, until a dark golden crust has formed, then turn and cook for another 3 minutes on the other side, watching the butter to make sure it does not burn and adjusting the heat if necessary. When done, transfer the chops to a warm platter and serve immediately.

(continued)

Breaded veal chops will fit with complete assurance into any menu, whether plain and sturdy or delicately balanced. They make an especially nice second course when preceded by one of the fine homemade pastas, such as Tortellini Filled with Parsley and Ricotta (page 162) with Tomato and Cream Sauce (page 163), or by Risotto with Zucchini (page 191) or Risotto with Asparagus (page 189). Potato Gnocchi (page 195) or Spinach and Ricotta Gnocchi (page 203) are also excellent choices for the first course. But you can just as easily serve a substantial soup, such as Beans and Pasta Soup (page 80), or macaroni pasta, such as Fusilli with Greamy Zucchini and Basil Sauce (page 106).

There is simply no vegetable that will not go with these chops. The tastiest accompaniment is Fried Eggplant (page 372) combined with Oven-Browned Tomatoes (page 389). Other good pairings are Sautéed Mushrooms with Garlic and Parsley (page 379), Sweet and Sour Onions (page 382), Sautéed Peas with Prosciutto, Florentine Style (page 383), and Sautéed Green Beans with Butter and Cheese (page 361).

Cotolette alla milanese

BREADED VEAL CUTLETS, MILAN STYLE

In Italian cooking, *cotolette*, or cutlets, are not so much the cut of meat as the method by which it is cooked. A *cotoletta* is often a slice of veal, cut like a *scaloppina*, but it can also be a slice of turkey or chicken breast, or beef, or even eggplant. It is dipped in beaten egg, dredged in bread crumbs, and fried in very hot oil.

For 6 persons

1½ pounds veal *scaloppine*, sliced ¼ inch thick and pounded flat	2 whole eggs, lightly beaten, in a soup plate

2 cups fine, dry unflavored
   bread crumbs, spread on
   a dinner plate or on waxed
   paper

Vegetable oil and butter,
   just enough to come ⅜
   inch up the side of the
   skillet (see note below)
¾ teaspoon salt
Lemon wedges

1. Dip each veal slice very lightly on both sides in the eggs and then into the bread crumbs. As you turn the cutlet over in the bread crumbs, tap it into the bread crumbs with the palm of your hand to get a better adherence of the crumbs to the meat. Shake off all excess loose crumbs and pile the breaded slices on a dish until you are ready to cook them. (You may prepare them up to this point a few hours ahead of time.)

2. Heat the oil and butter in a heavy skillet over medium-high heat. (To make sure the fat is hot enough, test it with the end of a cutlet. If it sizzles, it's ready.) Cook as many cutlets at one time as will fit in a single layer in the skillet. When they brown on one side, quickly turn them over. Remove them just as soon as they are brown and crisp on both sides, which will be very quickly. (Do not cook any longer than it takes to brown them or the meat will become dry.) Place the browned cutlets on paper towels, which will absorb any excess fat, and sprinkle with salt. Serve piping hot with lemon wedges, or with Red Sauce (page 30).

NOTE

The quantity of cooking fat obviously depends upon the size of the pan, but the proportions are always 2 parts of vegetable oil to 1 part of butter.

MENU SUGGESTIONS

Follow the ones given for Sautéed Breaded Veal Chops (previous page), but avoid tomatoes in the first course or vegetable if you are using the Red Sauce.

Nodini di vitello alla salvia

SAUTÉED VEAL CHOPS WITH SAGE AND WHITE WINE

For 4 persons

3 tablespoons vegetable oil
4 veal loin chops, cut ¾ inch
    thick
¾ cup all-purpose flour, spread
    on a dinner plate or on
    waxed paper

12 dried sage leaves
½ teaspoon salt
Freshly ground pepper, about
    4 twists of the mill
⅓ cup dry white wine
2 tablespoons butter

1. Heat the oil in a heavy-bottomed skillet over medium-high heat.

2. Turn the chops over in the flour, coating both sides, and shake off any excess. (Do not coat meat with flour until you are ready to sauté it. The flour becomes damp and the meat does not brown properly.)

3. Slip the chops and the sage into the hot oil. Cook for about 8 to 10 minutes all together, turning the chops two or three times so that they cook evenly on both sides. (Veal shouldn't cook too long or it will become dry. The meat is done when it is rosy pink on the inside when cut.) When cooked, remove to a warm platter and add salt and pepper.

4. Tilt the skillet and draw away most of the fat with a spoon. Add the wine and turn the heat to high. Boil rapidly until the liquid has almost completely evaporated and become a little syrupy. While boiling, loosen any cooking residue in the pan and add what juice the chops may have thrown off in the platter. When the wine has almost completely evaporated and thickened, turn the heat to very low and mix in the butter. Return the chops to the skillet for a few moments, turning them over in the sauce. Transfer them to a warm serving platter, pour the remainder of the sauce over them, and serve immediately.

MENU SUGGESTIONS

First course: Baked Rigatoni with Meat Sauce (page 110), Meat-Stuffed Pasta Rolls (page 149), Baked Green Lasagne with Meat Sauce (page 143), Homemade Macaroni (page 170) with Bolognese Meat Sauce (page 127), Spinach and Ricotta Gnocchi (page 201) or Italian Pancakes Filled with Spinach (page 177). A lovely vegetable accompaniment would be Braised Artichokes and Peas (page 347), Asparagus with Parmesan Cheese (page 356), or the Baked Stuffed Zucchini Boats (page 395).

Spezzatino di vitello alla salvia

VEAL STEW WITH SAGE AND WHITE WINE

The preferred cuts for Italian veal stew are the shoulder and the shanks. Avoid the round, which makes a dry and uninteresting stew.

For 4 persons

2 tablespoons finely chopped shallots or yellow onion	¾ cup all-purpose flour, spread on a dinner plate or on waxed paper
2 tablespoons vegetable oil	18 medium dried sage leaves
2 tablespoons butter	⅔ cup dry white wine
1½ pounds shank or shoulder of veal, boned and rather lean, cut into 1-inch cubes	½ teaspoon salt
	Freshly ground pepper, about 4 twists of the mill

1. In a deep skillet, sauté the shallots in the oil and butter over medium-high heat until translucent but not browned.

2. Dip the pieces of veal in the flour, coating them on all sides and shaking off excess flour. Add to the skillet, together with the sage leaves, and brown well on all sides. (If all the meat won't fit into the skillet at one time you can brown a few pieces at a time, but dip them in the flour only when you are ready to put them

in the skillet or the flour coating will get soggy and the meat won't brown properly.) Transfer the meat to a warm platter when browned.

3. When all the meat has been browned, turn up the heat to high, add the wine to the skillet, and boil briskly for about 30 seconds, scraping up and loosening any cooking residue in the pan. Turn the heat down to medium and add the browned meat, salt, and pepper. Cover and cook gently for about 1 hour, turning and basting the meat from time to time, adding a little warm water if necessary. The meat is done when it is tender at the pricking of a fork. Serve immediately.

NOTE

This stew can be prepared entirely ahead of time and refrigerated for several days in a Pyrex or enamelware container with a cover. It can then be warmed up, covered, in the same container, in a 325° preheated oven. Add 2 tablespoons of water when warming it up.

MENU SUGGESTIONS

Follow the first-course suggestion for Sautéed Veal Chops with Sage and White Wine (page 273). Also indicated would be Risotto with Asparagus (page 189), or Risotto with Zucchini (page 191). An ideal vegetable is Mushrooms with Cream (page 381), which, after cooking, can be mixed with the veal stew. The combination also makes a fine hot buffet dish.

Spezzatino di vitello coi piselli

VEAL STEW WITH TOMATOES AND PEAS

For 4 persons

2 tablespoons chopped shallots or yellow onion

3 tablespoons vegetable oil

2 tablespoons butter

1½ pounds boneless veal for stewing (see preceding recipe), cut into 1½-inch cubes

2 teaspoons salt

Freshly ground pepper,
about 6 twists of the mill

1 cup canned Italian tomatoes,
coarsely chopped, with
their juice

2 pounds fresh peas (unshelled
weight) or 1 ten-ounce
package frozen small peas,
thawed

1. Put the chopped shallots in a heavy casserole with the oil and butter and sauté over medium heat until pale gold.

2. Put in the pieces of veal, browning them well on all sides. (There are two points to bear in mind when browning the meat: it should be thoroughly dry, and it should not be crowded in the pot. If it does not all fit in at once, do a few pieces at a time. Remove the first batch as it is done and then add the others.)

3. Return all the meat to the pot, add 2 teaspoons salt, the pepper, and the chopped tomatoes with their juice. When the tomatoes begin to boil, cover the pot and adjust the heat so that the tomatoes are barely simmering. Cook until the veal is very tender when pricked with a fork, as little as 1 hour from the time you've covered the pot if it is very young, fine veal. (More often, however, it will be closer to 1½ hours. Actually, a little extra slow cooking doesn't do it any harm.)

4. The peas must be added to the stew before it is completely cooked. If you are using fresh peas, calculate 15 or more minutes' cooking time for the peas, depending on their size and freshness. Add them when the meat has begun to turn tender but is still rather firm. If you are using thawed frozen peas, add them when the veal is tender nearly through and through. Frozen peas take only about 5 minutes or less to cook. Taste and correct for salt.

NOTE

The stew can be prepared completely ahead of time and refrigerated for several days. Reheat over medium heat when ready to serve.

MENU SUGGESTIONS

A perfect choice for the first course is Risotto with Parmesan Cheese (page 181). Also to be recommended is Rice with Fresh

Basil and Mozzarella Cheese (page 194). If the occasion seems to call for a soup, try either Potato and Onion Soup (page 59) or Passatelli (page 70). No vegetable is required.

Vitello tonnato
COLD SLICED VEAL WITH TUNA SAUCE

This is one of the loveliest and most versatile of all cold dishes. It is an ideal second course for a summer menu, a beautiful antipasto for an elegant dinner, a very successful party dish for small or large buffets. It requires quite some time and patience in the preparation, but, since it must be prepared at least 24 hours in advance, you can set your own pace and make it at your convenience.

Vitello tonnato is common to both Lombardy and Piedmont, and there are many ways of making it. Most recipes call for braising the veal either partly or wholly in white wine. You may try it if you like. I find it gives the dish a tarter flavor than it really needs.

In this recipe, do not under any circumstances use prepared, commercial mayonnaise.

Veal tends to be dry. To keep it tender and juicy, cook it in just enough water to cover (the method indicated below—put the meat in, add water to just cover, and then remove the meat—is the simplest way to gauge the exact amount); add veal to its cooking liquid only when the liquid is boiling; *never* add salt to the liquid; allow the meat to cool in its own broth.

For 6 to 8 persons

2 to 2½ pounds lean, boneless veal roast, preferably top round, firmly tied	1 stalk celery, without leaves
	1 medium yellow onion
	4 sprigs parsley
1 medium carrot	1 bay leaf

THE TUNA SAUCE:

Mayonnaise (page 26),
made with 2 egg yolks,
1¼ cups olive oil, 2 to 3
tablespoons lemon juice,
¼ teaspoon salt
1 seven-ounce can Italian tuna
in olive oil

5 flat anchovy fillets
1¼ cups olive oil
3 tablespoons lemon juice
3 tablespoons tiny capers
Salt, if necessary

1. In a pot just large enough to contain the veal, put in the veal, the carrot, celery, onion, parsley, bay leaf, and just enough water to cover. Now *remove the veal and set aside*. Bring the water to a boil, add the meat, and when the water comes to a boil again, cover the pot, reduce the heat, and keep at a gentle simmer for 2 hours. (If you are using a larger piece of veal, cook proportionately longer.) Remove the pot from the heat and allow the meat to cool in its broth.

2. Prepare the mayonnaise according to the recipe on page 26, remembering that all ingredients for the mayonnaise must be at room temperature.

3. In a blender mix the tuna, anchovies, olive oil, lemon juice, and the capers at high speed for a few seconds until they attain a creamy consistency. Remove the mixture from the blender jar and fold it carefully but thoroughly into the mayonnaise. Taste to see if any salt is required. (None may be necessary, depending upon how salty the anchovies and capers are.)

4. When the meat is quite cold, transfer it to a cutting board, remove the strings, and cut into thin and uniform slices.

5. Smear the bottom of a serving platter with some of the tuna sauce. Arrange the veal slices over this in a single layer, edge to edge. Cover the layer well with sauce. Lay more veal over this and cover again with sauce; set aside enough sauce to cover well the topmost layer. (The more layers you make the better. It prevents the veal from drying.)

6. Refrigerate for 24 hours, covered with plastic wrap. (It keeps beautifully for up to 2 weeks.) Before serving you may garnish it with lemon slices, olive slices, whole capers, and parsley leaves.

(continued)

If you are using this as a second course, precede it with Cold Vegetable Soup with Rice, Milan Style (page 68), Rice and Peas (page 60), or Trenette with Potatoes and Pesto (page 142). No vegetable, but follow it with a simple salad, such as Green Bean Salad (page 412).

As an introduction to a memorable meal, follow it with Molded Risotto with Parmesan Cheese and Chicken-Liver Sauce (page 183), and follow the *risotto* with Pan-Roasted Squab (page 319).

Arrosto di agnello pasquale col vino bianco
ROAST SPRING LAMB WITH WHITE WINE

In most of Italy, lamb is a seasonal dish. It is usually consumed at Eastertime, when it is around four months old. The following traditional Easter recipe from Emilia-Romagna is not quite as highly flavored as Hothouse Lamb, Roman Style (page 281), but it brings out all the tenderness and delicacy of spring lamb.

For 4 persons

1¾ to 2 pounds spring lamb, preferably shoulder, including some chops	½ teaspoon rosemary leaves
	½ teaspoon salt
	Freshly ground pepper, about
3 tablespoons vegetable oil	6 twists of the mill
2 tablespoons butter	⅔ cup dry white wine
3 whole cloves garlic, peeled	

1. If the lamb is too large to fit into your largest saucepan in one piece, cut it in two or three parts. Wash in cold running water, and pat thoroughly dry with paper towels.

2. Heat the oil and the butter in the saucepan over medium-high heat. When the butter foam begins to subside, add the lamb, the

garlic, and the rosemary. Brown the lamb well on all sides. (Make sure the garlic doesn't become too brown. If you see that it is darkening too fast, set it on top of the lamb.)

3. When the lamb is nicely browned, especially on the skin side, add salt, pepper, and all the white wine. Turn the heat up to high for a minute or less, enough to turn the lamb over twice. Cover the pan, turn the heat down to low, and cook the lamb at a very gentle simmer for 1½ or 2 hours, turning the lamb from time to time. (If you find that there is not enough cooking liquid in the pan and the meat is sticking to the bottom, add 2 or 3 tablespoons of warm water.)

4. The lamb is done when it feels very tender when pierced by a fork and the meat begins to come away from the bone. Transfer the lamb to a warm serving platter. Tip the pan, drawing off with a spoon all but 1 or 2 tablespoons of fat. Add 2 tablespoons of water, raise the heat to high, and while the water evaporates scrape up and loosen all the cooking residue in the pan. Pour this over the lamb and serve immediately.

MENU SUGGESTIONS

As a first course, if you'd like to omit the pasta, you can serve Artichokes, Roman Style (page 337), Braised Artichokes with Mortadella Stuffing (page 343), or Fava Beans, Roman Style (page 359). If you are having pasta, these can be either antipasti or vegetable side dishes. For pasta, choose something robust, such as Bucatini with Pancetta, Tomatoes, and Hot Pepper (page 105), Homemade Pasta from Apulia (page 173) with Broccoli and Anchovy Sauce (page 174), Thin Spaghetti with Eggplant (page 98), Fusilli with Creamy Zucchini and Basil Sauce (page 106), or Baked Green Lasagne with Meat Sauce (page 143). Aside from the vegetables mentioned above, other suitable vegetables are Fried Finocchio (page 378) or Zucchini Fried in Flour-and-Water Batter (page 392).

Arrosto di agnello al ginepro

CASSEROLE-ROASTED LAMB WITH JUNIPER BERRIES

In this recipe the meat is simmered right from the start with the vegetables, wine, and flavorings. There is no browning and no liquid or cooking fat to add, because the meat supplies its own fat and juices as it cooks. There is practically nothing to do but watch the pot occasionally. Juniper berries, which are easily found at most spice counters, are absolutely essential to the full-bodied flavor of this dish. Most of the lamb commonly available throughout the year is mature lamb, and this method is particularly successful with it, because it transforms it into meat as tender as that of baby lamb or kid. Allow at least 3½ hours' cooking time.

For 4 persons

2½ pounds leg of lamb, preferably butt end, bone in
1 tablespoon chopped carrot
2 tablespoons chopped yellow onion
1 tablespoon chopped celery
1 cup dry white wine
2 cloves garlic, lightly crushed with a knife handle and peeled

½ teaspoon rosemary leaves
1½ teaspoons juniper berries
2 teaspoons salt
Freshly ground pepper, 4 to 6 twists of the mill

1. Put all the ingredients into a heavy casserole. Cover and cook on top of the stove at low heat for 2 hours, turning the meat every 45 minutes.

2. At this point the lamb should have thrown off a considerable amount of liquid. Set the cover askew, and cook for another 1½ hours at slightly higher heat. The meat should now be very tender at the pricking of a fork. If there is still too much liquid, uncover completely, raise the heat to high, and boil it until it is a little more concentrated. At the end the meat must be a rich brown in color.

3. Off the heat, tilt the casserole and draw off as much of the fat as you can with a spoon. (You can use it as cooking fat for Diced Pan-Roasted Potatoes, page 387.) If you are not serving the roast immediately, do not degrease until after you have reheated it.

MENU SUGGESTIONS

This is the most highly flavored of the three lamb roasts and requires a first course that is interesting but not too aggressive. I suggest Vegetable Soup (page 66), the Molded Risotto with Parmesan Cheese and Chicken-Liver Sauce (page 183), Cappellacci Filled with Sweet Potatoes and Parsley (page 168), or Bean Soup with Parsley and Garlic (page 79). As a vegetable: Fried Cauliflower (page 367), Fried Asparagus (page 358), Sautéed Spinach (page 388), or Sautéed Broccoli with Garlic (page 363).

Abbacchio alla cacciatora
HOTHOUSE LAMB, ROMAN STYLE

Abbacchio is very young, milk-fed lamb, taken when it is just one month old. Its flesh is nearly as pale as veal, and it is so delicate and tender that in texture it is almost closer to chicken than to lamb. In this recipe it is slowly pan roasted, and flavored with sage, rosemary, a faint amount of garlic, and anchovies. It is one of Rome's most celebrated specialties.

Such young lamb is never available in American markets, but some butchers here carry what they call hothouse lamb. It is two to three months old, somewhat older than *abbacchio*, but still entirely milk fed. If you find it, by all means try it. Cook it as directed here and you will come remarkably close to the taste of the best Roman *abbacchio*. If hothouse lamb is not available, don't give up. Any young lamb lends itself successfully to this recipe. What you should avoid is the coarser, stronger-tasting meat of mature lamb.

For 6 persons

2 tablespoons cooking fat,
  preferably lard
3 pounds shoulder and/or leg
  of very young lamb, boned
  and cut into 2-inch cubes
½ teaspoon salt
  Freshly ground pepper, 6 to
  8 twists of the mill
½ teaspoon chopped dried sage
  leaves

½ teaspoon finely chopped
  garlic
1 teaspoon chopped dried
  rosemary leaves
2 teaspoons all-purpose flour
½ cup vinegar
⅓ cup water
4 large anchovy fillets, chopped

1. In a saucepan, melt the lard over medium-high heat. Put in the lamb pieces and brown well on all sides.

2. Add the salt, pepper, sage, garlic, and rosemary and continue to cook briskly for another minute or so, long enough to turn all the pieces once.

3. Dust the lamb with flour, sifting it through a sieve. Continue cooking at lively heat, turning each piece once. The meat will have turned a rather dark color.

4. Add the vinegar and boil it briskly, turning up the heat, for 30 seconds. Add the water, cover the pan, lower the heat, and cook at a very gentle simmer for about 1 hour. (The exact cooking time depends entirely on the age of the lamb. When done it should be very tender at the pricking of a fork.) Turn the meat from time to time as it cooks. If there is not sufficient cooking liquid, add 2 to 3 tablespoons of water.

5. When the lamb is done, take 2 or 3 tablespoons of sauce from the pan and put it in a small bowl, together with the chopped anchovies. Mash the anchovies with a spoon or a pestle, then spoon over the lamb in the pan. Turn and baste the lamb with its sauce over very low heat for about 30 seconds. Transfer to a warm platter and serve immediately.

First course: Baked Semolina Gnocchi (page 198), Sliced Pasta Roll with Spinach Filling (page 152), Spaghetti with Garlic and Oil (page 103), or Pappardelle with Chicken-Liver Sauce (page 137). Vegetable: Crisp-Fried Whole Artichokes (page 344), Fava Beans, Roman Style (page 359), or Diced Pan-Roasted Potatoes (page 387).

Costolettine di agnello fritte

BABY LAMB CHOPS FRIED IN PARMESAN CHEESE BATTER

You will never know how succulent lamb chops can be until you've fried them in this egg-and-cheese batter. The crust, which is crisp and delicious, seals in all the sweetness and tenderness of young lamb. The younger the lamb you use, the sweeter and more delicate will be its flavor and texture in frying. But this recipe can be executed also with standard lamb. The chops must be no more than one rib thick. Have the butcher knock off the corner bone and remove the backbone, leaving just the rib. Ideally, he should flatten the eye of the chop for you, but as I've never found an American butcher willing to do this to lamb, avoid wrangling and do it yourself at home with a meat pounder or cleaver.

For 6 persons

12 single rib chops, partly boned and flattened as directed above

½ cup freshly grated Parmesan cheese, spread on a dish or on waxed paper

2 eggs, lightly beaten in a deep dish

1 cup fine, dry unflavored bread crumbs, spread on a dish or on waxed paper

Vegetable oil, enough to come ¼ inch up the side of the skillet

Salt

Freshly ground pepper, about 6 twists of the mill

(continued)

1. Turn both sides of the chops in the Parmesan cheese, then give the chops a tap to shake off the excess. Dip them immediately into the beaten eggs, letting any excess egg flow back into the dish. Then turn the chops in the bread crumbs, coating both sides and tapping them again to shake off all excess. (You can prepare the chops up to this point as much as an hour ahead of time, or, if you refrigerate them, even 3 or 4 hours. If refrigerated, allow to return to room temperature before frying.)

2. Heat the oil in the skillet over medium heat until it is very hot. Fry as many chops at one time as will fit loosely in the skillet. As soon as they have formed a nice crust on one side, season with salt and pepper and turn them. Add salt and pepper to the other side. Transfer to a warm platter as soon as the second side has formed a crust and do the next batch. (If it is truly young lamb and cut very thin, it should take, altogether, 4 to 5 minutes to cook. If the lamb is a little older or the chops are a bit thick, it may take a few moments longer.) Serve piping hot.

MENU SUGGESTIONS

Homemade pastas are ideal with these crisp, tender chops, but any soup, *risotto*, or macaroni will make a suitable first course, as long as it has no fish in it. Almost all vegetables are a suitable accompaniment, but particularly nice are Sautéed Peas with Prosciutto, Florentine Style (page 383), Fava Beans, Roman Style (page 359), the Celery and Potatoes Braised in Olive Oil (page 369), and Fried Zucchini with Vinegar (page 393).

Arrosto di maiale al latte

PORK LOIN BRAISED IN MILK

Whenever I teach this dish I am greeted by more or less polite skepticism, which usually turns to enthusiasm at the first taste. Pork cooked by this method turns out to be exceptionally tender and juicy.

It is quite delicate in flavor because it loses all its fat and the milk, as such, disappears, to be replaced by clusters of delicious, nut-brown sauce.

For 6 persons

2 tablespoons butter	1 teaspoon salt
2 tablespoons vegetable oil	Freshly ground pepper, 3 or
2 pounds pork loin in one	4 twists of the mill
piece, with some fat on it,	2½ cups milk
securely tied	

1. Heat the butter and oil over medium-high heat in a casserole large enough to just contain the pork. When the butter foam subsides add the meat, fat side facing down. Brown thoroughly on all sides, lowering the heat if the butter starts to turn dark brown.

2. Add the salt, pepper, and milk. (Add the milk slowly, otherwise it may boil over.) Shortly after the milk comes to a boil, turn the heat down to medium, cover, but not tightly, with the lid partly askew, and cook slowly for about 1½ to 2 hours, until the meat is easily pierced by a fork. Turn and baste the meat from time to time, and, if necessary, add a little milk. By the time the meat is cooked the milk should have coagulated into small nut-brown clusters. If it is still pale in color, uncover the pot, raise the heat to high, and cook briskly until it darkens.

3. Remove the meat to a cutting board and allow to cool off slightly for a few minutes. Remove the trussing string, carve into slices ⅜ inch thick, and arrange them on a warm platter. Draw off most of the fat from the pot with a spoon and discard, being careful not to discard any of the coagulated milk clusters. Taste and correct for salt. (There may be as much as 1 to 1½ cups of fat to be removed.) Add 2 or 3 tablespoons of warm water, turn the heat to high, and boil away the water while scraping and loosening all the cooking residue in the pot. Spoon the sauce over the sliced pork and serve immediately.

(continued)

This is a Bolognese dish, and is often preceded by Tagliatelle with Bolognese Meat Sauce (page 129) or Baked Green Lasagne with Meat Sauce (page 143). If this appears to be too substantial, try the Baked Semolina Gnocchi (page 198), or an assortment of Italian cold cuts. As a vegetable Fried Artichoke Wedges (page 346) or Crisp-Fried Whole Artichokes (page 344) are excellent accompaniments.

Arrosto di maiale all'alloro

ROAST PORK WITH BAY LEAVES

For 6 persons

2 pounds boneless pork loin	1 teaspoon whole peppercorns
3 tablespoons butter	3 bay leaves, medium size
2 tablespoons vegetable oil	½ cup red wine vinegar
Salt	

1. Choose a good heavy pot, preferably enameled cast iron, just large enough to contain the meat, and provided with a close-fitting lid. Heat the butter and oil together at medium-high heat. When the butter foam begins to subside, put in the meat and brown it well on all sides.

2. When the meat is well browned, salt it on all sides, then add the peppercorns, bay leaves, and vinegar. Turn up the heat for as long as it takes to scrape up all the cooking residue from the bottom. (Do not allow the vinegar to evaporate more than slightly.) Turn the heat down to low, cover the pot, and cook slowly for at least 2 hours, until a fork easily pierces the meat. (Check from time to time to make sure that the liquid in the pot has not completely dried up. If it has you can add, as required, 2 or 3 tablespoons of water.)

3. Place the meat on a cutting board and cut into slices ¼ to ⅜ inch thick. Arrange the slices, slightly overlapping, on a warm serving platter.

4. Tip the pot, removing most, but not all, the fat with a spoon. Remove the bay leaves and pour the sauce from the pot over the meat. (If there should be any cooking residue in the bottom of the pot, put in 2 tablespoons of water and scrape it loose over high heat. Add to the sauce.)

MENU SUGGESTIONS

This goes well with Escarole and Rice Soup (page 63), Vegetable Soup (page 66), Beans and Pasta Soup (page 80), or any of the chick-pea soups on pages 85–87. If you want a macaroni pasta, try Thin Spaghetti with Fresh Basil and Tomato (page 97), Penne with a Sauce of Tomatoes and Dried Wild Mushrooms (page 108) or Bucatini with Pancetta, Tomatoes, and Hot Pepper (page 105). Accompany with Sautéed Jerusalem Artichokes (page 352), Braised Artichokes and Leeks (page 348), or any of the finocchio dishes on pages 377–378.

Cotechino con le lenticchie
BOILED COTECHINO SAUSAGE WITH LENTILS

Cotechino has always been a specialty of that section of Emilia called Romagna, but now it is also made in other Emilian provinces, Modena especially. It is a large, fresh pork sausage about 3 inches in diameter and 8 to 9 inches long. The name cotechino comes from cotica, the Italian word for pork rind, which is an essential ingredient in this sausage. It also contains meat from the shoulder, cheek, and neck, and it is seasoned with salt, pepper, nutmeg, and cloves. There are slight variations, of course, according to the maker. In the finest cotechino only the pork rind is ground; the meat is mashed in a special mortar. A skillfully made cotechino when properly cooked is exquisitely tender, with an almost creamy texture, and it is more delicate in taste than you might expect from any pork sausage. Unfortunately, many Italian pork butchers in this country make *cotechino* according to their own lights, and the result is a sausage drier and sharper than it should be. From time to time one does find a reasonably good *cotechino*, and it is well worth searching for. *Cotechino* with lentils makes a wonderful country dish for family and friends, and it is specially heartening on a cold winter day.

For 6 persons

1 *cotechino* sausage	1 cup lentils, rinsed in cold water
1 tablespoon chopped yellow	and drained
onion	Salt
2 tablespoons vegetable oil	Freshly ground pepper, 4
1 tablespoon chopped celery	twists of the mill

1. Let the *cotechino* soak overnight, or at least 4 hours, in abundant cold water.

2. Put the *cotechino* in a stockpot large enough to contain it comfortably. Add at least 3 quarts of cold water, cover, and bring to a boil. Cook at a very slow boil for 2½ hours. (Do not prod it with a fork. You must not puncture the skin while it cooks.) When the *cotechino* is done, turn off the heat and allow it to rest in its cooking liquid for 30 minutes before serving. Do not remove it from its liquid until you are ready to slice it.

3. Start doing the lentils about 1½ hours after the *cotechino* has been cooking. Bring 1 quart of water to a simmer. Meanwhile, in a heavy-bottomed casserole, sauté the chopped onion, in the oil, over medium-high heat until pale gold in color. Add the chopped celery and sauté it for about 1 minute.

4. Add the lentils and stir until they are well coated with oil. Add enough simmering water to cover the lentils, turn the heat down to medium low so that the lentils cook at the gentlest simmer, cover the pot, and cook for 30 to 40 minutes, or until the lentils are tender. Add water from time to time so that the lentils are always just covered. (It will improve the taste of the lentils if, in addition to water, you use a ladleful or two of the liquid in which the *cotechino* is cooking.)

5. When the lentils are nearly done, do not add any more water. They must absorb all their cooking liquid before serving. Do not be concerned if some of the lentils burst their skins and become a bit mashed-looking. If there is still some liquid in the pot when they reach tenderness, uncover, turn up the heat, and quickly evaporate it while stirring the lentils. Add salt and pepper to taste.

6. Transfer the *cotechino* to a cutting board and cut into slices ½ inch thick. Spoon the lentils onto a heated platter and arrange the *cotechino* slices on top.

NOTE

If the lentils should cook much faster than anticipated and the *cotechino* is not yet ready, set them aside and warm them up before serving, over medium heat, uncovered, adding a small amount of *cotechino* broth.

MENU SUGGESTIONS

All this needs is a good soup to go before it: Passatelli (page 70), Rice and Celery Soup (page 62), or Escarole and Rice Soup (page 63).

Fagioli dall'occhio con salsicce

BLACK-EYED PEAS AND SAUSAGES WITH TOMATO SAUCE

For 4 persons

2 tablespoons chopped yellow onion
¼ cup olive oil
¼ teaspoon chopped garlic
⅓ cup chopped carrot
⅓ cup chopped celery
1 cup canned Italian tomatoes, coarsely chopped, with their juice

1 pound *luganega* sausage or other sweet sausage, such as bratwurst or breakfast sausage
1 cup dried black-eyed peas, soaked in lukewarm water for at least 1 hour before cooking
Salt and freshly ground pepper, if necessary

(continued)

1. Use an earthenware casserole if you have one. Otherwise, choose a heavy saucepan, preferably of enameled cast iron. Put in the chopped onion, along with the olive oil, and sauté over medium heat until pale gold. Add the garlic and sauté until it has colored lightly. Add the carrot and celery and cook for about 5 minutes, stirring occasionally. Add the chopped tomatoes with their juice, turn the heat down to medium low, and cook at a gentle, slow simmer for 20 minutes.

2. Preheat the oven to 350°.

3. Puncture the sausage skins in several places with a fork. If you are using *luganega,* cut it into 2½-inch lengths. Add the sausage to the pot and cook at a slow simmer for 15 minutes.

4. Add the peas and enough water to cover them well. Cover and bring to a steady simmer. Transfer to the middle level of the preheated oven and cook for 1½ hours, or until the peas are tender, remembering that cooking times vary according to the peas and some peas do cook faster than others. Look into the pot from time to time to make sure that there is enough cooking liquid. If there is not, you can add ½ cup warm water at a time, as needed. (If, on the contrary, the beans are cooked and the cooking liquid is too watery, return the pot to the stove, uncover, turn on the heat to high, and boil until the liquid is concentrated.)

5. Tip the pot and draw off most of the fat with a spoon. Taste the peas and correct for salt and pepper. (Seasoning varies greatly, according to the sausages.)

NOTE

If you are not serving it immediately, you can prepare the entire dish ahead of time. It keeps in the refrigerator for several days. Reheat either on the stove at low heat or in a 250° oven.

MENU SUGGESTIONS

Precede with a hot vegetable soup, as suggested for Boiled *Cotechino* Sausage with Lentils (page 289).

Coda alla vaccinara
OXTAIL BRAISED WITH WINE AND VEGETABLES

If you go to Rome and want to eat as the Romans do, you might include in your plans a meal at one of the *trattorie* near the slaughter-house where they specialize in this dish. *Coda alla vaccinara* is as genuinely Roman as its name. *Vaccinaro*, although now it means "tanner," was the old local name for "butcher." And truly it is a hearty butcher's dish. Oxtail is not for picky filet mignon eaters, but it will satisfy those who appreciate the flavor and body that meat always has when it comes from next to the joints and bones.

For 4 to 5 persons

½ pound pork rind
⅓ cup olive oil
1 tablespoon cooking fat, preferably lard
¼ cup chopped parsley
½ teaspoon chopped garlic
⅔ cup chopped yellow onion
⅔ cup chopped carrot
2½ pounds oxtail, cut at the joints and, if frozen, thawed overnight in the refrigerator

1½ cups dry white wine
½ cup canned Italian tomatoes, seeded, drained, and coarsely chopped
1½ teaspoons salt
Freshly ground pepper, 8 to 10 twists of the mill
1½ cups very coarsely chopped celery

1. Rinse the pork rind in cold water. Bring water to a boil in a pan. Drop in the pork rind. When the water returns to a boil, drain and let the rind cool. When cool, cut it into 1-inch long strips and set aside.

2. Preheat the oven to 350°.

3. Choose a heavy casserole, large enough to contain all the ingredients in the recipe. Put in the olive oil, lard, parsley, garlic, onion, and carrot. Sauté lightly over medium heat for 10 minutes, stirring frequently.

(continued)

4. Raise the heat to medium high, then add the oxtail pieces and the pork rind. Brown the meat well on all sides for about 8 minutes.

5. Add the wine, but pour it gradually, or it may boil over. Boil the wine for 2 to 3 minutes, turning the meat once or twice.

6. Add the chopped tomatoes, 1 cup water, salt, and pepper. When the contents of the casserole have come to a steady simmer, cover the pot and place it in the middle level of the preheated oven. Cook for 1½ hours, turning the meat every 30 minutes.

7. Add the cut-up celery to the casserole, mixing it well in the meat and juices. Cook for 45 minutes more in the oven, turning the contents of the pot at least twice. At this point, the meat should be very tender and come easily off the bone. (Some cooks cook the meat much longer and boil the celery before adding it to the meat. I find that 2¼ to 2½ hours are quite sufficient to make oxtail tender enough to cut with a fork. And boiling the celery results in a partial loss of the flavor that is characteristic of the dish.)

8. Before serving, tip the casserole and draw off as much fat as possible with a spoon.

NOTE

This dish can be prepared entirely ahead of time and warmed up on top of the stove at medium heat just before serving. It will keep in the refrigerator for several days.

MENU SUGGESTIONS

A good country soup is the best first course here: Lentil Soup (page 73), Bean Soup with Parsley and Garlic (page 79), or Beans and Pasta Soup (page 80). If you would rather have a pasta, choose either Spaghetti with Garlic and Oil (page 103) or Bucatini with Pancetta, Tomatoes, and Hot Pepper (page 105). No vegetables need accompany this dish, but follow it with a nice cleansing Mixed Salad (page 408) or Finocchio Salad (page 407).

Trippa alla parmigiana
HONEYCOMB TRIPE WITH PARMESAN CHEESE

To a great many Americans tripe is a mysterious and not particularly appealing dish. Actually, it is just a muscle, the stomach muscle, and a delicious one at that. Little of the meat we routinely eat is so savory, so succulently tender, or has such an appetizing fragrance as a well-prepared dish of tripe. To those who can approach a new experience without tension or preconceptions, I firmly recommend it. Fortunately, the greatest drawback to making tripe at home—its long and tedious scrubbing, soaking, and preliminary blanching—has been completely overcome by the appearance of ready-to-cook honeycomb tripe at many frozen-meat counters. This is an excellent product with which you can confidently prepare any of the great regional Italian tripe dishes.

For 6 persons

2 pounds frozen honeycomb tripe, thawed
1 small carrot
1 small onion
1 stalk celery
½ cup olive oil
3 tablespoons butter
½ cup chopped yellow onion
½ cup chopped celery
½ cup chopped carrot
2 cloves garlic, lightly crushed with a knife handle and peeled
1 tablespoon chopped parsley
¼ teaspoon chopped rosemary
⅔ cup dry white wine
1 cup canned Italian tomatoes, with their juice
Freshly ground pepper, about 8 to 10 twists of the mill
2 teaspoons salt
1 cup Homemade Meat Broth (page 10) OR ⅓ cup canned beef broth mixed with ⅔ cup water
¾ cup freshly grated Parmesan cheese

1. Rinse the tripe thoroughly under cold running water and set aside.

2. Bring 3 quarts of water to a boil with the whole carrot, onion,

and celery. Add the tripe, cover, and cook at a moderate boil for 15 minutes. Drain and place the tripe in a bowl with enough cold water to cover. Soak until the tripe is thoroughly cool, then cut it into strips ½ inch wide by 3 to 4 inches long. Set aside.

3. Preheat the oven to 325°.

4. In a heavy casserole put the olive oil, 1 tablespoon of the butter, and the chopped onion, celery, and carrot, and cook slowly over medium-low heat for about 5 minutes, or until the vegetables have slightly wilted. Add the crushed garlic, parsley, and rosemary and cook just long enough to stir everything well two or three times.

5. Add the tripe, stirring it into the vegetables and seasonings, and cook it for 5 minutes. Add the white wine and raise the heat to medium high, boiling the wine for 30 seconds.

6. Add the tomatoes and their juice, the pepper, salt, and broth and bring to a light boil. Cover the pot and bake in the middle level of the preheated oven for 2 to 2½ hours. (Look in on the tripe from time to time to make sure there is sufficient liquid in the pot. If the liquid is drying too fast, add 2 to 3 tablespoons of water.) Taste the tripe for doneness after 2 hours. It should be very tender but pleasantly chewy and easily cut with a fork.

7. When done, remove from the oven and swirl in the remaining 2 tablespoons of butter and the grated cheese. Serve piping hot.

NOTE

A more fiery version of the same dish can be achieved by adding ¼ teaspoon of chopped hot red pepper, or slightly more, to taste, before the tripe goes into the oven.

Tripe is just as delicious when reheated. It keeps perfectly in the refrigerator for 4 to 5 days.

MENU SUGGESTIONS

The earthy flavor of tripe goes best with a hearty soup such as Beans and Pasta Soup (page 80), any of the chick-pea soups on pages 85–87, or Vegetable Soup (page 66). If you want pasta, choose Spaghetti with Garlic and Oil (page 103). No vegetables are needed. Follow with Mixed Salad (page 408), Finocchio Salad (page 407), or Boiled Cauliflower Salad (page 413).

Animelle con pomodori e piselli

SWEETBREADS BRAISED WITH TOMATOES AND PEAS

In the Italian preparation of sweetbreads you must have a firm, light, patient hand to peel off the thin membrane in which they are wrapped. We don't soak them in water for several hours to whiten them because the Italian approach rarely alters or tones down the natural characteristics of an ingredient. In the version below the sweetbreads are very briefly blanched, sautéed in butter and oil, then cooked slowly with tomatoes and peas. They are quite tender when cooked and very delicate in flavor, somewhat tastier and firmer than brains. They are perfectly complemented by the sweet taste of very young peas.

For 4 to 6 persons

1½ pounds sweetbreads	⅔ cup canned Italian tomatoes,
½ carrot, peeled	coarsely chopped, with
1 stalk celery	their juice
1 tablespoon vinegar	2 pounds fresh, young peas
Salt	(unshelled weight) or 1
2½ tablespoons chopped shallots	ten-ounce package frozen
or yellow onion	small, early peas, thawed
4 tablespoons butter	Freshly ground pepper, 2 to
1 tablespoon vegetable oil	3 twists of the mill

1. Working under cold running water, peel off as much of the membrane surrounding the sweetbreads as you can. If you are patient and careful you should be able to pull virtually all of it off. When finished rinse the sweetbreads under cold running water.

2. In a saucepan put enough cold water to cover the sweetbreads later and add the carrot, celery, vinegar, and a pinch of salt. Bring the water to a boil, add the sweetbreads, and cook at a very gentle simmer for 6 minutes. Drain the sweetbreads and, while still warm, pull off any remaining bits of membrane. (The sweetbreads may be prepared a day ahead of time up to this point and refrigerated under plastic wrap.) When cold, cut the sweetbreads into smaller-than-bite-sized chunks, about 1 inch thick.

3. In a deep skillet or casserole, sauté the shallots, in the butter and oil, over medium heat until pale gold but not browned. Add the sweetbreads and sauté until lightly browned on all sides. Add the chopped tomatoes with their juice and continue cooking over moderate heat, keeping the tomatoes at a gentle simmer.

4. After 20 minutes add the shelled fresh peas, ½ teaspoon salt, and pepper, mixing well with the sweetbreads and tomato. (If you are using frozen peas wait another 15 minutes before adding the thawed peas.) Cover and cook at a gentle simmer for 20 more minutes. Taste and correct for salt and pepper, and serve while hot. (If the sauce is too thin, transfer the sweetbreads with a slotted spoon to a warm platter and rapidly reduce the sauce over high heat, then pour the sauce and peas over the sweetbreads and serve immediately.)

MENU SUGGESTIONS

Sweetbreads may also be served in individual pastry shells or over slices of toasted fine white bread. They can follow a first course of soup, pasta, or *risotto* that does not have a strong tomato presence. Risotto with Parmesan Cheese (page 181) would be an excellent choice. Avoid any spicy or very hearty first course that would be out of balance with the delicate taste of the sweetbreads.

Fegato alla veneziana
SAUTÉED CALF'S LIVER WITH ONIONS, VENETIAN STYLE

What you need for *fegato alla veneziana* is, above everything else, a butcher able and willing to slice calf's liver to an even thinness of ¼ inch. The thinner liver is, the faster it cooks, and the faster it cooks, the sweeter it tastes. This is the whole point of *fegato alla veneziana*. Another essential requirement is that the liver come from a very young, milk-fed animal, less than three months old. Liver from young calves is of a pale, clear, rosy color. As the animal gets older, the liver becomes darker, tougher, and sharper in taste. Of course, you can use the technique of *fegato alla veneziana* with what calf's liver you have available. But if you ever find access to younger liver and a cooperative butcher, don't pass up the opportunity to discover what a joy this dish can be at its best.

For 4 persons

1½ pounds calf's liver, very thinly sliced	Salt
3 tablespoons vegetable oil	Freshly ground pepper, about 6 twists of the mill
3 cups thinly sliced yellow onion	

1. Remove the thin skin tissue around the liver slices and any large gristly tubes. (Traditionally, liver for *fegato alla veneziana* is cut at this point into bite-sized pieces about 1½ inches wide. You may do this if you like. I find the larger slices easier to turn while cooking, and I skip this step, unless I am having Venetians to dinner.)

2. Choose a skillet that can later accommodate all the liver in a single layer without crowding. Put in all the oil and sliced onion and cook over medium-low heat for about 15 to 20 minutes. The onion should be limp and nicely browned. (You can prepare everything several hours ahead of time, up to and including this point.)

3. Remove the onion from the skillet with a slotted spoon or spatula, and set aside. Don't be concerned if two or three slivers of onion are left in the skillet. What is important is that you should still have oil in the skillet.

4. Turn the heat to high, and when the oil is very hot put in the liver. (The oil should be very hot in order to cook the liver rapidly.) As soon as the liver loses its raw, reddish color, turn it, add a large pinch of salt and some pepper, and return the onions to the skillet. Give everything one more turn, transfer to a warm platter, and serve immediately.

NOTE

It takes almost longer to read this than to cook the liver. If it is the proper thinness, the liver is done in less than a minute.

(*continued*)

MENU SUGGESTIONS

For a first course, it would be hard to improve on Rice and Peas (page 60). Rice and Lentil Soup (page 75), Risotto with Zucchini (page 191), and Risotto with Asparagus (page 189) are also good choices. If you want a vegetable, Fried Tomatoes (page 390) go well with liver.

Fegato di vitello fritto

FRIED BREADED CALF'S LIVER

For 4 persons

Vegetable oil, enough to thickly coat the bottom of the skillet	¾ cup fine, dry unflavored bread crumbs, spread on a dish or on waxed paper
2 tablespoons butter	Salt and freshly ground pepper to taste
1½ pounds thinly sliced calf's liver	Lemon wedges

1. Heat the oil and the butter in a skillet over high heat.

2. Press the slices of liver into the bread crumbs with the palm of your hand, turning to coat both sides. Shake off excess crumbs. As soon as the butter foam subsides, slip the breaded liver into the skillet.

3. When the liver is lightly and crisply browned on one side, turn it and do the other side. (If it is as thin as recommended, it should take about 30 seconds for each side. If it is thicker, it will take just a little longer.) When done, the liver should be pink and very tender inside.

4. As each slice is done, place on paper towels to drain and season with salt and pepper. Serve piping hot, with lemon wedges.

MENU SUGGESTIONS

First Course: any *risotto* with vegetables (pages 189–191) or Risotto with Parmesan Cheese (page 181). Other possibilities are Italian

Pancakes Filled with Meat Sauce (page 178), Conchiglie with Sausage and Cream Sauce (page 109), Beans and Sauerkraut Soup (page 75), or Spinach Soup (page 65). For a vegetable choose Sautéed Diced Eggplant (page 374) or Oven-Browned Tomatoes (page 389).

Cervella fritta
FRIED CALF'S BRAINS

This is the favorite way of doing brains in Italy. The brains are first cooked with vegetables, then sliced and fried. Frying points up their lovely texture. As one bites, the thin, golden armor of their crust gives way to yield the delectable core in all its tenderness.

For 4 persons

1 calf's brain (about 1 pound)	1 cup fine, dry unflavored bread
½ carrot, peeled	crumbs, spread on a dish
½ yellow onion, peeled	or on waxed paper
½ stalk celery	Vegetable oil, enough to
1 tablespoon vinegar	come ½ inch up the side
1 teaspoon salt	of the pan
1 egg, lightly beaten with 1	Lemon wedges
teaspoon salt, in a bowl	

1. Wash the brain thoroughly in cold water, then let soak in cold water for 10 minutes. Drain, and carefully remove as much as possible of the surrounding membrane and the protruding blood vessels.

2. Put the carrot, onion, celery, vinegar, and 1 teaspoon of salt in a saucepan with 6 cups of water and bring to a boil.

3. Drop in the brain, and when the water has returned to a boil cover the pan and adjust the heat so that the liquid bubbles very slowly but steadily. Cook for 20 minutes.

4. Drain, and let the brain cool completely. When cool, refrigerate for about 10 minutes, or until they are very firm. (You may

even prepare them ahead of time, in the morning, and refrigerate until shortly before you are ready to fry. If refrigerating brains for several hours, cover them with plastic wrap.)

5. Cut the brain into broad, larger-than-bite-size pieces, about ½ inch thick.

6. First dip the slices in egg, letting the excess flow back into the bowl, then turn them in bread crumbs.

7. Heat the oil in a skillet over high heat. When the oil is very hot, slip the coated slices into the pan. (Do not put in any more at one time than will fit loosely.) Fry until golden brown on one side, then do the other side. When a nice crust has formed on both sides, transfer to paper towels to drain. When all the slices are done, serve immediately, with lemon wedges on the side.

MENU SUGGESTIONS

Fried brains can be one of the components of Mixed Fried Meats, Vegetable, Cheese, Cream, and Fruit (page 333). If it is going to be a second course on its own, it can be preceded by a soup, such as Escarole and Rice Soup (page 63) or Spinach Soup (page 65), or by Fettuccine Tossed in Cream and Butter (page 130), Meat-Stuffed Pasta Rolls (page 149), Rice and Peas (page 60), or any *risotto*, except those with chicken livers or with clams. It can then be accompanied by any one of the fried vegetables, and Sautéed Green Beans with Butter and Cheese (page 361), Sautéed Mushrooms with Garlic and Parsley (page 379), or Sautéed Broccoli with Garlic (page 363).

Rognoncini trifolati al vino bianco
SAUTÉED LAMB KIDNEYS WITH WHITE WINE

When I started teaching I was not aware of the American aversion to organs. I found it out when my students nearly walked out on me the first time I taught this dish. They stayed on, however, and, after discovering how tasty and fine kidneys can be, many of them welcomed this addition to their repertoire. For anyone still unfamiliar with organs this delicate way of preparing kidneys could be a good way to embark on a most delicious experience.

For 4 to 6 persons

20 lamb kidneys

3 tablespoons vinegar

¼ cup vegetable oil

2 tablespoons finely chopped shallots or yellow onion

½ teaspoon finely chopped garlic

2 tablespoons finely chopped parsley

Salt to taste

Freshly ground pepper, 6 to 8 twists of the mill

½ teaspoon cornstarch

⅔ cup dry white wine

1. Split the kidneys in half and wash briefly under cold running water. To a china or earthenware bowl of water large enough to contain them add the vinegar, then the kidneys. Let the kidneys soak for at least 30 minutes, then drain and pat dry with paper towels. Cut them into very thin slices and try to remove as many of the small white vessels as possible.

2. Heat the oil in a heavy-bottomed skillet and sauté the shallots until pale gold. Add the chopped garlic, stir two or three times, add the parsley, and immediately after add the sliced kidneys.

3. Raise the heat to high, add salt and pepper, and stir so that the kidneys are well coated with the sautéed shallots and with the garlic and parsley. As soon as the kidneys have lost their raw red color, transfer them to a warm platter. (It is very important not to overcook kidneys. Tiny lamb kidneys, in particular, cook very rapidly.)

4. Mix the cornstarch into the wine and add to the skillet. Bring to a rapid boil over high heat, taking care to scrape up all the cooking residue stuck to the bottom of the pan. Add any juice the kidneys may have left in their platter. When the sauce starts to thicken, add the kidneys and stir quickly, cooking them just a moment more. Serve with their sauce while still hot.

(continued)

Any first course that has character but is not overbearingly sharp goes well with kidneys. Any of the following makes a good choice: Potato Gnocchi (page 195) with either Tomato Sauce III (page 95) or Gorgonzola Sauce (page 134), Cappelletti with Butter and Heavy Cream (page 159), Italian Pancakes Filled with Spinach (page 177), Rice and Peas (page 60). Vegetable: Braised Artichokes and Leeks (page 348) or Braised Artichokes and Peas (page 347).

Fegatelli di maiale con la rete
BROILED PORK LIVER WRAPPED IN CAUL FAT

This is a classic Tuscan dish, and it is delicious. Like all Tuscan grills it is extremely simple. The one important point to remember is not to overcook the liver. Perfectly broiled liver is pink, juicy, and sweet tasting. Caul fat, or pork net, is a fatty membrane enveloping the intestines. It acts as a self-baster for the liver. It is so inexpensive that it is well worth buying a large piece and utilizing the best parts of it for the wrappers.

For 6 persons

A large piece of caul fat (about 1 pound)	Salt and freshly ground pepper to taste
1½ pounds pork liver	Bay leaves

1. Preheat the broiler to its maximum.

2. Soak the caul fat in lukewarm water for 2 or 3 minutes, until it loosens up. Change the water a few times to rinse and clean the membrane. Lay the membrane on a dry cloth and carefully open it up. Cut the best parts of it into rectangles 5 by 7 inches. (Do not bother patching small pieces together.)

3. Remove any skin or tough, exposed vessels from the liver. Wash the liver in cold water and pat thoroughly dry. Cut it into sections

about 3 inches long, 2 inches wide, and ⅝ inch thick.

4. Season the sections of liver with a good pinch of salt and at least a grinding of pepper each. Place a bay leaf on each section and wrap each section with one of the caul-fat wrappers, tucking the ends under as you wrap. Fasten each piece of liver with a toothpick.

5. Place in the hot broiler, which should have been on for at least 15 minutes, so that it is searing hot when you put in the liver. Turn the liver after 2½ to 3 minutes. Do not cook more than 4 or 5 minutes all together. Serve piping hot.

MENU SUGGESTIONS

This dish is absolutely sensational cooked outdoors over charcoal. It can be part of a mixed grill with steaks and chops. Indoors, precede it with Bean Soup with Parsley and Garlic (page 79), Potato and Onion Soup (page 59), or Split Green Peas and Potato Soup (page 72). Accompany the liver with Cauliflower Gratinéed with Butter and Cheese (page 366), Swiss Chard Stalks with Parmesan Cheese (page 370), or Braised Artichokes and Leeks (page 348).

Fegatini di pollo alla salvia
SAUTÉED CHICKEN LIVERS WITH SAGE

For 6 persons

1½ pounds chicken livers	⅓ cup dry white wine
2 tablespoons finely chopped	Salt to taste
shallots or yellow onion	Freshly ground pepper,
¼ cup butter	about 4 twists of the mill
1 dozen dried sage leaves	

1. Examine the livers carefully for green spots and cut them out. Remove any bits of fat and wash the livers thoroughly in cold water. Dry well on paper towels.

(continued)

2. In a skillet, sauté the shallots in the butter over medium heat. When they turn pale gold, raise the heat and add the sage leaves and chicken livers. Cook over high heat for just a few minutes, stirring frequently, until the livers lose their raw, red color. Transfer the livers to a warm platter.

3. Add the wine to the skillet and boil briskly until it has almost completely evaporated. Scrape up and loosen any cooking residue in the pan. Add any liquid the livers may have thrown off in the platter, and allow it to evaporate.

4. Return the chicken livers to the pan, turn them rapidly for a few moments over high heat, add salt and pepper, and transfer to a warm serving platter. Serve immediately.

MENU SUGGESTIONS

These chicken livers go so well with Italian Mashed Potatoes with Parmesan Cheese (page 384) that you can dispense with a pasta first course without any regrets. You can precede them with Stuffed Mushrooms with Béchamel Sauce (page 46), Artichokes, Roman Style (page 337), or Baked Stuffed Zucchini Boats (page 395). If you want to vary this arrangement, choose Rice and Celery Soup (page 62) or Spinach Soup (page 65) as a first course and accompany the livers with Carrots with Parmesan Cheese (page 365).

Pollo arrosto in tegame

PAN-ROASTED CHICKEN WITH GARLIC, ROSEMARY, AND WHITE WINE

Reliable ovens are only a recent addition to the Italian kitchen, and, consequently, traditional roasts are done either on the spit or in a pan on top of the stove. In this recipe the chicken is entirely pan roasted, with just enough liquid to keep it from drying out. As in almost all Italian roasts, it is flavored with garlic and a hint of rosemary. It is one of the simplest and tastiest ways of doing chicken, and, if you use a young frying chicken, you should have the roasted chicken on the table in less than 45 minutes from the time you start preparing it.

For 4 persons

2 tablespoons butter
2 tablespoons vegetable oil
2 to 3 cloves garlic, peeled
1 frying chicken (2½ pounds), washed in cold water, quartered, and thoroughly dried in a towel
A small branch of fresh

rosemary, cut in two, or
½ teaspoon dried rosemary leaves
Salt
Freshly ground pepper, about 6 twists of the mill
½ cup dry white wine

1. Heat the butter and oil in a deep skillet or sauté pan over medium-high heat. When the butter foam begins to subside, add the garlic and the chicken quarters, skin side down. When the chicken is well browned on one side, turn the pieces over and add the rosemary. If the garlic starts to blacken, remove it. If, however, it stays a deep golden brown, leave it in until the chicken is cooked. Control the heat so that the cooking fat stays hot but doesn't burn.

2. When you have browned the chicken well on all sides, add a large pinch of salt, the pepper, and the wine. Allow the wine to bubble rapidly for 2 to 3 minutes, then lower the heat until it is just simmering, and cover the pan. Cook slowly until the chicken is tender at the pricking of a fork. (A young fryer should take about 30 to 35 minutes.) Turn the chicken two or three times while cooking. (If you see that the cooking liquid has dried up, you can add 1 to 2 tablespoons of water as needed.)

3. Transfer the chicken to a warm serving platter, removing the garlic from the pan if you haven't done it earlier. Tilt the pan, drawing off all but 2 tablespoons of fat with a spoon. Return the pan to high heat, adding 2 to 3 tablespoons of water, and scraping up the cooking juices in the pan. Pour these over the chicken and serve.

(continued)

MENU SUGGESTIONS

You can precede this with soup, such as Rice and Celery Soup (page 62), Escarole and Rice Soup (page 63), or Spinach Soup (page 65). If you'd like a pasta, any of these would be a good choice: Penne with a Sauce of Tomatoes and Dried Wild Mushrooms (page 108), Baked Rigatoni with Meat Sauce (page 110), Tagliatelle with Bolognese Meat Sauce (page 129), Meat-Stuffed Pasta Rolls (page 149), Risotto with Parmesan Cheese (page 181), Risotto with Meat Sauce (page 187), Rice and Peas (page 60). If the first course was soup, you can accompany the chicken with Diced Pan-Roasted Potatoes (page 387) or Italian Mashed Potatoes with Parmesan Cheese (page 384). If you had pasta, a good vegetable accompaniment would be Sautéed Green Beans with Butter and Cheese (page 361), Sautéed Peas with Prosciutto, Florentine Style (page 383), or Carrots with Parmesan Cheese (page 365).

Pollo arrosto al forno con rosmarino

ROAST CHICKEN WITH ROSEMARY

For 4 persons

3 cloves garlic, peeled	Salt
1 heaping teaspoon dried rosemary leaves	Freshly ground pepper, about 8 twists of the mill
1 frying chicken (about 2½ pounds), washed and thoroughly dried in a towel	¼ cup vegetable oil

1. Preheat the oven to 375°.

2. Put all the garlic and half the rosemary into the bird's cavity. Add a large pinch of salt and a few grindings of pepper.

3. Rub about half the oil over the outside of the chicken, and sprinkle with salt, some more pepper, and the rest of the rosemary.

4. Put the chicken and the rest of the oil in a roasting pan and place it in the middle level of the preheated oven. Turn the chicken

and baste it with the fat and cooking juices in the pan every 15 minutes. Cook for about 1 hour, or until the skin is well browned and crisp.

5. Transfer the chicken to a warm platter. Tip the pan and draw off all but 1 tablespoon of fat with a spoon. Place the pan over the stove burner, turn on the heat to high, add 1 or 2 tablespoons of water, and while it boils away scrape up all the cooking residue. Pour over the chicken and serve immediately.

MENU SUGGESTIONS

Follow the ones given for Pan-Roasted Chicken with Garlic, Rosemary, and White Wine (top of preceding page).

Pollo alla diavola

CHARCOAL-BROILED CHICKEN MARINATED IN PEPPER, OIL, AND LEMON

This peppery chicken should be very satisfying to an outdoor appetite. It is a famous Roman specialty that has now become popular in most of Italy. The chicken is opened flat, rubbed liberally with crushed peppercorns, and marinated in oil and lemon juice. Many cooks omit the lemon juice until the chicken is cooked, but I find that it enhances the texture and fragrance of the chicken when it goes in the marinade. If you are picnicking, you can prepare the chicken at home, put it in a plastic bag, stow it in a portable refrigerator or insulated food bag, and when your charcoal fire in the wilderness is ready the chicken is ready. Don't skimp on the pepper, or it won't be *alla diavola*, "hot as the devil."

Although charcoal is the ideal fire for chicken *alla diavola*, it is delicious even on an indoor broiler. Preheat the broiler to its maximum setting at least 15 minutes ahead of time.

(continued)

For 4 persons

1 broiling chicken (about 2 pounds)	3 tablespoons olive oil
⅓ cup lemon juice	2 teaspoons salt
1 tablespoon crushed pepper-corns	

1. Lay the chicken on a flat surface with the breast facing down and split it open along the entire backbone. Crack the breastbone from the inside. Spread the chicken as flat as you can with your hands. Turn it over so the breast faces you. Cut the wings and legs where they join the body, but without detaching them—just enough to spread them flat. Turn the chicken over again, with the inside of the carcass facing you, and pound it as flat as possible, using a cleaver or large meat flattener. It should have something of a butterfly shape.

2. Put the chicken in a deep dish. Pour the lemon juice over the chicken, then add the peppercorns and the olive oil. Cover the dish and let it marinate for at least 2 hours. Uncover and baste from time to time.

3. When the fire is ready, sprinkle the chicken with salt and place on the grill (which should be about 5 inches above the charcoal), skin side toward the fire. Broil until the skin has turned light brown, then turn it over on the other side, basting with marinade liquid from time to time. Turn it over after about 10 minutes and cook briefly once again on each side, until the thigh is tender at the pricking of a fork. (All together it should take about 35 minutes.) If the marinating liquid should run out before the chicken is done, baste with a teaspoonful of olive oil from time to time. Season with a pinch of crushed pepper before serving.

MENU SUGGESTIONS

If cooked outdoors, some or all of the Charcoal-Broiled Vegetables (page 400), would be lovely with this chicken. Indoors, a first course can be any soup, *risotto,* or pasta that does not have fish or cream in it. You can't go wrong with any vegetable, but a good combination is the Green Beans with Peppers and Tomatoes (page 362) or Fried Eggplant (page 372), together with Oven-Browned Tomatoes (page 389).

Pollo alla cacciatora

CHICKEN FRICASSEE WITH GREEN PEPPERS AND TOMATOES

For 4 or 5 persons

Frying chicken (2½ to 3 pounds), cut into 4 to 6 pieces
3 tablespoons vegetable oil
1 cup all-purpose flour, spread on a dinner plate or on waxed paper
Salt
Freshly ground pepper, 4 to 6 twists of the mill
⅔ cup dry white wine
⅓ cup thinly sliced yellow onion

1 green pepper, with seeds removed, cut into thin strips
1 medium carrot, sliced very thin
½ stalk celery, cut into thin strips
1 clove garlic, peeled and chopped very fine
⅔ cup canned Italian tomatoes, coarsely chopped, with their juice

1. Wash the chicken pieces in cold running water and pat dry very thoroughly with paper towels.

2. Choose a skillet large enough to contain all the chicken pieces comfortably, without crowding. Heat the oil in the skillet over moderately high heat. Turn the chicken pieces in the flour, coating both sides and shaking off the excess, and put in the skillet, skin side down. When one side has turned golden brown, turn the pieces over and brown the other side. When nicely browned on all sides, transfer them to a warm platter and add salt and pepper.

3. Tip the skillet and draw off most of the fat with a spoon. Turn the heat to high, add the wine, and boil rapidly until it is reduced by half. Scrape up and loosen any cooking residue in the pan. Lower

the heat to medium, add the sliced onion, and cook for about 5 minutes, stirring two or three times. Add the browned chicken pieces, all but the breasts. (Breasts cook faster, so they can be added later.) Add the sliced pepper, carrot, celery, garlic, and the chopped tomatoes and their juice. Adjust to a slow simmer and cover. After 9 to 10 minutes add the breasts and continue cooking until tender, about 30 minutes. Turn and baste the chicken a few times while cooking.

4. Transfer the chicken to a warm serving platter. If the sauce in the pan is too thin, raise the heat to high and boil it briskly until it thickens, stirring as it boils. Pour the sauce over the chicken and serve immediately.

NOTE

If prepared ahead of time, let the chicken cool in its sauce. When reheating, simmer very slowly, covered, for a few minutes, just until the chicken is hot.

MENU SUGGESTIONS

A good choice for a first course would be a simple Risotto with Parmesan Cheese (page 181). Other possibilities are Beans and Pasta Soup (page 80), Potato Gnocchi with Pesto (page 195), Rice with Fresh Basil and Mozzarella Cheese (page 194), or Tagliatelle with Bolognese Meat Sauce (page 129). No vegetable is called for, but instead of the usual raw salad you might serve Mixed Cooked Vegetable Salad (page 416).

Pollo coi funghi secchi
CHICKEN FRICASSEE WITH DRIED WILD MUSHROOMS

The key ingredient in this succulent dish is dried wild mushrooms. Nothing can be substituted for them that will yield the same full-flavored taste and rich woodsy aroma. The mushrooms with the most delicate flavor and finest texture are the creamy brown variety in large pieces. The very dark, crumbly chips are much cheaper but not quite so agreeable.

For 4 persons

1 ounce imported dried wild mushrooms

1 frying chicken (about 2½ pounds)

3 tablespoons vegetable oil

3 tablespoons butter

Salt and freshly ground pepper to taste

½ cup dry white wine

3 tablespoons canned Italian tomatoes, coarsely chopped

1. Place the mushrooms in ⅔ cup lukewarm water. Let soak at least 15 to 20 minutes.

2. Wash the chicken under cold running water. Cut into quarters and pat thoroughly dry.

3. Remove the mushrooms, reserving the water in which they have soaked. Filter the water by straining it through a paper towel placed in a fine sieve, and set aside. Rinse the mushrooms in cold running water three or four times, then chop them roughly and set aside.

4. In a heavy-bottomed skillet heat all the oil and 2 tablespoons of the butter. When the butter foam subsides, add the chicken quarters and brown them well on all sides over medium heat. Add salt and pepper, turning the chicken once or twice. Add the wine.

5. When the wine has evaporated add the chopped mushrooms, the water they have soaked in, and the chopped peeled tomatoes. Cover the skillet and cook at gentle heat for about 30 minutes, or until the chicken is tender. Turn the chicken pieces over from time to time.

6. Transfer the chicken to a warm platter. Tip the pan and draw off most of the fat with a spoon. If the sauce in the pan is too thin, boil it over high heat until it is concentrated. Off the heat, swirl in the remaining tablespoon of butter and pour the sauce over the chicken.

MENU SUGGESTIONS

A perfect first course would be Italian Pancakes Filled with Spinach (page 177). Other good choices: Baked Green Lasagne with Meat Sauce (page 143), Fettuccine with Gorgonzola Sauce (page 134), Conchiglie with Sausage and Cream Sauce (page 109), Creamy Potato Soup with Carrots and Celery (page 58), Cappellacci filled with Sweet Potatoes and Parsley (page 168), or Risotto with Luganega Sausage (page 188). For a vegetable: Fried Finocchio (page 378), Crisp-Fried Whole Artichokes (page 344), or one of the vegetables with butter and cheese, such as Carrots with Parmesan Cheese (page 365).

Petti di pollo

FILLETS OF BREAST OF CHICKEN

This is the Italian method of filleting chicken breasts. It produces very thin slices of chicken that cook very rapidly and remain extraordinarily juicy and tender. Once you've acquired the knack of separating the two muscles that make up each side of the breast the whole procedure becomes very simple. The result in terms of texture and flavor is so fine that you will probably adopt this method of filleting for any recipe calling for suprêmes of chicken.

1. Slip your fingers underneath the skin and pull it entirely away from the breast. It comes off quite easily. Be sure you also remove the thin membrane that adheres to the breast underneath the skin.

2. Run a finger along the broad upper part of the breast from the center bone toward the side and feel for an opening. You will find a spot where the finger enters easily without resistance. This is where the two muscles meet, and the probing, lifting action of your fingers has separated them. Detach them from the bone with a small sharp knife. You will obtain from each side of the breast two separate pieces, one small and tapered, the other flatter, larger, and somewhat triangular in shape.

3. The smaller piece has a white tendon that must be pulled out. With one hand grasp the tendon where it protrudes, with the other take a knife and push with the blade against the flesh where it meets the tendon. Pull the tendon out. It should come easily. Nothing else needs to be done to this piece.

4. Lay the larger piece on a cutting board with the side that was next to the bone facing down. Hold it flat with the palm of one

hand. With the other hand take a sharp knife and slice the breast with the blade moving parallel to the cutting board, thus dividing the piece into two even slices of half the original thickness. Watch both sides of the piece while slicing to make sure you are slicing it evenly.

You now have from each half breast three tender fillets ready for cooking.

To fillet a chicken breast, after skinning, run a finger along the broad upper part of the breast from the center bone toward the side and feel for an opening. You will find a spot where the finger enters easily. Detach the muscles from the bone with a small sharp knife.

When slicing the larger piece, make sure the side that was next to the bone is facing down. Hold it flat with the palm of one hand, and slice the breast parallel to the cutting board, dividing the piece into two even slices.

Petti di pollo alla senese

SAUTÉED CHICKEN BREAST FILLETS WITH
LEMON AND PARSLEY

For 4 or 5 persons

1 tablespoon vegetable oil	Freshly ground pepper, about
5 tablespoons butter	4 twists of the mill
3 whole chicken breasts, filleted	Juice of 1 lemon
as directed above	3 tablespoons chopped parsley
Salt to taste	1 lemon, thinly sliced

1. Heat the oil and 3 tablespoons of the butter in a skillet over medium-high heat. When the butter foam begins to subside, sauté the chicken fillets on both sides very briefly. (They will be cooked in 2 minutes at most.)

2. Remove the fillets to a warm platter and add salt and pepper.

3. Add the lemon juice to the skillet and turn on the heat to medium. Loosen all the cooking residue from the bottom of the pan, adding 1 or 2 tablespoons of water if necessary. Add the parsley and the remaining 2 tablespoons butter to the cooking juices. Stir three or four times. Lower the heat to a minimum and add the cooked chicken fillets, turning them over quickly in the sauce once or twice.

4. Transfer the fillets to a warm serving platter and pour the cooking juices from the skillet over them. Serve garnished with lemon slices.

MENU SUGGESTIONS

First course: Tortellini Filled with Parsley and Ricotta (page 162) with Tomato and Cream Sauce (page 163), Risotto with Dried Wild Mushrooms (page 185), or Spinach and Ricotta Gnocchi (page 201). Vegetable: Sautéed Peas with Prosciutto, Florentine Style (page 383), Fava Beans, Roman Style (page 359), or Sautéed Mushrooms with Garlic and Parsley (page 379).

Rollatini di petto di pollo e maiale
ROLLED BREAST OF CHICKEN FILLETS STUFFED WITH PORK

For 4 to 6 persons

2 cloves garlic, lightly crushed
    with a heavy knife handle
    and peeled
3 tablespoons vegetable oil
½ pound any lean cut pork,
    ground
Salt
Freshly ground pepper, about
    6 twists of the mill

1 teaspoon dried rosemary
    leaves
2 large whole breasts of chicken,
    filleted as directed on page
    312
2 tablespoons butter
½ cup dry white wine

1. In a skillet, sauté the crushed garlic cloves in the oil over medium heat. When the garlic has colored lightly, add the ground pork, a large pinch of salt, the pepper, and rosemary. Stir, and sauté the meat for 10 minutes, crumbling it with a fork as it cooks. Then, with a perforated ladle or slotted spoon, transfer the meat to a dish and allow to cool. Discard all but 2½ to 3 tablespoons of fat from the skillet.

2. Lay the chicken breast fillets flat and sprinkle very lightly with salt and pepper. Spread the sautéed ground pork on the fillets, and roll each fillet up tightly. Tie up each roll securely with string as though you were preparing miniature roasts. (You can prepare the dish up to this point several hours ahead of time.)

3. Add the butter to the skillet in which you cooked the pork and turn the heat up to medium high. When the butter foam begins to subside, put in the stuffed chicken rolls. Brown well on all sides, but do not overcook. Remember, it takes about 2 minutes to cook filleted chicken breasts. When the rolls are well browned, transfer them to a warm platter and remove the strings. Add the wine to the skillet, turn the heat to high, and loosen any cooking residue in the pan. When the wine has evaporated, pour the sauce over the chicken rolls, and serve hot.

(*continued*)

A first course that goes well here is Risotto with Dried Mushrooms (page 185). Other possibilities are Baked Semolina Gnocchi (page 198), Baked Rigatoni with Meat Sauce (page 110), or Penne with a Sauce of Tomatoes and Dried Wild Mushrooms (page 108). A good choice for vegetables would be Cauliflower Gratinéed with Butter and Cheese (page 366), Fried Cauliflower (page 367), Fried Finocchio (page 378), or Gratinéed Jerusalem Artichokes (page 353).

Cotoletta di tacchino alla bolognese
SAUTÉED TURKEY BREAST FILLETS WITH HAM, CHEESE, AND WHITE TRUFFLES

This is Bologna's most celebrated meat course, in which the delicate, almost neutral taste of veal or breast of turkey is used as a foil for perhaps the three finest products in the Italian larder: aged Parmesan cheese, sweet Parma ham, and the fresh white truffles of Alba. No one who has tasted this dish in Bologna in late fall, when the white truffles are in season, could possibly forget it. Of the three ingredients, only Parmesan cheese is available here, so it is obvious that our *cotoletta alla bolognese* will be only a distant cousin of the original. However, even with local materials, this is still a most attractive dish and well worth doing.

The old recipes call for thinly sliced veal or turkey breast to be lightly sautéed, then bound to slices of ham, truffles, and cheese, and simmered in beef stock or tomato sauce in a covered pan. Today the last step is omitted and the cutlet is run briefly into the oven just long enough to melt the cheese. This is an improvement over the old method, which tended to produce a flabbier texture and a less fresh-tasting liaison of the ingredients.

Fresh white truffles are virtually unobtainable here, except in New York for a short-lived moment in late November or early December, and at prohibitive prices. Canned white truffles, although expensive, are easily available throughout the year at all gourmet shops or by mail from Italian groceries and some department stores. Some cans contain marvelous truffles, while others, unfortunately, are nearly tasteless. The can should release a powerful fragrance when you open it, and the truffle should be a creamy beige color. It is a rather blind item, but you must take your chances, because the presence of truffles, however weakened by canning, is absolutely essential to *cotoletta alla bolognese*. Without it the dish is gross and banal, and you'd be better advised to invest time and effort in something more promising.

For 4 to 5 persons

1¼ pounds turkey breast, thawed if frozen

1 tablespoon vegetable oil

¼ cup butter

¾ cup all-purpose flour, spread on a dish or on waxed paper

Freshly ground pepper, about 4 twists of the mill

1 one-ounce can white Alba truffles, or more, if you are not daunted by the price

⅓ cup dry Marsala or dry white wine

2 tablespoons freshly grated Parmesan cheese

¼ pound thinly sliced prosciutto

6 ounces Parmesan cheese (approximately), cut into slivers or shavings using a vegetable peeler

1 tablespoon butter

1. Fillet the turkey breast, using the same method suggested for chicken breasts (page 312). Cut the fillets into slices ¼ inch thick.

2. Melt the butter and oil in a skillet over medium-high heat.

3. When the butter foam begins to subside, turn the turkey slices in the flour, coating both sides and shaking off any excess, and slip the turkey into the skillet. If the slices are no more than ¼ inch thick, they should cook very quickly, about 1 to 1½ minutes per side. Sauté as many slices at one time as will fit comfortably into the skillet, coating them with flour just before putting them in. As they are done, transfer to a warm platter and add the pepper.

4. Preheat the oven to 400°.

5. Open the can of truffles and pour the liquid it contains into the skillet. Turn on the heat to medium and stir for a minute or so, scraping up and loosening the cooking residue in the pan.

6. Add the Marsala or wine and partly exaporate it for a minute or two over medium heat. Stir it as it thickens.

7. Choose a baking dish that can accommodate all the turkey slices in a single layer. Smear the bottom with about 1 tablespoon of sauce from the skillet, then put in the turkey slices, laying them close together but not overlapping.

8. Distribute the grated cheese over the turkey, sprinkling a little over each slice, then cover each slice with prosciutto. Slice the truffles very thin, using a vegetable peeler, and distribute over the prosciutto. Cover each turkey slice with the slivered Parmesan cheese. (Some recipes suggest Fontina or Bel Paese cheese, but only Parmesan is part of an authentic *cotoletta alla bolognese*.) Pour the rest of the sauce from the skillet over the cheese and put a tiny dot of butter on each slice.

9. Place the dish in the uppermost level of the preheated oven for 6 to 8 minutes, or until the cheese melts. Serve piping hot from the same dish.

NOTE

The prosciutto and cheese should be sufficiently salty to make any addition of salt unnecessary. If, as sometimes happens, either the prosciutto or the Parmesan or both lack salt, salt can be added at the table.

MENU SUGGESTIONS

Tagliatelle with Bolognese Meat Sauce (page 129) is a natural combination with this dish, but other excellent choices would be Cappelletti with Butter and Heavy Cream (page 159), or Spinach and Ricotta Gnocchi (page 201). One or two fried vegetables would complete it to perfection: Fried Artichoke Wedges (page 346), and Fried Tomatoes (page 390).

Piccioncini in tegame
PAN-ROASTED SQUAB

For 4 to 6 persons (see note below)

4 fresh squab (about 1 pound each), cleaned and plucked

2 dozen medium-dried sage leaves

4 strips of *pancetta*, 1½ inches long, ½ inch wide, and ¼ inch thick

Salt and freshly ground pepper

3 tablespoons butter

2 tablespoons vegetable oil

⅔ cup dry white wine

1. Remove all the organs from the birds' interiors. Reserve the livers but discard the hearts and gizzards (or hold them for a *risotto*). Wash the squab in cold running water and pat dry thoroughly inside and out. Stuff the cavity of each bird with 2 sage leaves, 1 strip of *pancetta*, and 1 liver, and season with 2 pinches of salt and a twist of pepper.

2. In a skillet large enough to hold all the squab, heat up the butter and oil over medium-high heat. When the butter foam subsides, add the remaining sage leaves and then the squab. Brown the squab evenly on all sides and season with salt and pepper. Add the wine. Turn the heat up to high, allowing the wine to boil briskly for 30 to 40 seconds. While the wine is bubbling turn and baste the squab, then lower the heat to medium low and cover the skillet. Turn the birds every 15 minutes. They should be tender and done in 1 hour.

3. Transfer the squab to a warm platter. If you are serving ½ bird per person, halve them with poultry scissors. Tip the pan and draw off some of the cooking fat with a spoon. Add 2 tablespoons of warm water, turn the heat to high, and while the water evaporates scrape up and loosen any cooking residue in the pan. Pour over the squab and serve.

(continued)

A generous portion would be 1 whole squab per person. If you are having a substantial first course, however, ½ squab per person is quite adequate. The remaining squabs can be divided up for second helpings among the hungrier guests.

MENU SUGGESTIONS

The happiest accompaniment for squab and for any game is Polenta (page 204). When serving *polenta* you do not serve pasta as a first course. You can start the meal with very good-quality prosciutto, sliced thick, or with Artichokes, Roman Style (page 337), or Crisp-Fried Whole Artichokes (page 344). If you are not serving *polenta,* an excellent first course would be *risotto,* either Risotto with Dried Wild Mushrooms (page 185) or Molded Risotto with Parmesan Cheese and Chicken-Liver Sauce (page 183), Cappelletti in Broth (page 158), or Tortelloni with Butter and Cheese (page 167). A good vegetable side dish would be Sautéed Peas with Prosciutto, Florentine Style (page 383), Sweet and Sour Onions (page 382), Sautéed Finocchio with Butter and Cheese (page 377), or Sautéed Jerusalem Artichokes (page 352).

Coniglio in padella
STEWED RABBIT WITH WHITE WINE

Now that factory chicken has completely replaced free-roaming yard-raised chicken, one of the best tasting "fowls" you can eat is rabbit. Rabbit meat is lean and not as flabby as most chicken, and its taste is somewhere in between very good breast of chicken and veal. Frozen young rabbit of excellent quality is now widely available cut up in ready-to-cook pieces. It is so good that there is really little need to bother dismembering whole fresh rabbit. I recommend it without reservation.

In France and Germany rabbit is sometimes subjected to a lengthy preliminary marinade which gives it somewhat the taste of game and partly breaks down its texture. The method given here is very straightforward. Without sautéing, rabbit is stewed in practically nothing but its own juices. It is then simmered in white wine with a little rosemary and a touch of tomato. It is a familiar northern Italian approach, and it succeeds marvelously well in drawing out the delicate flavor of rabbit and in maintaining its fine texture intact.

For 6 persons

3 to 3½ pounds frozen cut-up rabbit, thawed overnight in the refrigerator (see note below)
½ cup olive oil
¼ cup finely diced celery
1 clove garlic, peeled
⅔ cup dry white wine

1½ teaspoons rosemary
2 teaspoons salt
Freshly ground pepper, 6 to 8 twists of the mill
1 bouillon cube
2 tablespoons tomato paste
¼ teaspoon sugar

1. Rinse the rabbit pieces in cold running water and pat thoroughly dry with paper towels.

2. Choose a deep covered skillet large enough to contain all the rabbit pieces in a single layer. Put in the oil, celery, garlic, and the rabbit, cover, and cook over low heat for 2 hours. Turn the meat once or twice, but do not leave uncovered.

3. After 2 hours, you will find that the rabbit has thrown off a great deal of liquid. Uncover the pan, turn up the heat to medium, and cook until all the liquid has evaporated. Turn the meat from time to time. When the liquid has evaporated, add the wine, rosemary, salt, and pepper. Simmer, uncovered, until the wine has evaporated. Dissolve the bouillon cube, tomato paste, and sugar in ⅔ cup warm water, pour it over the rabbit, and cook gently for another 12 to 15 minutes, turning and basting the rabbit two or three times. Serve immediately or reheat gently before serving.

NOTE

Do not use wild rabbit in this recipe, only rabbit raised for food.

If using fresh rabbit, soak in abundant cold water for 12 hours or more, then rinse in several changes of cold water and thoroughly pat dry. It may be refrigerated while soaking.

The rabbit may be prepared entirely ahead of time. When reheating, add 2 to 3 tablespoons of water and warm up slowly in a covered pan over low heat, turning the meat from time to time.

MENU SUGGESTIONS

Although this goes well with most soups—and *risotti,* except those with fish—your best choice for first courses is among the homemade pastas: Tagliatelle with Bolognese Meat Sauce (page 129), Baked Green Lasagne with Meat Sauce (page 143), or Cappelletti in Broth (page 158). A fine soup would be Passatelli (page 70). For vegetables, the most congenial are Fried Finocchio (page 378), Zucchini Fried in Flour-and-Water Batter (page 392), or Fried Artichoke Wedges (page 346).

Bollito misto
MIXED BOILED MEATS

When friends and acquaintances about to go to Italy ask what dishes they should eat, among my recommendations, especially if they are going to be in Emilia, Lombardy, or Piedmont, is *bollito misto,* mixed boiled meats. "*Boiled* meat?" they say, their incredulity soon overtaken by disdain. I am afraid it is a piece of advice that has done little to advance my reputation for culinary sagacity.

This makes me think of an episode in *The Passionate Epicure,* Marcel Rouff's legend of that prodigious gastronome, Dodin-Bouffant. Dodin had been the guest of the Prince of Eurasia, who, in the anxiety to parade the richness of his table before this most discerning of gourmets, overwhelmed him with a vulgar and grandiloquent display of pretentious courses. Dodin countered by inviting the Prince and some friends to dine with him at home. When his guests were seated, trembling in anticipation of the feast that awaited them, Dodin announced his menu. Not only was it astonishingly brief, but its principal course was to be a "boiled beef garnished with its own vegetables." This is what follows:

The Prince, reflecting that this meagre program would hardly have provided the first course of his ordinary meals, wondered inwardly whether he should countenance having been brought from so far in order to eat boiled beef which, at home, he left to the servants' hall. . . .

It arrived at last, that fearsome boiled beef, scorned, reviled, insulting to the Prince and to all gastronomy, Dodin-Bouffant's boiled beef, prodigiously imposing, borne . . . upon an immensely long dish . . . held so high aloft at arms' length, that at first the anxious guests could see nothing whatsoever. But when, cautiously and with purposeful slowness, it was placed upon the table there were several minutes of genuine astonishment. Each guest's return to self-possession was marked by personal rhythms and reactions. Rabaz and Magot mentally scourged themselves for having doubted the Master; Trifouille was seized with panic before the display of such genius; Beaubois trembled with emotion. As for the Prince of Eurasia, he wavered between the noble desire to create Dodin-Bouffant a Duke immediately, as Napoleon had wished to do for Corneille, a wild urge to offer the gastronome half his fortune and half his realm to take over the reins of his gustatory administration, the irritation of being taught a lesson which was now crystal clear, and his haste to cut into the marvel which laid before him its intoxicating promises.

The beef itself, lightly rubbed with saltpetre and then gone over with salt, was carved into slices of a flesh so fine that its mouth-melting texture could actually be seen. The aroma it gave forth was not only that of beef-juice smoking like incense, but the energetic smell of tarragon with which it was impregnated and the few, very few, cubes of transparent, immaculate bacon in the larding. The rather thick slices, their velvety quality guessed at by every lip, rested languidly upon a pillow made of a wide slice of sausage, coarsely chopped, in which the finest veal escorted pork, chopped herbs, thyme, chervil. . . . This delicate triumph of pork-butchery was itself supported by ample cuts from the breast and wing fillets of farm chickens, boiled in their own juice with a shin of veal, rubbed with mint and wild thyme. And, to prop up this triple and magnificent accumulation, behind the white flesh of the fowls (fed exclusively upon bread and milk), was the stout, robust support of a generous layer of fresh goose liver simply cooked in Chambertin. . . . Each guest was to extract, in one stroke, between spoon and fork, the quadruple enchantment which was his share. . . . Congenial wholehearted enjoyment could now give itself free rein. . . . They might abandon themselves, in all contentment, to the pleasures of taste, and to that sweet, confident friendship which beckons to well-born men after meals worthy of the name.

(*continued*)

An Italian platter of mixed boiled meats, although not as profusely aromatic as Dodin's boiled beef, has many points in common with it. Like Dodin's dish it includes veal, chicken, and a pork sausage, Modena's *zampone*. But what a sausage it is! No pork product in the world can approach its miraculously creamy texture or the poise of its perfectly balanced delicacy and savoriness. Dodin would have been enraptured. There is no *foie gras*, of course, but there is calf's head, which yields a very fine, tender, gelatinous supplement to the corpulence of the other meats.

Restaurants that feature *bollito misto* present it in a special cart, somewhat resembling an English roast beef cart, which carries the different meats in separate compartments filled with steaming broth. The meat is carved at tableside, as roast beef is in England, and served with a piquant green sauce or a red tomato and pepper sauce or both. In Italy, a proper *bollito misto* is virtually synonymous with a restaurant of the first rank.

The recipe given below is for a complete *bollito misto*. It is a fine recipe if you are serving at least eighteen people. If you are not, you will want to scale it down. You can reduce it by more than half simply by omitting the tongue and the *cotechino*. If any of the beef, chicken, or veal is left over, it can be cut up and used in a salad. The beef can also be used in the recipe on page 244.

For 18 persons or more

2 medium carrots, peeled
2 stalks celery
1 medium yellow onion, peeled
1 medium potato, peeled
½ green pepper, cored and seeded
1 beef tongue (about 3 to 3½ pounds)
2 pounds beef brisket, rump roast, or bottom round
2 tablespoons salt

3 tablespoons canned Italian tomatoes
2 pounds veal brisket, rump roast, or bottom round
½ calf's head
1 chicken (2½ pounds)
1 *cotechino* sausage, boiled separately, as directed on page 287, and kept warm in its own broth

1. Choose a stockpot or kettle large enough to hold all the above

ingredients, except for the *cotechino*. (It is very important in a *bollito misto* to have all the meats cook together because each lends part of its flavor to the others. However, if you just cannot manage in one pot, divide the vegetables in two parts, and cook the beef and tongue in one kettle, and all the other meats in another.) Since in an Italian *bollito* the meat is put into liquid that is already boiling, begin by putting all the vegetables, except the tomatoes, into the kettle and enough water to cover the meat later. Bring to a boil.

2. Add the tongue and beef brisket, cover, and return to a boil. Adjust the heat so that the liquid is just barely simmering. Skim off the scum that comes to surface for the first few minutes. Add the salt and the tomatoes.

3. After 1 hour of very slow simmering, remove the tongue for peeling. It is easier to peel the tongue if you can handle it while it is still very hot; otherwise wait a few moments for it to cool off slightly. Slit the skin all around the top of the tongue and peel it away with your fingers. (There is a second skin beneath this that does not peel off. It will be cut off later in one's own dish after the tongue has been sliced.) Trim away all the fat and gristle from the butt of the tongue, and return it to the pot.

4. Add the veal, then, when the veal has simmered for 1 hour, add the calf's head.

5. After another 45 minutes' simmering, add the chicken. When the chicken has simmered for 45 minutes to 1 hour, the *bollito* is done. Leave it in its broth, and it will stay warm enough to serve for 1 hour after you turn off the heat. If you are serving it much later, reheat by bringing the broth to a slow simmer for about 10 minutes. Turn the pieces of meat once or twice, changing their position in the kettle.

6. A steaming platter with an arrangement of all the boiled meats in slices is a beautiful and enticing thing to see. The juicy texture of boiled meat, however, is very short-lived outside of its broth. There are two solutions. One, slice only part of the meat and serve it, keeping the rest in the kettle until you are ready for another round. Or, even more successful, if less elegant, bring the kettle to the table (or transfer all the meat and enough broth to cover to a

large tureen), pull out one piece at a time, carving as much of it as desired, and then return it to the protection of its broth. The *cotechino,* as mentioned earlier, should be kept in its own broth until it is time to slice and serve it. Serve *bollito misto* with one of two sauces on the side: Piquant Green Sauce (page 29) or Red Sauce (page 30), or both, if you like.

NOTE
Calf's head is usually sold whole, but if you are on good terms with your butcher he should be willing to let you have a half. In case you've never used it before, calf's head is sold completely boned and ready for cooking. If the brains are included they should be removed. Use them for Fried Calf's Brains (page 299).

The following are approximate cooking times for the meats in this recipe, calculated from the moment the liquid they are in comes to a simmer:

beef—3½ hours	calf's head—1½ hours
tongue—3½ hours	chicken—45 minutes
veal—1¾ hours	

MENU SUGGESTIONS

Any light soup with a vegetable can precede *bollito misto.* An ideal combination is Passatelli (page 70), cooked in part of the *bollito's* broth, or Cappelletti in Broth (page 158).

Frittate

OPEN-FACED ITALIAN OMELETS

In some texts, the Italian *frittata* has become partly confused with French omelets. Actually, the technique for *frittata* differs in three very important ways from that for making omelets.

• Whereas an omelet is cooked very briefly over high heat, a *frittata* is cooked slowly over very low heat.

• An omelet is creamy and moist, just short of runny. A *frittata* is firm and set, although by no means stiff and dry.

• An omelet is rolled or folded over into an oval, tapered shape. A *frittata* is flat and perfectly round.

Because a *frittata* is cooked over low heat, there is less danger of sticking. You do not need to set aside a special pan for *frittate,* but it is essential to use a very good, heavy-bottomed skillet that transmits and retains heat evenly.

A *frittata* must be cooked on both sides. To do this, some people flip it in mid-air like a flapjack. Others turn it over on a dish and then slide it back into the pan. I have found that the least perilous and most effective way is to run it under the broiler for about 20 seconds to cook the top side once the underside is done.

You can incorporate into *frittate* an endless number of fillings, such as cheese, vegetables, herbs, and ham. The following *frittata al formaggio* illustrates the basic *frittata* technique, which remains exactly the same no matter what filling you use.

Frittata al formaggio
OPEN-FACED ITALIAN OMELET WITH CHEESE

For 4 persons

6 eggs (U.S. Extra Large)	1 cup freshly grated Parmesan
¼ teaspoon salt	cheese or Swiss cheese
Freshly ground pepper, about	3 tablespoons butter
4 twists of the mill	

1. Beat the eggs in a bowl until the yolks and whites are blended. Add the salt, pepper, and grated cheese, beating them into the eggs.

2. Melt the butter in a 12-inch skillet over medium heat. When the butter begins to foam, well before it becomes colored, add the

eggs and turn the heat down as low as possible. When the eggs have set and thickened and only the top surface is runny, about 15 minutes of very slow cooking, run the skillet under the broiler for 30 seconds to 1 minute, or until the top face of the *frittata* has set. (When done the *frittata* should be set, but soft. It should not be browned either on the bottom or top side.)

3. Loosen the *frittata* with a spatula and slide it onto a warm platter. Cut it into four pielike wedges and serve.

MENU SUGGESTIONS

In Italy, a *frittata* usually appears at the evening meal, which is the light meal of the day. It takes the place of meat or fowl and is preceded by a light soup, or a dish of prosciutto or assorted cold cuts. Here the situation is reversed, and *frittata* obviously makes a fine dish around which you can plan a light lunch. For a hearty country dinner, however, Open-Faced Italian Omelet with Cheese (page 327) can be a satisfying second course when preceded by Hot, Anchovy-Flavored Dip for Vegetables (page 42).

Frittata di carciofi

OPEN-FACED ITALIAN OMELET WITH ARTICHOKES

For 4 persons

1 large or 2 medium artichokes	Freshly ground pepper, 6 twists of the mill
1 teaspoon finely chopped garlic	
2 tablespoons olive oil	5 eggs (U.S. Extra Large)
2 tablespoons finely chopped parsley	3 tablespoons freshly grated Parmesan cheese
Salt	3 tablespoons butter

1. Trim the artichokes as directed on page 347. Then cut them lengthwise into the thinnest possible slices.

2. In a skillet, sauté the garlic, with all the oil, over medium heat until it has colored lightly. Add the sliced artichokes, the

parsley, a small pinch of salt, and half the pepper, and sauté for about 1 minute, or long enough to turn the artichokes two or three times. Add ⅓ cup water, cover the pan, and cook until the artichokes are very tender. If they are young and fresh, it may take just 15 minutes or less. (In this case there might be some water left in the pan. Uncover the pan and evaporate the water over high heat while stirring the artichokes.) If the artichokes are tough, it may take twice as long to cook them. (In which case, if all the water evaporates before they are done, add 2 or 3 tablespoons of water.) When done, drain them completely of oil and set aside to cool.

3. Beat the eggs in a bowl until the yolks and whites are blended. Add the artichokes, another small pinch of salt, the rest of the pepper, and all the grated cheese, and mix thoroughly.

4. In a 12-inch skillet, melt the butter over medium heat. When it begins to foam, and well before it becomes colored, add the egg-and-artichoke mixture, turn the heat down as low as possible, and proceed exactly as directed in Steps 2 and 3 of Open-Faced Italian Omelet with Cheese (page 327).

Frittata di asparagi

OPEN-FACED ITALIAN OMELET WITH ASPARAGUS

For 4 persons

1 **pound asparagus**	⅔ **cup freshly grated Parmesan**
5 **eggs (U.S. Extra Large)**	**cheese**
¼ **teaspoon salt**	3 **tablespoons butter**
Freshly ground pepper, 4 to	
6 twists of the mill	

1. Trim, peel, and boil the asparagus as directed on page 354; then drain and allow to cool.

2. Cut the cooled asparagus into ½-inch lengths, utilizing as much of the stalk as possible.

3. Beat the eggs in a bowl until the yolks and whites are blended.

(*continued*)

Add the cut asparagus and the salt, pepper, and grated cheese and mix everything thoroughly.

4. In a 10- or 12-inch skillet, melt the butter over medium heat. When it begins to foam, and well before it becomes colored, add the egg-and-asparagus mixture, turn the heat down as low as possible, and proceed exactly as directed in Steps 2 and 3 of Open-Faced Italian Omelet with Cheese (page 327).

Frittata con fagiolini verdi
OPEN-FACED ITALIAN OMELET WITH GREEN BEANS

For 4 persons

5 eggs (U.S. Extra Large)	1½ cups coarsely chopped boiled
½ teaspoon salt	green beans (see page 360)
Freshly ground pepper, 6 to	1 cup freshly grated Parmesan
8 twists of the mill	cheese
	3 tablespoons butter

1. Beat the eggs in a bowl until the yolks and whites are blended.

2. Add the salt, pepper, green beans, and grated cheese and mix thoroughly.

3. Melt the butter in a 12-inch skillet over medium heat. When it begins to foam, and well before it becomes colored, add the egg-and-green-bean mixture, making sure the green beans are evenly distributed, not bunched up all at one end. Turn the heat down as low as possible and proceed exactly as directed in Steps 2 and 3 of Open-Faced Italian Omelet with Cheese (page 327).

Frittata al pomodoro e basilico
OPEN-FACED ITALIAN OMELET WITH TOMATO, ONIONS, AND BASIL

For 4 persons

3 cups thinly sliced yellow onion
⅓ cup olive oil
1 cup canned Italian tomatoes, drained and roughly chopped
2 teaspoons salt
5 eggs (U.S. Extra Large)

2 tablespoons freshly grated Parmesan cheese
Freshly ground pepper, 6 twists of the mill
½ cup roughly chopped fresh basil
3 tablespoons butter

1. Cook the sliced onion, with all the oil, in a medium skillet over low heat until it is completely wilted and has turned a rich golden-brown color.

2. Add the tomatoes and ½ teaspoon of the salt. Raise the heat to medium and cook for 8 minutes, stirring frequently. Turn off the heat and tilt the pan, gathering the tomatoes and onion at the up-ended side of the pan to drain them of oil. When the oil has drained off, transfer the vegetables to a bowl and allow to cool.

3. Beat the eggs in a bowl until the yolks and whites are blended. Using a slotted spoon, add the tomatoes and onion, and then add the remaining 1½ teaspoons of salt, the grated cheese, pepper, and chopped basil, and beat everything into the eggs.

4. Melt the butter in a 12-inch skillet over medium heat. When the butter begins to foam, and well before it becomes colored, add the eggs, turn the heat down to minimum, and proceed exactly as directed in Steps 2 and 3 of Open-Faced Italian Omelet with Cheese (page 327).

Frittata di zucchine

OPEN-FACED ITALIAN OMELET WITH ZUCCHINI

For 4 persons

1 cup thinly sliced yellow onion	Freshly ground pepper, 7 or
¼ cup vegetable oil	8 twists of the mill
3 medium zucchini (or zucchini	6 fresh basil leaves, roughly
cores; see note below)	chopped, OR, if basil is not
½ teaspoon salt	in season, 1 tablespoon
4 eggs (U.S. Extra Large)	finely chopped parsley
⅔ cup freshly grated Parmesan	3 tablespoons butter
cheese	

1. Cook the sliced onion, with all the oil, in a medium skillet over low heat until it is completely wilted and has turned a rich golden-brown color.

2. While the onion is cooking, cut off the ends of the zucchini and wash thoroughly in cold water. If not absolutely fresh, with a very smooth glossy skin, peel the skin to remove all traces of imbedded soil. Slice into disks ¼ inch thick. If you are using zucchini cores, chop them roughly.

3. When the onion is cooked, add the zucchini and the salt. Cook over medium heat until lightly browned—or, if you are using the cores, until they have turned into a light-brown, creamy paste. When done, turn off the heat and tilt the pan lightly, pushing the zucchini and onion toward the upended side of the pan. When the oil has drained off, remove the vegetables to a bowl to cool.

4. Beat the eggs in a bowl until the yolks and whites are blended. Add the grated cheese and, with a slotted spoon, the zucchini and onion. Beat everything into the eggs, adding the pepper and basil or parsley at the end.

5. Melt the butter in a 10-inch skillet over medium heat. When the butter begins to foam, and well before it becomes colored, add the egg-and-zucchini mixture, turn the heat down as low as possible,

and proceed exactly as described in Steps 2 and 3 of Italian Open-Faced Omelet with Cheese (page 327).

NOTE

If you have made Zucchini Stuffed with Meat and Cheese (page 397), you can use the leftover cores of 6 or 7 zucchini for this recipe.

Il Grande Fritto Misto

MIXED FRIED MEATS, VEGETABLES, CHEESE, CREAM, AND FRUIT

Brillat-Savarin has given the very best description of frying, defining its action as that of a surprise. Perfectly fried food is "surprised" in hot fat, which quickly imprisons its natural flavor and texture intact within a crisp, light crust. Successful frying requires a generous quantity of very hot fat. Never add fat after you've started frying. Butter, even when clarified, does not tolerate very high temperatures, and it is not, as a rule, suitable for quick frying. The most convenient medium to use is vegetable oil.

Italians are the masters of the frying pan, and fried cheese, meat, vegetables, fruit, taken singly, are frequent components of an Italian meal. Moreover, in some sections of Italy, and in Emilia-Romagna in particular, an entire meal, from first course to fruit, can be based exclusively on fried dishes. This tour de force is known as *il grande fritto misto*. It is a menu that requires from its creator not just skill, but great self-abnegation. Fried foods must be consumed hot, and while the cook fries the guests eat. In Naples it is called *frienno magnanno*, "frying and eating," which is also used idiomatically as an equivalent of "said and done."

For obvious reasons, a *grande fritto misto*, like a *bollito misto*, is consumed more frequently these days in a restaurant than at home. But if you have help in the kitchen and feel like trying it, here is a list of recipes scattered throughout this book that you can pull together into a truly memorable meal.

The first course
Fried Mortadella, Pancetta, and Cheese Tidbits (page 48)

The second course
An assortment of as many as possible of the following, in reduced quantities:
Breaded Veal Cutlets, Milan Style (page 270), served cut into small squares
Baby Lamb Chops Fried in Parmesan Cheese Batter (page 283)
Fried Breaded Calf's Liver (page 298), served cut into small squares
Fried Calf's Brains (page 299)
Fried Artichoke Wedges (page 346)
Fried Asparagus (page 358)
Fried Tomatoes (page 390)
Fried Finocchio (page 378)
Zucchini Fried in Flour-and-Water Batter (page 392) and/or Fried Zucchini Blossoms (page 399)
Fried Cauliflower (page 367)
Fried Sweet Cream (page 444), an absolutely indispensable part of any *fritto misto*
Fried Polenta (page 206)

Desserts and fruit
Apple Fritters (page 435)

Le Verdure

VEGETABLES

I cannot imagine Italy without its vegetable stalls, filling ancient squares and animating dusty side streets with mounds of fabulous forms in purple, green, red, gold, and orange. In a land heavy with man's monuments, these are the soil's own masterworks.

Perhaps one day the vitality of these still-flourishing markets will be replaced by the pallor of deep-freeze counters, those cemeteries of food, where produce is sealed up in waxed boxes marked, like some tombstones, with photographs of the departed. But I hope it never happens. I would sooner be deprived of all the marvels of Michelangelo.

The quality of Italy's produce is matchless. Only that of France comes close. It is not surprising that, in Italian cooking, the richness and variety of vegetable dishes approaches that of the first courses. Sometimes a vegetable will even take the place of a first course, or of the second. Frequently a boiled vegetable, such as green beans or asparagus, is used as salad. Most often the vegetable'is a side dish. Except when fish is served, it is always an essential part of every meal.

In Italian cooking, vegetables can be boiled, braised, fried, sautéed, gratinéed, baked, and even broiled. Every one of these procedures is illustrated in this chapter, including a recipe for charcoal-broiled vegetables.

In a typically Italian approach, the vegetable is first boiled, then given a finish in the skillet or in the oven with butter and Parmesan cheese. Sometimes, instead of the butter-and-cheese treatment, a boiled vegetable such as spinach or broccoli is sautéed with garlic and olive oil. Frying is another favorite treatment for vegetables, and several examples are given, with different batters.

Trifolare is an expression you will find in all Italian cook books, and vegetables *trifolati* appear on nearly every restaurant menu. When vegetables are *trifolati*, they are thinly sliced and sautéed with garlic, oil, and parsley, a method very successful with mushrooms. You will find the recipe for it here, as well as a similar one for Jerusalem artichokes.

The Jerusalem artichoke is a native American tuber that is now happily settled in certain sections of northern Italy, where it is highly prized. In the following chapter you will be shown how it can be used in a salad.

There are three recipes for finocchio, a vegetable universally popular in Italy. Very good finocchio is available here, it is not terribly difficult to prepare, and it can be an enjoyable addition to your vegetable repertory.

The longest single section of this chapter deals with artichokes. Italians take great pleasure in this extraordinary relative of the thistle, and have found many fascinating ways to cook it. Among the recipes for artichokes given here you will find one of the oldest and still one of the best, *carciofi alla giudia* (crisp-fried whole artichokes), which dates back to Jewish cooking in the ghetto of ancient Rome.

Preparing and cooking vegetables takes time, patience, and care. Do not waste your efforts on second-rate materials. Buy carefully, avoiding any vegetable that is wilted, badly bruised, ill assorted, tired-looking, soggy, flabby, or overgrown. Shopping for good fresh vegetables in this country may be frustrating at times, but that does not mean that we must deliver ourselves up in thralldom to the frozen-food shelves. On any one marketing day there are always available two or more fresh vegetables of respectable quality. Limit yourself as much as possible to vegetables that are in season. They are more likely to be locally grown and fresher, or, at any rate, richer in flavor. Try not to decide in advance what you are going to cook but, rather, buy the best-quality vegetables you can find and then choose a recipe to suit.

Carciofi alla romana
ARTICHOKES, ROMAN STYLE

In Italy one finds two basic types of artichokes. One is purplish in color, with long, narrow, tapered leaves spiked at the tips. It is well worth looking out for if you are traveling in the northern and central part of Italy in the winter and spring because it is truly extraordinary in flavor and texture. However, it is not available here, so we will not discuss it further. The other type of artichoke is very common in the south, where it is called *mammola.* It has a stout, globe-like shape, it is green, and it is very similar to the artichokes found in this country. One of the most attractive and appetizing ways of preparing these artichokes is *alla romana,* Roman style, and it is particularly well suited to American artichokes.

For 4 persons

4 large artichokes	½ teaspoon crumbled mint
½ lemon	leaves
3 tablespoons finely chopped parsley	½ teaspoon salt
	½ cup olive oil
1½ teaspoons finely chopped garlic	

1. Artichokes *alla romana* are served with the stems attached, so be careful not to snap them off while trimming the artichokes. Begin preparing an artichoke by bending back and snapping off the outer leaves. Do not pull the leaves off all the way to the base, because the whitish bottom of the leaf is tender, and edible. As you get deeper

into the artichoke, the leaves will snap off farther and farther from the base. Keep pulling off leaves until you expose a central cone of leaves that are green only at the tips and whose paler, whitish base is at least 1½ inches high.

Slice at least an inch off the top of the entire central cone, eliminating all the green part. Don't be afraid to trim too much—you are eliminating only the tough, inedible portions. Rub with the lemon half, squeezing juice over the cut portions of the artichoke so that they won't discolor.

You can now look into the center of the artichoke, where you will find at the bottom some very small, pale leaves with prickly tips curving inward. Cut off all the little leaves and scrape away the fuzzy "choke" beneath them, being careful not to cut away any of the heart or the other tender parts. (A rounded point on the knife can be helpful.) Return to the outside of the artichoke and pare away the green parts of the leaves at the base, leaving only the white.

All there is left to trim now is the outer part of the stem. Turning the artichoke upside down, you will note from the bottom of the stem that the stem has a whitish core surrounded by a layer of green. Trim away all the green up to the base of the artichoke, keeping only the white part. Be careful not to detach the stem, and always rub the cut portions with lemon juice so that they will not discolor.

2. In a bowl, mix the chopped parsley, the chopped garlic, the mint leaves, and the salt. Set aside one-third of the mixture and press the rest into the cavity of each artichoke, rubbing it well into the sides of the cavity.

3. Choose a heavy-bottomed casserole just large enough to contain the artichokes, which are to go in standing, and provided with a tight-fitting lid. Place the artichokes, tops facing down and stems pointing upward, in the casserole. Rub the rest of the parsley, garlic, and mint mixture on the outside of the artichokes. Add all the oil and enough water to cover one-third of the artichoke leaves, *not* the stems. Soak two thicknesses of paper towels in water. (Since the moist towels help to keep steam that cooks the stems inside the pot, they must be wide enough to cover the casserole.) Place the towels

PREPARING AN ARTICHOKE

1. Taking care not to break the stem off, begin bending back and snapping off the outer green part of the leaves, letting only the whitish, tender bottom of each leaf remain—the edible portion. Use a lemon half to squeeze juice over the cut portions so they won't discolor.

2. As you get deeper into the artichoke, the leaves will snap off farther from the base. Keep snapping off leaves until you expose a central cone of leaves that are green only at the tips. The paler, whitish base of the leaves should be at least 1½ inches high.

(continued)

3. Slice about an inch off the top of the central cone, enough to eliminate all the green part.

4. In the center of the artichoke, you will see at the bottom some very small, pale leaves with purple, prickly tips curving inward. Using a knife with a rounded end, cut off all these little leaves and scrape away the fuzzy "choke" beneath them. Be careful not to cut away any of the heart or the other edible parts.

5. Pare away the green outer parts of the leaves at the base of the artichoke, leaving the white and continuing to rub the cut portions with the lemon half.

6. Taking care not to break the stem, trim away its outer green layer, leaving only the whitish core.

7. The finished product.

over the casserole and put the lid over the paper towels. Bend the corners of the towels back over the lid. Cook over medium heat for about 35 to 40 minutes, or until tender and easily pierced by a fork.

Cooking times vary according to the freshness and tenderness of the artichokes. (If the artichokes are tough and take long to cook, you may have to add 2 or 3 tablespoons of water from time to time. If they cook rapidly and there is too much water left in the pot, uncover and boil it away rapidly. Do not worry if the edges of the leaves next to the bottom of the pot start to brown; it improves their flavor.)

4. Transfer the artichokes to a serving platter, arranging them always with the stems pointing up. (Bear in mind that the stems are not merely decorative. They have an excellent flavor and they are to be eaten along with the rest of the artichoke.) Reserve the oil and juices from the pot and pour them over the artichokes just before serving. They should be served either lukewarm or at room temperature. The ideal temperature at which to serve them, if you can arrange it, is when they are no longer hot, but haven't quite completely cooled off.

NOTE

Try to prepare them the same day they are going to be eaten because, like most cooked greens, they lose part of their flavor when refrigerated.

MENU SUGGESTIONS

This is one of many vegetable dishes that Italians use primarily as an antipasto or even a first course, rather than a side dish. As an antipasto, it goes practically anywhere, preceding either a simple dish of spaghetti with tomato sauce or the elegant Fettuccine Tossed in Cream and Butter (page 130). As a first course it can lead to any roast, from beef to fowl.

Carciofi ripieni di mortadella

BRAISED ARTICHOKES WITH MORTADELLA STUFFING

For 4 persons

4 medium artichokes	1 egg
½ lemon	A small pinch of nutmeg
½ teaspoon finely chopped garlic	½ teaspoon salt
1 tablespoon chopped parsley	Freshly ground pepper, about 4 twists of the mill
½ cup chopped *mortadella*	2½ tablespoons fine dry bread crumbs
⅓ cup freshly grated Parmesan cheese	⅓ cup olive oil

1. Clean and trim the artichokes exactly as directed in step 1 of Artichokes, Roman Style (page 337), leaving the stems *on*. (Remember to rub with lemon, squeezing juice over the cut parts.)

2. In a mixing bowl, combine the garlic, parsley, *mortadella*, Parmesan cheese, egg, nutmeg, salt, pepper, and 1½ tablespoons of the bread crumbs. Mix thoroughly and divide into 4 equal parts.

3. Stuff the artichokes with the *mortadella* mixture, sealing the tops with the remaining bread crumbs.

4. Choose a deep casserole that can later accommodate the artichokes standing. Put in all the olive oil and the artichokes, laying them on their sides. Turn on the heat to medium, and slowly brown the artichokes on all sides. When nicely browned, stand the artichokes with their stems pointing up, put in ⅓ cup of water, and cover the casserole, placing between the cover and the pot a double thickness of water-soaked paper towels. Turn the heat down to low and cook for about 30 minutes. Test the hearts with a fork. If easily pierced, the artichokes are done. (If they are still firm, and there is no liquid left in the pot, add 1 or 2 tablespoons of water as needed. And don't worry if the leaves next to the bottom of the pot stick and darken.) When done, transfer the artichokes to a serving platter, pouring over them any juices left in the pot. Serve warm. Do not refrigerate or reheat.

(continued)

Follow the suggestions given for Artichokes, Roman Style (page 342).

Carciofi alla giudia
CRISP-FRIED WHOLE ARTICHOKES

There is a substantial tradition of native Jewish cooking in Italy, centered mainly on Ferrara in the north and Rome in the south. That of Rome goes back to the days of the Empire, which must make it, no doubt, the oldest Jewish cuisine in Europe. One of the dishes prized by both ancient and modern visitors to the ghetto is *carciofi alla giudia*. These are young Roman artichokes, trimmed of any hard leaves, flattened, and fried to a golden brown. The finished product is particularly beautiful, looking somewhat like an opened, dried chrysanthemum.

The frying is done in two stages. The artichokes are first fried at a lower temperature, to give the heat time to cook them thoroughly. They are then transferred to a pan with hotter oil, which is excited further by being sprinkled with cold water. This is what gives the leaves their crisp finish, while the heart remains moist and tender.

The best artichokes to use for this recipe are very young, tender artichokes.

For 6 persons

6 medium artichokes	Vegetable oil, enough to come
½ lemon	1½ inches up the sides of
½ heaping teaspoon salt	both pans
Freshly ground pepper, 6	
twists of the mill	

1. Trim the artichokes exactly as directed in Step 1 of Artichokes, Roman Style (page 337), but now leaving only a short stump of a stem. Keep the inside rows of leaves progressively longer, giving the artichoke the look of a thick, fleshy rosebud. Make sure, how-

ever, to cut off all the tough part of each leaf, because no amount of cooking will make it edible, and remember to rub all the cut edges of the artichoke with lemon juice to keep them from discoloring.

2. Turn the artichokes bottoms up, gently spread their leaves outward, and press them against your work surface to flatten them as much as possible without cracking them. Turn them right side up and season them with salt and pepper.

3. Heat the oil in a deep skillet (preferably earthenware) over medium heat. When it is hot, add the artichokes, with their leaves facing down. Cook for about 5 to 6 minutes, then turn the artichokes, adjusting the heat to make sure they don't fry too rapidly. Turn them every few minutes as they cook, until their bottoms feel tender at the pricking of a fork. Times vary greatly, depending on the artichokes, but it may take about 15 minutes if they are very young.

4. When the artichokes are tender, turn them so their leaves face the bottom of the pan and press firmly on them with a wooden spoon to flatten them some more.

5. Meanwhile, heat the oil in another deep skillet over high heat. When it is very hot, transfer the artichokes from the other pan, with the leaves always facing down. After they have fried at high heat for about 5 minutes, turn them so that the leaves face up, dip your hand in cold water, and shake the water into the hot oil, keeping at a distance from the pan because the oil will spatter.

6. Transfer the artichokes to paper towels to drain. Serve them piping hot, with the leaves facing up.

MENU SUGGESTIONS

This can be not only a side dish but also a hot antipasto or even a first course in any meal whose second course is meat or fowl. It goes particularly well with Hothouse Lamb, Roman Style (page 281) and Sautéed Lamb Kidneys with White Wine (page 300).

Carciofini fritti

FRIED ARTICHOKE WEDGES

For 4 to 6 persons

3 medium artichokes or 1
    ten-ounce package frozen
    artichoke hearts, thawed
½ lemon
1 tablespoon lemon juice
1 egg, lightly beaten, in a bowl
1 cup fine, dry unflavored bread
    crumbs, spread on a dish
    or on waxed paper

Vegetable oil, sufficient to
    come ¾ inch up the side
    of the skillet
Salt

1. If you are using fresh artichokes, detach and discard the stems; then prepare as directed on page 347, but cutting them into smaller wedges (about ¾ inch thick at the broadest point) and remembering to rub with lemon as you cut to keep the artichoke from discoloring. Drop in boiling water containing the 1 tablespoon lemon juice. Cook for 5 to 7 minutes, or until tender but not too soft. Drain and set aside to cool. (If you are using frozen artichokes, simply pat dry when thoroughly thawed.)

2. Dip the artichoke wedges into the egg, letting the excess flow back into the dish, then roll in the bread crumbs. (The artichokes may be prepared up to and including this point as much as 3 or 4 hours ahead of time.)

3. Heat the oil in a skillet until a haze forms over it. Slip the artichokes into the skillet, frying them on one side until a golden crust forms, then turning them until a crust has formed on all sides.

4. Transfer to paper towels to drain; then add salt. Serve while still hot.

MENU SUGGESTIONS

Fried artichoke wedges are a perfect accompaniment for any fried meat such as Breaded Veal Cutlets, Milan Style (270), Baby

Lamb Chops Fried in Parmesan Cheese Batter (page 283), or Fried
Breaded Calf's Liver (page 298). Like all fried vegetables, they fit
beautifully into any type of *fritto misto*. They are also a good accompaniment for Pan-Broiled Steak with Marsala and Hot Pepper Sauce
(page 239), Meat Loaf Braised in White Wine with Dried Wild
Mushrooms (page 249), Pork Loin Braised in Milk (page 284),
Sautéed Chicken Breast Fillets with Lemon and Parsley (page 314),
or Stewed Rabbit with White Wine (page 320).

Carciofi e piselli stufati
BRAISED ARTICHOKES AND PEAS

For 6 persons

2 large or 3 or 4 medium-small artichokes	weight) or 1 ten-ounce package frozen peas, thawed
½ lemon	
2 tablespoons chopped yellow onion	1 tablespoon chopped parsley
3 tablespoons olive oil	Salt
½ teaspoon finely chopped garlic	Freshly ground pepper, about 4 twists of the mill
2 pounds fresh peas (unshelled	

1. For this recipe you need to cut the artichokes lengthwise into
wedges about 1 inch thick at their widest point. It may be easier,
therefore, to first trim away the hard outer leaves and the green tips
as in Step 1 of Artichokes, Roman Style (page 337). Then cut
the artichoke into wedges and from there proceed to remove
the choke and the soft, white curling leaves directly above it. (You
may discard the stems, if you are so inclined, but it would be a pity,
because they have a tart, interesting flavor and can be quite tender.
If you use the stems, cut away the green outer layers, leaving just
the white inner core.) Remember as you prepare each artichoke to
rub it with the lemon, squeezing juice over the cut portions, or it
will discolor.

2. Put the chopped onion in a casserole with the olive oil and
sauté over medium-high heat until translucent. Add the garlic and

continue sautéing until it becomes lightly colored but not brown. Add the artichokes and ⅓ cup of water, cover, and cook over medium heat.

3. After 10 minutes add the shelled fresh peas, the chopped parsley, ½ teaspoon salt, pepper, and, if there is no more water in the pot, ¼ cup of warm water. Turn and mix the peas and artichokes. (If you are using frozen peas, add them only after the artichokes are almost completely tender, because they take only about 5 minutes to cook.) Cover and continue cooking over medium heat until the artichokes are tender all the way through. Test with a fork or, even better, taste, correcting for salt. (If there is too much water in the pot when the vegetables are cooked, uncover, raise the heat to high, and boil the water away rapidly.)

MENU SUGGESTIONS

Braised Artichokes and Peas is a perfect accompaniment to broiled and roasted meats, to roasted fowl, to sautéed veal *scaloppine*, and to Breaded Veal Cutlets, Milan Style (page 270). It does not go well with meats that are cooked in a cream- or milk-based sauce.

Carciofi e porri stufati

BRAISED ARTICHOKES AND LEEKS

For 6 persons

3 large artichokes or 5 or 6 small ones	¼ cup olive oil
½ lemon	Salt
4 large leeks, about 1¾ inches in diameter, or 6 smaller ones	Freshly ground pepper, about 4 twists of the mill

1. Prepare the artichokes as directed in Braised Artichokes and Peas (page 347), remembering to rub the lemon over the cut portion of each artichoke as you finish preparing it, or it will discolor.

2. Cut off the roots of the leeks, remove any leaves that are withered and discolored, and slice off a small part of the green tops. Slice the leeks into two lengthwise sections and wash thoroughly under cold running water.

3. Choose a casserole with a tight-fitting lid. Lay the leeks in the casserole, and add the oil and enough water to come 1 inch up the side of the pot. Cover and cook over moderate heat for 10 minutes. Add the artichoke sections, salt, pepper, and, if necessary, a little warm water. Continue cooking over moderate heat, turning the vegetables from time to time. The vegetables are cooked when they are tender. (Cooking times vary greatly according to the freshness and quality of the vegetable. The only way to tell is by piercing them with a fork or tasting a small piece. If they take long to cook, you will have to add a little warm water from time to time, but all the water must be absorbed by the time they finish cooking.)

MENU SUGGESTIONS

This dish is an ideal accompaniment to roasted meats and fowl, to Sautéed Chicken Breast Fillets with Lemon and Parsley (page 314), or Veal Scaloppine with Lemon Sauce (page 262) or with Marsala (page 261). Do not pair them with a second course carrying a cream or milk-based sauce.

Carciofi e patate
BRAISED ARTICHOKES AND POTATOES

For 4 to 6 persons

3 medium potatoes (about ¾ pound)

2 medium artichokes or 3 or 4 small ones

½ lemon

⅓ cup coarsely chopped yellow onion

5 tablespoons olive oil

¼ teaspoon finely chopped garlic

Salt

Freshly ground pepper, about 4 twists of the mill

1 tablespoon chopped parsley

(continued)

1. Peel the potatoes and wash in cold water. Cut into lengthwise wedges about ¾ inch thick at the broadest point.

2. Prepare the artichokes for cooking as directed in Braised Artichokes and Peas (page 347), remembering to rub the lemon over the cut portion of each artichoke as you finish preparing it, or it will discolor.

3. Choose a casserole just large enough for the artichokes and potatoes. Over medium heat sauté the onion in the olive oil until translucent. Do not let it color. Add the garlic and sauté until it colors lightly. Add the potatoes, artichokes, 1 teaspoon salt, pepper, and parsley and sauté long enough to turn everything two or three times.

4. Add ¼ cup of water, cover the pot, turn the heat down to medium low, and cook, turning the artichokes and potatoes from time to time, for about 40 minutes, or until the artichokes and potatoes are tender when pierced by a fork. (If, while they are still cooking, there is no liquid left in the pot, add 2 tablespoons of water as needed.) When done, taste and correct for salt. Serve warm.

MENU SUGGESTIONS

Follow those given for Braised Artichokes and Peas (page 348). In Italy you would use this as a side dish in a light evening meal, where the first course would not be pasta but a vegetable soup, or a rice-and-vegetable soup.

Topinambur

JERUSALEM ARTICHOKES

The Jerusalem artichoke is not an artichoke, nor has it ever seen Jerusalem. It is a tuber, the edible rootstock of a variety of the sunflower plant, native to Canada and the northern United States. Jerusalem is apparently a corruption of *girasole*, the Italian word for "sunflower." It is much prized in the Piedmont and Friuli regions of northern Italy, where it is called *topinambur*. It has an exquisite texture and a delicate flavor that faintly recalls that of artichoke hearts. It is delicious raw in salads (page 406), sautéed, or gratinéed. It is available usually from late fall through winter. If you find it at your market, buy one or two pounds of it, even though you might not be ready to cook it immediately. It easily keeps for a week or more in the refrigerator. It looks somewhat like ginger root, so be careful that what you are buying is Jerusalem artichoke. It is not easy to use up two pounds of ginger root, as I once found out to my dismay.

When buying Jerusalem artichokes, make sure they are as firm as possible, not spongy. Dig into one or two with your fingernail: if the color under the skin is pinkish, not the creamy white it should be, do not buy them. And peeling them will take half the time if you choose the least gnarled and twisted roots.

Jerusalem Artichokes

Topinambur trifolati
SAUTÉED JERUSALEM ARTICHOKES

For 6 persons

1½ pounds Jerusalem artichokes
¼ cup olive oil
1 teaspoon finely chopped
   garlic
Salt

Freshly ground pepper, about
  6 twists of the mill
1 tablespoon finely chopped
  parsley

1. Pare the artichokes with a potato peeler, or, if you don't object to the peel, scrub them thoroughly under cold running water with a stiff brush. Drop them into boiling salted water, the largest pieces first, the smallest last. As the water comes to a boil again, remove the artichokes and drain. Cut them into very thin slices, about ¼ inch thick. They should still be fairly hard.

2. In a skillet sauté the chopped garlic in the olive oil over medium heat. When the garlic has colored lightly, add the artichokes and stir. Add salt, the pepper, and the chopped parsley and stir again. Turn the artichokes a few times while cooking. They are done when quite tender at the pricking of a fork. Taste and correct for salt, and serve hot.

MENU SUGGESTIONS

Sautéed Jerusalem artichokes are a natural accompaniment for all roasts of veal or chicken, and they make a fine side dish for broiled meat. Try them also with Little Veal Bundles with Anchovies and Cheese (page 267), Sautéed Breaded Veal Chops (page 268), Fried Calf's Brains (page 299), or Sautéed Chicken Breast Fillets with Lemon and Parsley (page 314).

Topinambur gratinati
GRATINÉED JERUSALEM ARTICHOKES

For 4 persons

1 pound Jerusalem artichokes
Salt
Freshly ground pepper, about
4 twists of the mill

¼ cup freshly grated Parmesan
cheese
2½ tablespoons butter

1. Preheat the oven to 400°.

2. Peel or scrub the artichokes as directed in the preceding recipe. Drop them in boiling salted water, holding back the smaller pieces a few moments. Cook until tender but firm at the pricking of a fork. (Jerusalem artichokes tend to go from very firm to almost mushy in a brief span of time, so watch them carefully.) When done, drain and allow to cool.

3. Cut the artichokes into slices ½ inch thick. Arrange them in a buttered bake-and-serve dish so that they slightly overlap. Add salt and pepper, sprinkle the grated cheese over them, dot with butter, and place in the uppermost part of the preheated oven. Bake until a nice golden crust forms. Allow to settle briefly before serving.

MENU SUGGESTIONS

Gratinéed vegetables take easily to all roasts and broiled meats. They are also an excellent accompaniment to Pan-Broiled Steak with Marsala and Hot Pepper Sauce (page 239), Beef Braised in Red Wine Sauce (page 242), Sautéed Veal Scaloppine with Lemon Sauce (page 262) or with Marsala (page 261). There is actually no dish which they cannot accompany gracefully, but to avoid monotony, try not to pair them with those already containing cheese.

Asparagi

ASPARAGUS

HOW TO PREPARE AND BOIL ASPARAGUS

To have good cooked asparagus, you must first buy good raw asparagus. The surest sign that asparagus is over the hill is an open, droopy tip. It should always be tightly closed and firm. The stalk should feel crisp and look moist. You can buy early asparagus, if you don't mind the price, but avoid it at the end of its season, in late June.

Preparation Asparagus must be trimmed so as to make the entire spear edible. At the tip it is very tender, but it can be very tough at the base, with differing degrees of tenderness in between. The parts that must be eliminated are the very end and a thin layer of fibers surrounding the lower half of the spear.

Start by slicing off about 1 inch at the butt end. If, in cutting, you find the flesh hard, fibrous, and somewhat dry slice off more of the stalk until the exposed end is tender and moist. (If the asparagus is very young, it will not need to have much of the base sliced off. If it is older and drier you might have to cut as much as 1½ to 2 inches.) Now, using a sharp paring knife, trim away the tough, outer fibers. Start your cut at the base, going about ⅟₁₆ inch deep, and gradually tapering to nothing midway between the tip and the base. Remove any small leaves sprouting below the tip. Soak the trimmed asparagus in a basin of cold water for 10 minutes, then rinse in 2 or 3 fresh changes of cold water. It is now ready for cooking.

Cooking In Italy we partially boil and partially steam asparagus in a special cooker. Inside the cooker there is a separate, perforated liner that holds the spears upright and lifts out to remove the asparagus when it is cooked. While the butt of the spear is under boiling water, the tip is cooked by the rising steam. This method compensates for the difference between the butt and the tip so that both are cooked to an even degree of tenderness. The Italian asparagus cooker is available in all good housewares shops and departments, and I heartily recommend it to you. You can, however, cook asparagus almost equally well, as the French have always done, in a fish poacher, or in a deep, oval pot large enough to hold the spears horizontally. Here are directions for both methods.

Asparagus Cooked in the Italian Asparagus Cooker

1. Make a bundle of the asparagus, tying it in two places, one above the butts, the other below the tips.

2. Put enough cold water in the cooker to come 2½ inches up the side of the pot. Add 1 teaspoon of salt. Put in the asparagus bundle, cover, and cook at a steady, moderate boil for 15 to 20 minutes. Test the base of the asparagus with a sharp-pronged fork. If it is easily pierced it is done.

3. Transfer the asparagus bundle to an oval platter and remove the ties. Prop the platter up about 1 inch at one end so that the liquid thrown off by the asparagus runs down to the opposite end. This liquid is to be discarded when the asparagus has been well drained.

Asparagus Cooked Without an Asparagus Cooker

1. Make a bundle of the asparagus exactly as in Step 1 above.

2. Bring at least 4 quarts of water to a boil in a fish poacher or in a deep oval pot large enough to contain the asparagus horizontally. Add 2 teaspoons of salt. Wait a moment for the water to return to a rapid boil, then put in the asparagus. Cook the asparagus at a steady, moderate boil, uncovered, for 15 to 20 minutes. After 15 minutes test the base of the asparagus with a sharp-pronged fork. It is done when easily pierced.

3. Hook one or two forks under the bundle's ties and transfer it to an oval platter. Remove the string, loosening the asparagus, and proceed to drain it of its liquid as in Step 3 above.

Asparagi alla parmigiana
ASPARAGUS WITH PARMESAN CHEESE

One of spring's most exquisite gifts to the Italian table is young asparagus, first boiled, then briefly baked with fragrant, grated aged Parmesan cheese. Of all the many dishes called *alla parmigiana* this is an authentic specialty of Parma, which does not keep it from being a great favorite all over Italy, or even in France, where, curiously, it is called *à la milanaise*.

For 4 persons

2 pounds asparagus	⅔ cup freshly grated Parmesan
½ teaspoon salt	cheese
	5 tablespoons butter

1. Preheat the oven to 450°.
2. Trim, peel, and boil the asparagus as directed on page 354.
3. Smear the bottom of a rectangular bake-and-serve dish with butter. Arrange the boiled asparagus in the dish side by side, in slightly overlapping rows, setting the tips of the spears in one row over the butt ends of the ones in the row ahead. (Never cover the tips.) Sprinkle each row with salt and grated cheese and dot with butter before lapping the next row over it.
4. Bake on the uppermost rack of the oven for about 15 minutes, until a light, golden crust forms. Allow to settle a few minutes before serving.

MENU SUGGESTIONS

This is often served as a first course. It goes well before Rolled Stuffed Breast of Veal (page 254), Veal Rolls in Tomato Sauce (page 265), Roast Spring Lamb with White Wine (page 278), Hothouse Lamb, Roman Style (page 281), or Roast Chicken with Rosemary (page 306). If you are using it as a first course, you can dispense with green vegetables later and serve instead Diced Pan-Roasted Potatoes (page 387).

Asparagi alla parmigiana con uova fritte

ASPARAGUS WITH PARMESAN CHEESE AND FRIED EGGS

Serving asparagus *alla parmigiana* with fried eggs is a succulent enrichment of an already delectable dish. It can no longer, in fact, be considered a side dish. It has all the substance of a full second course and should be employed as such.

For 4 persons

2 pounds asparagus	Freshly ground pepper, about
8 eggs	8 twists of the mill
¼ cup butter	

1. Prepare the asparagus as directed in Asparagus with Parmesan Cheese (previous page).

2. After you remove the asparagus from the oven, fry the eggs in the butter.

3. Divide the asparagus into four equal parts and place on individual dishes. Slide two fried eggs over each portion of asparagus; then spoon the juices left in the baking dish over the asparagus and eggs. Grind pepper over the eggs and serve immediately.

NOTE

This dish, to be enjoyed, needs some abandonment of etiquette. Eat the asparagus with your fingers, holding it by the stem and swirling it in the eggs.

MENU SUGGESTIONS

Like a *frittata,* this can be the mainstay of a light but elegant lunch, preceded by a clear soup or Bresaola (page 47).

Asparagi fritti

FRIED ASPARAGUS

The sweet inner core under the crusty exterior of fried asparagus makes this one of the most delectable of all fried vegetables. Virtually no trimming is required because only the tips and the most tender part of the stalk are used.

For 4 persons

1 pound crisp, fresh asparagus
    Vegetable oil, enough to come
    ½ inch up the side of the
    skillet
1 egg, well beaten, in a deep,
    oval dish

1 cup fine, dry unflavored bread
    crumbs, spread on a dish
    or on waxed paper
½ teaspoon salt

1. Snap off the bottoms of the stems of the asparagus, leaving a stalk about 4 to 5 inches long, including the tips. Remove all the tiny leaves below the tips and wash the asparagus thoroughly in cold water. Pat dry with a towel.

2. Heat the oil in a skillet over high heat. When the oil is very hot, dip the asparagus in the beaten egg, roll it in the bread crumbs, and slide it into the skillet, doing just a few stalks at a time so that they are not crowded in the pan. When the asparagus has formed a crust on one side, turn it. When it has formed a crust on the other side, transfer with a slotted spatula to paper towels to drain, and add ½ teaspoon salt. When all the asparagus is done, taste and correct for salt and serve immediately.

MENU SUGGESTIONS

See Fried Artichoke Wedges (page 346). Fried Asparagus is a particularly nice side dish for Beef Braised in Red Wine Sauce (page 242).

Fave alla romana
FAVA BEANS, ROMAN STYLE

Fava beans usually appear in the vegetable markets from the middle of April until the end of June. They are best at the very beginning of their season when they are young and sweet and very small. In Italy, when they are at their peak, they are often served raw. The pods are brought whole to the table, and everyone shells his own and eats the beans, dipping them in salt. When eaten raw, fava beans are usually served at the end of the meal, replacing fruit. The raw fava bean has an intriguing bittersweet taste that usually turns very mellow and sweet when cooked. The Romans claim to have the best fava beans. There the beans are cooked with pork jowl (*guanciale*), and you will find them listed in the menus as *fave al guanciale*. Since pork jowl, as the Romans know it, is hard to come by here, I use *pancetta*, which is a totally successful substitute and is easily available in all Italian food shops.

For 4 persons

3 pounds small, young fava
  beans (unshelled weight)
2 tablespoons olive oil
2 tablespoons finely chopped
  yellow onion
1 slice rolled *pancetta*, ½ inch
  thick, cut into strips ¼
  inch wide

½ teaspoon salt
Freshly ground pepper, 3 or
  4 twists of the mill

1. Shell the fava beans and wash in cold water.
2. Heat the oil in a casserole and sauté the onion until translucent. Add the *pancetta* and sauté 30 seconds more.
3. Add the fava beans, salt, and pepper, and stir, coating them well. Add ⅓ cup water and cover the pot.
4. Cook over low heat. If the beans are very young and fresh

they will cook in 6 or 8 minutes. (If there is any water left, uncover the pot and raise the heat until it has evaporated.) Serve immediately.

MENU SUGGESTIONS

Fave al guanciale makes a very tasty antipasto. An unconventional but happy pairing is with Bresaola (page 47). As a side dish it goes beautifully with roasts of lamb, especially Hothouse Lamb, Roman Style (page 281), and with Baby Lamb Chops Fried in Parmesan-Cheese Batter (page 283).

Fagiolini verdi
GREEN BEANS

Very fresh, properly cooked green beans, used either as salad or vegetable, are one of the finest pleasures of the table. When you can appreciate the virtues of a salad of crisp beans, seasoned with nothing more than salt, olive oil, and lemon juice, you have understood Italian eating at its best—simple, direct, and inexhaustibly good.

When buying green beans, the best ones to look for are the smallest, youngest beans. They should be vividly green and should break with a snap, revealing a moist, meaty interior with very tiny, undeveloped seeds. Vegetable markets, in their tireless efforts to frustrate good cooking, often lump together beans of assorted sizes. These are practically impossible to cook evenly. If you have a choice, buy beans that are uniform in size.

COOKING GREEN BEANS

All it takes to cook green beans properly is plenty of salted boiling water and a readiness to drain them the moment they are tender but still crisp.

1. Snap both ends off the beans, pulling away any possible strings. Soak the beans in a basin of cold water for a few minutes, then drain.

2. For 1 pound of beans, bring 4 quarts of water to a boil. Add 1½ tablespoons salt. After a moment, when the water is boiling rapidly again, drop in the green beans. Hold the heat at high until the water returns to a boil, then regulate it so that the beans cook at a moderate boil. Do not cover. Since cooking times vary, depending on the size and freshness of the beans (very young, fresh beans may cook in 6 or 7 minutes, while larger, older ones may take 10 or 12), start tasting them after 6 minutes and drain them the moment they are tender but firm and crisp to the bite.

Boiled green beans can be used for salad (see page 412) or in the following recipe, which requires further cooking.

Fagiolini verdi al burro e formaggio
SAUTÉED GREEN BEANS WITH BUTTER AND CHEESE

For 6 persons

1 pound fresh, crisp green beans	Salt, as required
¼ cup butter	
¼ cup freshly grated Parmesan cheese	

1. Prepare and cook the green beans as directed above, being certain to drain them when they are tender but still crisp.

2. Put the green beans in a skillet with the butter and lightly sauté over medium heat for 2 minutes. Add the grated cheese and stir. Taste and correct for salt. Stir once or twice more, transfer to a warm platter, and serve immediately.

MENU SUGGESTIONS

Follow those for Gratinéed Jerusalem Artichokes (page 353). These green beans go particularly nicely with veal dishes, especially Sautéed Breaded Veal Chops (page 268) or Breaded Veal Cutlets, Milan Style (page 270).

Fagiolini verdi con peperoni e pomodoro

GREEN BEANS WITH PEPPERS AND TOMATOES

For 4 to 6 persons

1 pound green beans	⅔ cup canned Italian tomatoes,
1 green pepper	coarsely chopped, with
3 tablespoons olive oil	their juice
1 medium yellow onion, cut	1½ teaspoons salt
into slices about ¼ inch	Freshly ground pepper, 3 or
thick	4 twists of the mill

1. Snap off the ends of the green beans, pulling off any strings they may have. Wash in cold water and set aside.

2. Wash the green pepper in cold water, and, if you find the peel as disagreeable as I do, remove it with a potato peeler. Remove the core with all the seeds and slice the pepper into strips a little less than ½ inch wide. Set aside.

3. Heat the oil in a casserole and sauté the onion until translucent.

4. Add the strips of green pepper and the chopped tomatoes and cook over medium heat until the tomatoes separate from the oil and thicken into sauce, about 25 minutes.

5. Add the green beans, stir a few times until they are all well coated, and add ⅓ cup water, the salt, and the pepper. Cover and cook until tender, about 20 to 30 minutes, depending on the freshness and size of the green beans. Add 1 or 2 tablespoons of water from time to time if required. (If, however, at the end there is too much liquid in the pot, uncover, raise the heat to high, and boil it away quickly.) Taste and correct for salt.

NOTE

These green beans maintain their excellent flavor also when prepared ahead of time and warmed up.

These beans are a tasty accompaniment for broiled or roasted meats and for veal cutlets and other veal dishes, as long as these are not sauced with cream or with tomato.

Broccoli all'aglio
SAUTÉED BROCCOLI WITH GARLIC

For 4 to 6 persons

1 bunch fresh broccoli (about 1½ pounds)	¼ cup olive oil
Salt	2 tablespoons chopped parsley
2 teaspoons finely chopped garlic	

1. Cut off the tough butt end of the broccoli stalks, about ½ inch. With a sharp paring knife, peel off all the dark-green skin on the stalks and stems. (The skin is thicker around the larger part of the stalk, so you will have to cut deeper there.) Split the larger stalks in two, or if extremely large, in four, without cutting off the florets. Rinse well in 3 or 4 changes of cold water.

2. Bring 4 quarts of water to a boil with 1 teaspoon of salt. Drop in the broccoli and boil slowly until the stalks can be pierced easily by a fork, about 7 to 10 minutes, depending on the freshness of the broccoli. Drain and set aside. (You can prepare the broccoli several hours ahead of time up to this point, but do not refrigerate, because refrigeration impairs the flavor.)

3. Choose a skillet large enough to accommodate all the broccoli without much overlapping. Sauté the garlic in the olive oil over medium heat. As soon as the garlic colors lightly, add the broccoli, about 2 teaspoons salt, and the chopped parsley and sauté lightly for about 2 to 3 minutes. Turn the broccoli two or three times while cooking. Serve hot.

(continued)

Follow those for Sautéed Jerusalem Artichokes (page 353). Broccoli also goes well with Beef Patties with Anchovies and Mozzarella (page 245) and Casserole-Roasted Lamb with Juniper Berries (page 280).

Broccoli al burro e formaggio

SAUTÉED BROCCOLI WITH BUTTER AND CHEESE

For 4 to 6 persons

1 bunch fresh broccoli	½ cup freshly grated Parmesan
¼ cup butter	cheese
1 teaspoon salt	

1. Peel, wash, boil, and drain the broccoli as directed on page 363.

2. In a skillet large enough to accommodate all the broccoli without much overlapping, melt the butter over medium heat. When the butter foam begins to subside, add the boiled, drained broccoli and the salt, and sauté lightly for about 2 to 3 minutes, gently turning the broccoli two or three times. Add the grated cheese, turn the broccoli one more time, and serve.

Follow those for Gratinéed Jerusalem Artichokes (page 353).

NOTE

On many distressing occasions I have seen people eat the florets and leave the stalks on the plate. They are evidently under the impression that they are choosing the more delectable part. Actually, it is just the other way around.

Carote al burro e formaggio
CARROTS WITH PARMESAN CHEESE

For 6 persons

2 bunches carrots	¼ teaspoon sugar
5 tablespoons butter	3 tablespoons freshly grated
Salt to taste	Parmesan cheese

1. Peel the carrots and slice them into disks ⅜ inch thick. (The thin tapered ends can be cut a little thicker.) Put the carrots and butter in a skillet large enough to contain the carrots in a single layer and add enough water to come ¼ inch up the side of the pan. (If you have too many carrots for your largest pan, divide them equally between two skillets, using 2½ tablespoons of butter per skillet.) Cook over medium heat, uncovered.

2. When the liquid in the skillet has evaporated, add the salt and sugar. Continue cooking, adding 2 or 3 tablespoons of warm water as required but not too much at one time. The object is to obtain carrots that are well browned, wrinkled, and concentrated in texture and taste, which will take about 1 to 1½ hours of watchful cooking, depending on the carrots. When they begin to reach the well-browned, wrinkled stage do not add any more water, because there must be no liquid left at the end. (If you have been using two pans, the carrots reduce so much in volume that halfway through cooking they can be consolidated into a single pan.)

3. When cooked, add the grated Parmesan, stir once or twice over heat, and then transfer to a warm platter and serve immediately.

NOTE

This is a time-consuming dish, although not a complicated one. You can prepare it entirely ahead of time, however, stopping short of adding the Parmesan. Add the Parmesan only after reheating the carrots. Carrots cooked this way become very condensed in flavor, as they lose all their liquid, and very satisfying in texture.

(*continued*)

These carrots are a good accompaniment for all roasts, for broiled meats, for all sautéed veal dishes, for game—in short, for nearly all meats or fowl except those sauced with tomato.

Cavolfiore
CAULIFLOWER

A head of cauliflower should be very hard, its leaves should be fresh, crisp, and unmarked, and its florets should be compact and as white as possible. If speckled or slightly discolored, don't buy it. Fresh cauliflower keeps very nicely in the refrigerator for several days.

HOW TO BOIL CAULIFLOWER

Remove all the leaves from a head of cauliflower and cut a cross at the root end. Bring 5 quarts of water to a boil. (The greater the quantity of water you use, the faster cauliflower cooks and the sweeter it tastes.) Add the cauliflower and cook at a moderate boil, uncovered, for about 30 minutes, or until it is tender at the pricking of a fork. Drain immediately when cooked.

Boiled cauliflower can be served lukewarm or at room temperature as salad (page 413), or it can be gratinéed or fried.

Cavolfiore gratinato al burro e formaggio
CAULIFLOWER GRATINÉED WITH BUTTER AND CHEESE

For 6 to 8 persons

1 head cauliflower	2 teaspoons salt
(2 to 2½ pounds)	⅔ cup freshly grated Parmesan
¼ cup butter	cheese

1. Preheat the oven to 400°.

2. Boil the cauliflower as directed above, and when it has cooled detach the florets from the head. If they are rather large, divide them into two or three parts.

3. Choose a bake-and-serve dish large enough to hold the florets in a single layer. Smear the bottom with butter and arrange the florets so that they overlap slightly, like roof tiles. Sprinkle with salt and grated cheese and dot thickly with butter. Place on the uppermost rack of the preheated oven and bake for about 15 minutes, or until a light crust forms on top. Allow to settle a few moments before serving.

MENU SUGGESTIONS

Follow those for Gratinéed Jerusalem Artichokes (page 353).

Cavolfiore fritto
FRIED CAULIFLOWER

For 6 persons

1 head cauliflower
  (2 to 2½ pounds)
2 eggs, lightly beaten with 2
  teaspoons salt, in a bowl

1 cup fine, dry unflavored bread
  crumbs, spread on a dish or
  on waxed paper
Vegetable oil, enough to come
  ½ inch up the side of the
  pan

1. Boil the cauliflower as directed on page 366. When it has cooled, detach the florets from the head and cut into wedges about 1 inch thick at the widest point.

2. Dip the florets in egg, letting the excess flow back into the bowl, then turn them in bread crumbs. (They can be prepared up to and including this point a few hours ahead of time.)

3. Heat the oil in the skillet over high heat. When it is very hot, slip in the floret wedges, no more at one time than will fit loosely in the pan. Fry to a nice golden crust on one side; then turn them.

When both sides are done, transfer to paper towels to drain. Serve piping hot.

MENU SUGGESTIONS

Follow those for Fried Artichoke Wedges (page 346). Fried cauliflower is very nice also with Sautéed Chicken Livers with Sage (page 303), and Rolled Breast of Chicken Fillets Stuffed with Pork (page 315).

Coste di sedano alla parmigiana
BRAISED AND GRATINÉED CELERY WITH PARMESAN CHEESE

In this recipe, celery undergoes a nearly complete range of cooking procedures. It is first blanched, then briefly sautéed, braised in broth, and finished off in the oven. It is actually very much simpler than it sounds, and the result is a remarkably fine dish that is as elegant as it is delicious.

For 6 persons

2 large bunches crisp, fresh celery

3 tablespoons finely chopped yellow onion

3 tablespoons butter

¼ cup chopped *pancetta*, or prosciutto, or unsmoked ham

Salt

Freshly ground pepper, about 6 twists of the mill

2 cups Homemade Meat Broth (page 10) or 1 cup canned beef broth mixed with 1 cup water

1 cup freshly grated Parmesan cheese

1. Trim the tops of the celery and detach all the stalks from the bunches. Lightly peel the stalks to remove most of the strings. Cut the stalks into lengths of about 3 inches. Drop into 2 to 3 quarts of rapidly boiling water, and 2 minutes after the water returns to a boil, drain and set aside.

2. Preheat the oven to 400°.

3. Put the onion in a saucepan with the butter and sauté over medium heat until translucent but not browned.

4. Add the *pancetta*, stir, and sauté for about 1 minute.

5. Add the well-drained celery, a light sprinkling of salt, and the pepper and sauté for 5 minutes, turning the celery from time to time.

6. Add the broth, cover the pan, and cook at a gentle simmer until the celery is tender at the pricking of a fork. (If, when the celery is nearly done, there is still much liquid in the pan, uncover, raise the heat, and finish cooking while the liquid evaporates.)

7. Arrange the cooked celery in a bake-and-serve dish with the inner sides of the stalks facing up. Spoon the sautéed onion and *pancetta* from the pan over the celery, then add the grated cheese. Place the dish on the uppermost rack of the preheated oven and bake for 6 to 8 minutes, or until the cheese has melted and formed a slight crust. Allow to settle for a few moments, then serve directly from the baking dish.

MENU SUGGESTIONS

Follow those for Gratinéed Jerusalem Artichokes (page 353). This celery goes particularly well with Beef Braised in Red Wine Sauce (page 242), Rolled Stuffed Breast of Veal (page 254), and Rolled Breast of Chicken Fillets Stuffed with Pork (page 315).

Sedano e patate all'olio
CELERY AND POTATOES BRAISED IN OLIVE OIL

For 4 to 5 persons

5 medium potatoes, about 1¼ pounds	⅓ cup olive oil
	Salt
1 large bunch celery	2 tablespoons lemon juice

1. Peel the potatoes, wash them, and cut into halves.

2. Detach all the celery stalks. Since only the stalks are used in

this recipe, remove the leafy end entirely, and set aside the white, inner heart for use in a salad. Snap off a small piece from the narrow end of each stalk and pull down to remove as much of the celery strings as possible. Cut the stalks into 3-inch lengths and wash thoroughly in cold water.

3. Put the celery, olive oil, and ½ teaspoon of salt in a casserole and add enough water to cover. Cover the casserole and cook over medium heat for 10 minutes. Add the halved potatoes, 1 teaspoon of salt, and the lemon juice. (If there is not enough liquid to cover the potatoes, add water.) Cover and cook for 25 minutes. Test both the celery and the potatoes for tenderness with a fork. (Sometimes the celery lags, while the potatoes are already tender. If this happens, transfer the potatoes to a warm, covered dish, cover the casserole, and continue cooking the celery until tender.)

4. When the celery and potatoes are done the only liquid left in the pot should be oil. If there is still some water left, uncover the pot, raise the heat, and quickly evaporate it. If the potatoes were removed, return them to the casserole after boiling away the water. Cover, turn down the heat to medium, and warm up the potatoes for about 2 minutes. Taste and correct for salt. Serve hot.

MENU SUGGESTIONS

This is a good vegetable to choose when making up a meal without pasta. It is excellent with Open-Faced Italian Omelets (pages 326–332), with Veal Rolls in Tomato Sauce (page 265), and with Fried Calf's Liver (page 298).

Coste di biete alla parmigiana
SWISS CHARD STALKS WITH PARMESAN CHEESE

For 4 persons

2 bunches mature Swiss chard, the ones with the broadest stalks Salt	¼ cup butter ⅔ cup freshly grated Parmesan cheese

1. Pull off all the leaves from the Swiss chard stalks. Do not discard the leaves; they make an excellent salad (page 414). Wash the stalks in cold water, trimming away any remaining leaves, and cut them in lengths of about 4 inches.

2. Drop in abundant boiling salted water and cook for approximately 30 minutes. (They should be tender but firm because they will undergo additional cooking in the oven.)

3. Preheat the oven to 400°.

4. Smear a rectangular bake-and-serve dish with butter. Arrange a layer of stalks on the bottom of the dish, laying them end to end. Trim them to fit if necessary. Sprinkle lightly with salt and grated Parmesan cheese and dot with butter. Place another layer of stalks over this, season as above, and continue building up layers until you've used up all the stalks. The top layer should be generously sprinkled with Parmesan and well dotted with butter.

5. Place the dish in the upper third of the preheated oven. Bake for 15 minutes, or until the top layer acquires a light, golden crust. This dish is at its most agreeable in texture and flavor when warm, but not too hot, so allow it to settle and cool a bit before bringing to the table.

MENU SUGGESTIONS

Follow those for Gratinéed Jerusalem Artichokes (page 353).

Melanzane

EGGPLANT

Italian eggplants are very small, often just slightly larger than zucchini, whose shape they resemble. Similar eggplants are available here, but I have always found them rather sharp in flavor and do not recommend them. The most consistently good eggplant is the medium-sized one, weighing about 1½ pounds. The skin should be glossy, smooth, and intact. Avoid eggplants with skin that is opaque, discolored, or even slightly wrinkled. Fresh eggplants are resistant to the touch and compact, never spongy. They will keep in the refrigerator for 5 to 6 days.

The skin on American eggplant is quite tough, so it is best to peel it for any of the following recipes.

Melanzane fritte
FRIED EGGPLANT

Fried eggplant is the key ingredient in some very appealing Italian dishes, such as Eggplant, Parmesan Style (page 373) or Thin Spaghetti with Eggplant (page 98), and on its own it makes an excellent side dish. There are two points to remember in order to fry eggplant successfully:

• Before it can be cooked, eggplant must be drained of its excess moisture. This is done by salting it and letting it stand for 30 minutes.
• Eggplant must fry in an abundant quantity of very hot oil. When properly fried, it absorbs virtually none of the cooking fat. Never add oil to the pan while the eggplant is frying.

For 6 to 8 persons

2 to 3 medium eggplants	Vegetable oil, enough to come
(3 to 4½ pounds)	1 inch up the side
Salt	of the pan

1. Peel the eggplants and cut them lengthwise in slices about ⅜ inch thick. Set the slices upright in a pasta colander and sprinkle the first layer of slices liberally with salt before setting another layer next to it. Put a soup dish under the colander to collect the drippings and let stand at least 30 minutes.

2. Add enough oil to a large skillet to come 1 inch up the side of the pan. Turn on the heat to high. Take as many slices of eggplant as you think will fit in one layer in the skillet and dry them well with paper towels. When the oil is hot (test it with the end of one of the slices: it should sizzle), slide in the eggplant. Fry to a nice golden

brown on all sides, then transfer to a platter lined with paper towels to drain. Dry some more slices and continue frying until they are all done. (If you see that the eggplant is browning too rapidly, lower the heat.)

NOTE
Fried eggplant can be served hot or at room temperature.

MENU SUGGESTIONS

Combined with Oven-Browned Tomatoes (page 389), fried eggplant makes a marvelous accompaniment for Breaded Veal Cutlets (page 270).

Melanzane alla parmigiana
EGGPLANT, PARMESAN STYLE

For 4 persons

2 medium eggplants (about 3 pounds), sliced, drained of their moisture, and fried as directed in Fried Eggplant (page 372)	Salt
	1 whole-milk mozzarella cheese, coarsely grated on the largest holes of the grater
2 cups canned Italian tomatoes, drained, seeds removed, and coarsely chopped	4 to 5 tablespoons freshly grated Parmesan cheese
	1½ teaspoons orégano
	2½ tablespoons butter

1. Preheat the oven to 400°.

2. Line the bottom of a buttered bake-and-serve dish (10 inches square, or its rectangular equivalent) with a single layer of fried eggplant slices. Top this layer with chopped tomatoes. Add a pinch of salt, a generous sprinkling of grated mozzarella, a tablespoon of grated Parmesan cheese, and a pinch of orégano and cover with another layer of sliced eggplant. Continue building up layers of eggplant, tomatoes, and cheese until you've used up all the eggplant. The top layer should be eggplant. Sprinkle the remaining

Parmesan cheese over it and dot with butter. Place in the upper third of the preheated oven.

3. After 20 minutes pull out the pan and, pressing with the back of a spoon, check to see if there is an excess amount of liquid. If there is, tip the pan and draw it off with the spoon. Return to the oven for another 15 minutes. Allow it to settle and partly cool off before serving. It should not be piping hot.

NOTE

It can be prepared entirely ahead of time, refrigerated when cool, and warmed up several days later. It will still be good, although not quite as fragrant as the day you prepared it.

MENU SUGGESTIONS

Eggplant *parmigiana* is too hearty to be just a side dish. It can be a light luncheon on its own followed by a mixed green salad or, in a fully organized meal, it can precede Breaded Veal Cutlet (page 270), Fried Breaded Calf's Liver (page 298), or Baby Lamb Chops Fried in Parmesan Cheese Batter (page 283). It can also become a second course, preceded by Potato Gnocchi (page 195) with Genoese Basil Sauce for Pasta and Soup (page 139). Do not combine it with either heavily sauced or delicately flavored dishes. In restaurants it is often served at room temperature as a summer antipasto.

Melanzane al funghetto
SAUTÉED DICED EGGPLANT

This eggplant is called *al funghetto*, "mushroom style," because it is sautéed with olive oil, garlic, and parsley. This is the same technique as that used in making *funghi trifolati*, or "truffled" mushrooms (page 379), which are called "truffled" for obscure reasons of their own. Some people also add anchovies and orégano. I do not.

For 4 to 6 persons

2 medium eggplants (about 3
     pounds)
Salt
1 teaspoon finely chopped garlic
5 tablespoons olive oil

2 tablespoons finely chopped
     parsley
Freshly ground pepper, about
     6 twists of the mill

1. Peel the eggplant and cut it into 1-inch cubes. Put it in a colander and sprinkle liberally with salt. Toss and turn the eggplant cubes so that there is some salt on all of them. Allow to stand for at least 30 minutes, draining the eggplant of as much of its excess liquid as possible. Remove from the colander and blot with a paper towel.

2. In a skillet, over medium heat, sauté the garlic, with 4 tablespoons of the olive oil, until it colors lightly. Add the eggplant pieces, turning them frequently. At first the eggplant will absorb all the oil. Don't panic—turn the pieces rapidly and keep shaking the pan. Add 1 more tablespoon of oil after 5 minutes. (You will not need any more oil because as the eggplant cooks the oil will reappear on the surface.) After 10 or 12 minutes, add the chopped parsley and stir it well. Add the pepper and continue cooking until the eggplant is tender but firm, about 30 minutes, give or take a few minutes, depending on the eggplant. Taste and correct for salt; then spoon into a warm platter and serve.

NOTE

You can prepare the dish entirely ahead of time and when cool refrigerate in its cooking juices, under plastic wrap. When reheating, put it in a skillet (no additional oil is required) and warm it slowly over medium-low heat.

MENU SUGGESTIONS

Follow those for Sautéed Jerusalem Artichokes (page 352). Eggplant is also a tasty accompaniment for Thin Pan-Broiled Steaks with Tomatoes and Olives (page 241) and Veal Scaloppine with Tomatoes (page 264).

FINOCCHIO

Finocchio is a sweet variety of fennel, also known as Florence fennel. Most people have seen it in Italian vegetable markets, some may have had it raw in salads in Italian restaurants, but few know what a fine vegetable it is for cooking. It is sweeter cooked than raw, losing most of its slight taste of anise. It has an interesting flavor, gentle and forward at the same time, and its texture is quite similar to that of celery.

There are two basic types of finocchio. One is squat and bulbous, the other is flat and elongated. The squat, bulbous one is crisper, sweeter, and less stringy and should be the only kind used for salads. For cooking, either variety will do, although the stocky one always gives better results. Finocchio is generally available from late fall through early spring.

Finocchi al burro e formaggio
SAUTÉED FINOCCHIO WITH BUTTER AND CHEESE

For 4 persons

3 large finocchios or 4 to 5 small ones	Salt
5 tablespoons butter	3 tablespoons freshly grated Parmesan cheese

1. Cut away any wilted or bruised parts of the finocchio. Cut off and discard the tops and cut the bulbous lower parts into vertical slices no more than ½ inch thick. Wash thoroughly in cold water.

2. Put the sliced finocchio and the butter in a fairly broad saucepan, and add enough water barely to cover. Cook, uncovered, over medium heat. If there is too much finocchio for your pan, put in as much as it will hold, cover the pan, and cook for 5 to 8 minutes, or until the finocchio has wilted and come down in volume. Add the rest of the finocchio, mix well, cover the pan, and cook for 3 or 4 more minutes. Uncover the pan and cook, turning the finocchio from time to time, until it is tender at the pricking of a fork, from 25 to 40 minutes all together. You may add as much as ⅓ cup of warm water if it is necessary, but at the end the finocchio must have absorbed all the liquid and should have a glossy pale-gold color. Before removing from the heat, add salt to taste and the grated cheese. Mix well and transfer to a warm platter. Serve while hot.

NOTE

When cooked, the tender parts of finocchio will be soft but the firm ones rather crunchy. Don't try to eliminate this natural and interesting contrast in texture by cooking until the finocchio is all soft.

MENU SUGGESTIONS

Follow those for Gratinéed Jerusalem Artichokes (page 353). This finocchio is quite lovely with Roast Pork with Bay Leaves (page 286) and Meat Loaf Braised in White Wine with Dried Wild Mushrooms (page 249).

Finocchi all'olio
FINOCCHIO BRAISED IN OLIVE OIL

For 4 persons

3 large finocchios or 4 to 5 small ones	⅓ cup olive oil Salt

Follow the recipe for Sautéed Finocchio with Butter and Cheese (page 377). The procedure is identical, step for step, except that olive oil is substituted for butter and the grated cheese is completely omitted. While the procedure is the same, the taste and texture are quite different when finocchio is braised in olive oil. It is perhaps somewhat less elegant than finocchio done in butter, but it is sweeter, with a smoother texture.

MENU SUGGESTIONS

Finocchio all'olio is a suitable accompaniment for zesty dishes such as Pan-Broiled Steak with Marsala and Hot Pepper Sauce (page 239), Thin Pan-Broiled Steaks with Tomatoes and Olives (page 241), and Veal Scaloppine with Tomatoes (page 264).

Finocchi fritti
FRIED FINOCCHIO

For 4 persons

3 finocchios Salt 2 eggs, beaten lightly with ¼ teaspoon salt, in a bowl 1½ cups fine, dry unflavored bread crumbs, spread on a dish or on waxed paper	Vegetable oil, enough to come at least ½ inch up the side of the pan

1. Cut off the tops of the finocchios and trim away any bruised or discolored parts. Cut the finocchios lengthwise into slices about ⅜ inch thick. Wash thoroughly in several changes of cold water and drain.

2. Bring 3 quarts of water to a boil, add 1 teaspoon salt, then drop in the finocchio slices. First drop in the slices that are attached to part of the fleshy core, since these take a little longer to cook. After a minute or so drop in the others. Cook at a moderate boil until the core feels tender but firm at the pricking of a fork, about 6 to 10 minutes, depending on the finocchio. When done, drain and allow to cool.

3. Dip the cooled, parboiled finocchio slices in egg, then turn them in bread crumbs.

4. Heat the oil in the skillet over high heat. When the oil is quite hot, slip in as many finocchio slices as will fit loosely. Fry to a golden brown on one side, then on the other. Transfer to paper towels to drain. Taste and correct for salt.

MENU SUGGESTIONS

Follow those for Fried Artichoke Wedges (page 346). Fried finocchio is also particularly nice with Roast Spring Lamb with White Wine (page 278).

Funghi trifolati
SAUTÉED MUSHROOMS WITH GARLIC AND PARSLEY

Trifolare describes the classic Italian method of quickly sautéing sliced vegetables or meat in olive oil, garlic, and parsley. To these basic elements other flavors, such as anchovies or wine, are sometimes added. The term is derived from the word *trifola*, which in Lombardy and Piedmont means truffle. It is not exactly clear what the connection with truffles is, because there are no truffles in this dish. One explanation is that the ingredients are sliced thin, as one would slice truffles. Another is that anything cooked in this manner becomes so delicious it almost could be truffles.

(continued)

For 6 persons

1½ pounds crisp white mushrooms	Salt
1½ teaspoons finely chopped garlic	Freshly ground pepper, 5 to 6 twists of the mill
½ cup olive oil	3 tablespoons finely chopped parsley

1. Slice off the ends of the mushroom stems. Wipe the mushrooms clean with a damp cloth. If there are still traces of soil, wash very rapidly in cold running water and dry thoroughly with a towel. Cut into lengthwise slices ¼ inch thick.

2. Choose a large, heavy skillet that can later accommodate the mushrooms without crowding, and sauté the garlic in the olive oil over medium-high heat until it colors lightly but does not brown. Turn the heat up to high and add the mushrooms. When the mushrooms have absorbed all the oil, turn the heat down to low, add salt and pepper, and shake the pan, stirring and tossing the mushrooms. As soon as the mushroom juices come to the surface, which happens very quickly, turn the heat up to high again and cook for 4 to 5 minutes, stirring frequently. (Do not overcook, because the texture and flavor of mushrooms are not improved by prolonged cooking.)

3. Taste and correct for salt. Add the chopped parsley, stir rapidly once or twice, and transfer to a warm platter.

NOTE

Serve immediately if intended as a side dish. If prepared ahead of time and allowed to cool to room temperature, this makes an excellent antipasto.

MENU SUGGESTIONS

Follow those for Sautéed Jerusalem Artichokes (page 352).

Funghi alla panna

SAUTÉED MUSHROOMS WITH HEAVY CREAM

For 6 persons

1½ pounds mushrooms	Salt
1½ tablespoons finely chopped shallots or yellow onion	Freshly ground pepper, about 4 twists of the mill
2½ tablespoons butter	½ cup heavy cream
1½ tablespoons vegetable oil	

1. Slice off the ends of the mushroom stems. Wipe the mushrooms clean with a damp cloth. If there are still traces of soil, wash very rapidly in cold, running water, and dry thoroughly with a towel.

2. Cut the mushrooms into wedges, each section of which should be about ½ inch thick at the thickest point of the cap. (If the mushrooms are very small, cut them into halves or leave them whole.)

3. Choose a skillet large enough to hold the mushrooms later without crowding them. Over medium-high heat, sauté the chopped shallots in the butter and oil until pale gold in color. Raise the heat to high, and add the mushrooms. When the mushrooms have absorbed all the fat, turn the heat down to low. Add salt and pepper and stir-cook the mushrooms until their juices begin to come to the surface, in a few seconds. Raise the heat to high and cook for 3 to 4 minutes, shaking the pan and stirring the mushrooms frequently.

4. Add the heavy cream and cook for just 2 or 3 minutes longer, until part of the cream has been absorbed by the mushrooms and the rest has thickened slightly. Transfer the entire contents of the skillet to a warm platter and serve immediately.

MENU SUGGESTIONS

Possibly the most delicious way to serve these mushrooms is to mix them with Veal Stew with Sage and White Wine (page 273). Another lovely combination is with Sautéed Veal Chops with Sage and White Wine (page 272). Actually they will go beautifully with any veal dish, as long as they do not have to compete with a tart or tomatoey sauce.

Cipolline agrodolci

SWEET AND SOUR ONIONS

The secret of these delectably tart and sweet onions is not so much in the preparation, which is rapid and simple, as in the very long, slow cooking. It takes 2 to 3 hours of patient simmering to bring them to their peak, but it is well worth while because this is one of the most successful dishes of vegetables you can serve.

Since vinegar varies in strength and acidity, adjust the dose in this recipe according to the vinegar you are accustomed to using.

For 6 persons

3 pounds small white onions of uniform size	2 teaspoons sugar
¼ cup butter	¼ teaspoon salt
2½ tablespoons vinegar	Freshly ground pepper, 3 or 4 twists of the mill

1. In peeling the onions it can save you a great deal of time and tears if you first plunge them in boiling water for about 15 seconds. Remove just the outside skin and any dangling roots. Do not remove any of the onion layers, do not trim anything off the top, and leave the base of the root intact or the onions will come apart during the long cooking. Cut a cross into the root end.

2. Choose a skillet or a shallow enameled cast-iron pan large enough to contain the onions in a single layer. Put in the onions, the butter, and enough water to come an inch up the side of the pan. Cook over medium heat, turning the onions frequently, adding a little bit of warm water from time to time as the liquid evaporates. After about 20 minutes, when the onions begin to soften, add the vinegar, sugar, salt, and pepper. Turn the onions again. Continue to cook slowly for 2 hours or more, turning the onions frequently. Add a tablespoon or two of warm water as it becomes necessary. They are done when they have turned a rich, dark golden brown all over and are easily pierced by a fork. Serve while hot.

NOTE

If prepared ahead of time they can be reheated slowly before serving.

MENU SUGGESTIONS

This dish is a perfect accompaniment to almost any meat and fowl and it is particularly splendid with roasts. Avoid pairing it with any dish that is sharp in flavor, such as a spicy *pizzaiola* tomato sauce.

Pisellini alla Fiorentina

SAUTÉED PEAS WITH PROSCIUTTO, FLORENTINE STYLE

In Florence, the peas one uses for this recipe are very tiny, freshly picked, early peas. They cook quite rapidly and are very sweet and tender. No other kind of peas really works as well, but, if you can't find very young, fresh peas in the market, frozen tiny peas are to be preferred to mature, mealy fresh peas.

For 4 persons

2 cloves garlic, peeled
3 tablespoons olive oil
2 tablespoons prosciutto or
    pancetta, diced into ¼-
    inch cubes
2 pounds fresh, early peas
    (unshelled weight) or 1
    ten-ounce package frozen
    tiny peas, thawed

2 tablespoons finely chopped
    parsley
Salt
Freshly ground pepper, 4 or
    5 twists of the mill

1. Over medium-high heat sauté the garlic cloves in the olive oil until they have colored well.

2. Remove the garlic, add the diced prosciutto or *pancetta*, and sauté for less than a minute.

3. Add the peas, parsley, salt, and pepper, turn the heat down to medium, and cover the pan, adding 2 to 3 tablespoons of water only if you are using fresh peas. Cook until done, 5 minutes or less for

frozen peas, 15 to 30 minutes for fresh, which vary enormously. The only way to tell is to taste. While tasting, correct for salt. Serve immediately.

MENU SUGGESTIONS

These peas go well with practically any meat or chicken course, which is fortunate because this is one of the tastiest of all Italian vegetable dishes. Try them with Braised Veal Shanks, Milan Style (page 256), Sautéed Breaded Veal Chops (page 268), Baby Lamb Chops Fried in Parmesan-Cheese Batter (page 283), or Sautéed Chicken Breast Fillets with Lemon and Parsley (page 314).

Purè di patate

ITALIAN MASHED POTATOES WITH PARMESAN CHEESE

There is something about potatoes that seems rarely to have stimulated Italian cooks to a very high pitch of creativity. Rice has had a similar perplexing effect on the French, whose *risotti* are so unsatisfactory. There are one or two nice things we do with potatoes, however. *Gnocchi* is the most famous of these. Another is this luscious purée of potatoes made with butter, milk, and a substantial amount of fresh Parmesan cheese.

For 4 persons

1 pound boiling potatoes	⅓ cup freshly grated Parmesan
3 tablespoons butter	cheese
½ cup milk	Salt to taste

1. Put the potatoes, unpeeled, in a large pot with enough water to cover them well. Cover the pot, bring to a moderate boil, and cook until tender. (Do not test the potatoes too often with your fork, or they will become waterlogged.) Drain, and peel while still hot.

2. Bring water in the lower portion of a double boiler to a very slow simmer. Cut up the butter and put it in the upper portion. Purée the potatoes through a food mill directly into the upper pan.

3. In a separate pan, bring the milk to the verge of boiling. Turn the heat off just as it is about to boil.

4. Start beating the potatoes with a whisk or a fork, adding 2 to 3 tablespoons of hot milk at a time. When you have added half the milk, beat in the grated cheese. When the cheese has been very well incorporated into the potatoes, resume adding the milk without ceasing to beat, except to rest your arm for an occasional few seconds. The potatoes should become a very soft, fluffy mass, a state that requires a great deal of beating and as much milk as the potatoes will absorb without becoming thin and runny. (Some potatoes absorb less milk than others, so you must judge the correct quantity of milk as you are beating, both by taste and thickness of the mass.) As you finish adding the milk, taste and correct for salt. Serve piping hot.

NOTE

If necessary, you can prepare this up to 1 hour ahead of time. Just before serving, warm in the double boiler and beat in 2 or 3 tablespoons of very hot milk.

MENU SUGGESTIONS

The perfect marriage for this dish is with Sautéed Chicken Livers with Sage (page 303). Other congenial combinations are with Beef Braised in Red Wine Sauce (page 242), Rolled Stuffed Breast of Veal (page 254), Braised Veal Shanks, Trieste Style (page 257), and Sautéed Lamb Kidneys with White Wine (page 300). You will, of course, omit pasta from the same menu. Choose a light soup for the first course.

Patate spinose

POTATO CROQUETTES WITH CRISP-FRIED NOODLES

These tiny balls of mashed potatoes are fried with a coating of thin, crumbled noodles, which makes them look like large thistles. Not only is it an attractive dish, but also the creamy potato core and the crackly noodle surface offer an interesting and enjoyable contrast in textures.

(continued)

For 4 to 6 persons

1 pound boiling potatoes,
    unpeeled
1 tablespoon butter
1 egg yolk
1 teaspoon salt
⅛ teaspoon nutmeg

1 cup *fedelini* or *vermicelli*
    (hair-thin noodles), hand-
    crushed into fragments
    about ⅛ inch long
⅓ cup all-purpose flour
    Vegetable oil, enough to come
    ¼ inch up the side of the
    skillet

1. Put the unpeeled potatoes in a saucepan with enough cold water to cover them. Cover the pan and cook at a moderate boil until tender. Drain. Peel while still hot and mash through a food mill or potato ricer into a bowl.

2. Swirl the butter into the potatoes. Add the egg yolk, mixing it in with a fork very rapidly, lest the heat of the potatoes cook it. Add the salt and nutmeg and mix thoroughly again.

3. Combine the crumbled noodles and flour in a dish.

4. Put the oil in a 10-inch skillet and heat over medium-high heat. Shape the puréed potatoes into 1-inch balls, roll them in the noodles and flour, and slip them, a few at a time, depending on the size of the pan, into the hot oil. (Don't crowd them in the pan or they won't fry properly.) Fry, turning them on all sides, until a crisp, dark-

Potato Croquettes with
Crisp-Fried Noodles

golden crust has formed all around. Transfer with a slotted spoon to paper towels to drain. Serve hot.

MENU SUGGESTIONS

Follow the general indications for Italian Mashed Potatoes with Parmesan Cheese (page 384). These croquettes are also very nice with Pan-Broiled Steak with Marsala and Hot Pepper Sauce (page 239).

Dadini di patate arrosto

DICED PAN-ROASTED POTATOES

For 4 to 6 persons

1½ pounds boiling potatoes, not Idaho or other dry, mealy potatoes	5 tablespoons vegetable oil 2 tablespoons butter 2 teaspoons salt

1. Peel the potatoes, rinse in cold water, pat dry, and dice into ½-inch cubes.

2. Heat the oil and butter in a 12-inch heavy-bottomed or cast-iron skillet over medium-high heat. When the butter foam subsides, put in the potatoes and turn them until they are well coated with the cooking fat. Turn the heat down to medium and let the potatoes cook until a golden crust has formed on one side. Add the salt, turn them, and continue cooking and turning until every side has a nice crust. After 20 to 25 minutes, test them with a fork to see if they are tender. If not, turn the heat to low and cook until tender.

NOTE

These potatoes cannot be prepared ahead of time and reheated, but they stay crisp even when lukewarm. They are at their best, of course, piping hot.

MENU SUGGESTIONS

These are an ideal accompaniment to any roast, of meat or fowl. They are almost equally well matched with most sautéed dishes. Do avoid potato soups or *gnocchi* as a first course if you are going to have potatoes later.

Spinaci saltati
SAUTÉED SPINACH

For 4 to 6 persons

1½ to 2 pounds fresh spinach or 2 ten-ounce packages frozen whole-leaf spinach, thawed	Salt 2 cloves garlic, peeled ¼ cup olive oil

1. If you are using fresh spinach, discard any leaves that are not crisp and green. Snap off the hard, lower end of the stem on young spinach, remove the whole stem on more mature spinach. Soak it in a basin of cold water, dunking it with your hands several times. Lift out the spinach, being careful not to pick up any of the sand at the bottom of the basin. Change the water and repeat the operation. Continue washing in fresh changes of water until there is no more sand at the bottom of the basin.

Cook the spinach in a covered pan over medium heat with a pinch of salt and no more water than clings to the leaves after washing. It is done when tender, 10 minutes or more, depending on the spinach. Drain well but do not squeeze. (If you are using frozen spinach, simply cook the thawed spinach with a pinch of salt in a covered pan over medium heat for 1½ minutes; then drain.)

2. In a skillet, over medium-high heat, sauté the garlic cloves in the olive oil. When the garlic is well browned, remove it and add the drained, cooked spinach and about ½ teaspoon salt. Sauté for 2 minutes, turning the spinach frequently. Taste and correct for salt. Serve hot.

MENU SUGGESTIONS

Follow those for Sautéed Jerusalem Artichokes (page 353). This sautéed spinach is also very good with Veal Scaloppine with Tomatoes (page 264) and Casserole-Roasted Lamb with Juniper Berries (page 280).

Pomodori al forno
OVEN-BROWNED TOMATOES

In this recipe all the wateriness of fresh tomatoes is drawn off through long, slow cooking. What remains is a savory, concentrated essence of tomato.

Don't let the quantity of oil alarm you. Nearly all of it gets left behind in the pan.

For 6 persons

9 ripe, medium tomatoes or 6 large ones, such as the beefsteak variety	Salt to taste
	Freshly ground pepper, about 6 to 8 twists of the mill
3 tablespoons finely chopped parsley	6 tablespoons olive oil, or enough to come ¼ inch up the side
2 teaspoons finely chopped garlic	of the baking dish

1. Wash the tomatoes in cold water and slice them in half, across the width. If the variety of tomatoes you are using has a large amount of seeds, remove at least a part of them.

2. Preheat the oven to 325°.

3. Choose a flameproof baking dish large enough to accommodate all the tomato halves in a single layer. (You can crowd them in tightly, because later they will shrink considerably.) Arrange the tomatoes cut side up and sprinkle them with the parsley, garlic, salt, and pepper. Pour the olive oil over them until it comes ¼ inch up the side of the dish. Cook on top of the stove over medium-high heat until the tomatoes are tender, about 15 minutes, depending on the tomatoes.

4. When the tomato pulp is soft, baste with a little bit of oil, spooning it up from the bottom of the dish, and transfer the dish to the next-to-the-highest rack in the oven. From time to time baste the tomatoes with the oil in which they are cooking. Cook for about 1 hour, until the tomatoes have shrunk to a little more than half their original size. (The skins and the sides of the pan will be partly

blackened, but don't worry—the tomatoes are not burned.) Transfer to a serving platter, using a slotted spatula, leaving all the cooking fat behind in the pan. Serve hot or at room temperature.

NOTE

These tomatoes can be prepared several days ahead of time. Since they must be reheated, they should be refrigerated with all or part of their cooking fat. When refrigerating, cover tightly with plastic wrap. To reheat, return to a 325° oven for 10 to 15 minutes, or until warm.

MENU SUGGESTIONS

This dish is a tasty accompaniment to roasts and to Mixed Boiled Meats (page 322). You would never use it, of course, next to any dish already sauced or flavored with tomato. Nor does it get along well with cream or milk sauces. Its perfect marriage is with Fried Eggplant (page 372), when both are at their peak, in midsummer, and the two make a sensational combination as a side dish with Breaded Veal Cutlets (page 270).

Pomodori fritti
FRIED TOMATOES

I have not yet found a vegetable that does not take well to frying, and among all fried vegetables none can surpass tomatoes. They reach that perfect combination of outer crispness and inner juiciness that is always the goal when frying vegetables.

The best tomatoes for frying are those that are firm and meaty, with few seeds and as little water as possible.

For 4 persons

2 or 3 large tomatoes
1 cup all-purpose flour, spread on a dish or on waxed paper
1 egg, lightly beaten with ½ teaspoon salt, in a soup dish or small bowl

1 cup fine, dry unflavored bread crumbs, spread on a dish or on waxed paper
Vegetable oil, enough to come 1 inch up the sides of the pan
Salt, if necessary

1. Wash the tomatoes and cut them horizontally into slices ½ inch thick, discarding the tops. Remove the seeds, but handle the tomatoes gently, without squeezing them.

2. Turn the tomato slices lightly in the flour, dip them in egg, then dredge them well in bread crumbs.

3. Heat the oil over high heat. When the oil is very hot, slip in the tomatoes. When a dark golden crust has formed on one side, turn them and do the other side. When both sides have a nice crust, transfer them to paper towels to drain. Taste a little piece and correct for salt if necessary. Serve piping hot.

MENU SUGGESTIONS

Follow those for Fried Artichoke Wedges (page 346).

Zucchine

ZUCCHINI

Zucchini is one of the great favorites among Italian vegetables, and its first appearance in the markets in early spring is an event eagerly looked forward to in Italy. Its very delicate taste is sometimes mistaken for blandness, which some try to cover up with seasonings. In Italian recipes, however, its fine, distinct flavor is carefully nurtured and emerges quite clearly, undisguised.

WHAT TO LOOK FOR WHEN BUYING ZUCCHINI

Recognizing quality in raw zucchini can make all the difference between a successful dish and a tasteless one. Good zucchini are never very large. Do not buy any that are much broader than 1½ inches or longer than 6 inches. Unless you are going to stuff them, small, skinny zucchini that are 1 inch or less in diameter are the most desirable. Look for bright color and glossy skin, and avoid zucchini whose skin is mottled or discolored. Zucchini should feel very firm in your hands. If it is flabby and bends easily it is not fresh. When cut, the flesh of good, young zucchini should be crisp and show very tiny seeds.

CLEANING ZUCCHINI

Soak zucchini in a basin of cold water for 10 minutes, then scrub thoroughly under cold running water until the skin feels clean and smooth. Sometimes no amount of washing and scrubbing will loosen imbedded soil. If the skin feels gritty after scrubbing, peel it lightly with a vegetable peeler. Cut off and discard both ends of the zucchini. They are now ready for the preparation of any recipe.

Zucchine fritte con la pastella
ZUCCHINI FRIED IN FLOUR-AND-WATER BATTER

Zucchini fried in *pastella* is crisp and light and absolutely irresistible. *Pastella* is a flour-and-water batter that produces a thin, crackly coating that stays perfectly bonded to the zucchini and keeps it from absorbing any of the frying fat.

If you like fried onion rings, but loathe, as I do, the thick spongy wrapping in which restaurants usually present them, try them at home with *pastella*. It will be a revelation.

For 4 to 6 persons

1 pound zucchini	Salt
⅔ cup all-purpose flour	
Vegetable oil, enough to come ¾ inch up the side of the pan	

1. Clean the zucchini as directed on page 392. Cut them into lengthwise slices about ⅛ inch thick.

2. Put 1 cup of water in a soup plate and gradually add the flour, sifting it through a sieve and constantly beating the mixture with a fork until all the flour has been added. The batter should have the consistency of sour cream.

3. Heat the oil in the skillet over high heat. When the oil is very hot dip the zucchini slices in the batter and slip only as many as will fit loosely into the skillet.

4. When a golden crust has formed on one side of the zucchini slices, turn them over. When both sides have a nice crust, transfer the zucchini to paper towels to drain and sprinkle with salt. Continue in the same way until all the slices are fried. Serve piping hot.

MENU SUGGESTIONS

Follow those for Fried Artichoke Wedges (page 346).

Zucchine fritte all'aceto
FRIED ZUCCHINI WITH VINEGAR

For 4 to 6 persons

1 pound zucchini
Salt
Vegetable oil, enough to come
  ¼ inch up the side of the
  pan
1 cup all-purpose flour, spread
  on a dish or on waxed paper
2 to 3 tablespoons good-quality
  wine vinegar, preferably
  imported French vinegar

2 cloves garlic, lightly crushed
  with a heavy knife handle
  and peeled
Freshly ground pepper, about
  4 twists of the mill

1. Clean the zucchini as directed on page 392. Cut them into sticks about ¼ inch thick. Sprinkle with the salt and set aside for 30 minutes.

(continued)

2. When the 30 minutes have elapsed, the zucchini will have thrown off quite a bit of liquid. Drain them and pat them dry with a cloth or paper towels.

3. Heat the oil in a skillet over high heat. When the oil is quite hot, lightly dip the zucchini in flour and slip into the skillet. (Don't put too many in at one time. They should fit very loosely in the pan.) Turn them as they brown.

4. When the zucchini are a deep golden brown, transfer to a deep dish, using a slotted spoon. While they are still hot, sprinkle them with vinegar. You will hear them sizzle.

5. When all the zucchini are done, bury the garlic in their midst, and season with pepper. Serve at room temperature.

NOTE

After you've done these once, you can regulate the quantity of vinegar and garlic to suit your taste. I don't like any more than an intriguing suggestion of garlic, so I remove the cloves after about 5 minutes.

MENU SUGGESTIONS

In addition to being a superb accompaniment to meat, especially pork or sausages, these zucchini make an enticing antipasto. They are also a tasty side dish for a buffet.

Zucchine all'aglio e pomodoro
SLICED ZUCCHINI WITH GARLIC AND TOMATO

For 4 to 6 persons

1½ pounds zucchini
½ cup thinly sliced yellow onion
⅔ cup olive oil
1½ teaspoons coarsely chopped garlic
2 tablespoons chopped parsley

⅔ cup canned Italian tomatoes, coarsely chopped, with their juice
1 teaspoon salt
Freshly ground pepper, 4 to 6 twists of the mill
4 to 6 fresh basil leaves (optional)

1. Clean the zucchini as directed on page 392 and slice them into disks ⅜ inch thick.

2. Put the onion and oil in a flameproof bake-and-serve pan and sauté over medium heat until pale gold. Add the garlic and sauté until it colors lightly. Add the parsley, stir once or twice, then add the tomatoes and their juice. Cook at a steady simmer for 15 minutes.

3. Preheat the oven to 350°.

4. Add the sliced zucchini, salt, pepper, and basil. Cook until tender at the pricking of a fork, 20 minutes or more, depending on the age and freshness of the zucchini. (Do not overcook. The zucchini should be tender but firm.)

5. Transfer the pan to the uppermost level of the preheated oven for about 5 minutes, until the liquid the zucchini throws off while cooking has dried up. Serve immediately in the baking dish.

MENU SUGGESTIONS

Serve with any simple roast or with broiled meat. Avoid competition with a strong tomato or garlic presence.

Barchette di zucchine ripiene al forno
BAKED STUFFED ZUCCHINI BOATS

For 4 to 6 persons

8 to 10 young, very fresh, firm zucchini	Béchamel Sauce (page 28), made with 1 cup milk, 1½ tablespoons all-purpose flour, 2 tablespoons butter, and salt
Salt	
2 tablespoons butter	
1 tablespoon vegetable oil	1 egg
1 tablespoon finely chopped yellow onion	3 to 4 tablespoons freshly grated Parmesan cheese
3 or 4 slices unsmoked ham, chopped	A tiny pinch of nutmeg (optional)
Freshly ground pepper to taste	Fine, dry unflavored bread crumbs

(continued)

1. Clean the zucchini as directed on page 392. Slice off the ends and cut the zucchini into lengths of about 2½ inches. With a vegetable corer or peeler scoop out the zucchini from end to end, being careful not to perforate the sides. The thinned-out wall of the zucchini should not be less than ¼ inch thick. Set aside the pulp extracted from the inside of the zucchini.

2. Cook the hollowed-out zucchini in abundant boiling water, to which 1 teaspoon of salt has been added. Cook only until half done, or until lightly resistant when pierced by a fork. Drain and set aside.

3. Heat 1 tablespoon of butter and all the oil in a skillet. Sauté the chopped onion and chopped ham, and then add half the zucchini pulp, roughly chopped. Add salt and pepper and cook over high heat until the pulp turns creamy and acquires a mellow golden color. Lift away from the skillet with a slotted spoon or spatula, leaving all the cooking fat behind, and set aside.

4. Preheat the oven to 400°.

5. Prepare a thick béchamel sauce using the quantities indicated above, remembering that to make a béchamel thicker you simply cook it longer. As soon as the béchamel is ready, add the cooked zucchini pulp and quickly stir in the egg, the freshly grated Parmesan, and the optional pinch of nutmeg. Mix well, then set aside.

6. Smear the bottom of a rectangular bake-and-serve dish with butter. Split the cooked zucchini in half lengthwise and line them up in the dish, hollowed side facing up. Salt lightly, and fill each half zucchini with the béchamel–zucchini-core mixture. Sprinkle with bread crumbs and dot lightly with butter. (If you wish, you can wait up to a few hours before baking, but you must finish cooking the zucchini the same day or they will lose freshness.)

7. Bake in the upper third of the preheated oven for about 20 minutes, or until a light golden crust forms. Do not serve immediately but allow to settle until no longer steaming hot.

MENU SUGGESTIONS

Although this has been suggested elsewhere in the book as an elegant side dish, it also makes an excellent first course. Serve before

Beef Braised in Red Wine Sauce (page 242), any of the three lamb roasts on pages 278–281, Roast Pork with Bay Leaves (page 286), or Pan-Roasted Squab (page 319).

Zucchine con ripieno di carne e formaggio
ZUCCHINI STUFFED WITH MEAT AND CHEESE

For 4 to 6 persons

10 fresh, young zucchini about 1¼ to 1½ inches in diameter	½ pound lean beef, chopped
	1 egg
3 cups thinly sliced yellow onion	3 tablespoons freshly grated
3 tablespoons vegetable oil	Parmesan cheese
2 tablespoons chopped parsley	1 tablespoon chopped prosciutto,
2 tablespoons tomato paste	*mortadella, pancetta,* or
diluted with 1 cup of water	unsmoked ham
3 tablespoons milk	Salt
⅔ slice firm white bread, crust	Freshly ground pepper, 3 or
removed	4 twists of the mill

1. Clean the zucchini as directed on page 392. Slice off the ends and cut the zucchini into lengths of about 2½ inches. Hollow them out completely, removing the pulp with a vegetable corer or peeler, being careful not to perforate the sides. The thinned-out wall of the zucchini should not be less than ¼ inch thick. (You will not need the pulp in this recipe, but it would be a pity to throw it away because it makes a lovely *frittata* or an excellent *risotto.*)

2. Choose a covered skillet large enough to accommodate later all the zucchini in a single layer. Slowly cook the sliced onions in the oil until tender and considerably wilted.

3. Add the parsley, stirring it two or three times; then add the tomato paste diluted in water and cook slowly over low heat for about 15 minutes.

4. Warm the milk and mash the bread into it with a fork. Let cool.

5. In a mixing bowl put the chopped meat, the egg, the grated

cheese, the bread mush, and the chopped prosciutto or its substitute. Mix thoroughly with your hands. Add 1 teaspoon salt and the pepper.

6. Stuff the mixture into the hollowed-out zucchini sections, making sure they are well stuffed but not pushing too hard, to avoid splitting the zucchini. Put the zucchini into the skillet, turn the heat to medium low, and cover. Cook until done, from 40 minutes to 1 hour, approximately, depending on the quality of the zucchini. (You can tell for sure only by testing the zucchini. When done it should be tender, but not too soft.) Look in on the zucchini from time to time and turn them.

7. If, when the zucchini is cooked, there is too much liquid in the skillet, uncover, raise the heat to high, and boil away the excess liquid for a minute or two, turning the zucchini once or twice. Taste for salt, transfer to a serving platter, allow the zucchini to settle for a minute or two, and serve.

NOTE

This is a dish that has nothing to gain from being served the moment it is cooked. On the contrary, it actually improves in texture and flavor upon being reheated a day or two later. Always serve it warm, but not steaming hot.

MENU SUGGESTIONS

This is always served as a second course. It can be preceded by such antipasti as *bresaola* (page 47), Fried Mortadella, Pancetta, and Cheese Tidbits (page 48), or mixed Italian cold cuts. For a first course serve Spaghetti with Genoese Basil Sauce for Pasta and Soup (page 139), Risotto with Parmesan Cheese (page 181), or Rice with Fresh Basil and Mozzarella Cheese (page 194). This also makes an appetizing and easy-to-handle hot buffet dish.

Fiori di zucchine fritti

FRIED ZUCCHINI BLOSSOMS

Zucchini blossoms are extremely perishable, and for that reason they are not very frequently brought to market in America. But they do appear from time to time, and, if you should happen to come across these luscious orange flowers, do try them. They make an attractive and delectable dish that is extremely simple to prepare. The method for cooking zucchini blossoms is identical to that for Fried Zucchini in Flour-and-Water Batter (page 392).

For 4 to 6 persons

12 to 14 zucchini blossoms	The flour-and-water batter
Vegetable oil, enough to come	from page 392
¾ inch up the sides of the	Salt
skillet	

1. Wash the blossoms rapidly under cold running water and dry them gently on paper towels. If the stems are very long, cut them down to 1 inch in length. Cut the base of the blossom on one side, and open the flower flat, without dividing it.

2. Heat the oil over high heat. When it is very hot, dip the blossoms quickly in and out of the batter and slip them into the skillet. When they are golden brown on one side, turn them and cook them to golden brown on the other side. Transfer to paper towels to drain, sprinkle with salt, and serve promptly while still hot.

MENU SUGGESTIONS

Follow those for Fried Artichoke Wedges (page 346).

Verdura mista in gratticola
AN ITALIAN BARBECUE:
CHARCOAL-BROILED VEGETABLES

Americans have practically reinvented cooking over charcoal, but the uses to which all the marvelously practical barbecue equipment is put are incredibly few. Whenever our family goes barbecuing on a public campsite or picnic area, our grill topped with tomatoes, eggplant, peppers, onions, mushrooms, and zucchini is soon the object of ill-concealed wonderment as the only bright island in the midst of a brown atoll of hot dogs, hamburgers, and steaks.

Barbecuing vegetables is one of the most effective ways of concentrating their flavor. Charcoal-broiled peppers are all that peppers should be, and never are when done any other way. Zucchini turns out fresher-tasting than the most skillfully fried zucchini and is just as crisp and juicy. Even indifferent tomatoes are returned by the fire to their ancestral tomato taste and become nearly as full flavored as the vine-ripened tomatoes of San Marzano.

Doing vegetables need not interfere with the unquestioned pleasure of charcoal-broiled steak. Cook the vegetables in the first flush of the fire. When they are done, the fire is ready for broiling steak or whatever else you are having. With a full load of vegetables, calculate about 25 to 40 percent more coal than you would use ordinarily for steaks or hamburgers alone.

For 4 persons

1 large flat Spanish onion	Olive oil
2 sweet green or red peppers	Crushed peppercorns
2 large, firm, ripe tomatoes	1 teaspoon chopped parsley
1 medium eggplant	(optional)
Salt	⅛ teaspoon chopped garlic
2 medium fresh, young, firm,	(optional)
glossy zucchini	½ teaspoon fine, dry unflavored
¼ pound very fresh and crisp	bread crumbs (optional)
mushrooms	

1. Remove the outer, crackly skin of the onion, but do not cut off the point or the root. Divide it in half horizontally.

2. Wash the peppers in cold water and leave whole.

3. Wash the tomatoes in cold water and divide in two horizontally.

4. Wash the eggplant in cold water, then cut in half lengthwise. Without piercing the skin, make shallow cross-hatched cuts, spaced about 1 inch apart, in the eggplant flesh. Sprinkle liberally with salt and stand the halves on end in a colander for at least 15 minutes to let the bitter juices drain away.

5. Wash the zucchini thoroughly in cold water. Cut off the ends; then cut the zucchini into lengthwise slices about ⅜ inch thick.

6. Wipe the mushrooms clean with a damp cloth. Unless they are very small, detach the caps from the stems. You are now ready to light the fire.

7. When the highest flames have died down, place the onion on the grill, cut side down. Place the peppers on the grill as well, laying them on one side. After 4 or 5 minutes check the peppers. The skin toward the fire should be charred. When it is, turn another side of the peppers toward the fire, at the same time drawing them closer together to make room for the tomatoes and eggplant (see Step 10 below). Continue turning the peppers, eventually standing them on end, until all the skin is charred. Remove them from the grill and peel them while they are as hot as you can handle. Cut them into 2-inch strips, discard the seeds, put the cut-up peppers in a bowl, and add at least 3 tablespoons of olive oil plus large pinches of salt and cracked peppercorns. Toss and set aside.

8. While the peppers are still cooking, check the onion. When the side facing the fire is charred, turn it over with a spatula, taking care not to separate the rings. Season each onion half with 1 tablespoon of olive oil and ½ teaspoon of salt. Move to the edge of the grill, making sure there is some burning charcoal underneath.

9. When the onion is done, in about 15 to 20 minutes, it should be well charred on both sides. Scrape away part of the blackened surface and cut each half in 4 parts. Add it to the bowl of peppers, tossing it with another pinch of salt and cracked pepper. (The onion will be quite crunchy, which makes a nice contrast with the peppers,

but it will also be very sweet, with no trace of sharpness.)

10. When you first turn the peppers (see Step 7 above), make room for the tomatoes and eggplant. Place the tomatoes, cut side down, on the grill. Check them after a few minutes, and if the flesh is partly charred, turn them. Season each half with ½ teaspoon of olive oil, a small pinch of salt, and the optional parsley, garlic, and bread crumbs and cook until they have shrunk by half and the skin is blackened.

11. Shake off any liquid from the eggplant. Pour 1 tablespoon of olive oil over each half and place it on the grill with the cut side facing the fire. Allow it to reach a deep brown color, but don't let it char, which would make it bitter. Turn the eggplant over and season each half with another tablespoon of olive oil. From time to time as it cooks, pour ½ teaspoon of oil in between the cuts. The eggplant is done when it is creamy tender. Do not cook it beyond this point or it will become bitter.

12. When the eggplant is nearly done, put the zucchini slices on the grill. As soon as they have browned on one side turn them over and cook until done, 5 to 8 minutes. Remove to a shallow bowl and season with a large pinch of salt, pepper, and about ½ tablespoon of oil.

13. When you turn the zucchini over, put the mushrooms on the grill. These cook very quickly, about 1 minute to a side, including the stems. Add them to the bowl of zucchini and season the same way.

NOTE

It is unfortunate that the length of this recipe makes it appear so forbidding. It is actually about as simple to execute as grilled hamburgers and hot dogs. The whole secret lies in mastering the sequence in which the vegetables are put on the grill. Aside from that, there is very little to do except watch them. The fire does nearly all the work. The entire process should take about 35 minutes.

Le Insalate

SALADS

THERE are two basically different dishes that appear in an Italian meal, both of which are called salads.

One contains cold cooked fish, meat, or chicken, and occasionally rice, mixed with either raw or cooked vegetables. Although it is called a salad, it is usually served as an antipasto, a first course, or even a second course but rarely, if ever, as the salad course. A choice group of these salads appears later in this chapter.

The true salad course is something else entirely, with a special and fixed role. It is served invariably after the second course, signaling the approaching end of the meal. It releases the palate from the spell of the cook's inventions, and leads it to sensations of freshness and purity, to a rediscovery of food in its natural and artless state.

In this kind of salad, vegetables and greens are used raw or boiled, alone or mixed. Its composition changes with the seasons. There are always some greens available throughout the year, but in fall and winter salads raw finocchio and artichokes are frequently dominant. Boiled asparagus and green beans appear in the spring, followed by new potatoes. Then there are tart and nutty wild field greens, and in the warmer months zucchini, both raw and cooked, and tomatoes.

ITALIAN DRESSING

There is absolutely nothing mysterious about the dressing for an Italian salad. The ingredients are salt, olive oil, and wine vinegar. Pepper is optional, and lemon juice is occasionally substituted for vinegar.

Italians would find any discussion of something called "salad dressing" very puzzling. Although the term could be translated, it would have little currency. For Italians, salad dressing is not an element separate from the salad; it is not added on to the greens as you might add a sauce to pasta. Dressing is a process rather than an object, a verb rather than a noun. It is the act that transforms greens and vegetables into salad.

There are many old folk sayings that illustrate this. According to one of them, to make a good salad you need four persons: a judicious one with the salt, a prodigal one with the oil, a stingy one with the vinegar, and a patient one to mix it. You do not need to know very much more than that to make a proper Italian salad. There is no way to give precise proportions of salt, oil, and vinegar. It takes less oil to dress green beans than an equivalent amount of lettuce. Asparagus and potatoes take more vinegar, tomatoes and cucumber more salt. Other factors that vary are the fruitiness and density of the oil, the acidity and bouquet of the vinegar, and even the character of the salt. The only foolproof method is to taste and correct the salad before serving it.

Do not begin to dress the salad until it is quite dry. Water dilutes the flavor of the dressing. You can use a special wire basket to shake the greens dry, if you like. My own method is to wrap the greens in a towel, gather the corners of the towel in one hand, and give it a few vigorous jerks over the sink.

Seasonings and oil and vinegar are never mixed in advance. They are poured directly on the salad in the following order:

First: Sprinkle the salt. Do not overdo it. You can add more salt later if necessary.

Second: Add the oil. There should be enough oil to coat the salad greens or vegetables and give them a surface gloss, but not so much as to form a pool at the bottom of the bowl, which would make the salad soggy.

Third: Add the vinegar. This is the hardest ingredient to judge. A few drops too much will ruin a salad. There must be just a hint of tartness, enough to be noticed but not so much as to grab your attention.

Toss the salad thoroughly and repeatedly, taking care not to bruise and blacken delicate greens such as field lettuce. Taste and correct for oil, salt, or vinegar. Serve immediately. Never allow salad to sit and steep in its seasonings.

From time to time you can add other seasonings to sharpen the flavor of the salad and to avoid monotony. Shredded fresh basil leaves or chopped parsley go very well into an Italian salad. They are particularly nice with tomatoes and cucumbers.

For zest you can add chopped shallots or thinly sliced onion. After the onion is sliced very thin it should be soaked in two or more changes of cold water for at least ½ hour before putting it in the salad. This helps to sweeten it.

To add the heartiness of garlic to a salad rub a small piece of bread with a lightly crushed garlic clove. Discard the garlic and add the bread to the salad. After the salad has been seasoned, dressed, and thoroughly tossed, remove and discard the bread.

Note on oil and vinegar: To call any oil that is not pure olive oil salad oil is a contradiction in terms. Tasteless vegetable oils merely grease the greens. The flavor of the olive is absolutely indispensable to a good salad, and the denser and fruitier the olive oil is the better.

The choice of vinegar is also very important. It should be wine vinegar, preferably red, with all the characteristics of good wine: strength, flavor, and a well-developed bouquet. A fine vinegar should not be spiked with tarragon or other herbs, any more than you would make a fruit-flavored "pop" wine out of good Burgundy. Most familiar brands of vinegar, unfortunately, do not measure up to these standards. However, most specialty food shops, and many of the better supermarkets, do stock good French wine vinegar. It can be ordered by mail from many department stores, such as Blooming-dale's in New York. It is certainly not cheap, but a little goes a long way, and it will make all the difference in the world to your salads.

Insalata di spinaci e topinambur
JERUSALEM ARTICHOKE AND SPINACH SALAD

For 4 persons

½ pound Jerusalem artichokes	Olive oil
½ pound very young, crisp spinach	Red wine vinegar, preferably imported French vinegar
Salt and freshly ground pepper, a liberal quantity, to taste	

1. Soak the artichokes for a few minutes in cold water, then scrub them thoroughly under running water or peel them, if you object to the hard bite of the peel. Cut into the thinnest possible slices, and put into a salad bowl.

2. Detach the stems from the spinach, pulling them off, in one motion, together with the thin central stalk on the underside of the leaves. Wash the spinach in a basin of cold water, changing water frequently until it shows no more trace of soil. Drain, shaking off as much water as possible from the leaves. Wrap the spinach in a dry cloth and give it a few sharp, brusque jerks to drive away any remaining moisture. Tear the leaves in two or three parts and add to the salad bowl.

3. When ready to serve, toss with salt, pepper, enough olive oil to coat, and just a dash of vinegar.

Insalata di carote
SHREDDED CARROT SALAD

No salad takes so little to prepare as this excellent carrot salad. Its tart, gently bracing taste is particularly welcome after a hearty, robust meal.

For 4 persons

5 to 6 medium carrots	6 tablespoons olive oil
1 teaspoon salt	1 tablespoon lemon juice

1. Peel and wash the carrots, and grate them on the largest holes of the grater.

2. When ready to serve, add the salt, olive oil, and lemon juice. Toss thoroughly and serve immediately.

Finocchio in insalata
FINOCCHIO SALAD

When finocchio is eaten alone, as it is here, neither vinegar nor lemon is used in the dressing.

For 3 or 4 persons, depending on the size of the finocchio

1 medium squat, bulbous finocchio	Olive oil
Salt	Freshly ground pepper

1. Cut off the tops of the finocchio and remove any bruised, discolored, or wilted outside stalk.

2. Cut off about ⅛ inch or less from the base; then cut the finocchio horizontally into the thinnest possible slices. (The slices will be in the form of rings, some half, some whole.)

3. Wash the finocchio slices thoroughly in cold water, then dry them well in a towel. Toss in a salad bowl with salt, an abundant quantity of oil, and a liberal grinding of pepper.

MENU SUGGESTIONS

A salad of finocchio is ideal after any substantial meat dish and is especially appropriate after roast pork.

Insalata mista
MIXED SALAD

Everyone makes mixed salads, but the Italian ones seem to have an equilibrium and a freshness that many others lack. This is because even the most wildly assorted salad is never a catchall. It is assembled with an intuitive but nonetheless precise feeling for the correct proportions of greens and vegetables. There is never the monotony of too much green pepper, carrot, artichoke, celery. There is just enough, so that what is missing from one mouthful of salad is suddenly and delightfully present in the next.

The ingredients for the salad given below can be found, all at one time, at only certain moments of the year. When one or more is not available, substitute for it, in approximately equal proportions, whatever is currently in season.

Prepare all the greens and vegetables in any order you like, and add them to the salad bowl as they are ready. Save the tomatoes for last, however, or they may get crushed and watery. Note that

arugola, listed below, is known in Italian as *ruchetta* or *rucola*. Its true English equivalent is "rockets." "Arugola" is 100 percent Italian-American.

For 6 persons

2 small carrots, or 1 large one
1 finocchio, of the squat, bulbous variety
½ medium green pepper
1 celery heart
½ head curly chicory, Boston lettuce, or escarole, or 1 head Bibb lettuce
½ small bunch lamb's tongues or field lettuce
½ small bunch arugola

1 medium artichoke
½ lemon
3 or 4 scallions, thinly sliced, or ½ red Bermuda onion, sliced and presoaked as directed on page 405
1 large or 2 small tomatoes
Salt
Olive oil
Red wine vinegar, preferably imported French vinegar

1. Wash and peel the carrots, and shred them on the largest holes of the grater.

2. Trim the finocchio and slice it into thin rings, as directed on page 377. Wash thoroughly and dry well in a towel.

3. Remove the inner pulp and seeds from the pepper. Peel with a sharp vegetable peeler and cut into very thin strips.

4. Strip the celery heart of any leaves, then slice it crosswise into narrow rings, about ¼ inch thick.

5. If you are using curly chicory or escarole, discard all the outer, dark green leaves. Detach all the leaves from the head and tear them by hand into small, bite-sized pieces. Let them soak in one or two changes of cold water in a basin for 15 to 20 minutes, or until the water shows no trace of soil. Drain and dry thoroughly in a towel or a salad basket. If you are using Bibb lettuce, handle it very gently because it bruises easily and discolors.

6. Trim away the stems of the lamb's tongues and arugola, tear the larger leaves in two or more pieces, and soak, drain, and dry as directed above for lettuce.

7. Discard the artichoke stem, and trim the artichoke as directed for Artichokes, Roman Style (page 337), trimming a little more off the top than you would ordinarily to make sure only the tenderest

part goes into the salad and remembering to rub the cut parts with juice from the half lemon. Cut the trimmed artichoke lengthwise into the thinnest slices you can.

8. Add the presoaked onion slices.

9. Cut the tomatoes into small chunks or narrow wedges, removing some of the seeds if there is an excess.

10. When ready to serve, sprinkle liberally with salt and add enough oil to coat all the ingredients well and a dash of vinegar. Toss thoroughly but not roughly, and serve immediately.

NOTE

Other raw vegetables you can use are red cabbage, Savoy cabbage, or regular cabbage. Cabbage should be finely shredded. Add white or small red radishes, thinly sliced. Substitute cucumber for carrot. (Never have the two at one time; somehow they are not compatible.) Also, young zucchini may be used raw. They should be thoroughly scrubbed and washed or even lightly peeled, and cut into matchsticks.

Panzanella

BREAD AND VEGETABLE SALAD WITH ANCHOVIES

This salad was originally the poor man's dinner in parts of Tuscany and Rome. In the traditional version, two- or three-day-old bread is soaked in water, squeezed, and added to the salad in amounts proportioned to one's hunger. This procedure is quite successful with good, solid Tuscan country bread. I do not find it very appealing, however, when made with supermarket bread. I much prefer this version, however decadent it may be, in which the waterlogged bread is replaced by crisp squares of bread fried in olive oil.

For 4 persons

½ clove garlic, peeled and chopped	½ teaspoon salt
	5 tablespoons olive oil
4 flat anchovy fillets	1 tablespoon red wine vinegar
1 tablespoon capers	

¼ sweet green, yellow, or red pepper, cored, seeded, and diced

½ recipe Fried Bread Squares for Soup (page 88), but fried in olive oil rather than vegetable oil

Freshly ground pepper, 5 to 6 twists of the mill

½ cucumber, peeled and diced into ½-inch cubes

1 medium, firm, meaty tomato, preferably peeled, and cut into ½-inch chunks

½ red Bermuda onion, thinly sliced and soaked as directed on page 405

1. Mash the garlic, anchovies, and capers to a pulp in a mortar or in a bowl. Put into a salad bowl.

2. Add the salt, olive oil, vinegar, and sweet pepper and blend thoroughly with a fork.

3. Add the fried bread squares, pepper, cucumber, tomato, and onion and toss thoroughly. Taste and correct for seasoning and chill for 30 minutes before serving.

MENU SUGGESTIONS

Although this can be served on occasion after the second course, it is more suitable as an antipasto or a first course in a fresh and tasty summer meal.

Insalata di asparagi
ASPARAGUS SALAD

When asparagus is at the peak of its flavor, one of the favorite ways of eating it in Italy is as salad. No other way of preparing it brings one so close to the essential asparagus taste. The very finest asparagus should be chosen, because it will confront the palate thinly clothed in a light dressing of oil and vinegar. It is never mixed with any other salad vegetables.

(continued)

For 4 to 6 persons

2 pounds asparagus

Salt and freshly ground pepper
to taste

⅓ cup olive oil

3 tablespoons red wine vinegar
(approximately), depending
on taste and the vinegar

1. Peel and boil the asparagus as directed on page 354. When the asparagus is done it should be spread on a platter, leaving one end of the platter free. Prop up the end under the asparagus. After about 30 minutes some liquid will have collected at the other end of the platter. Discard it and rearrange the asparagus on the platter.

2. Add salt and pepper to taste. Season liberally with olive oil, and add the vinegar, taking into account the fact that asparagus requires a great deal of vinegar. Tip the platter in several directions so that the seasoning is evenly distributed. Serve either lukewarm or at room temperature, but never chilled.

NOTE

An alternative to seasoning the asparagus in the platter is to provide everyone with the seasonings mixed in individual shallow bowls, into which they will dip the asparagus.

Fagiolini verdi in insalata

GREEN BEAN SALAD

For 4 persons

1 pound green beans

Salt

Olive oil

Lemon juice

1. Trim, wash, and boil the beans as directed on page 360.

2. Put the beans in a salad bowl and add salt to taste. Add enough olive oil to give all the beans a thin glossy coating. Add lemon juice to taste. (The salad should be just slightly, not aggressively, tart.) Toss well and serve immediately.

NOTE

Boiled green beans may be served slightly lukewarm or at room temperature, but never chilled.

MENU SUGGESTIONS

This salad may be served after any second course of meat, fowl, or fish.

Cavolfiore lesso in insalata
BOILED CAULIFLOWER SALAD

For 6 to 8 persons

1 head cauliflower (about 2 pounds)	Olive oil
Salt to taste	Red wine vinegar, preferably imported French vinegar

1. Boil the cauliflower as directed on page 366.

2. Before the cauliflower cools, detach the florets from the head, dividing all but the smallest ones into two or three parts.

3. Put the florets into a salad bowl and season very liberally with salt, oil, and vinegar. Taste and correct for all three. (Cauliflower takes a great deal of seasoning.) Toss the florets carefully so as not to mash them and serve either lukewarm or at room temperature.

NOTE

If you cannot use the whole head for salad, season only what you need and refrigerate the rest. It can be made into gratinéed cauliflower (page 366), or fried (page 367) a day or two later.

MENU SUGGESTIONS

Cauliflower salad can follow any meat dish, but preferably not those that include tomato.

Swiss Chard

Insalata di biete cotte
BOILED SWISS-CHARD SALAD

Cooked Swiss chard leaves make a lovely, sweet salad that is particularly nice after pork or lamb. If the chard is mature and has large, white stalks, these can be utilized in Swiss Chard Stalks with Parmesan Cheese (page 370).

For 4 to 6 persons

2 **bunches young Swiss chard or**	**Olive oil**
the leaves of 3 large bunches	1 **or more tablespoons lemon**
of mature Swiss chard	**juice**
Salt	

1. If you are using young chard, detach the stems. If you are using mature chard, pull the leaves from the stalks, discarding any wilted or discolored leaves. Wash in a basin of cold water, changing the water frequently until it shows no trace of soil.

2. Put the chard in a pan with whatever water clings to the leaves. Add 1 teaspoon salt, cover, and cook over medium heat until tender, about 15 to 18 minutes from the time the liquid starts to bubble.

3. Drain in a pasta colander and gently press some of the water out of the chard with the back of a fork. Place in a salad bowl.

4. Serve cool (not refrigerated) or lukewarm, seasoning with salt, oil, and lemon only when ready to serve.

Insalata di zucchine
ZUCCHINI SALAD

An excellent demonstration that zucchini has a fine and distinctive flavor of its own is this salad of boiled zucchini. For a successful salad, it is absolutely essential that you choose young, fresh, firm zucchini. See the recommendations on buying zucchini on page 391.

For 6 persons

6 small to medium zucchini
3 large cloves garlic, lightly crushed with a heavy knife handle and peeled
½ cup olive oil
2 to 3 tablespoons red wine vinegar, preferably imported French vinegar

2 tablespoons chopped parsley
Freshly ground pepper, about 8 twists of the mill
Salt to taste

1. Clean the zucchini as directed on page 392.
2. Bring 4 to 5 quarts of water to a boil, then drop in the zucchini. Cook at a moderate boil until tender but not soft and easily pierced by a fork—about 30 minutes, more or less, depending on the zucchini, from the time the water returns to a boil.
3. When done, drain, cut off the ends, and cut, lengthwise, into halves.
4. While it is still hot, rub the zucchini flesh with the crushed garlic cloves. Arrange the zucchini, flesh side up, in a single layer on a platter. Prop up the platter at one end so that while the zucchini cools any excess liquid will gather at the other end. Do not refrigerate.
5. When the zucchini are cool, discard the liquid from the platter and season with oil, vinegar, parsley, and pepper, adding salt only when just ready to serve, to prevent the zucchini from continuing to throw off liquid.

Insalatone

MIXED COOKED VEGETABLE SALAD

The sequence of steps indicated below is more or less arbitrary. Actually, all the ingredients can be prepared contemporaneously. This salad is at its most agreeable when its components are still slightly lukewarm. If you must prepare any part of it ahead of time, keep it at room temperature, do not refrigerate.

For 4 to 6 persons

3 medium boiling potatoes	Salt
5 medium yellow onions	Olive oil
2 medium sweet green, yellow, or red peppers	Red wine vinegar, preferably imported French vinegar
6 ounces green beans	Freshly ground pepper
1 8¼-ounce can small whole beets, drained	

1. Preheat the oven to 400°.

2. Boil the potatoes with their skins on, until tender. Cooking time varies greatly with size and type of potato. Peel while hot, and cut into ¼-inch slices. Put into a salad bowl.

3. Put the onions, with their skins on, on a baking sheet, then into the upper third of the oven. Cook until they are tender all the way to the center at the pricking of a fork. Skin them, cut them each into three or four sections, and add to the salad bowl.

4. Broil and peel the peppers exactly as directed in Peppers and Anchovies (page 37). When peeled, cut the peppers into strips 1 inch wide, removing all the seeds and pulpy core. Add to the salad bowl.

5. Cook the beans until tender but firm, as directed on page 360. Drain and add to the salad bowl.

6. Cut the drained canned beets into halves if they are very tiny, into quarters if they are larger. Add to the bowl.

7. Add the seasonings, being liberal with the oil and pepper and

stingy with the vinegar. Taste and correct for salt. Serve immediately.

MENU SUGGESTIONS

This salad is the ideal accompaniment to all broiled meats, and it can be served at the same time as the second course, in place of vegetables. It also goes well with fish, either broiled or poached. It can even stand on its own as a light summer meal, adding to it if you wish hard-boiled eggs, anchovy fillets, or tuna.

Insalata di tonno e fagioli
TUNA AND BEAN SALAD

Although this famous salad has been given often enough before in Italian cook books, it is included here because no survey of Italian salads can fail to take notice of it. Moreover, while most of the English versions suggest scallions, in this recipe we follow the traditional Tuscan use of red onion. It is a small difference but a significant one, because the crunchiness of onion is a delightful and essential relief for the creaminess of beans and the tenderness of tuna.

For 4 persons

1 cup dried white kidney beans, Great Northern beans, or other white beans OR 1 twenty-ounce can precooked similar beans

½ Bermuda onion, thinly sliced and soaked in water for 1 hour (see page 405)

Salt to taste

1 seven-ounce can Italian tuna or other tuna packed in oil, drained

⅓ cup olive oil

2 teaspoons red wine vinegar, or more, according to taste and the strength of the vinegar

Freshly ground black pepper to taste (optional)

1. If using uncooked beans, cook them as directed on page 78. Drain.

(continued)

2. Put them, or the drained canned beans, into a salad bowl. Add the onion and season with salt to taste. Add the tuna, breaking it into large flakes with a fork. Add oil, vinegar, and the optional pepper. Toss thoroughly and serve.

MENU SUGGESTIONS

This makes a very agreeable second course for a summer meal. It can be preceded by Cold Vegetable Soup with Rice, Milan Style (page 68), Spaghetti with Tomato Sauce with Marjoram and Cheese (page 95), Spaghetti with Genoese Basil Sauce for Pasta and Soup (page 139), or Thin Spaghetti with Fresh Basil and Tomato Sauce (page 97). It can also be part of mixed antipasti for any meal with a rustic flavor, and is an excellent dish to add to a buffet.

Insalata russa con gamberi
SHRIMP AND VEGETABLE SALAD

This salad is beautiful to look at, absolutely delicious, and very simple to execute. It does take time and patience to get the ingredients cleaned, boiled, and diced, but it can all be prepared and completed well in advance, whenever you are not pressed for time.

For 6 persons

1 pound medium shrimps, unpeeled
1 tablespoon red wine vinegar
¼ pound green beans
2 medium potatoes
2 medium carrots
⅓ ten-ounce package frozen peas, thawed
6 small canned red beets, drained and dried on paper towels

2 tablespoons gherkins in vinegar, preferably French *cornichons*, cut up
2 tablespoons capers, the smaller the better
3 tablespoons olive oil
2 teaspoons red wine vinegar, preferably imported French vinegar
Salt
2½ cups Mayonnaise (page 26)

1. Wash the shrimps. Put them, whole and unpeeled, in boiling salted water. Add the tablespoon of vinegar to the water and cook for 4 minutes. Allow the shrimps to cool; then shell and devein them and set aside.

2. Snap the ends off the green beans, pulling away any possible strings. Rinse them and drop them into rapidly boiling salted water. Taste them early and drain them as soon as they are tender but still firm, in as little as 8 minutes if they are very young and fresh.

3. Rinse the potatoes and boil them with the peel on. When they are easily pierced with a sharp fork, drain them and peel them while they are still hot.

4. Scrape or peel the carrots clean and drop them in boiling salted water. Do not overcook. Drain when tender and set aside.

(continued)

Insalata russa

5. Drop the frozen peas into boiling salted water and cook very briefly, not more than a minute or a minute and a half. Drain and set aside.

6. When the vegetables have cooled, set aside a very small quantity of each (potatoes excepted), which you will need later for garnishing, and cut up the rest as follows: the green beans into pieces ⅜ inch long; the potatoes, carrots, and beets diced into ⅜-inch cubes. The peas, of course, stay whole. Cut up the capers also if these are not the very tiny ones. Put all the ingredients, including the cut-up gherkins or *cornichons,* in a mixing bowl.

7. Set aside half the shrimps. Cut up the rest and mix with the vegetables. Season with the olive oil, wine vinegar, and ½ teaspoon salt. Add 1 cup of the mayonnaise and mix thoroughly. Taste for salt and correct.

8. Turn the mixture over onto a serving platter. Shape it into a shallow, flat-topped, oval mound pressing with a rubber spatula to make sure the surface is smooth and uniform. Now spread the remaining mayonnaise over the entire surface of the mound. Use the spatula to make it as smooth and even as possible. Indentations or deep pockets will spoil the effect.

9. Now decorate the mound. Here is one way of doing it. Place a thin carrot disk on the center of the mound. Put a pea in the center of the carrot. Make a rosette of shrimps around the carrot, placing the shrimps on their side, nestling one around the other. Over the rest of the flat surface scatter flowers made using carrots for the center button, beets for the petals, green beans for the stems. Emboss the sides of the mound with the remaining shrimps, heads and tails imbedded in the salad, backs arching away. There are limitless ways in which you can use shrimps and vegetables to decorate this salad. Use your imagination! Caution: if you are preparing this many hours or a day in advance decorate with beets at the last moment before serving. Their color has a tendency to run.

NOTE

This dish should be refrigerated at least 30 minutes before serving.

This is a wonderfully cool dish for a summer day, splendid for a buffet, and a magnificent antipasto for an important meal.

When it is used as antipasto, it can be followed by Fettuccine with White Clam Sauce (page 135), Trenette with Potatoes and Pesto (page 142) (omitting the potatoes), or Risotto with Clams (page 192). The second course should be a beautiful Fish Broiled the Adriatic Way (page 224) or Baked Striped Bass and Shellfish Sealed in Foil (page 212), substituting red snapper for the striped bass. It can also be handled as a second course. Precede it with Baked Oysters with Oil and Parsley (page 32), Broiled Mussels and Clams on the Half Shell (page 34), and/or Fettuccine with White Clam Sauce (page 135). Alone, it is an exquisite midnight snack with champagne, followed by A Bowl of Macerated Fresh Fruit (page 453). It is worth staying up for.

Insalata di mare
HERB-FLAVORED SEAFOOD SALAD

This may well be the most popular cold seafood dish in Italy. Every region has its own version, each slightly differing in ingredients and seasonings. The one thing they all have in common, and the most notable characteristic of this dish, is the delectable juxtaposition of the varied textures of such crustaceans as shrimps, *scampi*, and *cannocchie* and such mollusks as clams, mussels, scallops, squid, and octopus. You can try making your own combinations, as long as they result in a variety of delicate tastes and interesting textures.

For 6 persons

½ pound medium shrimps, preferably the very tiny shrimps from Maine or the Pacific, if available	Salt
	2 medium carrots, peeled and washed
7 tablespoons vinegar	2 stalks celery, washed
	2 medium yellow onions, peeled

(continued)

½ pound squid, cleaned as
    directed on page 230
1 pound octopus tentacles,
    peeled like the squid
¼ pound sea scallops
1 dozen mussels, cleaned as
    directed on page 56
1 dozen littleneck clams, the
    tiniest you can find, washed
    and scrubbed as directed
    on page 53
6 black Greek olives, pitted and
    quartered
6 green olives, pitted and
    quartered

⅓ cup broiled sweet red pepper
    (page 37), cut into strips
    ½ inch wide
¼ cup lemon juice
½ cup olive oil
    Freshly ground pepper, about
    6 twists of the mill
1 good-sized clove garlic, lightly
    crushed with a knife handle
    and peeled
¼ teaspoon dried marjoram or
    ½ teaspoon fresh

1. Wash the shrimps in cold water, but don't shell them. Bring 2 quarts of water with 2 tablespoons of vinegar and 1 teaspoon of salt to a boil. Drop the shrimps into the boiling water and cook for 2 minutes after the water returns to a boil. (Very tiny shrimps may take 1½ minutes or less, depending on size.) Drain. When cool, peel and devein the shrimps and cut into rounds ½ inch thick. If very, very tiny, leave whole. Set aside.

2. Using two separate pots, put 3 cups of water, 2 tablespoons of vinegar, 1 teaspoon of salt, 1 carrot, 1 celery stalk, and 1 onion in each pot. Bring to a boil. Add the squid and their tentacles to one pot and the octopus tentacles to the other, and cover. Cook at a slow, steady boil, testing the squid with a knife or sharp-pronged fork for tenderness after 20 minutes. Drain when tender, and when cool cut into strips ⅜ inch wide and 1½ inches long. Test the octopus tentacles for tenderness after 40 minutes. Drain when tender, and when cool cut into disks ⅜ inch thick. Set aside.

3. Rinse the scallops in cold water. Bring 2 cups of water, with 1 tablespoon of vinegar and ½ teaspoon of salt, to a boil. Add the scallops and cook for 2 minutes after the water returns to a boil. Drain, and when cool cut into ½-inch cubes. Set aside.

4. In separate covered pans, heat the mussels and clams over high heat until their shells open. Detach the mussels from their shells and set aside. Detach the clams from their shells and rinse them one by one in their juice to remove any possible sand.

5. Combine all the seafood in a mixing bowl. Add the quartered olives, the red pepper, the lemon juice, and the olive oil and mix thoroughly. Taste and correct for salt, and add pepper, the crushed garlic clove, and the marjoram. Toss and mix all the ingredients thoroughly. Allow to rest for at least 2 hours, and retrieve the garlic before serving.

NOTE

You can prepare this salad many hours ahead of time, if you like, but it is best if it is not refrigerated. If you absolutely must refrigerate it, cover it tightly with plastic wrap. Remove from the refrigerator well in advance of serving so that it has time to come to room temperature.

MENU SUGGESTIONS

Its fragrance and cool, fresh taste make this an ideal summer dish. It can be served as antipasto for a multicourse fish dinner, or as a first course in a simpler dinner followed by Fish Broiled the Adriatic Way (page 224), Red Snapper with Sautéed Mushrooms (page 217), or Pan-Roasted Mackerel with Rosemary and Garlic (page 216).

Insalata di riso con pollo
RICE AND CHICKEN SALAD

Cold boiled rice and cheese are the basic ingredients of a number of salads that are very popular in Italy, particularly in the summer. They can be varied with the addition of cold chicken, shrimp, lobster, finely diced cold boiled beef or veal, or cold, diced hot dogs, which in Italy are called *wurstel*. These salads are never served after the second course, but are offered as an antipasto, a first course, or as the basis of a light hot-weather lunch.

(continued)

For 4 to 6 persons

  1 tablespoon salt
  1 cup raw rice

  1 teaspoon Dijon or German
      mustard
  ½ teaspoon salt
  2 teaspoons red wine vinegar
  6 tablespoons olive oil

½ cup finely diced Swiss cheese
¼ cup black olives, pitted and
    diced
2 tablespoons green olives, pitted
    and diced
¼ cup sweet red, yellow, or
    green pepper, seeded, cored,
    and diced

3 tablespoons diced sour
    gherkins, preferably French
    cornichons
1 whole breast of a young
    chicken, boiled and diced
    into ½-inch cubes

1. Bring 2 quarts of water to a boil. Add the 1 tablespoon salt; then drop in the rice. When the water returns to a boil, adjust the heat so that it simmers gently. Stir the rice, cover, and cook for 10 to 12 minutes or more, until *al dente*, firm to the bite.

2. Drain the rice, rinse in cold water, and drain thoroughly once more.

3. Put the mustard, 1 teaspoon salt, and vinegar into a salad bowl. Blend well with a fork, then add the oil, incorporating it into the mixture.

4. Add the drained rice and toss with the dressing.

5. Add the remaining ingredients, mix thoroughly, and serve cool, but not refrigerator cold.

Il Formaggio

THE CHEESE COURSE

SALAD, cheese, and fruit, in that order, are the three courses that gradually cleanse the palate of the taste of cooking and bring an Italian meal to a natural close.

The simple, universal combination of cheese and good crusty bread is beyond discussion. But here are a few other ways in which cheese is served at an Italian table.

Parmesan

There is no more magnificent table cheese than a piece of aged, genuine *parmigiano-reggiano,* when it has not been allowed to dry out and it is a glistening, pale-straw color. It is frequently combined with the fruit course and eaten together with peeled ripe pears, or with grapes.

Gorgonzola

When it is soft, ripe, and mild, gorgonzola is one of the world's loveliest blue cheeses. Italians sometimes mash it into a paste with some sweet butter, or simply spread butter on the accompanying bread. (This is one of the rare occasions when Italians have bread and butter during a meal.) When gorgonzola is not overripe, it develops extraordinary flavor and texture if it is wrapped in aluminum foil and sent into a 250° oven for 2 to 3 minutes before serving.

Provola affumicata

This is smoked mozzarella, and looks exactly like any other mozzarella, except that it has a tanned skin. Remove the skin, slice the cheese into thin strips, and serve with good olive oil and a liberal amount of freshly ground pepper.

Cheese and olive oil

The combination of cheese and olive oil, as above, is a favorite one for both mild and pungent cheeses. A soft, white, full-flavored cheese called Robiola is mashed through the largest holes of a food mill, and the resulting strands are soaked in olive oil for a day or more. It can be refrigerated, but must be served at room temperature. There is no Robiola available here, but the same treatment is very effective with Taleggio or Fontina. I have found it to be astonishingly successful with Boursault cheese.

I Dolci e la Frutta

DESSERTS AND FRUIT

ITALIANS take their sweets and their apéritifs away from the dining table, at a pastry shop or café. Drinks, except for wine and liqueurs, do not belong on an Italian table, and desserts but rarely.

When the palate has traveled the peaks and valleys of an Italian meal with its first courses, second courses, side dishes, salads, and cheese, all it needs is the pause and refreshment of some fresh fruit. Of course there are circumstances in which a dessert does appear. These are almost always special occasions, either a religious holiday or a family celebration, such as a wedding. But these sweets, save those from Sicily, are, both in substance and appearance, modest, earthbound creations.

Italy does indeed produce some of the most luscious and beautiful desserts in Europe, as it has for centuries. But this is the work of pastry cooks. It is rarely done even in restaurant kitchens, and practically never at home.

Elaborate desserts do not have a significant part in Italian cooking or in the design of an Italian meal. For that reason there is no notice taken of them in this chapter. What you will find instead are some very plain but excellent traditional cakes and puddings, coffee and fruit ices, and a very good coffee ice cream. There is also a simple home version of that delicious Tuscan specialty *zuccotto*, and what is probably the most elegant dessert in the home repertory, the chest-nut-and-cream Monte Bianco.

In addition to desserts, there are two recipes for fresh fruit. In my opinion, these are the ones that take the cake, if that is the correct expression.

A RICE CAKE AND TWO PUDDINGS

Here are three traditional desserts based on such modest staples as rice, semolina, and bread. The rice cake is the most famous one of the three. It is a specialty of Bologna, where it was customary to serve it only at Easter, with lively rivalry among those families that claimed to have the most delicious cake. The recipe given here is an authentically venerable one, belonging to Bolognese friends, who have had it in their family for generations.

None of the three desserts is a very glamorous creation. Their virtue is in their nostalgic, homespun flavor, their plain, straightfor-ward goodness that seldom palls or cloys.

Torta di riso
RICE CAKE

For 6 to 8 persons

1 quart milk
¼ teaspoon salt
2 or 3 strips of lemon peel, yellow part only
1¼ cups of granulated sugar

⅓ cup raw rice, preferably Italian Arborio rice
4 eggs plus 1 yolk
½ cup almonds, skinned, toasted, and chopped as directed on page 450

⅓ cup candied citron or, if not
    available, candied lemon
    peel, coarsely chopped
2 tablespoons rum

Butter
Fine, dry unflavored bread
    crumbs

1. Put the milk, salt, lemon peel, and sugar in a medium-sized saucepan and bring to a boil.

2. As the milk comes to a boil, add the rice and mix with a wooden spoon. Cook, uncovered, at the lowest possible simmer for 2¾ hours, stirring occasionally. The mixture should become a dense, pale-brown mush, into which much of the lemon peel will have been absorbed, but remove any large, visible pieces. Set aside and allow to cool.

3. Preheat the oven to 350°.

4. Beat the 4 whole eggs and the egg yolk in a large bowl until the yolks and whites are blended. Beat in the rice-and-milk mush a spoonful at a time. Add the chopped toasted almonds, the candied fruit, and the rum. Mix all the ingredients thoroughly.

5. Smear butter generously on the bottom and sides of a rectangular 6-cup cake pan and then sprinkle with bread crumbs, shaking off excess crumbs. Pour the mixture from the bowl into the pan and bake in the middle level of the preheated oven for 1 hour.

6. Remove the cake from the oven and let it cool to lukewarm. Put a platter over the pan, turn the pan over on the platter, give it a few vigorous taps, and lift it away. Serve the cake at least 24 hours after making it.

NOTE

This cake keeps improving for several days after it is made. Do not refrigerate if you are using it the next day.

Budino di semolino caramellato
GLAZED SEMOLINA PUDDING

For 6 to 8 persons

½ cup plus ⅔ cup granulated sugar

Generous ⅓ cup small seedless raisins

2 cups milk

¼ teaspoon salt

⅓ cup semolina

1 tablespoon butter

1 tablespoon rum

¼ cup mixed candied fruit, chopped into ¼-inch pieces

Grated peel of 1 orange

All-purpose flour

2 eggs

1. Choose a 6-cup metal mold. (A simple cylindrical shape is the easiest to work with.) Put the ½ cup sugar and 2 tablespoons water in the mold and bring to a boil over medium heat. Do not stir, but tilt the mold forward and backward from time to time until the syrup turns a light-brown color. Remove from heat immediately and tip the mold in all directions to give it an even coating of caramel. Keep turning until the caramel congeals, then set aside.

2. Put the raisins in a bowl with enough lukewarm water to cover and soak for at least 15 minutes.

3. Preheat the oven to 350°.

4. While the raisins are soaking, put the milk and salt in a saucepan over low heat. When the milk is just about to come to a boil, add all the semolina in a thin stream, stirring rapidly with a wooden spoon. Continue cooking, without ceasing to stir, until the semolina has thickened sufficiently to come away from the sides of the pan as you stir. Turn off the heat, but continue stirring for another 30 seconds to make sure the semolina won't stick.

5. Add the ⅔ cup sugar and stir, then add the butter and rum and stir. Add the candied fruit and grated orange peel, stirring them evenly into the mixture.

6. Drain the raisins and dry with a cloth. Put them in a sieve and sprinkle them with flour while shaking the sieve. When the

raisins are lightly floured, mix them with the other ingredients in the pan.

7. Add the eggs, beating them very rapidly into the semolina mixture. Pour the mixture into the caramelized mold and bake in the middle level of the preheated oven for 40 minutes. Remove from the oven and cool.

8. When the pudding is cold, refrigerate for 10 minutes to give it extra firmness. To unmold, first very briefly warm the bottom and sides of the mold over low heat to loosen the caramel, then place a dish over the mold, turn the two upside down, and give the mold a few sharp taps and downward jerks. It should lift away easily.

Budino di pane caramellato
GLAZED BREAD PUDDING

For 6 to 8 persons

½ plus ⅓ cup granulated sugar	½ cup small seedless raisins
2½ cups roughly cut-up stale, lightly toasted, crustless, good-quality white bread	All-purpose flour
	¼ cup pine nuts
¼ cup butter	3 egg yolks
2 cups milk	2 egg whites
	¼ cup rum

1. Caramelize an 8-cup rectangular cake pan as directed in Step 1 of Glazed Semolina Pudding (opposite page), using the ½ cup granulated sugar.

2. Put the bread and the butter in a large mixing bowl.

3. Heat the milk, and as soon as it comes to a boil pour it over the bread and butter. Let the bread soak without mixing, and allow to cool.

4. Put the raisins in a bowl with enough warm water to cover and soak for at least 15 minutes.

5. Preheat the oven to 375°.

(continued)

6. When the bread is cool, beat it with a whisk or a fork until it is an even, soft mass.

7. Drain the raisins, and squeeze them dry in a cloth. Put them in a sieve and dust them with flour while lightly shaking the sieve. Add them to the bowl with the bread mass.

8. Add the ⅓ cup sugar, pine nuts, and egg yolks to the bowl and mix all the ingredients thoroughly.

9. Beat the egg whites until they form stiff peaks, then fold them gently into the mixture in the bowl.

10. Pour the contents of the bowl into the caramelized pan and place it in the middle level of the preheated oven. After 1 hour turn the heat down to 300° and bake for 15 more minutes.

11. While the pudding is still warm, pierce it in several places with a toothpick, and gradually pour 2 tablespoons of the rum over it. When the rum has been absorbed, place a platter on the pan, turn the pan over on the platter, give it a few sharp downward jerks, and lift it away. Pierce the top of the pudding in several places with a toothpick and pour the rest of the rum over it.

NOTE

Plan to serve the pudding the day after you make it. It improves in texture and flavor as it rests. You can refrigerate it for several days, but always take it out sufficiently ahead of time to serve it at room temperature.

Torta Sbricciolona
CRUMBLY CAKE

For 6 persons

1⅓ cups all-purpose flour	2 egg yolks
⅔ cup cornmeal	¼ pound butter, softened to
⅝ cup granulated sugar	room temperature
Grated peel of 1 lemon	1 tablespoon confectioners'
4 ounces almonds, skinned	sugar
and dried as directed on	
page 438 and ground	
to powder in a blender	

1. Preheat the oven to 375°.

2. In a bowl mix the flour, the cornmeal, the granulated sugar, the grated lemon peel, and the powdered almonds. Add the two egg yolks and work the mixture with your hands until it breaks up into little crumbly pellets. Add the softened butter, working it in with your fingers until it is completely incorporated into the mixture. (At first it may seem improbable that all the ingredients can ever be combined, but after mixing for a few minutes, you'll find that they do hang together, although forming a very crumbly dough.)

3. Smear the bottom of a 10-inch round baking pan with butter. Crumble the mixture through your fingers and into the pan until it is all uniformly distributed. Sprinkle the top with confectioners' sugar and place in the upper third of the preheated oven for about 40 minutes.

NOTE

This cake has a very crusty and crumbly consistency, which is part of its charm, but if you prefer to have it available in neat serving portions you can cut it into sections before it cools completely and hardens. It keeps beautifully for several days after baking.

This is an ideal cake to take with a glass of chilled dessert wine or in the afternoon with tea or coffee.

Chiacchiere della nonna
SWEET PASTRY FRITTERS

The dough for these fritters is cut into ribbons, then twisted into bows and fried in lard. For the sake of those who are put off by lard I've tried frying them in every other fat, but they do not really come off as well. There is nothing terribly subtle about them, but they are very nice to have at the end of a hearty, homey meal or at any time of the afternoon or evening with friends over a glass of *vin santo* or other dessert wine.

(continued)

For 4 to 6 persons

1⅔ cups all-purpose flour	2 tablespoons white wine
Lard	¼ teaspoon salt
1 tablespoon granulated sugar	Confectioners' sugar
1 egg	

1. Combine the flour, ¼ cup lard, 1 tablespoon sugar, the egg, wine, and salt and knead into a smooth, soft dough. Put the dough in a bowl, cover, and allow to rest at least 15 minutes.

2. Roll out the dough with a rolling pin to a thickness of ⅛ inch, then cut into ribbons about 5 inches long and ½ inch wide. Twist into simple bowlike shapes.

3. In a skillet, over high heat, melt enough lard to come 1 inch up the sides of the pan. When it is quite hot, add the pastry bows. (Do not put in any more at one time than will fit loosely in the skillet.) When they are a nice, deep gold on one side, turn them

Sweet Pastry Fritters

over. When both sides are done, transfer to paper towels to drain, and sprinkle liberally with confectioners' sugar. They may be served hot or cold.

NOTE

If kept in a dry place, they maintain their crispness for several days.

Frittelle di mele renette
APPLE FRITTERS

For 4 persons

3 apples, any firm, sweet eating variety	⅔ cup all-purpose flour
¼ cup granulated sugar	Vegetable oil, enough to come ½ inch up the side of the skillet
2 tablespoons rum	
1 lemon peel, grated	Confectioners' sugar

1. Peel the apples, core them, and cut them into slices ⅜ inch thick. (The slices should look like miniature cartwheels, each with a hole in the middle.)

2. Put ¼ cup sugar, the rum, and lemon peel into a bowl and add the apple slices. Let the apples macerate for at least 1 hour.

3. Make a batter of the flour and 1 cup water, according to the directions in Step 2 of Zucchini Fried in Flour-and-Water Batter (page 393).

4. Pour enough oil into a skillet to come at least ½ inch up the side of the pan. Turn the heat on high.

5. Pat the apple slices dry with paper towels. Dip them in the batter, and when the oil is very hot slip them into the skillet. (Do not put in any more at one time than will fit loosely in the skillet.) When they are golden brown on one side, turn them. When both sides are nicely browned, transfer the fritters to paper towels to drain. Sprinkle with confectioners' sugar. Serve hot.

Il Diplomatico
RUM-AND-COFFEE-FLAVORED CHOCOLATE LAYER CAKE

The marvelous thing about this dessert is that it requires no baking, and you can put in a little less rum or a little more chocolate, add or subtract an egg, and you'll still come up with a successful and delicious cake. It is practically foolproof. In its easygoing approach and its knack for transforming simple ingredients and procedures into a most enjoyable concoction, it is quintessentially Italian. It will, however, lose character if you use the blander American coffee instead of Italian espresso.

For 6 to 8 persons

4 eggs	1 teaspoon granulated sugar

THE RUM MIXTURE (to be repeated as often as necessary using the same proportions):

5 tablespoons rum	5 teaspoons granulated sugar
1¼ cups strong espresso coffee (see How to Make Italian Coffee, page 455)	5 tablespoons water

1 sixteen-ounce pound cake	6 ounces semisweet chocolate drops or chopped-up squares

THE FROSTING:

4 ounces semisweet chocolate drops or chopped-up squares	Whipped cream and maraschino cherries or walnuts for garnish
1 teaspoon butter	

1. Preheat the oven to 250°.

2. Separate the eggs and beat the yolks together with 1 teaspoon of the sugar until the yolks turn pale yellow.

3. Line a 9-inch baking pan or any equivalent container with buttered waxed paper, extending it up the sides and above the rim. Combine the rum, coffee, 5 teaspoons sugar, and 5 tablespoons water in a soup dish. Cut the pound cake into slices ¼ inch thick. Soak each slice in the rum-and-coffee mixture and place it on the bottom and along the sides of the baking pan, until it is completely

lined with rum-soaked pound cake. (You've got to be quick about dipping the slices in and out of the mixture before they get too soggy to handle.) If you run out of rum mixture, prepare more, following the same proportions.

4. In a small saucepan, melt the chocolate in the oven. (I have found this the easiest and least problem-fraught method of melting chocolate, especially when using chocolate drops. If you have another method you are happy with, by all means use it.) Mix the melted chocolate into the beaten egg yolks. Whip the egg whites until they form stiff peaks. First combine 1 tablespoon of the beaten egg whites with the egg yolks and chocolate, mixing normally, then add the rest of the egg whites, folding them with care into the mixture.

5. Spoon the entire mixture over the rum-soaked pound cake in the pan. Cover the mixture with more slices of pound cake dipped in the rum-and-coffee soak. (Don't worry about how the cake looks at this point. What you are looking at is the bottom, and the rest will be completely covered by frosting.) Refrigerate overnight.

6. The following day turn the pan over on a flat serving platter, holding your thumbs on the protruding waxed paper. The pan should lift away easily, leaving the waxed-paper-covered cake on the platter. Carefully peel off the waxed paper. The cake is now ready for the frosting.

7. The customary frosting for *il diplomatico* is chocolate. In a preheated 250° oven, melt 4 ounces of chocolate in a small saucepan together with 1 teaspoon of butter. Cover the entire exposed surface of the cake with the melted chocolate. Refrigerate for an hour or less until the chocolate hardens. Decorate with curls of whipped cream topped with maraschino cherries and/or walnuts. Since you can prepare *il diplomatico* a week or ten days ahead of time, add the whipped-cream decorations just before serving.

NOTE

For a lighter texture and more delicate taste you can substitute whipped cream for the chocolate frosting. Whip 1½ cups very cold heavy cream together with 2 teaspoons of granulated sugar until it is stiff. Cover the entire exposed surface of the cake with cream. Decorate with candied fruit arranged in simple patterns. Cream is always best when freshly whipped, but, if necessary, it can be refrigerated for one or two days.

ZUCCOTTO

Zuccotto is a dome-shaped Florentine specialty inspired, it is said, by the cupola of Florence's Duomo. Whether that is true or not, I don't know, but it is a fact that almost anything hemispherical seems to remind Florentines of Brunelleschi's ever-present dome. Zuccotto used to be found only in Florentine cafés and pastry shops, but it is now mass-produced and distributed all over Italy. It requires no baking or any special confectionery skills, yet it is an extremely presentable and successful dessert.

For 6 persons

2 ounces shelled, unskinned almonds

2 ounces shelled whole filberts or hazelnuts

1 ten- to twelve-ounce pound cake

3 tablespoons Cognac or other grape brandy

2 tablespoons maraschino liqueur

2 tablespoons Cointreau

5 ounces semisweet chocolate drops

2 cups very cold heavy whipping cream

¾ cup confectioners' sugar

1. Preheat the oven to 400°.

2. Drop the almonds into boiling water and boil for 20 seconds. Drain. With your fingertips, squeeze the almonds out of their skins. Place the peeled almonds on a baking sheet and put in the oven to dry for about 2 minutes. Remove from the oven and chop them roughly. Set aside.

3. Place the filberts on a baking sheet and put in the oven for 5 minutes. Remove them from the oven and rub off as much of their skin as you can with a rough, dry towel. (Don't worry if it doesn't all rub off.) Chop roughly and set aside.

4. Reset the oven thermostat to 250°.

5. Choose a 1½-quart, perfectly round-bottomed hemispherical bowl, and line it with a layer of damp cheesecloth.

6. Cut the pound cake in slices ⅜ inch thick. Cut each slice on the diagonal, making of it two triangular sections. There will be crust on two sides of the triangle. Moisten each section with a sprinkling of the cordials and place it against the inside of the bowl, its narrowest end at the bottom, until the inside of the bowl is completely lined with moistened sections of pound cake. Where one side of the section has crust on it, have it meet the crustless side of the section next to it, because when the dessert is unmolded the thin lines of crust running down the sides should form a sunburst pattern. Make sure that the entire inside surface of the bowl is entirely lined with cake. If there are any gaps, fill them in with small pieces of moistened cake. (Don't worry about the appearance of the dessert. A little irregularity is part of its charm.)

(*continued*)

Zuccotto

7. Split or coarsely chop 3 ounces of the chocolate drops. Then, in a chilled mixing bowl, whip the cold heavy cream together with the powdered sugar until it is stiff. Mix into it the chopped almonds, filberts, and chocolate drops. Divide the mixture into two equal parts. Set aside one half and spoon the other half into the cake-lined bowl, spreading it evenly over the entire cake surface. This should leave a still unfilled cavity in the center of the bowl.

8. Melt the remaining 2 ounces of chocolate drops in a small pan in the 250° oven. Fold the melted chocolate into the remaining half of the whipped-cream mixture. Spoon it into the bowl until the cavity is completely filled. Even off the top of the bowl, cutting off any protruding pieces of cake. Cut some more ⅜-inch slices of pound cake, moisten them with the remaining cordials, and use them to seal off the top of the bowl. Trim the edges until they are perfectly round. Cover the bowl with plastic wrap and refrigerate overnight, or up to 1 or 2 days.

9. Cover the bowl with a flat serving dish and turn it upside down. Lift off the bowl and carefully remove the cheesecloth. Serve cold.

Monte Bianco
PURÉED CHESTNUT AND CHOCOLATE MOUND

This is an especially lovely winter dessert. The mound of puréed chestnuts and chocolate topped with whipped cream is supposed to recall Monte Bianco, a mountain in the Italian Alps whose upper slopes are always snow clad. It can be decorated in many charming ways, using those paper or balsa-wood figures of skiers, Santas, and firs that are readily found in party-supply shops. It cannot be prepared too long in advance because the chestnuts turn tart in taste. It can certainly be prepared in the morning for the evening, however.

For 6 persons

1 pound fresh chestnuts
Milk, enough to cover
A tiny pinch of salt
6 ounces semisweet chocolate
    drops or chopped-up squares

¼ cup rum
2 cups very cold heavy whipping
    cream
2 teaspoons granulated sugar

1. Wash the chestnuts in cold water. Chestnuts have a flat side and a round bellying side. Being careful not to cut into the chestnut meat itself, make a horizontal cut in each chestnut starting on one end of the flat side, coming across the entire width of the round side and terminating just past the other edge of the flat side; the cut should not go all the way around and meet. (This method loosens both the shell and the inside skin while the chestnuts boil and makes peeling them a fast and simple task.)

2. Place the chestnuts in a pot with abundant cold water, cover, bring to a boil, and cook for 25 minutes. Peel the chestnuts while still very warm, pulling them out of the hot water a few at a time, and making sure to remove both the outer shell and the wrinkled inner skin.

3. Preheat the oven to 250°.

4. Put the peeled chestnuts in a saucepan with just enough milk to cover, and a pinch of salt. Boil slowly, uncovered, for 15 minutes more or less until the milk is entirely absorbed. The chestnuts should be tender but not mushy.

5. Put the chocolate drops or chopped-up chocolate squares in a small saucepan and place in the 250° oven until melted.

6. Purée the chestnuts through a food mill into a bowl and mix with the melted chocolate and the rum. Pass this mixture through the mill again, using the largest holes available, letting it drop directly onto a round serving platter. Start dropping it close to the dish with a circular movement, beginning at the edge of the dish, and as it piles up gradually move upward and toward the center. You should end up with a cone-shaped mound. Do not pat it or attempt to shape it.

7. Whip the cream with the sugar. Use half the whipped cream to

cover the top of your mound, coming about two-thirds of the way down. It should have the natural look of a partially snow-covered mountain, so do not strive for smoothness and regularity, but let the cream come down the mound at random in peaks and hollows. When serving the dessert, bring the remaining half of the whipped cream to the table for anyone who would like to have a bit more "snow" on his portion.

Monte Bianco

Spuma di cioccolata
COLD CHOCOLATE FOAM

For 6 persons

6 ounces semisweet chocolate drops	2 tablespoons rum
2 teaspoons granulated sugar	⅔ cup very cold heavy whipping cream
4 eggs, separated	
¼ cup strong espresso coffee (see How to Make Italian Coffee, page 455)	

1. In a 250° oven, melt the chocolate in a small saucepan.

2. Add 2 teaspoons of sugar to the egg yolks and beat with a whisk or the electric mixer until they become pale yellow. By hand mix in the melted chocolate, the coffee, and the rum.

3. Whip the cream in a cold bowl until it is stiff, then fold it into the chocolate-and-egg-yolk mixture.

4. Whip the egg whites until they form stiff peaks, then fold into the mixture. When all the ingredients have been gently but well combined by hand, spoon the mixture into glass or crystal goblets, custard cups, or any other suitable and attractive serving container. Refrigerate overnight. (This dessert can be prepared even 3 or 4 days ahead of time, but after 24 hours it tends to wrinkle and lose some of its creaminess.)

NOTE

Don't exceed the recommended amounts of rum and coffee, or you may find a liquid deposit at the bottom of the dessert.

Zabaglione
ZABAIONE

Zabaione must not cook over direct heat. It is necessary to have a double boiler. Since it is desirable that the upper part have a heavy bottom, you might use an enameled cast-iron saucepan or other heavy ware and hold it over water simmering in any other kind of pot. Be sure to choose a large enough pot—the mixture increases greatly in volume as you beat.

For 6 persons

4 egg yolks	½ cup dry Marsala
¼ cup granulated sugar	

1. Put the egg yolks and the sugar in your heavy-bottomed pot and whip them with a wire whisk (or an electric mixer) until they are pale yellow and creamy.
2. In a slightly larger second pot, bring water to the brink of a simmer, not a boil.
3. Place the pot with the whipped-up egg yolks over the second pot. Add the Marsala and continue beating. The mixture, which will begin to foam, and then swell into a light, soft mass, is ready when it forms soft mounds.
4. Spoon it into goblets, cups, or champagne glasses and serve immediately.

Crema fritta
FRIED SWEET CREAM

This cream requires substantially more flour than would a regular custard cream, otherwise it would not be firm enough for frying. In order for the flour to become evenly and smoothly blended, the cream must cook very slowly over very low heat, and you will have to stir virtually without interruption the entire time it is cooking. It takes patience, but it is not very hard work, and part of the time you can let your mind run on other thoughts while you are doing it. It is best to prepare it in the morning for the evening, or even a day ahead of time.

For 6 persons

3 eggs	1 cup fine, dry unflavored bread
½ cup granulated sugar	crumbs, spread on a dish
½ cup all-purpose flour	or on waxed paper
2 cups milk	Vegetable oil, enough to come
2 small strips lemon peel, yellow	1 inch up the side of the
part only	skillet

1. Off the heat, in the upper part of a double boiler, beat 2 of the eggs together with the sugar until the eggs are well blended and the sugar almost completely dissolved.

2. Still off heat, add the flour to the eggs 1 tablespoon at a time, mixing thoroughly, until the eggs have absorbed all the flour.

3. While you are doing this, bring the milk to the edge of a boil in another pan. When the eggs and flour have been thoroughly mixed, add the hot milk very gradually, about ¼ cup at a time, beating it into the mixture. When all the milk has been well blended with the eggs and flour, add the lemon peel.

4. Unite the two parts of the double boiler and put it over very low heat. The water in the lower half must come to only the gentlest of simmers. Begin to stir, slowly but steadily. Fifteen minutes after the water in the lower pan has started to simmer, you may raise the heat slightly. Continue cooking and stirring for about 25 minutes more. When done, the cream should be thick and smooth and have no taste of flour.

5. Pour the cream onto a slightly moistened large platter, spreading it to a thickness of about 1 inch, and let it cool completely. (If you are going to use it the following day, refrigerate it, when cool, under plastic wrap.)

6. When the cream is cold, cut it into diamond-shaped pieces about 2 inches long. Beat the remaining egg lightly in a soup dish

or small bowl. Dredge the pieces in bread crumbs; then dip them in egg; then dredge them in bread crumbs again.

7. Heat the oil in the skillet over high heat. When the oil is very hot, slide in the pieces of cream. Fry them until a dark, golden crust forms on one side; then turn them and do the other side. When there is a nice crust all around, transfer them to paper towels to drain. Serve piping hot.

MENU SUGGESTIONS

Aside from its role in Mixed Fried Meat, Vegetables, Cheese, Cream, and Fruit (page 333), fried cream is an excellent accompaniment for many single meat courses. Serve it somewhat as you might a potato croquette. It goes beautifully with Sautéed Breaded Veal Chops (page 268) or Breaded Veal Cutlets (page 270), Fried Breaded Calf's Liver (page 298), or Baby Lamb Chops Fried in Parmesan Cheese Batter (page 283). It is also, of course, a delectable hot dessert after any meal.

Gelato agli amaretti
VANILLA ICE CREAM WITH MACAROONS

For this preparation you should use imported Italian macaroons. They are packed two to a wrapper, and that is why the quantities given below are for double macaroons. If you cannot find Italian macaroons where you live, you can order them from the specialty food shops of many large-city department stores. They keep crisp almost indefinitely.

For 4 persons

8 double macaroons, ground
5 tablespoons strong espresso
    coffee (see How to Make
    Italian Coffee, page 455)

1 tablespoon ground dry
    espresso coffee, powdered
    in a blender
1 pint vanilla ice cream
2 double macaroons soaked in 1
    tablespoon rum for garnish

1. Mix the ground macaroons with the brewed coffee until the

macaroons are thoroughly moistened. Mix in the coffee powder.

2. Line a small dome-shaped bowl with lightly buttered waxed paper. Spread a little less than half the ice cream along the sides and bottom of the bowl. Spread the macaroon mixture over the ice cream, then cover with the rest of the ice cream. Place in the freezer for at least 4 hours before serving.

3. To serve, turn the bowl over on a plate, lift away the bowl, and gently remove the waxed paper. Garnish, pressing the four parts of the rum-soaked macaroons into the sides of the ice cream. When cut into 4 portions, there should be a macaroon to each portion.

Gelato spazzacamino

VANILLA ICE CREAM WITH POWDERED COFFEE AND SCOTCH

This is not just window dressing for plain ice cream. It is a combination of unexpected textures and flavors that act upon each other with extraordinary success. Everyone must have a favorite way of serving ice cream. This one is mine.

The doubly roasted taste of espresso coffee is essential here. Grind regular espresso coffee in the blender at high speed until it is a fine powder. You can make a substantial quantity at one time and keep it in a tightly closed jar.

For 1 person

2 scoops vanilla ice cream	1 tablespoon Scotch whisky
2 teaspoons ground dry espresso coffee, powdered in a blender	

Spoon the ice cream into individual shallow bowls, sprinkle 2 teaspoons of coffee powder over each serving, and over it pour the whisky.

NOTE

The quantities of coffee and whisky given are suggestions. Regulate them according to taste.

Gelato di caffè con la cioccolata calda

ESPRESSO COFFEE ICE CREAM WITH
HOT CHOCOLATE SAUCE

For 6 persons

4 egg yolks

⅔ cup granulated sugar

1½ cups espresso coffee, made
using milk in place of water
(see How to Make Italian
Coffee, page 455)

1 cup heavy cream

THE CHOCOLATE SAUCE:

⅔ cup heavy cream

2 tablespoons cocoa

4 teaspoons granulated sugar

1. Beat the egg yolks and sugar until they become a pale-yellow cream.

2. Combine the coffee and heavy cream and mix into the beaten egg yolks until uniformly blended. Warm the mixture in a saucepan over low heat, stirring constantly until it swells to nearly twice its original volume.

3. Pour into freezer trays without the ice-cube grids. When cool, stir thoroughly and place in the freezer for at least 5 hours. Stir every 30 to 40 minutes.

4. Just before serving, prepare the sauce by combining the heavy cream, cocoa, and sugar in a small saucepan and stirring it over low heat for about 6 minutes, or until it becomes a smooth, thick cream.

5. Spoon the ice cream, which should be quite firm but not rock hard, from the freezer trays into individual bowls. Pour the hot sauce over each serving and serve immediately.

Granita di caffè con panna
COFFEE ICE WITH WHIPPED CREAM

A *granita* is a dessert ice made of very fine-grained frozen crystals of coffee or fruit syrup. By far the most popular *granita* in Italy is *granita di caffè*, coffee ice. It is usually taken at a café after lunch, and, as you sit outdoors on a steamy afternoon watching life flow by, you let the *granita* melt between tongue and palate, spoonful by spoonful, until the inside of your mouth feels like an ice cavern dense with coffee flavor.

It should go without saying that you use only Italian espresso coffee to make *granita di caffè*.

For 6 to 8 persons

2 cups espresso coffee (see How
   to Make Italian Coffee, page
   455)
2 tablespoons sugar, or more to
   taste

Freshly whipped cream, made
   with 1 cup heavy cream and
   2 teaspoons sugar (optional)

1. Put all the coffee in a pitcher and dissolve the sugar in it while it is still hot. Taste and correct for sweetness. Do not make it very sweet because sugar weakens its flavor.

2. Remove the ice-cube grids from two freezer trays and pour the coffee into the trays. When the coffee is cold, put the trays in the freezer and set a timer at 15 minutes.

3. When the timer rings, remove the trays from the freezer and stir the contents to break up the ice crystals. (Ice forms first at the sides of the tray. It is important that you break this up thoroughly each time before it becomes solid.) Return to the freezer, and set the timer again for 15 minutes. When the timer rings repeat the operation and reset the timer for 10 minutes. The next time set the timer for 8 minutes, and continue to stir the coffee every 8 minutes for the next 3 hours. If you are not ready to serve the *granita* immediately,

continue stirring every 8 minutes until just before serving. Serve in a glass, goblet, or crystal bowl, topped with whipped cream, if desired.

NOTE

By exactly the same procedure, you can make orange ice (*granita di arancia*), using 2 cups freshly squeezed orange juice and 1 tablespoon granulated sugar, and lemon ice (*granita di limone*), using ½ cup freshly squeezed lemon juice, 1½ cups water, and ¼ cup granulated sugar.

Croccante
CARAMELIZED ALMOND CANDY

Croccante is the same thing as French praline, except that it is usually less sweet. It is an excellent candy, so very much better than commercial brittle. Crushed or powdered it is marvelous in desserts or as topping for ice cream. In an airtight jar or tightly wrapped in aluminum foil it keeps almost indefinitely.

Yield: About 2½ cups, if crushed or powdered

6 ounces (about 1½ cups) shelled, unskinned almonds	1 heaping cup granulated sugar A potato, peeled

1. Preheat the oven to 450°.
2. Drop the almonds in boiling water. Twenty seconds after the water returns to a boil, drain the almonds. Squeeze the almonds out of their skins with your fingers and spread them on a baking sheet. Toast them in the preheated oven for 6 minutes, until they are a light brown. (Make sure they don't burn.) If you prefer to do them under the broiler, watch them closely—it will take only a few seconds. Chop the toasted almonds until the slivers are half the size of a grain of rice.
3. Put the sugar and ¼ cup water in a small, preferably thin-bottomed pan. Melt the sugar over medium-high heat, without stirring, but tilting the pan occasionally. When the melted sugar becomes a light golden color, add the chopped almonds and stir constantly until

the almonds turn a deep tawny gold. Pour out *immediately* on a greased sheet of aluminum foil. Cut the potato in half and use the flat side to spread out the hot mixture to a thickness of ⅛ inch.

4. If you want to use it as candy, cut it into 2-inch diamond shapes before it cools. When cool, lift off and wrap each piece tightly in aluminum foil. Store in a dry cupboard, where it will keep indefinitely. (For use in desserts, it can be ground coarsely in a mortar or pulverized in a blender when it has cooled. Store in an airtight jar. Do not refrigerate.)

Frullati di frutta
FRESH FRUIT WHIPS

These are not served in Italy after meals, but they are a refreshing and nourishing accompaniment to a light summer snack. Italians, who, as a rule, eat nothing for breakfast, will sometimes have a *frullato* in the middle of the morning to tide them over until lunch. If you are traveling in Italy with the children and are enjoying an afternoon Campari at a sidewalk café, this is a nice refreshment to order for them. If they are very young children, you can ask the waiter to omit the liqueur.

For 2 persons

⅔ cup milk	1½ teaspoons sugar
1 banana or a comparable quantity of fresh strawberries, peaches, apricots, etc. (see note below)	3 tablespoons crushed ice
	2 tablespoons maraschino liqueur

Whip all the ingredients in the blender at high speed until the ice has completely dissolved. Serve immediately.

NOTE

All the fruit except the banana must be washed in cold water, and all except berries must be peeled. Peaches and apricots, of course, must be pitted.

Arance tagliate

MACERATED ORANGE SLICES

Among all the ways in which a meal can be brought to a happy close, there is none, I think, that surpasses a dish of sliced oranges. Their bright, joyous color is an instant promise of refreshment, which they maintain by loosening from our taste buds the thick traces of the preceding courses, leaving nothing but happy memories and a fragrantly clean palate.

For 4 persons

6 eating oranges, such as navel, temple, or tange-orange	5 tablespoons granulated sugar
Grated peel of 1 medium lemon	Juice of ½ medium lemon

1. Peel just four of the oranges, using a very sharp knife. Take care to remove all the white spongy pulp and also as much as possible of the thin skin beneath.

2. Cut the oranges horizontally into thin slices about ⅜ inch thick. Pick out any seeds. Put the slices into a shallow serving bowl or deep platter and then grate the lemon peel into the bowl. (Avoid grating the white pulp beneath the peel.) Add the sugar. Squeeze the other two oranges and add their juice to the bowl. Add the lemon juice. Turn the orange slices over a few times, being careful not to break them up. Cover the bowl with a dish and refrigerate for at least 4 hours, or even overnight. Serve chilled, turning the slices once or twice in the macerating liquid just before serving.

NOTE

You may add more sugar if you like the oranges much sweeter. Some people add 2 or 3 tablespoons of maraschino or Curaçao just before serving. I do not because I find it interferes with the fragrance of the lemon peel. Try it both ways, if you like, and decide for yourself.

Ananas al maraschino
PINEAPPLE SLICES WITH MARASCHINO

It isn't without some embarrassment that I include this recipe for what is little more than pineapple slices out of a can. It is quite popular with many Italian restaurants, and before coming to this country I was certain that it was commonly served by all Americans. Pineapple is certainly not Italian; in Italy it is, in fact, very expensive canned and prohibitive fresh. When I first started serving it here, however, I discovered that people were startled by this version. It doesn't really have any pretensions, but if you like pineapple you might want to try this simple Italian approach.

For 1 person

2 slices canned pineapple, with
　 2 tablespoons of their syrup
1 maraschino cherry

1 tablespoon maraschino liqueur,
　 or more to taste

Put 2 slices of pineapple in an individual dish or saucer. Place the cherry in the center, in the hole. Add 2 tablespoons of the syrup from the can, and 1 tablespoon of maraschino liqueur. Refrigerate for 2 hours or more. Serve chilled.

Macedonia di frutta
A BOWL OF MACERATED FRESH FRUIT

The name *macedonia* is borrowed from a region in southern Europe that includes parts of Yugoslavia, Bulgaria, and Greece. It is an area known for the mixture of races that populates it, and its name is well taken for this dish, whose success depends upon the variety of its components.

The indispensable ingredients are apples, pears, bananas, and orange and lemon juice. To these you should add a generous sam-

454   DESSERTS AND FRUIT

pling of seasonal fruits, choosing them for the diversity of their colors, fragrances, and textures. In Italy, when *macedonia* is made in summer, we always add peaches. Italian peaches are silken in texture and immensely fragrant. I have never found comparable peaches here, but there is a thoroughly acceptable substitute in ripe mango. If it is locally available, I strongly recommend your using it.

For 8 persons or more

1½ cups freshly squeezed orange juice

Grated peel of 1 medium lemon, yellow part only

2 to 3 tablespoons freshly squeezed lemon juice, or to taste

2 apples

2 pears

2 bananas

1½ pounds of assorted other fruit, such as cherries, apricots, nectarines, plums, peaches, grapes, mango, cantaloupe, honeydew melon

6 tablespoons to ½ cup granulated sugar, according to taste

½ cup maraschino liqueur (optional)

1. In a large serving bowl (a tureen or punch bowl) put the orange juice, the grated lemon peel, and the lemon juice.

2. If you are using grapes, wash them and detach them from the clusters. Add seedless grapes whole to the bowl. Cut the other varieties in half and remove the seeds before adding them to the bowl. The cherries, too, must be pitted before they are put in.

3. All the other fruit must also be washed, then peeled, cored or pitted, and cut into ½-inch cubes. Add each fruit to the bowl as you cut it, so that the juice in the bowl will keep it from discoloring. (Remember, do not put in any unpeeled fruit, except for grapes, cherries, and berries.)

4. When all the fruit is in the bowl, add the sugar and the optional maraschino. Mix thoroughly. Cover the bowl with a dish and refrigerate for at least 4 hours or even overnight. Serve chilled, mixing three or four times before serving.

NOTE

For full flavor and fragrance, fruit should be ripe. Don't use any overripe fruit, however, or it will become mushy. It is better not to use strawberries for the same reason. If you really want strawberries in the dish, add them just 30 minutes before serving.

HOW TO MAKE ITALIAN COFFEE

Italian coffee has so many admirers throughout the world that it does not need additional appreciation from these pages. Aside from its merits as a drink, however, it is by far the best coffee to use in any dessert in which coffee is an ingredient, and for Italian desserts in particular it has absolutely no substitute.

Making Italian coffee at home is incredibly easy and quick. All you need is double-roasted espresso coffee and an Italian coffeepot. All Italian coffeepots, whatever their special design might be, share the same working principle. Water is heated to a boil in one chamber of the pot, then filtered through the ground coffee and collected in a second, serving chamber.

The traditional coffeepot, which may or may not have been invented in Naples, is known in Italy nonetheless as *la napoletana*. Neapolitans, in fact, consider themselves supreme custodians of the secret of good coffee, and, without any doubt, no one in Italy makes better coffee.

The *Moka*

The *Napoletana*

HOW TO MAKE COFFEE WITH THE *NAPOLETANA*

1. Fill the bottom half of the pot, the one *without* the spout, with cold water up to the tiny escape hole near the top.

2. Insert the metal filter for the coffee. Fill with coffee until it forms a mound, but do not tamp the coffee down. Always fill the filter to capacity.

3. Tightly screw on the top of the filter.

4. Place the empty half of the pot, with the spout pointing *downward,* over the filter, and snap the pot shut, pushing upper and lower halves together.

5. Place the pot over medium heat exactly as you assembled it, with the spout on top, pointing downward.

6. When you see steam leaking out of the escape hole on the side, turn the pot over and turn off the heat. The spout should now be at the bottom, pointing upward. It will take several minutes for all the water to filter through into the bottom chamber.

NOTE

Some Neapolitans do not assemble the pot in advance. First they boil the water in the lower half of the pot, then they insert the coffee filter, attach the other half of the pot, and turn the pot over. Their explanation is that, by assembling the pot in advance, the heat of the water before it reaches a boil dissipates some of the coffee's flavor.

HOW TO MAKE COFFEE WITH THE *MOKA*

There is another, more modern type of pot that works faster and also makes first-rate coffee. In Italy it is known as *la moka.*

1. Fill the bottom chamber of the pot with cold water up to the small, round safety valve.

2. Put in the coffee filter and fill exactly as with the *napoletana,*

up to capacity, forming a mound, but without pressing the coffee down.

3. Screw on the top of the filter.

4. Screw the upper half of the pot on tightly and place over medium heat. (In this system, hot water is drawn up through the filter and into the upper chamber, so that there is no turning over to do.) For best results, keep the lid open.

5. When the coffee begins to emerge, lower the heat to a minimum. (By reducing the speed at which the water seeps through the coffee, you concentrate the flavor.) When the chamber is nearly filled, close the lid. When you hear the coffee sputtering, it is all done. Turn off the heat.

NOTE

Italian coffee should never be reheated.

AFTERTHOUGHTS

What people do with food is an act that reveals how they construe the world. It is no coincidence that the same country that produced the Confucian system of ethical conduct imposes on the ingredients of its cooking a rigid discipline of cut and shape. The work of art that is a Japanese meal is a natural legacy of the only society where aesthetics, at one time, entirely governed life. And the achievement of classic French cuisine, its logic, the marvelous subtlety of its discoveries, could have occurred only in the country of Descartes and Proust.

The world of the Italians is not a phenomenon that needs to be subdued, reshaped, arranged in logical patterns. It is not a challenge to be won. It is there simply to be enjoyed, mostly on its own terms. What we find in the cooking of Italy is a serene relationship between man and the sources of his existence, a long-established intimacy between the human and natural orders, a harmonious fusion of man's skills and nature's gifts. The Italian comes to his table with the same open heart with which a child falls into his mother's arms, with the same easy feeling of being in the right place.

The essential quality of Italian food can be defined as fidelity to its ingredients, to their taste, color, shape, and freshness. In the Italian kitchen, ingredients are not treated as promising but untutored elements that need to be corrected through long and intricate manipulation and refined by the ultimate polish of a sauce. The methods of Italian cooking are not intended to improve an ingredient's character, but rather to allow it as much free and natural development as the tasteful balance of a dish will permit. The taste of Italian cooking is discreetly measured but frank. Flavors are present and undisguised, but never overbearing. Pastas are never swamped by sauce. Portions are never so swollen in size as to tax our capacity for enjoyment.

Because Italian cooking simply does not come off without raw materials of the freshest and choicest quality, it is sometimes the most costly of the world's cuisines to produce. But it is probably the one whose satisfactions are the most accessible to the home cook. Although a few of the recipes require a little practice and some manual dexterity, there is not a single dish in this book that is beyond the competence of any moderately alert person. Italian cooking techniques are disciplined by tradition, but they allow an individual approach to food that is spontaneous, immediate, and uncomplicated. Italian cooking does not lend itself well to the regimentation of professional chefs. When Aristotle said that a work of art should imitate the motions of the mind and not an external arrangement of facts, he was anticipating a definition of the art of the Italian home cook. In Italy the source of the very best Italian food is the home kitchen. There is no reason why this should not be equally true here.

And so this book comes to a close. And with it, a long year's work, the exasperating and sometimes almost intolerable task of fixing the fluid intuitions of half a lifetime of cooking within the step-by-step frames of a recipe. Although frequently I felt like a gymnast forced to retrace his twists and somersaults in slow motion, I wrote, tested, rewrote each recipe until it was as clear and reliable as I was able to make it. I hope they will work as well in your kitchen as they have in mine. I cannot expect from anyone a total conversion to Italian cooking, but if even a few of these dishes together with their proper placement within an Italian meal become a natural part of your life at table, I shall feel handsomely rewarded for my efforts.

Index

Abbacchio alla cacciatora, 281
Acciughe, 35–37
    peperoni e, 37
Agnello, 278–284
    abbacchio alla cacciatora, 281
    fritte, costolettine di, 283
    al ginepro, arrosto di, 280
    pasquale col vino bianco, arrosto
        di, 278
Almond candy, caramelized, 450
Ananas al maraschino, 453
Anchovy (-ies), 35–36
    and broccoli sauce for orecchiette
        and other pasta, 174
    -flavored dip for vegetables,
        hot, 42
    in oil, 36
    and peppers, 37
Animelle con pomodori e piselli, 295
Antipasti, 31–50
    acciughe, 35
        e peperoni, 37
    bagna caôda, 42
    bastoncini di carota marinati, 41
    bocconcini fritti, 48

Antipasti (cont'd)
    bresaola, 47
    bruschetta, 49
    carciofi alla giudia, 344
    carciofi ripieni di mortadella, 343
    carciofi alla romana, 337
    cozze e vongole passate ai ferri,
        34
    fave alla romana, 359
    funghi ripieni, 46
    funghi trifolati, 379
    gamberetti all'olio e limone, 39
    insalata di funghi e formaggio, 47
    insalata di mare, 421
    insalata di riso con pollo, 423
    insalata russa con gamberi, 419
    insalata di tonno e fagioli, 417
    ostriche
        alla moda di Taranto, 32
        alla parmigiana, 33
    panzanella, 410
    polenta col gorgonzola, 207
    pomodori
        coi gamberetti, 39
        ripieni di tonno, 38

Antipasti (*cont'd*)
  salame di tonno, 222
  trota marinata all'arancio, 220
  uova sode in salsa verde, 45
  vitello tonnato, 276
  zucchine fritte all'aceto, 393
Appetizers, 31–50
  anchovy (-ies), 35
    -flavored dip for vegetables,
      hot, 42
    and peppers, 37
  artichokes, Roman style, 337
  braised artichokes with
      mortadella stuffing, 343
  bread and vegetable salad with
      anchovies, 410
  carrot sticks, tasty, 41
  cold sautéed trout in orange
      marinade, 220
  cold sliced veal with tuna sauce,
      276
  crisp-fried whole artichokes,
      344
  fava beans, Roman style, 359
  fried zucchini with vinegar, 393
  hard-boiled eggs with piquant
      sauce, 45
  herb-flavored seafood salad, 421
  mortadella, pancetta, and cheese
      tidbits, fried, 48
  mushroom(s)
    and cheese salad, 47
    stuffed, with Béchamel sauce,
      46
  mussels and clams on the half
      shell, broiled, 34
  oysters, baked
    with oil and parsley, 32
    with Parmesan cheese, 33
  polenta with gorgonzola, 207
  rice and chicken salad, 423
  salmon foam, cold, 33

Appetizers (*cont'd*)
  sautéed mushrooms with garlic
      and parsley, 379
  shrimp and vegetable salad,
      419
  shrimps with oil and lemon, 39
  tomatoes, stuffed
    with shrimp, 39
    with tuna and capers, 38
  tuna and bean salad, 417
  tuna salami, 222
Apple fritters, 435
  for mixed fry, 333
Arance tagliate, 452
Artichoke(s)
  crisp-fried whole, 344
  for hot anchovy-flavored dip, 43
  Jerusalem, 350–353
    gratinéed, 353
    sautéed, 352
    and spinach salad, 406
  and leeks, braised, 348
  with mortadella stuffing,
      braised, 343
  and peas, braised, 347
  and potatoes, braised, 349
  Roman style, 337
  wedges, fried, 346
    for mixed fry, 333
Asparagi, 354–358
  fritti, 358
  insalata di, 411
  alla parmigiana, 356
    con uova fritte, 357
Asparagus, 354–358
  fried, 358
    for mixed fry, 333
  for hot anchovy-flavored dip, 44
  how to prepare and boil, 354
  with Parmesan cheese, 356
    and fried eggs, 357
  salad, 411

Bagna caôda, 42
Barbecue, Italian: charcoal-broiled
  vegetables, 400
Basil sauce for pasta and soup,
  Genoese, 139
Bass, baked striped, and shellfish
  sealed in foil, 212
Bay leaves, 9
Bean(s)
  dried, cooking of, 78
  fava, Roman style, 359
  green, 360–363
    with butter and cheese,
      sautéed, 361
    how to cook, 360
    with peppers and tomatoes, 362
    salad, 412
  and pasta soup, 80
  and sauerkraut soup, 75
  soup with parsley and garlic, 79
  and tuna salad, 417
Béchamel sauce, 28
Beef
  braised in red wine sauce, 242
  leftover boiled, with sautéed
    onions, 244
  meatballs, 247
  meat loaf braised in white
    wine with dried wild
    mushrooms, 249
  mixed boiled meats, 322
  patties with anchovies and
    mozzarella, 245
  steak(s)
    broiled the Florentine way, 238
    pan-broiled with Marsala and
      hot pepper sauce, 239
    thin pan-broiled with tomatoes
      and olives, 241
Biete
  cotte, insalata di, 414
  alla parmigiana, coste di, 371

Black-eyed peas and sausages with
  tomato sauce, 289
Blossoms, fried zucchini, 399
  for mixed fry, 333
Bocconcini fritti, 48
Bollito misto, 322
Bollito rifatto con le cipolle, il, 244
Brains, fried calf's, 299
  for mixed fry, 333
*Branzino al cartoccio con frutti di
  mare,* 212
Bread
  pudding, glazed, 431
  Roman garlic, 49
  squares, fried, for soup, 88
  and vegetable salad with
    anchovies, 410
Bresaola, 47
Broccoli
  and anchovy sauce for orecchiette
    and other pasta, 174
  with butter and cheese, sautéed,
    364
  with garlic, sautéed, 363
  for hot anchovy-flavored dip, 43
Broccoli, 363–364
  all'aglio, 363
  al burro e formaggio, 364
Brodetto di papi, il, 235
Broth, 10
  homemade meat, 10
Bruschetta, 49
Bucatini with pancetta, tomatoes,
  and hot pepper, 105
Bucatini all'Amatriciana, 105
Budino
  di pane caramellato, 431
  di semolino caramellato,
    430

Cabbage soup, red, 82
Caffè, 455

Cake(s)
  crumbly, 432
  rice, 428
  rum-and-coffee-flavored
    chocolate layer, 436
Calamari, 228–235
  fritti, 234
  e piselli alla livornese, 230
  ripieni stufati al vino bianco,
    232
Calf's brains, fried, 299
  for mixed fry, 333
Calf's head
  mixed boiled meats, 322
Calf's liver
  fried breaded, 298
    for mixed fry, 333
  sautéed with onions, Venetian
    style, 296
Candy, caramelized almond, 450
Cannellini con aglio e prezzemolo,
    zuppa di, 79
Cannelloni, 149
Cappellacci
  with butter and cheese, 170
  filled with sweet potatoes and
    parsley, 168
  with meat sauce, 170
Cappellacci del Nuovo Mondo, 168
Cappelletti
  in broth, 158
  with butter and heavy cream, 159
  filled with meat and cheese, 155
Cappelletti, 155–160
  in brodo, 158
  con la panna, 159
Carciofi(ni), 337–350
  fritti, 346
  alla giudia, 344
  e patate, 349
  e piselli stufati, 347
  e porri stufati, 348

Carciofi(ni) (cont'd)
  ripieni di mortadella, 343
  alla romana, 337
Cardoons for hot anchovy-flavored
    dip, 43
Carota(e)
  al burro e formaggio, 365
  insalata di, 406
  marinati, bastoncini di, 41
Carrot(s)
  for hot anchovy-flavored dip, 44
  with Parmesan cheese, 365
  shredded, salad, 406
  sticks, tasty, 41
Cauliflower, 366–368
  fried, 367
    for mixed fry, 333
  gratinéed with butter and
    cheese, 366
  how to boil, 366
  salad, boiled, 413
Cavolfiore, 366–368
  fritto, 367
  gratinato al burro e formaggio,
    366
  lesso in insalata, 413
Cavolo nero, zuppa di, 82
Ceci
  e maltagliati, zuppa di, 87
  e riso, zuppa di, 86
  zuppa di, 85
Celery
  for hot anchovy-flavored dip,
    44
  with Parmesan cheese, braised
    and gratinéed, 368
  and potatoes braised in olive oil,
    369
  and rice soup, 62
Cervella fritta, 299
Chard, Swiss
  filling for tortelloni, 164

Chard, Swiss (*cont'd*)
  salad, boiled, 414
  stalks with Parmesan cheese,
      371
Cheese
  course, 425
  gorgonzola, 425
  and meat filling for cappelletti,
      155
  and meat stuffing for zucchini, 397
  and meats, vegetables, cream, and
      fruit, mixed fried, 333
  and mortadella and pancetta
      tidbits, fried, 48
  and olive oil, 426
  Parmesan, 425
  provola affumicata, 426
Chestnut and chocolate mound,
      puréed, 440
Chiacchiere della nonna, 433
Chick-pea(s)
  and pasta, 87
  and rice soup, 86
  soup, 85
Chicken
  charcoal-broiled, marinated in
      pepper, oil, and lemon, 307
  fillets of breast of, 312
    rolled, stuffed with pork, 315
    sautéed, with lemon and
        parsley, 314
  fricassee
    with dried wild mushrooms,
        310
  with green peppers and tomatoes,
      309
  livers with sage, sautéed, 303
  mixed boiled meats, 322
  pan-roasted, with garlic, rose-
      mary, and white wine, 304
  and rice salad, 423
  roast, with rosemary, 306

Chocolate
  and chestnut mound, puréed,
      440
  foam, cold, 443
  layer cake, rum-and-coffee-
      flavored, 436
Chops
  baby lamb, fried in Parmesan-
      cheese batter, 283
  Veal
    with sage and white wine,
        sautéed, 272
    sautéed breaded, 268
Cipolle, zuppa di patata e, 59
Cipolline agrodolci, 382
Clam(s)
  and mussels on the half shell,
      broiled, 34
  soup, 53
  with mushrooms, velvety, 54
Coda alla vaccinara, 291
Coffee
  espresso ice cream with hot
      chocolate sauce, 448
  ice with whipped cream, 449
  Italian, preparation of
    with the *Moka*, 457
    with the *Napoletana*, 457
Conchiglie with sausage and cream
      sauce, 109
*Conchiglie con il sugo per la
      gramigna*, 109
Coniglio in padella, 320
Coste
  di biete alla parmigiana, 370
  di sedono alla parmigiana, 368
Costolette
  alla milanese, 268
Costolettine di agnello fritte, 283
Cotechino sausage
  boiled, with lentils, 287
  mixed boiled meats, 322

Cotechino con le lenticchie, 287
*Cotoletta di tacchino alla
        bolognese*, 316
Cotolette alla milanese, 270
Cozze
    e vongole passate ai ferri, 34
    zuppa di, 56
Cream
    fried sweet, 444
    and meats, vegetables, cheese,
        and fruit, mixed fried, 333
Crema fritta, 444
Crespelle, 175
    alla fiorentina, 177
    con il ragù, 178
Croccante, 450
Croquettes, potato, with crisp-fried
        noodles, 385
Crostini di pane per minestra, 88
Cutlets, breaded veal, Milan style,
        270

Desserts, 427–455
    cakes
        crumbly, 432
        rice, 428
        rum-and-coffee-flavored
            choco-layer, 436
    chestnut and chocolate mound,
            puréed, 440
    chocolate foam, cold, 443
    fritters
        apple, 435
        sweet pastry, 433
    ice, coffee, with whipped cream,
            449
    ice cream
        espresso coffee, with hot
            chocolate sauce, 448
        vanilla, with macaroons, 446
        vanilla, with powdered coffee
            and Scotch, 447

Desserts (*cont'd*)
    puddings
        glazed bread, 431
        glazed semolina, 430
    sweet cream, fried, 444
    zabaione, 444
    zuccotto, 438
Diplomatico, il, 436
Dolci
    budino
        di pane caramellato, 431
        di semolino caramellato, 430
    chiacchiere della nonna, 433
    crema fritta, 444
    croccante, 450
    diplomatico, il, 436
    frittelle di mele renette, 435
    gelato
        agli amaretti, 446
        *di caffè con la cioccolata
            calda*, 448
        spazzacamino, 447
    granita di caffè con panna, 449
    Monte Bianco, 440
    spuma di cioccolata, 443
    torta
        di riso, 428
        Sbricciolona, 432
    zabaglione, 444
    zuccotto, 438
Dried beans, cooking of, 78

Egg(s)
    hard-boiled, with piquant sauce,
            45
    open-faced Italian omelets,
            326–333
        with artichokes, 328
        with asparagus, 329
        with cheese, 327
        with green beans, 330

Egg(s), open-faced Italian omelets (*cont'd*)
  with tomato, onions, and basil, 331
  with zucchini, 332
  pasta, homemade, 111–126
    basic recipe, 113
    ingredients for, 113
    utensils for, 112
Eggplant, 372–376
  fried, 372
  for Italian barbecue, 400
  Parmesan style, 373
  sautéed diced, 374
Equipment, 20–23
  cutting tools, 21
  pots and pans, 20
Escarole and rice soup, 63

Fagioli
  insalata di tonno e, 417
  dall'occhio con salsicce, 289
Fagiolini verdi, 360–363
  al burro e formaggio, 361
  in insalata, 412
  con peperoni e pomodoro, 362
Fagottini di vitello leccabaffi, 267
Fava beans, Roman style, 359
Fave alla romana, 359
Fegatelli di maiale con la rete, 302
Fegatini di pollo alla salvia, 303
Fegato
  di vitello fritto, 298
  alla veneziana, 296
Fettine di manzo alla sorrentina, 241
Fettuccine, 121, 130–137
  with gorgonzola sauce, 134
  tossed in cream and butter, 130
  with white clam sauce, 135
Fettuccine, 121, 130–137
  all'Alfredo, 130

Fettuccine (*cont'd*)
  al gorgonzola, 134
  al sugo di vongole bianco, 135
Fillet of sole with piquant tomato sauce, 219
Finocchio, 376–379
  braised in olive oil, 378
  with butter and cheese, sautéed, 377
  fried, 378
  for mixed fry, 333
Finocchi(o), 376–379
  al burro e formaggio, 377
  fritti, 378
  insalata, 407
  all'olio, 378
Fiorentina, la, 238
Fish
  anchovy(-ies)
    -flavored dip for vegetables, 42
    in oil, 37
    and peppers, 37
  bass, baked striped, and shellfish sealed in foil, 212
  broiled the Adriatic way, 224
  clam soup, 53
    velvety, with mushrooms, 54
  halibut, poached with parsley sauce, 214
  mackerel, pan-roasted with rosemary and garlic, 216
  mussel(s)
    and clams on the half shell, broiled, 34
    soup, 56
  oysters, baked
    with oil and parsley, 32
    with Parmesan cheese, 33
  red snapper with sautéed mushrooms, 217
    see also baked striped bass and shellfish sealed in foil, 212

470   INDEX

Fish (cont'd)
salmon foam, cold, 33
seafood salad, herb-flavored,
421
shrimp(s)
brochettes, Adriatic style, 226
with oil and lemon, 39
tomatoes stuffed with, 38
sole, fillet of, with piquant
tomato sauce, 219
soup, my father's, 235
squid, 228–237
braised in white wine, stuffed,
232
fried, 234
with tomatoes and peas,
stewed, 230
trout in orange marinade,
sautéed, 220
tuna
and bean salad, 417
and capers, tomatoes stuffed
with, 38
salami, 222
Formaggio, 425–426
Frittata (e), 326–333
di asparagi, 329
di carciofi, 328
con fagiolini verdi, 330
al formaggio, 327
al pomodoro e basilico, 331
di zucchine, 332
Frittelle di mele renette, 435
Fritters
apple, 435
for mixed fry, 333
sweet pastry, 433
Fritto misto, il grande, 333
Fruit
macerated
fresh, 453
orange slices, 452

Fruit (cont'd)
and meats, vegetables, cheese,
and cream, mixed fried,
333
pineapple slices with maraschino,
453
whips, fresh, 451
Frullati di frutta, 451
Frutta
ananas al maraschino, 453
arance tagliate, 452
frullati di, 451
macedonia di, 453
Funghi, 379–381
e formaggio, insalata di, 47
alla panna, 381
ripieni, 46
trifolati, 379
Fusilli with creamy zucchini and
basil sauce, 106
Fusilli alla pappone, 106

Gamberi (etti)
dell'Adriatico, spiedini di, 226
insalata russa con, 419
all'olio e limone, 39
pomodori coi, 39
Garganelli, 170
Gelato
agli amaretti, 446
di caffè con la cioccolata calda,
448
spazzacamino, 447
Genoese basil sauce for pasta
and soup, 139
Gnocchi, 195–203
green
in broth, 202
gratinéed with butter and
cheese, 201
with tomato and cream sauce,
202

Gnocchi (cont'd)
  potato, 195
  semolina baked, 198
  spinach and ricotta, 200
Gnocchi, 195–203
  di patate, 195
  alla romana, 198
  verdi
    in brodo, 202
    al burro e formaggio, 201
    con sugo di pomodoro e
      panna, 202
Gorgonzola cheese, 425
Granita di caffè con panna, 449
Green bean(s), 360–363
  with butter and cheese,
    sautéed, 361
  how to cook, 360
  with peppers and tomatoes, 362
  salad, 412
Green gnocchi
  in broth, 202
  gratinéed with butter and
    cheese, 201
  with tomato and cream sauce,
    202
Green sauce, piquant, 29
Green and yellow noodles with
    cream, ham, and
    mushroom sauce, 132

Halibut with parsley sauce,
    poached, 214

Ice, coffee, with whipped cream,
    449
Ice cream
  espresso coffee, with hot
    chocolate sauce, 448
  vanilla
    with macaroons, 446

Ice cream, vanilla (cont'd)
    with powdered coffee and
      Scotch, 447
Insalata
  di asparagi, 411
  di biete cotte, 414
  di carote, 406
  cavolfiore lesso in, 413
  fagiolini verdi in, 412
  finocchio in, 407
  di mare, 421
  mista, 408
  di riso con pollo, 423
  russa con gamberi, 418
  di spinaci e topinambur, 406
  di tonno e fagioli, 417
Insalatone, 416
Italian
  barbecue: charcoal-broiled
    vegetables, 400
  coffee, 455
  pancakes, 175–177
    filled with meat sauce, 178
    filled with spinach, 177

Jerusalem artichoke(s)
  gratinéed, 353
  sautéed, 352
  and spinach salad, 406
Jota, la, 75

Kidneys with white wine, sautéed
    lamb, 300

Lamb
  baby chops fried in Parmesan-
    cheese batter, 283
  casserole-roasted with juniper
    berries, 280
  hothouse, Roman style, 281
  sautéed kidneys with white
    wine, 300

Lamb (cont'd)
 roast spring, with white wine,
  278
Lasagne, baked green, with meat
  sauce, 143
Lasagne verdi al forno, 143
Leeks and artichokes, braised,
  348
Lenticchie
 e riso, zuppa di, 75
 zuppa di, 73
Lentil
 and rice soup, 75
 soup, 73
Liver(s)
 calf's
  fried breaded, 298
  fried breaded, for mixed fry,
   333
  sautéed with onions, Venetian
   style, 296
 chicken, sautéed with sage,
  303
 pork, wrapped in caul fat,
  broiled, 302
Luganega sausage, 11

Macaroni, homemade, 170
Macedonia di frutta, 453
Machine, pasta, 123
Mackerel, pan-roasted with
  rosemary and garlic, 216
Maiale
 all'alloro, arrosto di, 286
 cotechino con le lenticchie,
  287
 fagioli dall'occhio con salsicce,
  289
 al latte, arrosto di, 284
Maionese, 26
Maltagliati, 121
Marjoram, sweet, 19

Manzo, 238–242
 bistecca alla diavola, 239
 fiorentina, la, 238
 alla sorrentina, fettine di, 241
Mayonnaise, 26
Meat(s)
 balls, 247
 and cheese filling for cappelletti,
  155
 and cheese stuffing for zucchini,
  397
 loaf braised in white wine with
  dried wild mushrooms,
  249
 mixed boiled, 322
 sauce
  Bolognese style, 127
  filling for Italian pancakes, 178
 -stuffed pasta rolls, 149
 and vegetables, cheese, cream,
  and fruit, mixed fried, 333
 see also Beef, Lamb, Oxtail, Pork,
  Poultry, Rabbit, Specialty
  Cuts
Melanzane, 371–376
 fritte, 372
 al funghetto, 374
 alla parmigiana, 373
Minestra di sedano e riso, 62
Minestrina
 di spinaci, 65
 tricolore, 58
Minestrone, cold or hot, with
  pesto, 69
Minestrone, 66–69
 freddo alla milanese, 68
 di Romagna, 66
Monte Bianco, 440
Mortadella, 11
 and pancetta and cheese tidbits,
  fried, 48
 for mixed fry, 333

Mortadella (*cont'd*)
  stuffing for braised artichokes, 343
Mushroom(s)
  and cheese salad, 47
  dried wild, 12
  for Italian barbecue, 400
  sautéed
    with garlic and parsley, 379
    with heavy cream, 381
  stuffed, with Béchamel sauce, 46
Mussel(s)
  and clams on the half shell, broiled, 34
  soup, 56
My father's fish soup, 235

Noodles, green and yellow, with cream, ham, and mushroom sauce, 132

Olive oil, 13
Omelets, open-faced Italian, 326–333
  with artichokes, 328
  with asparagus, 329
  with cheese, 327
  with green beans, 330
  with tomato, onions, and basil, 331
  with zucchini, 332
Onion(s)
  for Italian barbecue, 400
  and potato soup, 59
  sweet and sour, 382
Orange slices, macerated, 452
Orecchiette, 173
Orégano, 19
Ossobuco alla milanese, 256
Ostriche
  alla moda di Taranto, 32
  alla parmigiana, 33

Oxtail braised with wine and vegetables, 291
Oysters, baked
  with oil and parsley, 32
  with Parmesan cheese, 33

Pagello con i funghi trifolati, 217
Paglia e fieno alla ghiotta, 132
Pancakes
  Italian, 175
  filled
    with meat sauce, Italian, 178
    with spinach, Italian, 177
Pancetta, 13
  and mortadella and cheese tidbits, fried, 48
  for mixed fry, 333
Panzanella, 410
Pappardelle, 121
  with chicken-liver sauce, 137
Pappardelle, 121
  con il ragù di fegatini, 137
Parmesan cheese, 425
Parsley, 15
  sauce for poached halibut, 214
Passatelli, 70
Pasta, 89–179
  and beans soup, 80
  bucatini with pancetta, tomatoes, and hot pepper, 105
  and chick-peas, 87
  conchiglie with sausage and cream sauce, 109
  fusilli with creamy zucchini and basil sauce, 106
  homemade, from Apulia, 173
  homemade egg
    basic recipe, 113
    broccoli and anchovy sauce for orecchiette and other pasta, 174

Pasta, homemade egg (*cont'd*)
  cappellacci
    with butter and cheese, 170
    filled with sweet potatoes
      and parsley, 168
    with meat sauce, 170
  cappelletti
    in broth, 158
    with butter and heavy
      cream, 159
    filled with meat and
      cheese, 155
  cooking, 126
  fettuccine
    with gorgonzola sauce, 134
    tossed in cream and butter,
      130
    with white clam sauce, 135
  flat, 120–123
    fettuccine, 121
    maltagliati, 121
    pappardelle, 121
    quadrucci, 123
    tagliarini, 121
    tagliatelle, 120
    tagliolini, 121
  Genoese basil sauce for, 139
  ingredients for, 113
  lasagne, baked green, with
    meat sauce, 143
  macaroni, 170
  meat sauce, Bolognese style,
    127
  noodles, yellow and green,
    with cream, ham, and
    mushroom sauce, 132
  pappardelle with chicken-
    liver sauce, 137
  preparation using pasta
    machine, 123
  roll, sliced, with spinach
    filling, 152

Pasta, homemade egg (*cont'd*)
  rolls, meat-stuffed, 149
  shells, yellow, stuffed with
    spinach fettuccine, 145
  spinach, 126
  storage of, 125
  tagliatelle with Bolognese
    meat sauce, 129
  tortellini, 160
    filled with parsley and
      ricotta, 162
    tomato and cream sauce
      for, 163
  tortelloni
    with butter and cheese,
      167
    with butter and heavy
      cream, 168
    filled with Swiss chard, 164
    with tomato and cream
      sauce, 168
  trenette with potatoes and
    pesto, 142
  utensils for, 112
 how to cook, 89
 pancakes, Italian, 175
  filled with meat sauce, 178
  filled with spinach, 177
 penne with a sauce of tomatoes
    and dried wild
    mushrooms, 108
 rigatoni, baked, with meat sauce,
    110
 spaghetti with tuna sauce, 102
 thin spaghetti
  with anchovy and tomato
    sauce, 101
  with eggplant, 98
  with fresh basil and tomato
    sauce, 97
  with red clam sauce, 100
 tomato sauces for, 92

Pasta, 89–179
  "ajo e ojo," 103
  bucatini all'Amatriciana, 105
  cannelloni, 149
  cappellacci, 168
    del Nuovo Mondo, 168
  cappelletti, 155
    in brodo, 158
    con la panna, 159
  conchiglie con il sugo per la
      gramigna, 109
  fettuccine, 121, 130–137
    all'Alfredo, 130
    al gorgonzola, 134
    al sugo di vongole bianco, 135
  fusilli alla pappone, 106
  garganelli, 170
  lasagne verdi al forno, 143
  orecchiette, 173
  paglia e fieno alla ghiotta, 132
  pappardelle con il ragù di
      fegatini, 137
  penne al sugo di pomodoro e
      funghi secchi, 108
  rigatoni al forno col ragù, 110
  rotolo di, il, 152
  scrigno di Venere, lo, 145
  spaghetti
    alla carrettiera, 97
    al tonno, 102
  spaghettini
    con le melanzane, 98
    al sugo di pomodoro e
        acciughe, 101
    alle vongole, 100
  tagliatelle, 120
    alla bolognese, 129
  tortellini, 160
    di prezzemolo, 162
  tortelloni
    di biete, 164
    al burro e formaggio, 167

Pasta (cont'd)
  trenette col pesto, 142
  all'uovo fatta in casa, 111
  e fagioli, 80
Pastry fritters, sweet, 433
Patata(e), 384–387
  arrosto, dadini di, 387
  e cipolle, zuppa di, 59
  purè di, 384
  spinose, 385
Patties, beef, with anchovies and
    mozzarella, 245
Peas
  black-eyed, and sausage with
      tomato sauce, 289
  and artichokes, braised, 347
  with prosciutto, sautéed,
      Florentine style, 383
  and rice, 60
Penne with a sauce of tomatoes
    and dried wild
    mushrooms, 108
Penne al sugo di pomodoro e
    funghi secchi, 108
Pepper, 16
Peppers
  and anchovies, 37
  sweet
    for hot anchovy-flavored dip,
        44
    for Italian barbecue, 400
Perch, see Trout in orange
    marinade
Pesce
  branzino al cartoccio con frutti
      di mare, 212
  brodetto di papi, il, 235
  calamari
    fritti, 234
    e piselli alla livornese, 230
    ripieni stufati al vino bianco,
        232

Pesce (*cont'd*)
  ai ferri alla moda dell'Adriatico,
    224
  gamberi dell'Adriatico, spiedini
    di, 226
  pagello con i funghi trifolati, 217
  sgomberi in tegame con
    rosmarino e aglio, 216
  da taglio con salsa di prezzemolo,
    214
  tonno, salame di, 222
  trota marinata all'arancio, 220
Pesto, 139–142
  blender, 140
  making for the freezer, 142
  mortar, 141
Petto(i) di pollo
  e maiale, rollatini di, 315
  alla senese, 314
Petto di vitello arrotolato, 254
Piccioncini in tegame, 319
Pineapple slices with maraschino,
    453
Piquant green sauce, 29
Piselli secchi e patate, zuppa di, 72
Pisellini alla fiorentina, 383
Polenta, 203–208
  basic method for making, 204
  with butter and cheese, 206
  fried, 206
  with gorgonzola, 207
  with meat sauce, baked, 208
  with sausages, 205
Polenta, 203–208
  al burro e formaggio, 206
  fritta, 206
  col gorgonzola, 207
  con la luganega, 205
  pasticciata, 208
Pollo, 304–318
  arrosto
    al forno con rosmarino, 306

Pollo, arrosto (*cont'd*)
  in tegame, 304
  alla cacciatora, 309
  alla diavola, 307
  coi funghi secchi, 310
  insalata di riso con, 423
  petto(i) di, 313–316
    e maiale, rollatini di, 315
    alla senese, 314
Polpette alla pizzaiola, 245
Polpettine, 247
Polpettone alla toscana, 249
Pomodoro(i), 389–391
  al forno, 389
  fritti, 390
  coi gamberetti, 39
  ripieni di tonno, 38
  sughi di, 92–96
Pork
  cotechino sausage, boiled, with
    lentils, 287
  liver, broiled, wrapped in caul
    fat, 302
  loin braised in milk, 284
  roast, with bay leaves, 286
  sausages and black-eyed peas
    with tomato sauce, 289
  stuffing for rolled breast of
    chicken fillets, 315
Potato(es)
  and artichokes, braised, 349
  and celery braised in olive oil,
    370
  croquettes with crisp-fried
    noodles, 385
  diced pan-roasted, 387
  gnocchi, 195
  and onion soup, 59
  with Parmesan cheese, Italian
    mashed, 384
  soup with carrots and celery,
    creamy, 58

Potato(es) (cont'd)
  and split green pea soup, 72
Poultry, see Chicken, Turkey,
      Squab
Provola affumicata cheese, 426
Pudding
  bread, glazed, 431
  semolina, glazed, 430

Quadrucci, 123

Rabbit, stewed, with white wine,
      320
Radishes for hot anchovy-flavored
      dip, 44
Ragù, 127
  di fegatini, 137
Red cabbage soup, 82
Red sauce, 30
Red snapper with sautéed
      mushrooms, 217
  See also Baked striped bass
      and shellfish sealed in foil,
      212
Rice, 16
  cake, 428
  and celery soup, 62
  and chicken salad, 423
  and chick-pea soup, 86
  and escarole soup, 63
  and lentil soup, 75
  and peas, 60
Ricotta, 17
  and parsley filling for tortellini,
      162
  and semolina gnocchi, 200
Rigatoni, baked, with meat sauce,
      110
Rigatoni al forno col ragù, 110
Riso(i), 16
  e bisi, 60
  filante con la mozzarella, 194

Riso(i) (cont'd)
  minestra di sedano e, 62
  con pollo, insalata di, 423
  torta di, 428
  zuppa di scarola e, 63
Risotto, 179–195
  with asparagus, 189
  basic technique, 180
  with clams, 192
  with dried wild mushrooms, 185
  with fresh basil and mozzarella
      cheese, 194
  with luganega sausage, 188
  with meat sauce, 87
  Milan style, 184
  molded, with Parmesan cheese
      and chicken-liver sauce,
      183
  with Parmesan cheese, 181
  with zucchini, 191
Risotto, 179–195
  con gli asparagi, 189
  coi funghi secchi, 185
  con la luganega, 188
  alla milanese, 184
  alla parmigiana, 181
    con il ragù di fegatini,
      anello di, 183
  col ragù, 187
  riso filante con la mozzarella,
      194
  con le vongole, 192
  con le zucchine, 191
Rognoncini trifolati al vino bianco,
      300
Rollatini di vitello al pomodoro,
      265
Romano cheese, 17
Rosemary, 18
Rotolo di pasta, il, 152

Sage, 18

Salad(s), 403–425
  asparagus, 411
  bread and vegetable, with
      anchovies, 410
  carrot, shredded, 406
  cauliflower, boiled, 413
  finocchio, 407
  green bean, 412
  Jerusalem artichoke and spinach,
      406
  mixed, 408
  mushroom and cheese, 47
  rice and chicken, 423
  seafood, herb-flavored, 421
  shrimp and vegetable, 418
  Swiss-chard, boiled, 414
  tuna and bean, 417
  vegetable, mixed cooked, 416
  zucchini, 415
Salame di tonno, 222
Salmone, spuma fredda di, 33
Salmon foam, cold, 33
Salsa
  balsamella, 28
  maionese, 26
  rossa, 30
  verde, 29
Sauce(s)
  Béchamel, 28
  broccoli and anchovy, for
      orecchiette and other
      pasta, 174
  butter and cheese, 167
  chicken livers, 137
  clam
    red, 100
    white, 135
  cream and butter, 130
  Genoese basil, for pasta and
      soup, 139
  gorgonzola, 134
  mayonnaise, 26

Sauce(s) (*cont'd*)
  meat, Bolognese style, 127
  parsley, for poached halibut, 214
  piquant green, 29
  prosciutto, mushrooms, and
      cream, 132
  red, 30
  sausage and cream, 109
  tomato
    anchovy and, 101
    and dried wild mushrooms, 108
    and cream, 163
    fresh basil and, 97
    I, 93; II, 94; III, 95
    with marjoram and cheese, 95
    pancetta, tomatoes, and hot
        pepper, 105
    with rosemary and pancetta,
        96
  tuna
    for cold sliced veal, 276
    for spaghetti, 102
  zucchini and basil, 106
Sauerkraut and beans soup, 75
Sausage
  and black-eyed peas with tomato
      sauce, 289
  cotechino, boiled, with lentils,
      287
  luganega, 11
  mixed boiled meats, 322
  mortadella, 11
Scaloppine, veal, 260–268
  "bundles" with anchovies and
      cheese, 267
  rolls in tomato sauce, 265
  sautéed
    with lemon sauce, 262
    with Marsala, 261
  with tomatoes, 264
Scaloppine di vitello, 260–268
  al limone, 262

Scaloppine de vitello (cont'd)
  al Marsala, 261
  alla pizzaiola, 264
Scarola e riso, zuppa di, 63
"*Schinco,*" *lo,* 259
Scrigno di Venere, lo, 145
Seafood salad, herb-flavored, 421
Sedano, 368–371
  alla parmigiana, coste di, 368
  e patate all'olio, 369
  e riso, minestra di, 62
Semolina, 18
  gnocchi, baked, 198
  pudding, glazed, 430
Sfoglia, la, 111
Sgomberi in tegame con rosmarino
    e aglio, 216
Shellfish
  and baked striped bass sealed in
    foil, 212
  see also Clams, Mussels,
    Oysters, Shrimp
Shrimp(s)
  brochettes, Adriatic style, 226
  with oil and lemon, 39
  tomatoes stuffed with, 39
  and vegetable salad, 418
Sole, fillet of, with piquant tomato
    sauce, 219
Sogliola con pomodoro e capperi,
    filetti di, 219
Soup(s), 53–89
  bean(s)
    with parsley and garlic, 79
    and pasta, 80
    and sauerkraut, 75
  chick-pea(s), 85
    and pasta, 87
    and rice, 86
  clam, 53
  escarole and rice, 63
  fish, my father's, 235

Soup(s) (*cont'd*)
  garnish
    fried bread squares, 88
    Genoese basil sauce for, 139
  lentil, 73
    and rice, 75
  minestrone, cold or hot, with
    pesto, 69
  mussel, 56
  passatelli, 70
  potato
    with carrots and celery,
      creamy, 58
    and onion, 59
  red cabbage, 82
  rice
    and celery, 62
    and peas, 60
  spinach, 65
  split green pea and potato,
    72
  vegetable with rice, Milan style,
    cold, 68
Spaghetti(ni)
  with garlic and oil, 103
  thin
    with anchovy and tomato
      sauce, 101
    with eggplant, 98
    with fresh basil and tomato
      sauce, 97
    with red clam sauce, 100
  tomato sauces for, 92
  with tuna sauce, 102
Spaghetti(ni)
  "*ajo e ojo,*" 103
  alla carrettiera, 97
  con le melanzane, 98
  al sugo di pomodoro e acciughe,
    101
  al tonno, 102
  alle vongole, 100

Specialty cuts
    calf's brains, fried, 299
    calf's liver
        fried breaded, 298
        sautéed, with onions, Venetian
            style, 296
    chicken livers, sautéed, with
        sage, 303
    lamb kidneys, sautéed, with
        white wine, 300
    pork liver, wrapped in caul fat,
        broiled, 302
    sweetbreads braised with
        tomatoes and peas, 295
    tripe, honeycomb, with Parmesan
        cheese, 293
Spezzatino di vitello
    coi piselli, 274
    alla salvia, 273
Spiedini di gamberi dell'Adriatico,
    226
Spinach
    fettuccine, yellow pasta shells
        stuffed with, 145
    filling
        for Italian pancakes, 177
        for sliced pasta roll, 152
    for hot anchovy-flavored dip, 43
    and Jerusalem artichoke salad,
        406
    pasta, 126
    and ricotta gnocchi, 200
    sautéed, 388
    soup, 65
Spinaci
    minestrina di, 65
    saltati, 388
    e topinambur, insalata di, 406
Split green pea and potato soup,
    72
Spuma di cioccolata, 443
Squab, pan-roasted, 319

Squid, 228–237
    fried, 234
    my father's fish soup, 235
    stuffed, braised in white wine,
        232
    with tomatoes and peas, stewed,
        230
Steak(s)
    broiled the Florentine way, 238
    pan-broiled, with Marsala
        and hot pepper sauce, 239
    thin pan-broiled with tomatoes
        and olives, 241
Stew, veal
    with sage and white wine, 273
    with tomatoes and peas, 274
Stracotto al Barolo, 242
Sugo(hi)
    di broccoli e acciughe, 174
    per la gramigna, 109
    di pomodoro, 92
        e acciughe, 101
        e funghi secchi, 108
        e panna, 163
    di vongole bianco, 135
Sweet potato and parsley filling for
    cappellacci, 168
Sweetbreads braised with
    tomatoes and peas, 295
Swiss chard
    filling for tortelloni, 164
    salad, boiled, 414
    stalks with Parmesan cheese, 370

Tacchino alla bolognese, cotoletta
    di, 316
Tagliarini, 121
Tagliatelle, 120
    with Bolognese meat sauce, 129
Tagliatelle, 120
    alla bolognese, 129
Tagliolini, 121

Tomato(es)
  fried, 390
    for mixed fry, 333
  for Italian barbecue, 400
  oven-browned, 389
  sauces for pasta, 92–96
    with marjoram and cheese, 95
    with rosemary and pancetta, 96
  stuffed
    with shrimp, 39
    with tuna and capers, 38
Tonno
  e fagioli, insalata di, 417
  pomodori ripieni di, 38
  salame di, 222
Topinambur, 350–353
  gratinati, 353
  insalata di spinaci e, 406
  Trifolati, 352
Torta
  di riso, 428
  Sbricciolona, 432
Tortellini, 160–162
  filled with parsley and ricotta, 162
  tomato and cream sauce for, 163
Tortellini, 160–162
  di prezzemolo, 162
Tortelloni, 164–168
  with butter and cheese, 167
  with butter and heavy cream, 168
  filled with Swiss chard, 164
  with tomato and cream sauce, 168
Tortelloni, 164–168
  di biete, 164
  al burro e formaggio, 167
Trenette with potatoes and pesto, 142
Tripe, honeycomb, with Permesan cheese, 293

Trippa alla parmigiana, 293
Trota marinata all'arancio, 220
Trout, cold sautéed, in orange marinade, 220
Tuna
  and bean salad, 417
  salami, 222
  sauce for cold sliced veal, 276
  tomatoes stuffed with capers and, 38
Turkey breast fillets, sautéed, with ham, cheese, and white truffles, 316

Uvoa sode in salsa verde, 45

Vanilla ice cream
  with macaroons, 446
  with powdered coffee and Scotch, 447
Veal
  "bundles" with anchovies and cheese, 267
  chops, sautéed
    breaded, 268
    with sage and white wine, 272
  cold sliced, with tuna sauce, 276
  cutlets, breaded, Milan style, 270
  mixed boiled meats, 322
  pan roast of, 252
  rolled stuffed breast of, 254
  rolls in tomato sauce, 265
  scaloppine, 260–268
    with lemon sauce, sautéed, 262
    with Marsala, sautéed, 261
    with tomatoes, 264
  shanks, braised
    Milan style, 256
    Trieste style, 259
  stew
    with sage and white wine, 273
    with tomatoes and peas, 274

Vegetables
  See name of vegetable
  and bread salad with anchovies,
    410
  for Italian barbecue, 400
  for hot anchovy-flavored dip,
    44
  and meats, cheese, cream, and
    fruit, mixed fried, 333
  minestrone, cold or hot, with
    pesto, 69
  mixed cooked, salad, 416
  and shrimp salad, 418
  soup, 66
    with rice, Milan style, cold,
      68
Verdura mista in gratticola, 400
Vitello
  arrosto di, 252
  arrotolato, petto di, 254
  costolette di, alla milanese, 268
  cotolette alla milanese, 270
  leccabaffi, fagottini di, 267
  nodini di, alla salvia, 272
  ossobuco alla milanese, 256
  al pomodoro, rollatini di, 265
  scaloppine di, 261–265
    al limone, 262
    al Marsala, 261
    alla pizzaiola, 264
  "*Schinco,*" lo, 259
  spezzatino di
    coi piselli, 274
    alla salvia, 273
  tonnato, 276
Vongole
  e cozze passate ai ferri, 34
  vellutata, zuppa di, 54
  zuppa di, 53

Water, 19
Whips, fresh fruit, 451

Yellow
  and green noodles with cream,
    ham, and mushroom sauce,
    132
  pasta shells stuffed with spinach
    fettuccine, 145

Zabaglione, 444
Zucchine, 391–399
  all'aglio e pomodoro, 394
  fritte
    all'aceto, 393
    con la pastella, 392
  fritti, fiori di, 399
  insalata di, 415
  ripiene al forno, barchette di, 395
  con ripieno di carne e formaggio,
    397
Zucchini, 391–399
  blossoms, fried, 399
    for mixed fry, 333
  boats, baked stuffed, 395
  cleaning, 392
  fried
    in flour-and-water batter, 392
    for mixed fry, 333
    with vinegar, 393
  salad, 415
  sliced, with garlic and tomato,
    394
  stuffed with meat and cheese,
    397
  what to look for when buying,
    391
Zuccotto, 438
Zuppa
  di cannellini con aglio e
    prezzemolo, 79
  di cavolo nero, 82
  di ceci, 85
    e maltagliati, 87
    e riso, 86

Zuppa (cont'd)
   Jota, la, 75
   di lenticchie, 73
     e riso, 75
   minestra
     crostini di pane per, 88
     di scarola e riso, 63
   minestrina
     di spinaci, 65
     tricolore, 58

Zuppa (cont'd)
   minestrone
     freddo alla milanese, 68
     di Romagna, 66
   passatelli, 70
   pasta e fagioli, 80
   di patate e cipolle, 59
   di piselli secchi e patate, 72
   risi e bisi, 60
   di vongole, 53

A NOTE ABOUT THE AUTHOR

Marcella Hazan was born in Cesenatico, a fishing village on the Adriatic in Emilia-Romagna, Italy's foremost gastronomic region. After receiving her doctorates from the University of Ferrara in natural sciences and in biology, she lived and traveled throughout Italy. In 1967 she and her husband, Victor, an Italian-born American, came to New York, and shortly thereafter Mrs. Hazan started giving lessons in Italian cooking in her New York apartment. Since the publication of *The Classic Italian Cook Book*, her reputation as America's premier teacher of Northern Italian cooking has grown throughout the country.

A NOTE ABOUT THE ILLUSTRATOR

George Koizumi, the illustrator, was born in Chicago of Japanese descent and studied at the Pratt Institute in Brooklyn. He worked for two years as a graphics designer in Amsterdam, Holland, and since then has worked in New York City.

A NOTE ON THE TYPE

The text of this book was set in Caledonia, a Linotype face designed by W. A. Dwiggins. It belongs to the family of printing types called "modern faces" by printers—a term used to mark the change in style of type letters that occurred about 1800. Caledonia borders on the general design of Scotch Modern, but is more freely drawn than that letter.

Composed, printed and bound by
The Haddon Craftsmen, Scranton, Pennsylvania.

Typography by Lydia Link
Binding design by Margaret Wagner

Notes

Notes